T0329928

DEMANDING
DEVALUATION

A volume in the series
Cornell Studies in Money
edited by Eric Helleiner and Jonathan Kirshner

A list of titles in this series is available at www.cornellpress.cornell.edu.

DEMANDING DEVALUATION

Exchange Rate Politics in the Developing World

David A. Steinberg

CORNELL UNIVERSITY PRESS   ITHACA AND LONDON

Cornell University Press gratefully acknowledges support from the College of
Arts and Sciences, the Department of Political Science, and the Oregon Humanities
Center, University of Oregon, which aided in the publication of this book.

First published 2015 by Cornell University Press
Printed in the United States of America

Steinberg, David A., 1980– author.
    Demanding devaluation : exchange rate politics in the developing world /
David A. Steinberg.
        pages cm — (Cornell studies in money)
    Includes bibliographical references and index.
    ISBN 978-0-8014-5384-7 (cloth : alk. paper)
1. Foreign exchange rates—China—Political aspects.   2. Foreign exchange
rates—Developing countries—Political aspects.   I. Title.   II. Series: Cornell
studies in money.

    HG3978.S74 2015
    332.4'56—dc23

                                                                    2014039460

Cornell University Press strives to use environmentally responsible suppliers
and materials to the fullest extent possible in the publishing of its books. Such
materials include vegetable-based, low-VOC inks and acid-free papers that are
recycled, totally chlorine-free, or partly composed of nonwood fibers. For further
information, visit our website at www.cornellpress.cornell.edu.

Cloth printing   10 9 8 7 6 5 4 3 2 1

For Sarah

Contents

Figures

Tables

Acknowledgments

This book could not have been written without the support of many friends, family members, and colleagues. I began working on this project at Northwestern University. During and since my time at Northwestern, Hendrik Spruyt has provided inspiration, encouragement, and exceptional advice on this project. Ben Schneider has been very generous with his time and energy, and his many challenging questions helped me refine and improve this work considerably. I am deeply indebted to Victor Shih for his camaraderie and for going way beyond the call of duty in order to help me develop a better understanding of Chinese politics. Anne Sartori provided many excellent suggestions on the project, especially regarding its methodology. I also received helpful comments from Sean Gailmard, Jim Mahoney, and Kathleen Thelen. My colleagues Toby Bolsen, Diego Finchelstein, Rick Hay, Olivier Henripin, Patrick Johnston, and Sebastian Karcher helped me formulate many of the preliminary ideas in this book and provided useful distractions from work.

The University of Pennsylvania's Christopher H. Browne Center for International Politics provided a fun and intellectually stimulating environment to work on this book. There, I benefited from conversations over lunch and happy hour with many individuals and owe special thanks to Avery Goldstein and Ed Mansfield for their support and mentorship. The Browne Center also funded a book workshop where I received outstanding comments from Jeff Frieden, Steph Haggard, Ed Mansfield, and other attendees; their input made the book much stronger. I thank the Browne Center for financial support and participants in the workshop for their guidance.

At the University of Oregon, I received helpful comments on this work from Gerry Berk, Alison Gash, Ron Mitchell, Nick Thompson, and participants in the "Junior League" workshop. Special thanks are due to Karrie Koesel and Lars Skalnes, who read multiple chapters and provided tons of great advice. I also benefited from the stellar research assistance of several Oregon graduate students: Thibaud Henin, Yongwoo Jeung, Zhuo Li, Kevin O'Hare, Gulce Tarhan, and Patrick Van Orden.

This research also benefited from comments from many other colleagues, including David Bearce, Bill Bernhard, Jeff Colgan, Randy Henning, Ashley Jester, Andrew Kerner, Patrick Leblond, James Morrison, Angela O'Mahony, Tom Pepinsky, Maggie Peters, Molly Roberts, David Singer, Felicity Vabulas, and Stefanie Walter. I thank the editors at Cornell University Press—Roger Haydon, Eric Helleiner, and Jonathan Kirshner—for their guidance, as well as two anonymous reviewers for their extraordinarily detailed, constructive comments that greatly improved the manuscript.

This book would not have been possible without the generous help of many people in Argentina and China who took the time to answer my questions. Victor Shih provided extensive support, without which field research in China would have been impossible. Simon Rabinovitch also gave excellent guidance on my research in China, and Haiyan Duan and Kai Kang were helpful research assistants. My research in Argentina owes much to the help of Sebastián Etchemendy, Jesús Monzón, and especially to Diego Finchelstein and his family. I thank the following institutions for their financial assistance: the Social Sciences and Humanities Research Council of Canada; the Graduate School and the Buffett Center for International and Comparative Studies at Northwestern University; the Christopher H. Browne Center for International Politics at the University of Pennsylvania; and the College of Arts and Sciences at the University of Oregon.

Portions of chapter 4 originally appeared in David A. Steinberg and Victor C. Shih, "Interest Group Influence in Authoritarian States: The Political Determinants of Chinese Exchange Rate Policy," *Comparative Political Studies* 45, no. 11 (2012): 1405–1435. I thank Sage Publications and Victor Shih for granting me permission to reuse this material.

My biggest debt of gratitude is to my family for their enduring support. I greatly appreciate the support of my in-laws, Rhonda and Larry, and wish that Larry had a chance to read this book. I have no doubt that he would have found much to object to. My sister, Jessica, is a close friend who has been there for me as long as I can remember. This book could not have been completed without the exceptional generosity and loving support of my parents, Buddy and Graciela. Finally, I will never be able to adequately repay my wife Sarah for everything she does for me. The last few years that I spent working on this book would have been far less enjoyable were it not for Sarah. For that, I dedicate this book to her.

Abbreviations

ABM: *Asociación de Bancos de México* (Association of Mexican Banks)

ACFTU: All China Federation of Trade Unions

ADEFA: *Asociación de Fábricas de Automotores* (Association of Automotive Makers [Argentina])

ADIMRA: *Asociación de Industriales Metalúrgicos de la República Argentina* (Association of Metallurgical Industries of Argentina)

BCRA: *Banco Central de la República Argentina* (Central Bank of the Argentine Republic)

CANACINTRA: *Cámara Nacional de la Industria de Transformación* (National Chamber of Industrial Transformation [Mexico])

CASS: Chinese Academy of Social Sciences

CCE: *Consejo Coordinador Empresarial* (Business Coordinating Council [Mexico])

CCP: Chinese Communist Party

CGE: *Confederación General Económica* (General Economic Confederation [Argentina])

CGT: *Confederación General del Trabajo* (General Confederation of Labor [Argentina])

CMHN: *Consejo Mexicano de Hombres de Negocios* (Mexican Council of Businessmen)

CONCAMIN: *Confederación de Cámaras Industriales* (Confederation of Industrial Chambers [Mexico])

CONCANACO: *Confederación de Cámaras Nacionales de Comercio, Servicios y Turismo* (Confederation of National Chambers of Commerce, Services, and Tourism [Mexico])

CTM: *Confederación de Trabajadores de México* (Confederation of Mexican Workers)

FKTU: Federation of Korean Trade Unions

GDP: gross domestic product

ILO: International Labour Organization

IMF: International Monetary Fund

INDEC: *Instituto Nacional de Estadística y Censos* (National Institute of Statistics and Censuses [Argentina])

ISI: import substitution industrialization

MOC: Ministry of Commerce (China)

NDRC: National Development and Reform Commission (China)

OECD: Organization for Economic Co-operation and Development

OEP: open-economy politics

PBC: People's Bank of China

PBSC: Politburo Standing Committee (China)

PPP: purchasing power parity

PRI: *Partido Revolucionario Institucional* (Institutional Revolutionary Party [Mexico])

SDPC: State Development and Planning Commission (China)

SDR: special drawing rights

UIA: *Unión Industrial Argentina* (Argentine Industrial Union)

Introduction

During most of the last twenty years, China's government has intervened in the foreign exchange market to suppress the value of China's currency, the renminbi. This policy of undervaluing the renminbi gives Chinese firms a competitive advantage over their foreign rivals. As a result of China's interventions in the foreign currency market, it takes more renminbi to buy each dollar, and Chinese citizens find it expensive to import goods from abroad. China's "undervalued" exchange rate therefore has similar effects to more traditional protectionist instruments, such as tariffs. Some believe that China's currency manipulation is "the largest protectionist measure maintained by any major economy since the Second World War" (Bergsten 2010). China's undervalued exchange rate also makes Chinese goods cheaper for consumers in the United States and elsewhere, and has been a major driving force behind the astonishing growth of China's exports, which increased over 1400% between 1990 and 2006 (see figure 0.1). This has been a colossal boon to Chinese businesses, but it has been an equally large burden for China's foreign competitors, such as the United States. China's undervalued exchange rate is also highly problematic for some groups within China, such as consumers who cannot afford imports. But it is undeniable that China's undervalued exchange rate has contributed to China's miraculous development and helped bring millions out of poverty.[1] Aided by rapid export growth, the income of the average Chinese citizen was more than four times higher in 2006 than in 1990.

---

1. Rodrik (2010) and Herrerias and Orts (2011) discuss the important effects of undervaluation on Chinese economic growth.

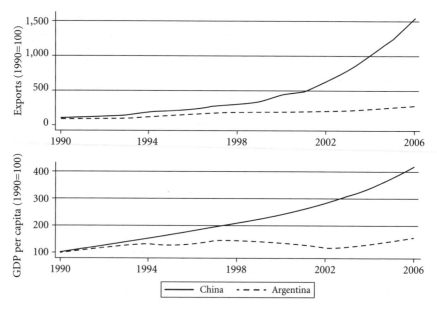

Figure 0.1. Economic performance in China and Argentina, 1990–2006. Data are from World Bank (2010).

China was not the first developing country to reap the rewards of an under-valued exchange rate. South Korea followed a similar exchange rate policy in the 1960s and 70s, and achieved equally remarkable results. Despite the posi-tive examples set by China, Korea, and others, few countries in the developing world have followed this path. In fact, many governments in the developing world do the exact opposite: intervene in the foreign exchange market to keep their exchange rates strong and "overvalued." This occurs in spite of the fact that keeping the exchange rate overvalued usually inflicts serious damage on national economies.

Argentina provides a clear example of a country that has repeatedly overval-ued its exchange rate and suffered as a result. During the 1990s, Argentina's overvalued exchange rate made it affordable for middle-class consumers to import Gucci handbags and go on vacation in Miami, and helped businesses pay off their foreign debts with ease. Unfortunately, Argentina's overvalued ex-change rate also made the country's goods prohibitively expensive, and its export growth was relatively slow as a result. Due in part to a lack of external competitiveness, economic growth in Argentina was mediocre throughout the 1990s. Even worse, overvaluation in the 1990s contributed to a massive eco-nomic crisis that led to a 22% fall in average incomes between 1998 and 2002. Argentine officials attempted to keep the exchange rate undervalued in the aftermath of the 2002 crisis, but the peso did not remain undervalued for long. Overvaluation in Argentina has created serious economic problems once again, and ultimately contributed to another financial crisis in January 2014. Argentina's poor performance and China's stellar success obviously result from a multitude of factors. There is little doubt, though, that exchange rate policy has contributed to these outcomes.

Whereas the economic effects of undervalued exchange rates are well understood, the political sources of undervalued exchange rates remain elusive. It is far from obvious why some policymakers undervalue their country's exchange rates while others choose to overvalue despite the widely recognized problems that overvaluation brings. The purpose of this book is to explain why a relatively small number of developing countries keep their exchange rates undervalued while many more overvalue their exchange rates.

The origins of exchange rate policy lie at least in part in a country's domestic political arrangements. Two characteristics of domestic political systems influence the exchange rate level: (1) the power of the manufacturing sector and (2) the design of national labor and financial market institutions. Exchange rates tend to be most undervalued in countries with powerful manufacturing sectors and state-controlled labor and financial systems. Manufacturing sectors that have many power resources tend to have substantial influence over exchange rate policy decisions. State control of labor and finance enables state leaders to push most of the costs of an undervalued exchange rate onto workers and banks. When both factors are present, as they are in China, the manufacturing sector is likely to prefer an undervalued exchange rate and often has the ability to convince policymakers to adopt this policy. By contrast, in countries like Argentina, where the state cannot control labor and finance, undervalued exchange rates can be costly for manufacturing firms, and manufacturers' opposition to undervaluation often discourages politicians from adopting this policy. Finally, when the manufacturing sector controls few power resources, as in countries such as Iran, low levels of societal support for undervaluation discourage policymakers from sustaining an undervalued exchange rate. Understanding why countries undervalue their exchange rates requires close attention to domestic political processes, especially the preferences and political influence of the industrial sector. Using both quantitative data on over one hundred countries and detailed case studies of five developing countries, this book provides strong evidence in support of this domestic political explanation of undervalued exchange rates.

Why Don't We See More Undervalued Exchange Rates?

Developing countries, as a group, have favored overvalued exchange rates to undervalued ones since at least the 1960s. Economists have frequently observed this tendency. To take just one example, an article by economists Pick and Vollrath (1994, 556) observes that "in developing countries, exchange rates are usually overvalued."[2] International financial institutions also judge overvaluation to be much more common than undervaluation: "only twice has the IMF [International Monetary Fund] found that a country has deliberately undervalued its currency, while it has found hundreds of cases of countries overvaluing their currencies" (Frankel and Wei 2007, 586).

More systematic data buttress these observations. Table 0.1 displays data on one widely used measure of exchange rate over/undervaluation. Positive (negative) values on this measure indicate that the exchange rate is more appreciated (depreciated) than one would expect based on a country's economic fundamentals. The data indicate that the typical country in Asia had an undervalued exchange rate in 2007, the most recent year for which data are available for a large sample of countries. However, exchange rates tended toward overvaluation in all four other developing regions: Africa, Eastern Europe, Latin America, and the Middle East.

It should be noted at the outset that measuring exchange rate undervaluation is hardly straightforward. No measure is perfect, and the one used in table 0.1 is no exception. In fact, the data in the table probably underestimate the true tendency toward overvaluation of exchange rates. As chapter 2 discusses in greater detail, this measure is constructed such that the mean level of over/undervaluation equals zero in each year. If the majority of developing countries adopt policies that keep their exchange rates overvalued, as many observers believe, then this measure understates the true degree of overvaluation for each country.[3]

Why have countries as diverse as Latvia, Turkey, Venezuela, and Zambia all converged on overvalued exchange rates? The popularity of overvaluation across these disparate countries and regions stands at odds with many leading theories of international relations and political economy. One major ambition of this book is to understand why overvalued exchange rates are more prevalent than undervalued exchange rates in the developing world.

The popularity of overvalued exchange rates is of more than purely intellectual interest. It is also a major driver of poverty and underdevelopment. Economists

---

2. Frenkel and Taylor (2007, 279), Edwards (1989, 78), Huizinga (1997, 273), and Todaro and Smith (2003, 571) provide similar descriptions.

3. Despite this limitation, this measure is very useful for comparing levels of over/undervaluation across countries and over time, which is the main way that this book utilizes this data.

TABLE 0.1. Exchange rate overvaluation in five developing regions (%)

	REAL EXCHANGE RATE OVERVALUATION
All developing countries	7.7
Asia	−14.7
Eastern Europe	24.4
Latin America	7.6
Middle East and North Africa	18.1
Sub-Saharan Africa	10.6

Note: Overvaluation was constructed by the author using data from Heston et al. (2009) and following the methodology of Rodrik (2008). Positive (negative) values on this variable indicate that the exchange rate is overvalued (undervalued). Cell entries are the median value for each group. A more detailed description of this variable is provided in chapter 2.

have long recognized the harmful effects of overvalued exchange rates. The IMF has actively encouraged developing countries to depreciate their exchange rates since the 1970s (Polak 1991).[4] In the 1990s, the maintenance of a "competitive" (i.e., non-overvalued) exchange rate was codified as one of the ten elements of the "Washington Consensus" (Williamson 1990).

Some recent economic theories go further and argue not only that overvaluation harms growth but also that undervaluing the exchange rate actually increases economic growth. A large number of statistical studies confirm that countries with undervalued exchange rates tend to grow more rapidly than those with market-valued or overvalued exchange rates.[5] Three plausible explanations have been offered for this finding. First, undervaluation leads to "export surges" (Freund and Pierola 2012). Since exports are a component of gross domestic product, more exports mean higher economic growth if all else is equal. Second, undervaluation encourages firms to invest in complex, technologically advanced industries, which increases productivity and ultimately growth (Rodrik 2008). A third theory posits that undervaluation promotes growth because it reduces real wages and thereby increases aggregate investment rates (Levy-Yeyati, Sturzenegger, and Gluzmann 2013). Regardless of the mechanism, an abundance of evidence indicates

---

4. The IMF's intermittent effort to encourage China to appreciate its exchange rate since 2003 is, therefore, unusual.

5. See, for example, Béreau, Villavicencio, and Mignon (2012), Berg and Miao (2010), Cottani, Cavallo, and Khan (1990), Dollar (1992), Easterly (2001), Levy-Yeyati, Sturzenegger, and Gluzmann (2013), Gluzmann, Levy-Yeyati, and Sturzenegger (2012), Mbaye (2013), Razin and Collins (1999), and Rodrik (2008). Although these studies typically use a continuous measure of over/undervaluation, the Béreau et al., Berg and Miao, Mbaye, Razin and Collins, and Rodrik studies investigate potential nonlinearities and find that, relative to market-valued exchange rates, overvaluation reduces growth while undervaluation increases growth.

that countries with undervalued exchange rates grow faster than those with over-valued exchange rates.

High average rates of growth are not the only benefit of undervaluation. Un-dervalued exchange rates also help countries sustain high growth rates for longer periods of time (Berg, Ostry, and Zettelmeyer 2012; Johnson, Ostry, and Subra-manian 2006) and make growth rates less volatile (Acemoglu et al. 2003). Lower rates of unemployment are another benefit of undervalued exchange rates. Em-ployment rises because undervaluation makes it cheaper to hire workers compared to using alternative inputs, such as imported capital goods (Frenkel and Ros 2006; Gluzmann, Levy-Yeyati, and Sturzenegger 2012; Levy-Yeyati, Sturzenegger, and Gluzmann 2013). Finally, undervalued exchange rates are among the most effec-tive policies available for preventing national financial crises (Reinhart and Rog-off 2009; Frankel and Saravelos 2012). Although not sufficient for successful de-velopment, the avoidance of overvalued exchange rates is probably a necessary condition for sustained economic growth (Bresser-Pereira 2008; Eichengreen 2007; Frenkel and Taylor 2007).

It is perplexing that large numbers of developing countries adopt exchange rate policies that impede their long-run development. A growing literature pos-its that policymakers' ideas and understandings about the economy determine their decisions about economic policy. In this view, political decision makers adopt whichever exchange rate policies they believe are best for the national economy.[6] The fact that developing countries "frequently suffer from recurring episodes of real exchange rate overvaluation . . . [is] puzzling, because it can hardly be the case that developing country policy makers do not know how to reverse over-valuations, or that they believe that real exchange rate overvaluation generally improves economic efficiency and welfare" (Huizinga 1997, 273). Since most ex-change rate policymakers realize that undervalued exchange rates are superior to overvalued ones, policymakers' ideas about exchange rate policy cannot explain why so many of them overvalue their exchange rates.

The rarity of undervalued exchange rates also stands at odds with standard interest-based theories of political economy, often referred to as the "open-economy politics" approach (Lake 2009). An undervalued exchange rate is a form of protectionism that, like a tariff or subsidy, provides local producers with a com-

---

6. Helleiner (2005), McNamara (1998), Morrison (2015), Moschella (2015) and Odell (1982) pres-ent theories along these lines to explain exchange rate policy. This type of argument has also been applied to other issue-areas, such as welfare states (Blyth 2002), capital controls (Chwieroth 2007), and trade policy (Morrison 2012). Related research on financial policy focuses on other ideational factors, such as social conventions (Nelson and Katzenstein 2014), national identity (Helleiner 2003), and perceptions of legitimacy (Kirshner 2003). However, these latter variables have received less schol-arly attention. I focus on the most common version of this approach but accept the possibility that these other ideational factors might influence exchange rate policy.

petitive edge over their foreign rivals. Interest group theories widely assume that politicians find protectionist policies virtually irresistible because protectionism benefits concentrated and well-organized interest groups.[7] Along these lines, many scholars assert that the beneficiaries of an undervalued exchange rate—exporters and import-competing firms—are more powerful than the opponents (Broz and Frieden 2001, 333; Eichengreen 1996, 152; Frieden 1997, 85; Henning 2006, 123). According to conventional wisdom, the benefits of an overvalued exchange rate are "spread out broadly among the population. These benefits often don't seem large enough to create a viable constituency . . . In contrast, exporters are a powerful political block, and the costs of currency appreciation hit them directly in the gut. Their complaints tend to resonate much more with politicians" (Prasad 2014, 16). By overvaluing their exchange rates, the majority of developing countries are going against the interests of what many political economists believe are the most powerful interest groups within these countries. Traditional interest-based theories have difficulty explaining why undervalued exchange rates are not very common.

Realist and mercantilist theories of international politics also have difficulty making sense of the why overvalued exchange rates are so popular. Many observers assume that "improvement[s] in competitiveness resulting from devaluation . . . are likely to be welcomed in our still mercantilist world" (Cooper 1975, 72). Realists and mercantilists believe that policymakers favor undervalued exchange rates and other protectionist policies because this increases a state's wealth and power at the expense of its trading partners (Gilpin 2001, 90). From this perspective, overvaluing the exchange rate is completely perverse. Overvaluation is equivalent to subsidy on imports and a tax on exports (Broz and Frieden 2001). When a government chooses to overvalue its exchange rate it is choosing to provide favorable treatment to foreign industries over domestic ones. Overvaluation does not just thwart the national interest; it also furthers other nations' interests. The frequent adoption of "anti-protectionist" exchange rate policies, which impose both absolute and relative losses on national economies, begs for an explanation.

The Argument in Brief

My political explanation of undervalued exchange rates, which is fleshed out in greater detail in chapter 1, has two main aims: (1) to explain the general tendency toward overvalued exchange rates in the developing world and (2) to explain why certain developing countries buck this trend and keep their exchange rates

---

7. The political advantage of protectionist interest groups is a common explanation for the ubiquity of protectionist trade policies (e.g., Schattschneider 1935; Ehrlich 2007).

undervalued. To answer these questions, I developed what I refer to as a "conditional preference theory." The label for this theory highlights two of its main contributions. The first is an assertion that the preferences of powerful interest groups are a major driving force behind exchange rate policy. The second contribution is to show that those preferences are context-dependent, meaning that an interest group favors different types of exchange rate policies across different political, economic, and institutional contexts. I argue that politicians rarely undervalue their currencies because most interest groups dislike undervaluation most of the time, and that undervaluation is most likely in countries where powerful interest groups do prefer this policy.

Exchange rates are inescapably political because it is government officials who are primarily responsible for the valuation of exchange rates. Government officials have numerous instruments that they can—and indeed do—use to control the value of their exchange rate. These instruments include intervening in foreign exchange markets, altering interest rates, changing tax rates and government spending levels, and regulating international capital flows. Should they choose to do so, governments are capable of keeping their exchange rates "undervalued," meaning that the currency is below its market value and domestic goods are cheaper than foreign goods. Governments are also capable of keeping their exchange rate "overvalued," which refers to a situation in which domestic goods are more expensive than foreign goods.

Why do more policymakers choose to use these policy instruments to maintain an overvalued exchange rate instead of an undervalue one? When politicians choose whether or not to undervalue their exchange rate, one consideration stands above the rest: the need for domestic political support. This imperative arises because national leaders that lack support from powerful interest groups do not remain national leaders for long. Politicians, therefore, choose exchange rate policies favored by the most powerful interest groups—groups with the most economic resources, strongest organizations, and highest levels of prestige.

Politicians frequently forego undervaluation because, even though undervalued exchange rates contribute to the long-run development of an economy, they often have some harmful effects on powerful interest groups over the short run. Many interest groups, from labor unions to banks and construction companies, oppose undervalued exchange rates because undervaluation makes it more expensive for these groups to purchase foreign imports or to pay off their foreign debts.[8] Of course, some groups do benefit from an undervalued exchange rate.

---

8. Frieden's (1991a) seminal theory convincingly argues that nontradable industries, such as services and banking, oppose undervaluation. Others argue that labor opposes an undervalued exchange rate because it reduces their real wages (Cooper 1971; Dornbusch and Edwards 1991).

Manufacturing firms and others that produce internationally tradable goods benefit from an undervalued exchange rate because it gives them a competitive edge over their foreign rivals (Frieden 1991a).

However, even though an undervalued exchange rate benefits the manufacturing sector in some ways, undervaluation does not necessarily increase manufacturing firms' profits. Undervaluation also harms manufacturing firms in various ways. An undervalued exchange rate increases the costs of manufacturers' imported inputs. Undervaluation also increases the debt burdens of manufacturing firms that borrow in dollars or another foreign currency. The process of maintaining an undervalued exchange rate often requires central banks to purchase foreign currency and sell domestic bonds, which pushes up domestic interest rates and makes it more expensive for manufacturing firms to borrow money from local banks. Increased labor costs are another common consequence of an undervalued exchange rate: when faced with an undervalued currency, workers naturally demand higher wages to help them increase their purchasing power; if a firm must raise its employees' wages, these added costs may outweigh any benefits from undervaluation. Therefore, industrialists are hardly stalwart proponents of undervalued exchange rates. They are likely to favor an undervalued exchange rate in some circumstances, but not in others. One major reason why so few policymakers undervalue their exchange rates is that their constituents typically dislike this policy.

Although interest-based theories of international political economy typically assume that actors' policy preferences are fixed and immutable, some scholars, such as McNamara (1998) and Helleiner (2005), have recognized that the manufacturing sector's exchange rate preferences are context dependent. I advance this important insight in a new direction. Whereas McNamara and Helleiner suggest that the contextual nature of preferences renders interest-based approaches of little help in explaining exchange rate policymaking, I show that a (slightly) more complex interest group theory is very useful for analyzing exchange rate politics.[9] To do so, this book explores how certain contextual factors help determine whether the manufacturing sector supports or opposes an undervalued exchange rate. The approach followed here is broadly similar to that of Henning (1994), which shows that one contextual factor—the structure of financial markets—can transform the exchange rate preferences of banks. Although Henning's study focuses on a

---

9. Helleiner (2005, 41) argues that "private sector preferences vis-à-vis exchange rate regimes are highly context-specific, and thus not easily modeled on the kinds of 'rationalist' deductive models" that are often employed. Similarly, McNamara (1998, 7) suggests that her findings "cast doubt" on the usefulness of interest-based approaches because these theories "fail to address the high degree of uncertainty about the microeconomic costs of different monetary regimes and the contextual nature of actor's preferences."

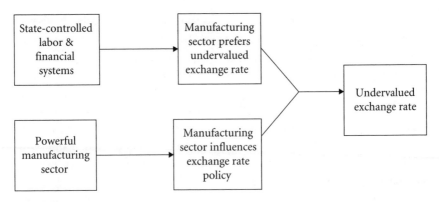

Figure 0.2. Causal model.

different interest group (the financial sector) and a different set of countries (advanced industrialized nations), it provides compelling evidence that contextual variables can influence preferences in a systematic fashion. Along these lines, my conditional preference theory aims to demonstrate that exchange rate preferences are not constant, but they are coherent.

This book brings attention to the important ways that institutions influence preferences. A variety of different institutional arrangements are likely to determine whether the manufacturing sector prefers an undervalued exchange rate. In this book, I focus special attention on labor and financial market institutions. Their importance stems from the fact that undervalued exchange rates often increase firms' labor and financing costs, and these two factors comprise a large share of the total costs of many manufacturing firms.

I argue that institutional structures that expand state policymakers' control over labor and financial markets increase support for undervaluation. When the state controls the financial system, policymakers can channel cheap credit to industrial firms. Thus, an undervalued exchange rate is less likely to push up industrialists' borrowing costs in state-controlled financial systems than in private financial systems. Institutions that enhance state control over labor markets, such as legal restrictions on organized labor, suppress wage costs for industrial firms. Undervalued exchange rates are likely to be profitable for manufacturing firms in countries with state-controlled labor institutions because wage rates are unlikely to rise following an exchange rate devaluation. By contrast, when policymakers are unable to control and repress workers, undervalued exchange rates are likely to push up wage rates and manufacturers' costs. Other things being equal, increased state control over labor and financial markets strengthens the manufacturing sector's support for undervaluation.

By bolstering the demand for undervalued exchange rates, state-controlled labor and financial-market systems can encourage policymakers to undervalue their exchange rates. Although preferences are hugely important, they do not determine exchange rate policy on their own. Power also matters.

This book pays particular attention to the preferences and power of the manufacturing sector because this sector plays a unique role in developing countries. Manufacturing is the archetypal tradable industry, and therefore one of the strongest potential beneficiaries of an undervalued exchange rate.[10] Additionally, the manufacturing sector often has exceptional political clout. There are two main reasons for this. First, most policymakers in developing countries covet industrial development, a good that only manufacturing firms can deliver. Second, manufacturing firms' large size and geographic proximity to one another provides them with organizational advantages over other sectors (Bates 1981; Bellin 2002). There are also more pragmatic reasons to focus on this one interest group. While there is strong agreement that the manufacturing sector plays an important role in exchange rate politics, the nature of that role is poorly understood. My manufacturing-centered theory does not provide a complete explanation of exchange rate politics, but an in-depth analysis of the manufacturing sector delivers large analytical payoffs because it greatly improves our understanding of this key player.

Policymakers have strong incentives to undervalue the exchange rate when the manufacturing sector supports this policy *and* this sector is politically influential. The political influence of the manufacturing sector depends upon this sector's "power resources" (Korpi 1985).[11] When the manufacturing sector controls a large amount of economic, organizational, and normative resources, policymakers have strong incentives to keep the exchange rate at whichever level industrialists prefer. The manufacturing sector is likely to have limited influence on exchange rate policy when other interest groups have more power resources. In this latter case, policymakers are likely to overvalue the exchange rate in adherence to the demands of other, more powerful, interest groups. Since the manufacturing sector is more likely to support undervalued exchange rates when labor and financial markets are state controlled, my conditional preference theory predicts a tendency for exchange rates to be most undervalued in countries that combine a powerful manufacturing sector with state-controlled labor and financial institutions. Figure 0.2 summarizes the argument graphically.

---

10. Chapter 1 explains why agriculture, though also a tradable sector in principle, is not always tradable in practice.

11. Following Cox and Jacobson (1973), this book maintains a sharp distinction between "power," which refers to an actor's internal attributes, and its "influence," defined as an interest group's control over policy outcomes.

Implications and Scope of the Argument

The conditional preference theory has three important implications for our understanding of the global political economy. First, it forces us to take politics seriously. The theory suggests that an adequate understanding of global economic trends requires us to look beyond economics and to pay close attention to politics and political incentives.

Second, the theory points to some important limitations of prevailing theories of interest group preferences, which assume that "interests are determined largely by a unit's production profile or position in the international division of labor" (Lake 2009, 231). The conditional preference theory suggests that an interest group's production profile cannot fully explain its preferences. This book shows that largely identical groups prefer different exchange rate policies in different situations. Scholars need to be more sensitive to the ways in which contextual factors influence preferences.

Finally, my theory suggests that institutions may be even more important than is often appreciated. The consensus among scholars of international political economy is that institutions matter because they "aggregate preferences"—they determine which interest groups influence policy (Moravcsik 1997; Milner 1998; Lake 2009; Rogowski 1999). By contrast, my theory suggests that institutional structures do not merely determine how preferences get aggregated. Institutions also play a more profound role: they influence what interest groups want. Historical institutionalists have previously recognized that institutions can shape preferences, but the field of international political economy has largely ignored this important insight.[12]

Before proceeding, it is important to clarify that my theory applies only to developing countries (i.e., low- and middle-income countries), and is not intended to apply to the advanced industrialized economies.[13] The exchange rate level has different—and generally more important—effects on developing countries. Undervalued exchange rates are more beneficial, in terms of economic growth, in developing countries than in countries that are already highly developed (Mbaye 2013; Rodrik 2008). At the same time, undervalued exchange rates also impose larger costs on developing countries. For example, developing countries are more heavily reliant on foreign-currency debt (Eichengreen, Hausmann, and Panizza 2005), and undervaluation makes it harder to repay these debts. Developed and

---

12. Henning (1994) and Farrell and Newman (2010) are rare examples of IPE scholarship that recognize this important point. For further discussion of historical institutionalist theories of preferences, see Fioretos (2011), Steinmo (1989), Thelen (1999), and Thelen and Steinmo (1992).

13. The advanced industrial countries consist of the Australia, Canada, Japan, New Zealand, the United States, and the eighteen countries that make up Western Europe.

developing countries also have very different political structures, and the specific institutional variables highlighted by my theory are much rarer in the developed world.[14] While my general arguments about the importance of interests and institutions should also apply to the industrialized world, the specifics are likely to be quite different in developed countries. Excluding the developed countries helps me provide a more detailed understanding of the politics of undervalued exchange rates in the developing world, where the stakes of this policy are highest.

Evaluating the Argument

In order to corroborate my theory it is necessary to demonstrate that it provides an accurate explanation of both *when* and *how* undervalued exchange rates emerge. The conditional preference theory argues that undervalued exchange rates are most likely when the manufacturing sector is powerful and the state controls labor and financial markets. I argue that governments undervalue in these conditions as a result of two distinct causal processes: (1) powerful manufacturing sectors have high degrees of *political influence* over exchange rate policy; and (2) the manufacturing sector has a *preference* for undervalued exchange rates in countries with state-controlled labor and financial systems. Since no single method is sufficient for evaluating every aspect of the conditional preference theory, this book examines different types of data to assess various aspects of the theory. This book combines national-level quantitative data, firm-level survey data, and qualitative case studies of five different countries to provide a comprehensive evaluation of my conditional preference theory.

As a first cut, it is necessary to examine general patterns in exchange rate valuation across countries and over time. To this end, I gathered data on the exchange rate level, the power of the manufacturing sector, and state control of labor and financial systems for a large sample of developing countries between 1975 and 2006. This quantitative dataset is crucial for assessing whether my theory accurately explains variation in the degree of exchange rate undervaluation across countries.

Quantitative data is also useful for assessing whether the preferences of the manufacturing sector are context dependent. To help answer this question, I utilize a survey of more than two thousand manufacturing firms from over fifty countries fielded by the World Bank in 1999. This survey, which asked firms their opinions about exchange rates, provides a unique opportunity to investigate whether

---

14. According to Cingranelli and Richards's (2010) data, no developed state severely restricted labor rights in 2006. In Micco, Panizza, and Yañez's (2007) dataset, no developed state owned more than 26% of its country's bank assets in 2002, the most recent year with wide data coverage.

TABLE 0.2. Summary statistics of the five cases (%)

COUNTRY	MANUFACTURING/ GDP	STATE-OWNED BANKS	LABOR RESTRICTIONS	OVERVALUATION
China (1993–2009)	33	100	100	−38
South Korea (1961–1979)	20	57	100	−21
Argentina (1966–2012)	27	35	0	14
Mexico (1970–1994)	22	24	0	−3
Iran (1953–1997)	9	43	100	25

Note: Overvaluation was constructed by the author using data from Heston et al. (2009), following the methodology of Rodrik (2008). Positive (negative) values indicate that the exchange rate is overvalued (undervalued). Manufacturing/GDP is manufacturing production as a percentage of gross domestic product, using data from World Bank (2010). State-owned banks indicates the percentage of bank assets held by state-owned banks; data are from Micco et al. (2007) for all countries except South Korea, whose data are obtained from La Porta et al. (2002). Labor restrictions indicates the percentage of years in which governments prohibited strikes or unionization and is coded based on Cingranelli and Richards (2010). Cingranelli and Richards's data starts in 1981 and therefore there is no data for Korea during the period of interest; since Korea is coded as being labor restrictive for every year from 1981 to 1985, and labor restrictions were similar, if not stricter, in the previous period, I imputed the values accordingly. Cell entries are the mean value for each group, except for labor restrictions, which indicates the percentage of observations for that country coded as restrictive. Chapter 2 provides more details for each variable.

manufacturing firms favor undervaluation and if labor and financial market institutions influence this preference.

These two sets of statistical analyses are extremely valuable for detecting when countries undervalue the exchange rate and when firms support such policies. However, quantitative analyses are less helpful at identifying the causal mechanisms that influence exchange rate policy and produce the correlations observed in the quantitative datasets. Qualitative case studies are better suited to this end. The case studies in this book illuminate why and how state-controlled labor and financial institutions influence interest group preferences, and whether interest groups truly impact government decisions about exchange rates. This book examines the politics of undervalued exchange rates in five countries: China, Argentina, South Korea, Mexico, and Iran. The analyses of China and Argentina are based upon field research in these countries.[15] The case studies of Korea, Mexico, and Iran rely primarily upon the large secondary literatures on these countries.

Table 0.2 provides summary statistics for the main variables of interest in each of the five countries. Although the case studies use much richer information to code these cases, these quantitative indicators are useful for initial comparison. Table 0.3 classifies the five cases according to whether they have weak or powerful

---

15. I gathered data in Argentina in August 2007 and September–November 2008, and in China during July–August 2008 and March–April 2009. During that time, I conducted elite interviews and collected primary documents.

TABLE 0.3. Case selection

LABOR AND FINANCIAL MARKET INSTITUTIONS	MANUFACTURING SECTOR	
	WEAK	*POWERFUL*
PRIVATELY-CONTROLLED		Argentina (1966–2012) Mexico (1970–1994)
STATE-CONTROLLED	Iran (1953–1997)	China (1993–2009) Korea (1961–1979)

manufacturing sectors and whether the state controls labor and financial markets. In two of the cases, China and South Korea, a powerful manufacturing sector coexists with state control over the financial and labor system. Two other cases, Argentina and Mexico, mix powerful manufacturing sectors with privately controlled labor and financial systems. Finally, Iran has a weak manufacturing sector and state-controlled labor and financial markets.[16] Countries with weak manufacturing sectors and states that lack control over their labor and financial systems would provide little analytical leverage because exchange rate policy is "overdetermined" in such cases.[17] For this reason, this book does not include case studies of the latter type of country. I also do not include cases where the state controls one type of market but not the other; my theoretical expectations are more ambiguous in such cases.

I chose dates for the case studies based upon major political and economic turning points within each country. Since these countries underwent "critical junctures" at different times, each case study covers a different period of time.[18] The studies of Argentina, Korea, and Iran begin with radical changes in each country's political regime. The Chinese and Mexican case studies start with the inauguration of a new President that initiates a major change to their country's economic model. The case studies of Argentina and China are brought as far forward in time as was feasible. The other three cases end with important changes in government. For each country, I divide the analysis into several different sub-periods, which means that there are multiple "cases" per country.

---

16. I focus on two cases of a powerful manufacturing sector with private controlled institutions and one case with the opposite combination because the former type is more important theoretically. Most theories expect industrialists to support undervaluation under these conditions. My conditional preference theory expects this type of country to overvalue its exchange rate because industrialists are likely to oppose undervaluation in this context. As my theory makes fewer unique predictions in the combination epitomized by Iran, it is less essential to study multiple such cases.

17. Hence, Mahoney, and Goertz (2004) call these "irrelevant cases."

18. The decision to start and end each case study according to when each country experiences a critical juncture follows the classic comparative historical approach of Collier and Collier (1991).

Exchange rate policy in these cases largely fits the expectations of the conditional preference theory. China and South Korea maintained undervalued exchange rates for extended periods of time. By contrast, Argentina, Iran, and Mexico experienced multiple episodes of overvaluation during the periods covered, and these countries rarely kept their exchange rates undervalued for more than a few years' time. This is the most important difference in exchange rate policy across these five cases.

These contrasting exchange rate outcomes are reflected in the final column of Table 0.2, which presents data on average rates of over/undervaluation for each country. Exchange rates in China and South Korea were highly undervalued on average. In Argentina and Iran, by contrast, the exchange rate was considerably overvalued in the average year in the sample. By this metric, Mexico falls in between the other cases. According to Table 0.2, Mexico's exchange rate was, on average, mildly undervalued between 1970 and 1994. However, as noted earlier, this measure likely underestimates the actual degree of overvaluation. More importantly, one exceptional period—the debt crisis of 1982–89, when Mexico's exchange rate was highly undervalued—skews Mexico's average. Excluding this crisis period, the Mexican peso was 6% overvalued on average in the remaining seventeen years. The Mexican case does not fit the theory quite as well as the other cases, but is a reasonably good fit because Mexico's exchange rate was overvalued on several separate occasions during this twenty-five year period.

The selection of cases that broadly conform to the argument was not accidental. In fact, I intentionally selected cases where the exchange rate level was broadly consistent with the relationship hypothesized by my theory.[19] This research design would be utterly useless if I was using these cases to evaluate whether my explanatory variables are correlated with an undervalued exchange rate (King, Keohane, and Verba 1994, 142–146). However, this is decidedly not the purpose of these case studies. Since the quantitative analyses are used to evaluate my theory's ability to explain variation in exchange rate valuation across countries, little would be gained by repeating this exercise with small-N case studies.

The goal of the case studies is entirely different: to evaluate which mechanisms are responsible for the association between undervaluation and a country's domestic political arrangements. Whereas the quantitative analyses are useful for understanding the relationship *across* countries, the principal focus of the case studies are on the political dynamics *within* individual countries. In other words, this book does not use case studies to assess *whether* these variables are associated with

---

19. To be clear, none of the countries provides a perfect fit with the theory. Each case includes at least one brief period in which exchange rate outcomes deviated from my theoretical expectations. These outlier periods are useful for illuminating the role of other causal factors and clarifying some potential limitations and scope conditions for my argument.

undervaluation. They are used instead to determine *why* these variables are correlated. These cases help assess whether the effects of these explanatory variables are truly causal or merely spurious. The principal outcomes of interest for the case studies are the preferences of the manufacturing sector and the degree to which the manufacturing sector influences policy choices—outcomes that were unknown to the author prior to conducting the research for this book. Cases that typify a cross-case relationship (AKA "on-the-line" cases) are ideal for illuminating the causal mechanisms that produce these cross-national relationships.[20] This is especially true when one combines within-case qualitative research with cross-case quantitative research, as in this book.[21]

The five countries were selected from the universe of on-the-line cases based upon two main considerations. First, I chose cases that pose relatively "hard" tests for the theory being evaluated. Second, this book focuses on a group of countries that cover a diverse range of political, social, and economic circumstances. Focusing on a diverse group of hard cases increases the likelihood that the evidence found in these cases is generalizable.[22]

China is one of the countries where interest group preferences are least likely to influence exchange rate policy. Many scholars believe that Chinese policymakers are relatively immune from interest group pressures because the Chinese state is highly authoritarian and autonomous (e.g., Kaplan 2006, 1193; Liew and Wu 2007, 23; Shih 2007, 1243; Wang 2003, 170). Thus, evidence that interest groups impact exchange rate policy in China would provide particularly strong support for my argument that interest group preferences influence whether exchange rates are undervalued.

The extremely diverse political and economic contexts that Argentina has experienced over the past fifty years make it a useful case to examine in detail. The case study of Argentina covers democratic and authoritarian regimes; governments

---

20. A "*typical case* study focuses on a case that exemplifies a stable cross-national relationship . . . . Because the typical case is well explained by an existing model, the puzzle of interest to the researcher lies *within* that case. Specifically, the researcher wants to find a typical case of some phenomenon so that he or she can better explore the causal mechanisms at work in a general, cross-case relationship" (Seawright and Gerring 2008, 299).

21. Lieberman's (2005, 444) influential article on mixed method research strategies suggests that, after finding statistical evidence in favor of a hypothesis, "scholars should only select cases for further investigation that are *well predicted* by the best fitting statistical model . . . [I]n this instance SNA [small-N analysis] provides a check for spurious correlation and can help to fine-tune a theoretical argument by elaborating causal mechanisms . . . The primary goal is to assess the strength of a *particular* model. As such, there is little value to the pursuit of cases that are not well predicted by the model."

22. Bennett (2008) and Eckstein (1975) suggest that generalizability will be greatest in "hard" or "least-likely" cases. The most different case method, wherein researchers examine cases that have similar values on the explanatory variable(s) but are otherwise dissimilar, "provide[s] the strongest basis for generalization" (Seawright and Gerring 2008, 298).

of the left, center, and right; and both protectionist and liberal economic models. As a result, the Argentine case is uniquely suited for assessing whether or not the conditional preference theory holds in different political and economic circumstances.

South Korea and Mexico, while similar to China and Argentina with respect to the main variables of interest, were selected in part because they differ in a number of other important respects. Korea faced a very different international political and economic environment in the 1960s and 1970s than China does today.[23] Korea and China also have different political regime types: Korea had a military dictatorship in this period while China has had a single-party dictatorship.[24] Argentina and Mexico's political and economic structures also differ in several notable regards: Mexico had a single-party regime in the period examined while Argentina has had either democratic or military regimes; and Argentina exports large amounts of food while Mexico's main primary sector export is oil.[25] Our confidence in the theory should increase if, despite these political and economic differences, similar political dynamics are observed in China and Korea and in Argentina and Mexico.

Iran is a useful case of a weak manufacturing sector and state-controlled institutions because these features persisted for decades despite a radical change to the Iranian political system in 1979. To the extent that the preferences and political influence of the manufacturing sector differed little when Iran was ruled by a US-backed monarchy and when it was governed by an anti-American theocracy, one should be more confident in the generalizability of these findings. Overall, this eclectic research design, which combines two types of quantitative data with qualitative case studies of five countries, greatly improves our understanding of the politics of undervalued exchange rates.

The Plan of the Book

The next chapter develops the conditional preference theory in greater detail. There, I argue that undervalued exchange rates are relatively uncommon because they are unpopular with powerful domestic interest groups. That chapter also presents my hypotheses about when interest groups and policymakers are most likely

---

23. Stubbs (1999) argues that the geopolitical environment encouraged the adoption of export oriented industrialization policies in East Asia during the 1960s.

24. Steinberg and Malhotra (2014) argue that single-party structures contribute to undervalued exchange rates.

25. O'Donnell (1978) and Richardson (2009) posit that reliance on food exports contributed to overvaluation in Argentina.

to support undervalued exchange rates, which are tested in the remaining chapters.

Chapter 2 uses two different cross-national quantitative datasets to test the theory. First, I examine which countries are most likely to maintain undervalued exchange rates, using data on as many as one hundred twenty developing countries from 1975 to 2006. The data indicate that exchange rates are most undervalued when countries combine powerful industrial sectors with state control over labor and financial markets. Second, I analyze survey data of about two thousand manufacturing firms from over fifty countries in the year 1999 to understand whether and when industrialists favor undervalued exchange rates. These analyses show that manufacturing firms are more supportive of undervalued exchange rates in countries with state-controlled labor and financial systems than they are in other conditions.

The following three chapters present the qualitative case studies. Chapter 3 shows that lobbying by the powerful manufacturing sector is a major reason why China kept its exchange rate undervalued for most of the 1993–2009 period. Chapter 4, which turns to Argentina and its repeatedly overvalued exchange rate, finds that the powerful manufacturing sector has frequently lobbied against policymakers' attempts to maintain an undervalued exchange rate, and their opposition helps explain why Argentina has not sustained an undervalued exchange rate.

Chapter 5 turns to Korea, Mexico and Iran. Like their counterparts in China, Korean policymakers in the 1960s and 1970s used their control over labor and financial markets to increase industrialists' support for an undervalued exchange rate. Korea's powerful industrialists also provided crucial political backing for President Park's decision to maintain an undervalued exchange rate. Mexican exchange rate politics bears many similarities to Argentine exchange rate politics: Mexican industrialists frequently opposed undervalued exchange rates, and their preferences encouraged Mexican policymakers to overvalue the peso. Iran's weak manufacturing sector typically favored an undervalued exchange rate. Although they received their preferred exchange rate policy in the 1960s and 70s, Iranian manufacturers had insufficient clout to prevent an overvalued exchange rate in the 1950s, 80s, or 90s.

The conclusion summarizes the main findings and discusses some of the book's implications for scholars and policymakers. I suggest that the scholarly literature on political economy would benefit from reconceptualizing the relationship between interests and institutions and paying more attention to how contextual factors shape preferences. I end by discussing a key policy implication of my findings: the potential for certain types of institutional reforms to contribute to better exchange rate policies.

A CONDITIONAL PREFERENCE THEORY OF UNDERVALUED EXCHANGE RATES

Economists overwhelmingly agree that overvalued exchange rates are detrimental to developing economies, and yet large numbers of developing countries overvalue their exchange rates. And despite compelling evidence that undervalued exchange rates can be highly beneficial for development, comparatively few developing countries have undervalued their exchange rates for an extended period of time. This chapter explains why. I answer two main questions here. First, why do more developing countries adopt overvalued exchange rates than undervalued exchange rates? Second, why do some developing countries diverge from most of their peers and keep their exchange rate undervalued?

To answer these important questions, this chapter presents a "conditional preference theory," which contends that the preferences of powerful interest groups are the most important driver of exchange rate policy. Those preferences, however, are not fixed or constant, as is often assumed. Rather, preferences for undervalued exchange rates are influenced by a country's institutional context.

After first providing some background information about exchange rate economics, this chapter develops the conditional preference theory in four main steps. First, I explain why powerful interest groups, defined as societal actors that control many power resources, influence government decisions regarding exchange rate levels. This chapter places special emphasis on one interest group: the manufacturing sector. The manufacturing sector is not the only interest group that influences exchange rate policy, but there are strong reasons to single it out for particular attention. Focusing on the manufacturing sector helps this book develop one of its key theoretical arguments: that the preferences of this interest group vary across countries. Moreover, the manufacturing sector has an oversize influence on exchange rate policy in many (though certainly not all) developing countries. As one of the strongest potential beneficiaries of an undervalued exchange rate, manufacturers' preferences and political influence can be decisive. I hypothesize that the manufacturing sector's influence over exchange rate policy is an increasing function of the amount of power resources that it controls.

After explaining why and how powerful interest groups matter, I examine interest groups' preferences. Most interest groups have at least some reasons to dislike undervalued exchange rates. Even interest groups that benefit from undervaluation in some ways are usually harmed by undervaluation in other ways. For example, undervaluation gives manufacturing firms a competitive edge over their foreign rivals, but it also raises the costs of their imported inputs and increases their debt burdens. As a result, many manufacturing firms are no more than "conditional supporters" of undervalued exchange rates: sometimes they favor undervaluation, other times they oppose undervaluation. The lack of consistent support for an undervalued exchange rate is one key reason that few developing countries undervalue their exchange rates.

In the third major step in the argument, I explain why institutions influence interest groups' preferences. I argue that the type of exchange rate policy that an interest group favors depends on a country's institutional arrangements. Here, I focus on labor and financial market institutions, specifically whether rules and decision-making procedures give the state control over workers and banks. State-controlled labor and financial systems insulate manufacturing firms from some of the costs of an undervalued exchange rate, which increases their demands for undervaluation.

The final step in the argument puts together the two main pieces of the story—power and preferences—to explain when exchange rates are most likely to be undervalued. Undervalued exchange rates are most likely when state-controlled labor and financial structures coincide with a powerful manufacturing sector. When both factors are present, industrialists are likely to demand an undervalued exchange rate and policymakers have strong incentives to comply with these demands. Absent one or more of these factors, support for undervaluation tends to be more limited, making this a precarious political strategy.

The Economics of Undervalued Exchange Rates: A Brief Overview

What Is an "Undervalued" Exchange Rate?

Before analyzing how political factors influence exchange rate policy, one needs to understand a few key economic concepts. Most casual discussions of exchange rates refer to the *nominal exchange rate*, which is defined as the quantity of domestic currency required to purchase one unit of foreign currency. A rise in this ratio, defined as a nominal "depreciation," indicates that foreign currency is more expensive; more "pesos" (i.e., home currency) are required to buy one "dollar" (i.e., foreign currency). A fall in the exchange rate is a nominal "appreciation," which means that foreign currency is cheaper; fewer pesos are needed to buy one dollar.

Most people care about the relative price of foreign and domestic goods, not the relative price of currencies. Car enthusiasts in the United States, for instance, care about how much it costs to import a Ferrari from Italy and not just how many euros they can get for each greenback. Thus, when speaking of exchange rate valuation, the true outcome of interest is typically the *real exchange rate*: the price of a basket of foreign goods relative to the price of that same basket of domestic goods. Typically, the real exchange rate is defined as the nominal exchange rate (e) multiplied by the ratio of foreign to domestic prices ($e \times P_F / P_D$). The real exchange rate tells you how much one unit of currency can buy in the domestic economy (P_D) relative to how much it can buy abroad ($e \times P_F$). Counterintuitively, a rise in the real exchange rate is a real depreciation, meaning that foreign goods have become more expensive relative to domestic goods. Decreasing the real exchange rate is defined as a real appreciation; foreign goods are now (relatively) cheaper than before. Throughout the book, unless I explicitly specify otherwise, the terms "exchange rate level" and "exchange rate value" refer to the real exchange rate.

Finally, it is not simply the level of the real exchange rate that matters, but the *degree of overvaluation or undervaluation*. There are several ways to conceptualize exchange rate over/undervaluation, but "purchasing power parity" (PPP) is the most widespread and useful benchmark. When the real exchange rate is at its PPP level, a basket of domestic goods costs the same amount as an identical basket of foreign goods ($e \times P_F = P_D$). An exchange rate is overvalued when residents can buy more foreign goods than domestic goods ($e \times P_F < P_D$). It is undervalued when domestic goods are cheaper than foreign goods ($e \times P_F > P_D$).

The aim of this book is to explain the political factors that influence the real exchange rate, which is defined as the relative price of domestic and foreign goods. Real exchange rates range in value from highly overvalued to highly undervalued. The exchange rate is defined as overvalued (undervalued) when foreign goods are cheap (expensive) relative to domestic goods.

The theory that I will develop aims to explain why developing countries do or do not keep their exchange rates undervalued for prolonged periods of time. Tunisia provides a clear illustration of a persistently undervalued exchange rate. The Tunisian government kept its exchange rate undervalued throughout the 1990–2007 period by depreciating its exchange rate in small and steady increments. I am less interested in explaining why some countries experience undervaluation for only brief periods of time. As I will discuss, short-lived episodes of undervaluation often result from capital flight and currency crises, not from intentional government policies. Post-Soviet Russia epitomizes this dynamic. Financial crises in 1992 and 1998 rapidly depreciated Russia's exchange rate and left it highly undervalued, but Russia's exchange rate appreciated and became overvalued again within a few years after each crisis. Even though Russia's real exchange rate was 27% undervalued on average between 1990 and 2007, Russia was anything but a model of undervaluation during this period because the ruble was overvalued on multiple occasions and its depreciations were not a result of official policy. The important question raised by this case is why Russia, like so many developing countries, does not keep its exchange rates undervalued for long. This is the question that the conditional preference theory seeks to answer.

The Economic Effects of Undervalued Exchange Rates

Undervalued exchange rates have a mixture of positive and negative effects on the economy. Since the costs of undervaluation are typically more concentrated and immediate than many of the benefits, it is useful to start the discussion there. Three costs of undervaluation are particularly salient.

First, undervalued exchange rates reduce the purchasing power of local businesses and consumers (Broz and Frieden 2001; Walter 2008). When the exchange rate is undervalued, imported goods are more expensive. This reduces workers' real wages because it means that a person's salary is not able to purchase as much food, clothing, or other goods from abroad. Likewise, firms that rely on imported inputs into production—for example, a Bangladeshi garment company that uses cotton from Benin—find their input costs increasing with undervaluation. Higher costs for imported goods might, in turn, push up prices for locally made goods and increase the overall rate of inflation.

Second, an undervalued exchange rate makes foreign debts more burdensome. Many individuals and businesses in developing countries take out loans from foreign countries that they must repay in foreign currency terms. For example, 700,000 Hungarians took out home mortgages that were denominated in Swiss francs (Alderman 2011). Undervalued exchange rates increase foreign debt burdens because local debtors need more units of domestic currency to pay off a given amount of foreign debt (Pepinsky 2009; Walter 2008; Woodruff 2005). Hungarian homeowners learned this lesson when Hungary's currency, the forint, depreciated against the Swiss franc; as a result, paying off their mortgages took up a bigger share of their forint-denominated salaries than beforehand.

An undervalued exchange rate imposes a third cost on local households and businesses: higher domestic borrowing costs. As I explain in more detail in the next section, in order to keep the exchange rate undervalued, central banks typically adopt "sterilized" foreign exchange interventions, meaning that they purchase foreign currency by selling domestic bonds (Calvo, Leiderman, and Reinhart 1996; Reinhart and Reinhart 1998). When a government sells large volumes of sterilization bonds, investors become more worried that the government will not honor its debt obligations. Therefore, governments must pay investors a higher interest rate to get them to purchase their bonds. Sterilized foreign exchange interventions therefore lead to large spikes in interest rates (Frankel 1997; Reinhart and Reinhart 1998). For instance, when Colombia's central bank started to sterilize heavily in the 1990s, interest rates on short-term loans increased from 23% to 47% (Reinhart and Reinhart 1998, 108). Higher domestic interest rates make it costlier for households to purchase big-ticket items like cars and they make business investments more expensive and less profitable. Due to the rising cost of capital, sterilized interventions often reduce investment in plants and equipment (Reinhart and Reinhart 1998, 109). In short, sustaining an undervalued currency is achieved by selling more government bonds, which raises borrowing costs.

External competitiveness is the most direct benefit of undervalued exchange rates (Frieden 1991a). Undervalued exchange rates make a country's products cheaper in world markets, which tends to increase exports. They also make foreign goods more expensive for local consumers, which encourages them to purchase more domestically produced goods.

By improving external competitiveness, undervalued exchange rates can bring substantial long-run benefits to an economy. As discussed in the introduction, many studies find that economic growth tends to be faster in countries with undervalued exchange rates than in those with market-valued or overvalued exchange rates. Some economists believe that undervaluation promotes growth because it encourages firms to invest in high-productivity tradable industries, which increases economy-wide productivity rates (Rodrik 2008). Others believe that undervaluation increases economic growth because it lowers labor costs, which allows firms to increase their investment rates (Levy-Yeyati, Sturzenegger, and Gluzmann 2013). Undervaluation also leads to more stable growth rates: undervaluation ensures that countries maintain positive trade balances, which reduces a country's vulnerability to capital flight and financial crises (Acemoglu et al. 2003; Reinhart and Rogoff 2009). Lower unemployment is another benefit of undervaluation: undervalued exchange rates lower wages relative to foreign imports and encourage firms to hire more workers (Frenkel and Ros 2006).

Undervalued exchange rates, then, have a variety of effects on the national economy, both negative and positive. The negative effects include higher costs for imports and increased costs of foreign and local debts. The main direct benefit of undervaluation is external competitiveness, but undervalued exchange rates also have numerous indirect long-term positive effects.

How Politicians Control Exchange Rates

An adequate understanding of exchange rate misalignments requires attention to politics. It is "political actors"—government officials that select national economic policies—rather than "market actors," such as currency speculators, that ultimately choose whether a country sustains an undervalued exchange rate. For this reason, the political calculations of policymakers must be front and center in any theory of undervalued exchange rates.

The real exchange rate is a "policy variable" that is within the control of government policymakers (Eichengreen 2007; Frieden 1997; Rodrik 2008). Governments that attach the highest priority to undervaluation should always be capable of maintaining an undervalued exchange rate.[1] Jeffry Frieden (1997, 82) forcefully argues that "there is no such thing as a technically unsustainable exchange rate. There is no level of the exchange rate that cannot be maintained for purely economic reasons." While it can be costly to sustain a misaligned exchange rate, "authorities always have the option" of doing so (Frieden 1997, 83). Policymakers are able to undervalue their exchange rates because all governments have a variety of policy instruments at their disposal that can be used to control their real exchange rate.

To maintain an undervalued exchange rate, policymakers must first get the exchange rate to an undervalued level, and then keep it there. The first step, depreciating the real exchange rate, can be accomplished in one of two ways. The most common way is to devalue the nominal exchange rate. All else equal, depreciating the domestic currency leads to a depreciation of the real exchange rate.[2] A second way to depreciate the real exchange rate is to adopt contractionary monetary and fiscal policies, such as high interest rates, high tax rates, and low levels of government spending. Contractionary macroeconomic policy decreases domestic prices and, holding other things constant, causes the real exchange rate to depreciate. Since 2008, Estonia, Latvia, and Lithuania all depreciated their real exchange rates via austerity-induced deflations.

---

1. The evidence overwhelmingly supports this idea that exchange rates diverge from their equilibrium values for long periods of time (see Rogoff 1996; Taylor and Taylor 2004).

2. Nominal depreciations contribute to real exchange rate depreciations as long as prices do not increase as rapidly as the currency depreciates, which tends to be the case empirically (Campa and Goldberg 2005; Choudhri and Hakura 2006).

Once the real exchange rate is undervalued, policymakers must then keep it undervalued. The most important way to do so is through central bank intervention in the foreign exchange market.[3] When the exchange rate is undervalued, there is an excess supply of foreign currency. Central banks must purchase this excess foreign currency to prevent appreciation of the nominal exchange rate. However, purchasing foreign currency increases the money supply, which puts upward pressure on domestic prices, threatening to erode the real exchange rate's undervaluation. The most common way for central banks to limit inflationary pressure is through "sterilized" foreign exchange interventions—purchasing foreign currency by selling bonds (Calvo et al. 1996; Reinhart and Reinhart 1998).[4] Czech Republic, Egypt, and Kenya were among the many countries whose governments purchased foreign currency and sold securities as part of their efforts to avoid an appreciation of the real exchange rate during the 1990s (Reinhart and Reinhart 1998).

Policymakers often adopt a number of additional policies to sustain an undervalued exchange rate. Contractionary fiscal policies, such as tax hikes and spending cuts, are often required to prevent real exchange rate appreciation (Reinhart and Reinhart 1998; Calvo, Leiderman, and Reinhart 1996). Tight fiscal policies are important because they keep domestic inflation low relative to foreign inflation. For instance, persistent fiscal surpluses were one of the key ingredients that helped Botswana's government keep its exchange rate undervalued (Harvey and Lewis 1990).

Some countries also intensify restrictions on capital inflows to reduce real appreciation.[5] When investors bring money into the economy, this increases the demand for the local currency, causing its value to strengthen. Restrictions on capital inflows can reduce these inflows and limit currency appreciation (Ghosh et al. 2012; Reinhardt, Ricci, and Tressel 2013). In the wake of the 2008 global financial crisis, policymakers in Brazil and Korea imposed controls on capital inflows to prevent their exchange rates from becoming overvalued (Gallagher 2015).

Just because governments are able to maintain an undervalued exchange rate does not mean that they are equally capable of sustaining an overvalued exchange

---

3. Although there has been a clear trend toward more flexible exchange rates since the 1970s, most developing countries continue to intervene in the foreign exchange market. Only four developing countries (Democratic Republic of Congo, South Africa, Turkey, and Zambia) had freely floating exchange rates in 2006 while the remaining 140 developing countries continued to intervene in the foreign exchange markets (Ilzetzki, Reinhart, and Rogoff 2008).

4. When the government sells bonds, it acquires currency that used to circulate, which reduces inflationary pressures. Sterilized intervention is effective when capital mobility is imperfect, which is a realistic assumption for virtually all developing countries (Frankel 1997; Reinhart and Reinhart 1998).

5. Many developing countries have removed restrictions on international capital flows since the 1980s, but according to Karcher and Steinberg's (2013) dataset, the vast majority (111 of 153 developing countries) maintained some capital controls in 2006.

rate. On the contrary, a government's ability to control the exchange rate is "decidedly asymmetric: Authorities have a variety of tools to blunt pressures that would otherwise lead to an appreciation of the home currency. Efforts to stem a depreciation of the home currency, in contrast, typically run aground against a strong tide of investor unwillingness to hold an asset expected to decline in value" (Reinhart and Reinhart 2008, 2). Governments wanting to keep their exchange rate undervalued face few obstacles to success because the amount of foreign currency that governments can purchase is effectively limitless. It can be harder for governments to keep the exchange rate overvalued because it is possible for them to run out of foreign currency (Mohanty and Turner 2005, 60). Not infrequently, overvalued exchange rates lead to large-scale capital flight, which drains the central bank of its foreign currency reserves and causes the exchange rate to depreciate rapidly. Governments can raise interest rates to stave off capital flight and prevent exchange rate devaluation. However, even if high interest rates successfully prevent the nominal exchange rate from depreciating, interest rate increases often cause prices to fall, which also depreciates the real exchange rate. Policymakers that want to keep their exchange rate overvalued can do so in most, but not all, circumstances.

In short, policymakers that are determined to keep their exchange rates undervalued have numerous policy instruments that they can use to this end. Those that want to undervalue their exchange rates can devalue the exchange rate, adopt contractionary fiscal policies, engage in sterilized foreign exchange interventions, and restrict capital inflows. This is undoubtedly a tall order. But policymakers do not lack the technical capacity to keep their exchange rates undervalued.[6] Undervaluation may be costly, but it is possible. The main obstacles to doing so are the economic costs and political unpopularity of these measures. As a result, it is essential to understand the motivations of the political actors that control the exchange rate.

Interest Groups and Undervalued Exchange Rates
Why Interest Groups Influence Exchange Rate Policy

In order to understand why undervalued exchange rates are rare, one must consider the goals of those that decide the exchange rate's level: politicians.[7] Most

---

6. To be clear, I am not suggesting that government officials have precise control over their exchange rate's level. They may not be able to maintain an exchange rate that is, say, exactly 20% undervalued. But they are able to control whether the exchange rate is undervalued or not.

7. Politicians, not central bankers, are the key decision makers on exchange rate policy in developing countries. Even "independent" central banks do not typically have the authority to determine

politicians should want to keep their exchange rate at or below its market rate because economies grow slowly and suffer from frequent financial crises when the exchange rate is overvalued. No policymaker is likely to find these outcomes desirable. Even a kleptocratic dictator should find the damaging effects of over-valued exchange rates unappealing; slower growth means less loot for klepto-crats and their cronies (Olson 1993).

Yet, clearly policymakers do not always select policies that are best for the over-all economy, and exchange rate policy is no exception. Politicians are concerned with maintaining social support for their exchange rate policies, and they are unlikely to undervalue the exchange rate unless this decision wins them support from powerful domestic interest groups. Policymakers may want to adopt ex-change rate policies that promote long-term development, but they need short-term political support for their policies. Interest group support typically trumps other objectives when it comes to exchange rate policymaking.

The starting premise of the conditional preference theory is that societal interest groups strongly influence exchange rate policy. That is, interest group preferences help determine whether policymakers maintain an undervalued exchange rate. Throughout this book, I use the term "influence" to refer to an actor's ability to bring about favorable policy outcomes. An interest group is said to exert influence over exchange rate policy when the government's exchange rate policies would have been different in the absence of that group's support for the adopted policy.

Why are interest groups able to influence exchange rate policy? The answer is simple: political leaders require societal support for their exchange rate policies. Their survival in office depends on such support. Neither dictators nor demo-cratic rulers are likely to remain in power if they choose policies that receive no support from key interest groups (Bueno de Mesquita et al. 2003). Politicians would be taking excessive political risks if they maintained an undervalued exchange rate in a country where interest groups universally opposed this policy.

Societal interest groups have a variety of tools that they can use to influence government decisions with respect to exchange rate policy. Interest groups can reward leaders for adopting favorable exchange rate policies and they can punish rulers that maintain unfavorable exchange rate policies. Lobbying and direct pres-sure are one set of tactics that interest groups can use to encourage political deci-sion makers to adopt their preferred exchange rate policy. For example, in a de-mocracy, organized interest groups can punish unresponsive leaders by instructing their members to vote for the leaders' opponents in primary and general elec-

---

the objectives of monetary policy, but only to independently manipulate policy levers to achieve their objectives. Rather, it is political leaders and other political officials that determine whether an under-valued exchange rate is a major policy objective.

tions. Organized interests may also make campaign contributions to politicians that promise more favorable exchange rate policies. In countries with an independent media, interest groups may also attempt to sway public opinion by publicly lambasting unfriendly politicians.

Interest groups can also influence exchange rate policy in authoritarian regimes, though they use different means to do so. Interest groups can use their connections with bureaucrats and party elites to promote alternative candidates or factions of single-party dictatorships. In military regimes, interest groups that are unhappy with exchange rate policy can encourage other members of the armed forces to replace the sitting ruler, or they can help democratic movements overthrow the junta altogether. The collapse of Indonesia's military regime in the late 1990s provides an example: currency devaluation harmed certain business groups, and their declining support for the Suharto regime hastened its demise (Pepinsky 2009).

It is also possible for interest groups to influence exchange rate policy through more indirect channels, sometimes without even trying. Policymakers may seek to anticipate an interest group's reaction to policy changes. Political decision makers have incentives to avoid policy changes that they expect will generate unfavorable outcomes, such as a reduction in certain types of investment (Lindblom 1977; Hacker and Pierson 2002; Fairfield 2010).[8] The financial sector in the United States provides a helpful illustration: one reason American banks receive favorable financial policies is that bank failures would have disastrous effects on the rest of the American economy, and thus on policymakers' political standing. Along the same lines, politicians have every incentive to avoid an undervalued exchange rate if they expect that undervaluation would damage an interest group whose success is vital to the economy's well-being. An interest group in that situation could influence exchange rate policy without even lobbying.

Simply put, interest groups control various "carrots" and "sticks" that give them influence over exchange rate policy. Interest groups that are pleased with exchange rate policies can use their resources to support incumbent rulers and help them fend off political rivals. Societal actors that are displeased with the government's exchange rate policies can punish political decision makers in various ways and make it more difficult for them to retain office. Policymakers have an incentive to maintain exchange rate policies that are favored by interest groups that can advance or impede their political fortunes. There are certainly some politicians that ignore these political incentives because they are, depending on one's perspective, courageous or foolish. That being said, most exchange rate policymakers prioritize domestic political support over economic development and other objectives.

---

8. This type of indirect influence is often referred to as "structural power." For reasons explained shortly, I avoid this term and reserve the term "power" to refer to an actor's resources.

Power Resources and Political Influence

Different interest groups often have opposing interests when it comes to the exchange rate level. Any interest group theory must, therefore, explain which interest groups are likely to win battles over exchange rate policy. In other words: What determines an interest group's influence over exchange rate policy?

Political influence is determined by many factors. I focus here on one important variable: power. "Powerful" interest groups should have more influence over exchange rate policy than less powerful groups. Since power is a contested concept, it is important to be clear about my definition of power. While power and influence are often used as synonyms, I sharply distinguish between the two terms.[9] I adopt a "power resources approach," which defines power as the "resources that actors can control to advance their claims and to defend their interests" (Korpi 2006, 172).[10] From this perspective, an interest group is defined as powerful when it controls more resources than other interest groups. At least three types of power resources are relevant for an interest group's ability to influence exchange rate policy: economic, organizational, and normative resources.

Economic resources are the first, and most straightforward, type of power resource (Baldwin 1979; Korpi 1985, 2006). Interest groups that control more wealth, own more physical capital, and employ more people are likely to have more sway over exchange rate policy decisions than those with fewer of these economic resources.[11] There are a number of reasons why economic resources should increase political influence. Groups with more income have more funds to dedicate to campaign contributions and to hire lobbyists. Interest groups that control a larger share of the economy's wealth receive more attention from the media and the public, which should make their lobbying efforts more successful. Finally, interest groups that command more economic resources have a larger impact on employment, tax revenue, and overall economic growth. Thus, policymakers should be especially concerned with ensuring that large industries are economically successful, and should provide them with more favorable policies as a result.

The second type of power resource, which I label "organizational resources," refers to an interest group's ability to overcome collective action problems and lobby effectively. There are several components to an actor's organizational resources. One important factor for economic interest groups is their industrial structure: industries composed of a small number of large firms will have an eas-

---

9. In differentiating between power and influence, I follow Cox and Jacobson (1973), among others.

10. Korpi (1985) presents a compelling defense of the "power resources" approach.

11. Baumgartner et al. (2009, ch. 11), Gilens and Page (2014), and Weymouth (2012) provide compelling evidence that economic resources increase policy influence.

ier time organizing and lobbying than industries that are made up of a large num-ber of small firms (Olson 1965). Second, business associations provide an impor-tant avenue through which groups of firms can lobby and influence policy (Fairfield 2010; Schneider 2004; Weymouth 2012). Sectors that have already constructed effective business associations should, therefore, have greater influence over ex-change rate policy. An industry's relationship with political decision makers, such as legislators, bureaucrats, and political parties, are a third type of organizational resource that should increase influence over exchange rate policy (Fairfield 2010). Previous research demonstrates that politically connected firms receive more fa-vorable policies in a variety of issue areas, including tax breaks, subsidized credit, and government bailouts (Adhikari, Derashind, and Zhang 2006; Faccio, Masu-lis, and McConnell 2006; Khwaja and Mian 2005; Malesky and Taussig 2009). The same should hold true for exchange rate policy: sectors that have ties to political decision makers should have more success convincing policymakers to keep the exchange rate at their preferred level.

"Normative power resources" are a third type of power resource that should increase groups' influence over exchange rate policy (Korpi 1985, 34). Norma-tive power resources encompass various types of nonmaterial resources, such as the social status or prestige of an interest group.[12] Interest groups that societies hold in high esteem should find it easier to convince policymakers to adopt pol-icies that benefit them. By contrast, groups should be less likely to win favorable public policies when government officials and the public believe that they are un-worthy of public assistance.

This discussion suggests that an interest group's influence over exchange rate policy—i.e., its ability to alter government decisions about exchange rates—should increase with the amount of economic, organizational, and normative resources that it controls. It also implies that the balance of power between various domes-tic interest groups should influence the exchange rate level. Policymakers are likely to undervalue their exchange rate when the interest groups that favor undervalu-ation are powerful. Undervalued exchange rates should be rare when opponents of this policy are powerful.

The Importance of the Manufacturing Sector

Exchange rate policy should depend on the balance of power between all of the interest groups with a stake in the matter. However, when it comes to exchange rate policy in developing countries, some interest groups are more decisive than

---

12. This kind of nonmaterial resource is similar to what Nye (2004) calls a "soft-power resource."

others. The influence of one group often stands above the rest: namely, the manufacturing sector. Randall Henning (1994, 28; 2006, 123) suggests that "the manufacturing sector merits special attention" in the study of exchange rate politics because it has large stakes in the issue and because it is "often well represented in the policy process."

The manufacturing sector is widely viewed as a privileged interest group in the developing world. Manufacturing is not the only interest group that matters, nor is it the most important interest group in all countries. But the political power of the manufacturing sector has particularly important consequences for whether an undervalued exchange rate is politically viable. Eva Bellin (2002, 11) points out that "private sector industrialists have long been perceived by social scientists, from Marxists to liberals, as uniquely positioned to control the state's policy direction." This influence should be as substantial for exchange rate policy as for any policy issue.

My theory places the power and preferences of the manufacturing sector at the center of the analysis. Doing so provides an admittedly incomplete picture of the story, but a detailed analysis of the manufacturing sector is very useful in other ways. Paying close attention to the manufacturing sector helps to generate a more accurate understanding of how this important—and widely misunderstood—group influences exchange rate policymaking. The remainder of this section provides an overview of the power resources of the manufacturing sector, explains why they have extensive influence over exchange rate policy in many developing countries, and when that influence should be strongest.

Industrialists typically have more organizational power than other interest groups in developing countries. The manufacturing sector is typically composed of a small number of large firms. Moreover, these firms tend to locate in close proximity to one another in cities. These attributes make it easier for the manufacturing sector to organize and lobby the state for favorable policies (Bates 1981). By contrast, agricultural producers tend to be spread out across the countryside, and the number of farmers in a developing country is typically very large.[13] The service sector also tends to comprise a large number of small firms, thwarting their capacity for collective action.[14] All else equal, the manufacturing sector's ability to lobby the state for favorable policies surpasses that of other sectors.

---

13. According to Bates (1981, 88), most African nations have fewer than 1,000 manufacturing firms, and most manufacturing subsectors have fewer than ten firms. By contrast, countries like Tanzania and Kenya have over a million farmers each. Producers of nonagricultural commodities tend to lack influence for a different reason: states often own these firms and use them to promote political and social goals, rather than economic ones such as profit maximization (Radetzki 2008, 166–173).

14. For instance, in the World Bank Enterprise Survey (2002–2006), the median manufacturing firm in the developing world had 30 permanent employees (n = 43,650). The equivalent figure for service and construction firms was 12 (n = 22,488).

The manufacturing sector also wields tremendous normative power resources throughout the developing world. Policymakers and citizens often equate industrialization with development and modernity (Amsden 2001; Bates 1981; Tybout 2000). As Bates (1981, 3–4) explains: "Foremost among the social objectives of governments in the developing areas is to shift the basis of their economies away from the production of agricultural commodities and toward the production of manufactured goods." In developing countries that have an existing industrial base, the state typically aspires to transform its industrial sector and to manufacture more innovative, technologically sophisticated products with the highest value-added (Evans 1995; Gereffi, Humphrey, and Sturgeon 2005). A state's ability to achieve these objectives depends on the actions of entrepreneurs in the manufacturing sector, which further bolsters their political influence (Bellin 2002). There is a widespread belief in developing countries that what is good for industry is good for the nation. These normative resources help the manufacturing sector triumph over other sectors in distributional conflicts.

The manufacturing sector's organizational and normative resources set it apart from other sectors, but this does not imply the manufacturing sector should have a strong influence over exchange rate policy in all developing countries. Power resources vary across countries, and political influence is likely to vary accordingly. First, even though, as a general tendency, the organizational and normative power resources of the manufacturing sector exceed those of other sectors, this is not always the case. In countries where manufacturers have relatively few organizational and normative resources, their influence is likely to be more limited. Second, the manufacturing sector's control over economic resources varies considerably from one country to the next. The manufacturing sector is unlikely to have much influence over exchange rate policy when its economic resources are limited. It is likely to have a strong impact on exchange rate policy decisions when it controls a large share of economic resources relative to other interest groups (Blomberg, Frieden, and Stein 2005; Frieden 2002; Frieden, Ghezzi, and Stein 2001; Frieden, Leblang, and Valev 2010; Singer 2010, 312).

To summarize, the preferences of powerful interest groups influence whether a country's exchange rate is overvalued or undervalued. The preferences of the manufacturing sector are of particular importance. Manufacturers tend to control many organizational and normative power resources; when these power resources are combined with substantial economic resources, the manufacturing sector's influence over exchange rate policy should be unparalleled. However, despite widespread recognition that manufacturers are important players in the exchange rate arena, their preferences are poorly understood. According to conventional wisdom, the "industrial sector . . . has an *un*ambiguous interest in a competitively valued currency" (Henning 1994, 27). The next section shows that this is not the case, and that a more accurate understanding of the preferences of the manufacturing sector goes a long way toward explaining why undervalued exchange rates are rare.

Interest Group Preferences

Even though an undervalued exchange rate is good for the long-run health of the economy, there is often little societal support for this policy. Many interest groups oppose undervalued exchange rates because they experience large costs and negligible benefits from an undervalued exchange rate in the short run. Some important groups, such as the manufacturing sector, certainly benefit directly from an undervalued exchange rate. However, since undervalued exchange rates also increase their operating costs, these groups tend to be no more than "conditional supporters" of an undervalued exchange rate.[15] Hence, preferences for undervalued exchange rates are often context-dependent, rather than constant.[16] Since the manufacturing sector often has exceptional levels of political influence, its failure to unconditionally support undervaluation is especially consequential. The overall lack of enthusiastic support for an undervalued exchange rate helps explain why exchange rates are rarely undervalued.

A Simple Model of Exchange Rate Valuation Preferences

This section presents a simple framework for deducing interest group preferences vis-à-vis an undervalued exchange rate. I assume that actors focus on how undervalued exchange rates affect their profits/income over the short or medium term, but they do not weigh its effects far into the future as heavily. This framework derives preferences for undervalued exchange rates based on two actor characteristics.

The first characteristic is the degree of "tradability": whether the product one sells can be easily traded across national borders. Frieden's (1991a) path-breaking study emphasizes this distinction between tradable and nontradable industries as the main determinant of exchange rate level preferences. Retail, banking, and services, such as haircuts, are examples of nontradable industries. Manufactured goods, from toothbrushes to televisions, are tradable. Tradability determines

---

15. Other scholars, such as Helleiner (2005), Henning (1994), McNamara (1998), and Walter (2008), have also observed that some interest groups have context-specific exchange rate preferences.

16. The term "preference," as used here, refers to an actor's policy preferences, or what Frieden (1999) calls "preferences over outcomes." When I say that preferences are context-dependent, I mean that the ideal level of the real exchange rate varies from one context to another. The theory assumes that actors' "primitive preferences," such as the desire for higher income, are constant.

whether undervalued exchange rates are beneficial. Undervaluation benefits tradable producers because it increases these firms' international competitiveness. Increasing an economy's external competitiveness has little effect on nontradable firms because they, by definition, do not compete with foreign producers. Frieden's sectoral theory hypothesizes that tradable industries prefer undervalued exchange rates and nontradable industries prefer overvalued exchange rates.

The characteristics of a firm's inputs are as important as the nature of its output. The more a firm relies on importable inputs and debt, the larger the costs of an undervalued exchange rate. Since undervalued exchange rates make imports more expensive, they increase the operating costs of firms that use imported production inputs. In fact, all internationally tradable inputs whose prices are set in world markets, even if they are not directly obtained from foreign suppliers, become more expensive when the exchange rate depreciates (Bodnar and Gentry 1993). Likewise, firms whose borrowing is denominated in foreign currency see their debt burdens increase when the exchange rate is undervalued. Finally, firms that rely on domestic debt are also hurt by undervalued exchange rates because undervaluation tends to push up local interest rates.

Two main factors determine an actor's exchange rate preferences: the degree of tradability of a firm's product or service, and its reliance on imported inputs and debt. These two attributes produce four possible types of actors.[17] Table 1.1 summarizes how these actor characteristics affect exchange rate valuation preferences. Firms that produce tradable goods and do not use importable inputs and bank debt should strongly support undervalued exchange rates because undervaluation improves these firms' competitiveness but has no effect on their production costs. By contrast, nontradable industries that are heavily reliant on debt and importable inputs should strongly oppose undervalued exchange rates because undervaluation increases their costs without enhancing their competitiveness. The other two combinations produce more ambiguous preferences. Undervalued exchange rates have little effect, either positive or negative, on nontradable firms that use few inputs and debt, causing them to be indifferent to the exchange

---

17. The degree of product differentiation is a third variable that influences support for undervalued exchange rates (Broz and Frieden 2001). However, it is less central than the other two attributes because it does not determine *whether* undervaluation is beneficial, only *how much* it is beneficial. As explained below, in note 20, incorporating this issue reinforces the conclusion that few groups benefit from an undervalued exchange rate. Previous studies also divide tradable firms according to whether they are import-competing or export-oriented (Frieden 1991a). I ignore this distinction because, as Frieden (1991a) points out, export orientation should influence preferences for a stable exchange rate, but not for an undervalued exchange rate; both import-competing and export-oriented firms gain competitiveness when the exchange rate is undervalued. A second reason to not focus on export orientation is the strong potential for reverse causality: the exchange rate level influences whether a firm can profitably export its products and therefore whether it is an export-oriented or import-competing firm (Oatley 2010).

TABLE 1.1.   Exchange rate preferences

| TRADABILITY | RELIANCE ON DEBT AND IMPORTABLE INPUTS | |
	LOW	HIGH
LOW	Indifferent	Overvalued
HIGH	Undervalued	Conditional

TABLE 1.2.   Summary of interest group preferences

INTEREST GROUP	TRADABILITY	RELIANCE ON DEBT AND IMPORTABLE INPUTS	PREFERRED EXCHANGE RATE LEVEL
Service sector	Low	High	Overvalued
Financial sector	Low	High	Overvalued
Labor	Low	High	Overvalued
Primary sector	Variable	Variable	Divided
Manufacturing sector	High	High	Conditional

rate's level. On the other hand, tradable producers with a high dependence on debt and importable inputs receive both large benefits and large costs from undervaluation. Although undervaluation has ambiguous effects on this last group's profit, they are hardly indifferent to the exchange rate's level; they are better characterized as conditional supporters of undervaluation.

The remainder of this section assesses the degree to which five different actors support or oppose undervalued exchange rates. Table 1.2 summarizes the attributes and preferences of these five groups. A clear message emerges from this discussion: few interest groups strongly and consistently favor an undervalued exchange rate.

The Service Sector

The service sector, which includes everything from restaurants to real estate, is the archetypal nontradable industry. These service-sector firms do not compete for customers with companies in foreign countries. Table 1.3 shows that the average service and construction firm exports a mere 5% of its sales. As a result, these industries benefit little from an undervalued exchange rate. However, most service providers rely on some importable inputs: the local restaurant may buy their vegetables or fish from a foreign country and construction companies may import cement from abroad. Many service-sector firms also borrow from banks to finance their investments. According to table 1.3, over one-quarter of this sector's inputs are imported and over 10% of their investments are financed by local bank borrowing. Undervaluation is anathema to firms in the service sector because it increases their costs without improving their competitiveness.

The Financial Sector

The financial sector opposes undervaluation because it is a nontradable industry that is often highly dependent on foreign capital. When the exchange rate depreciates, banks in emerging economies face serious difficulties paying off their foreign creditors and are likely to go bankrupt (Pepinsky 2009; Woodruff 2005; Walter 2008). Undervaluation also makes it more expensive for bankers to purchase assets from abroad (Frieden 1991a). Undervalued exchange rates may also have indirect negative effects on the financial sector: banks earn low rates of return on foreign reserves and/or sterilization bonds, which often account for a large share of their assets when the exchange rate is undervalued (Cruz and Walters 2008, 671; Standard Chartered 2008c).

Labor

Labor is another group that tends to dislike undervalued exchange rates. An undervalued exchange rate increases the price of imports and increases the price of domestically produced tradable goods relative to nontradable goods. Thus, basic consumer items like clothing, food, and oil are more expensive when the exchange rate is undervalued. Since workers typically consume more tradable than nontradable items, undervaluation decreases real wage levels (Cooper 1971; Edwards 1989; Huizinga 1997; Levy-Yeyati, Sturzenegger, and Gluzmann 2013).

In addition, most workers are employed in nontradable industries: the service sector, which is more labor intensive than other industries, employs over half of the workforce in the majority of developing countries (Bearce and Hallerberg 2011). Thus, for most laborers, undervaluation also reduces their employers' profitability and increases the likelihood that they experience wage cuts or layoffs. On the other hand, it is unclear that even the minority of workers that are employed in export-oriented industries are able to capture much, if any, of the gains from an undervalued exchange rate. For example, low real wages were the most noticeable effect of undervaluation on workers in East Asia's exporting factories (Deyo 1989). Overall, labor opposes undervalued exchange rates because lower real wages are the main short-run effect of this policy.[18]

---

18. Although undervaluation has one important benefit for labor—higher aggregate employment—this tends to occur over the long run as firms substitute foreign capital for labor (Frenkel and Ros 2006). This effect is too indirect, uncertain, and long term to be salient for most individuals.

The Primary Sector

The primary sector comprises producers of agriculture and primary commodities such as oil and minerals. This sector encompasses various types of actors with distinct exchange rate preferences. In principle, primary goods are tradable and some developing countries export large volumes of primary goods, but this is not always the case in practice. Many farmers live in remote areas, and the high cost of transporting goods from rural areas makes some parts of agriculture a de facto nontradable industry (Broz, Frieden, and Weymouth 2008, 433). The primary sector also varies greatly in terms of its reliance on importable inputs and debt. Land and labor are the main production inputs for some primary producers. However, many primary producers are quite capital-intensive. For example, farmers often use imported tractors and fertilizers in the production process. Similarly, producers of commodities such as lumber and mining often need to undertake massive fixed investments, which makes them sensitive to interest rates and the price of imported inputs (Forbes 2002).

Due to these important variations, positions on exchange rate policy vary widely within the primary sector. Export-oriented primary producers are strong advocates of undervaluation in some countries, particularly when they do not rely on imported inputs. For example, Ghanaian cocoa producers and Colombian coffee exporters supported undervalued exchange rates (Bates 1981, 1997). On the other hand, many primary firms rely on imported inputs and, as a result, may oppose undervaluation, as was the case for Turkey's agricultural sector (Waldner 1999, 109–116). Finally, exchange rate valuation has little effect on subsistence farmers who produce nontradable goods without any reliance on imported inputs or debt. Some agricultural and commodity firms strongly support undervalued exchange rates; other firms in this sector only conditionally support undervaluation; still others are indifferent to the exchange rate's level. The primary sector is a divided one when it comes to the level of the exchange rate.[19]

The Manufacturing Sector

Most manufacturing firms produce tradable goods, use large volumes of importable inputs, and borrow from domestic and foreign banks. Table 1.3 provides data from the World Bank's Enterprise Survey, a large survey of private firms fielded between 2002 and 2006, which supports this characterization. The second col-

---

19. Consistent with this view, Forbes (2002) finds that devaluations do not have consistent effects on the long-term profits of commodity firms. This effect depends on firms' capital-intensity and the degree to which devaluation pushes up interest rates.

TABLE 1.3. Characteristics of service and manufacturing firms

	SERVICES AND CONSTRUCTION	MANUFACTURING	TEXTILE MANUFACTURING	AGRO-INDUSTRIAL MANUFACTURING	CAPITAL GOODS MANUFACTURING	CONSUMER GOODS MANUFACTURING
Exports	5.2% (n=22,134)	21.9% (n=44,999)	33.7% (n=12,128)	18.1% (n=9,142)	17.2% (n=12,713)	17.4% (n=10,761)
Imported inputs	28.7% (n=11,928)	31.5% (n=24,315)	39.9% (n=6,710)	19.3% (n=5,362)	34.6% (n=7,528)	28.2% (n=4,426)
Local bank borrowing	10.6% (n=12,544)	20.2% (n=26,839)	19.6% (n=5,848)	20.7% (n=5,848)	20.1% (n=7,742)	20.7% (n=6,154)
Foreign currency borrowing	4.4% (n=6,723)	14.7% (n=18,263)	15.2% (n=5,163)	15.5% (n=3,456)	17.8% (n=4,917)	10.2% (n=4,714)

Note: Data are from The World Bank, Enterprise Survey (2002–2006). Firms in high-income OECD countries are excluded. Exports equals the percentage of production that is exported either directly or indirectly. Imported inputs is the percentage of inputs that are imported either directly or indirectly. Local bank borrowing is the percentage of finance for new investment from local banks. Foreign currency borrowing is the percentage of total borrowing denominated in foreign currency. Textile manufacturing includes producers of textiles, leather, or garments. Agro-industrial manufacturing includes producers of agro-industry, food, and beverages. Capital goods manufacturing includes producers of metals and machinery, chemicals and pharmaceuticals, and plastics. Consumer goods manufacturing includes producers of electronics, wood and furniture, paper, sporting goods, other manufacturing, automobiles, and other transport equipment.

umn of table 1.3 presents data for the entire manufacturing sector. The data indicate that the average manufacturing firm exports over one-fifth of its production, which is far more than service-sector firms and illustrates that many manufacturing goods are tradable. Manufactured goods also tend to be produced with a high quantity of importable components (Campa and Goldberg 1997). For example, automobile producers use large volumes of imported machinery and steel in the production process (Sturgeon, Van Biesobroeck, and Gereffi 2008). Table 1.3 shows that the average manufacturing firm in the Enterprise Survey sample imports almost a third of its inputs. A third characteristic of the manufacturing sector is its heavy borrowing from local banks, with 20% of manufacturing firms' new investments financed from borrowing from local banks. Lastly, table 1.3 shows that 15% of manufacturers' debts are denominated in foreign currency.

These characteristics are remarkably consistent across all the major manufacturing subsectors. The next four columns in table 1.3 provide data for four groups of manufacturing firms: textiles, agro-industrial, capital goods, and consumer goods manufacturers. The similarities across these subsectors are far more striking than their differences. All four manufacturing industries produce tradable goods and rely on imported inputs and debt. The typical firm in each of these manufacturing subsectors fits into the lower right quadrant of table 1.1.

Due to these attributes, undervaluation simultaneously increases many manufactured firms' revenues as well as their expenses, with ambiguous effects on the profits of these firms. Since manufactured goods must compete against foreign products, an undervalued exchange rate can provide these firms with much-needed competitive advantages.[20] However, undervaluation is also potentially problematic for many industrialists because it makes it more expensive for them to purchase their inputs and increases their debt burdens. Due to these two important but cross-cutting effects, many in the manufacturing sector are conditional supporters of an undervalued exchange rate. Industrialists should support undervaluation at least some of the time because of its large benefits. However, the costs are

---

20. However, this benefit may be small for manufacturing firms because some manufactured goods, such as electronics, are differentiated in terms of product quality, meaning that the quality of the product influences its price. Since the prices of differentiated goods are less sensitive to the exchange rate's level, producers of differentiated manufactured goods receive relatively small benefits from an undervalued exchange rate (Broz and Frieden 2001; Helleiner 2005; Kinderman 2008). Foreign ownership is another factor that might reduce manufacturing firms' sensitivity to the exchange rate level (Frieden 1994, 86; Kinderman 2008). Since multinational corporations have interests in multiple economies, they may be less concerned about any individual country's exchange rate level. Even with the growth of multinational corporations in recent years, less than 10% of manufacturing firms are majority foreign-owned (Enterprise Survey, 2002–2006). Foreign firms also tend to be less politically influential: "the problem of developing countries, at least in the area of exchange rates, is not that multinational enterprises have been too politically powerful but that they have not been strong enough to influence policy" (Herbst 2000, 219).

likely to outweigh the benefits at other times, causing manufacturers to oppose undervaluation. In short, many manufacturing firms have context-dependent preferences for undervalued exchange rates.

A brief glance at the historical record confirms that the manufacturing sector has supported undervalued exchange rates in some circumstances and opposed undervalued exchange rates at other junctures. Chile in the early 1980s and Taiwan in the late 1990s are two of the many cases in which industrialists lobbied policymakers to undervalue the exchange rate (Silva 1993, 551; Walter 2008, 421). There have also been numerous instances in which manufacturing firms have opposed undervalued exchange rates. Mexican industrialists lobbied against exchange rate devaluation in the early 1990s (Kessler 1998). Turkish industrialists "objected vociferously" to their country's devaluation in 1970 (Waldner 1999, 116). Peruvian manufacturing firms also regularly "pushed for . . . a stronger (appreciated) currency" (Pascó-Font and Ghezzi 2001, 251). The manufacturing sector's preferred exchange rate level varies greatly across countries.

What determines whether the manufacturing sector favors undervaluation or opposes it? I suggest that cross-country differences in the manufacturing sector's preferences are mostly caused by the varying national contexts that this sector finds itself in. Variation in the manufacturing sector's production profile cannot fully explain why preferences vary across countries. The production profile of the manufacturing sector is quite similar from one country to the next. In virtually all developing countries, a substantial share of the manufacturing sector produces tradable goods and relies on imported inputs and debt. Regardless of whether a country's manufacturing sector focuses on making metals or microchips, undervaluation is likely to have an ambiguous effect on their profits. As I will explain shortly, one contextual factor—labor and financial market institutions—shapes this sector's preferences.

Preferences and the Rarity of Undervalued Exchange Rates

This investigation into interest group preferences for undervalued exchange rates reveals one striking pattern: there is typically more societal support for an overvalued exchange rate than an undervalued one. It is widely recognized that labor, services, and finance oppose undervalued exchange rates. An equally important but less widely recognized fact is that tradable firms are often reluctant to support an undervalued exchange rate. Tradable firms are often indifferent, or even opposed, to undervalued exchange rates because this policy increases their input costs and debt burdens. The manufacturing sector is often no more than a conditional supporter of undervalued exchange rates.

This lack of interest group support for undervaluation discourages policymakers from keeping their exchange rates undervalued. One of my main arguments is that low levels of interest group support help explain why undervalued exchange rates have been relatively uncommon in the developing world. The preferences of the manufacturing sector are particularly important. Since the manufacturing sector is often one of the most powerful interest groups in many developing countries, manufacturers' failure to staunchly and consistently support an undervalued exchange rate discourages many policymakers from pursuing undervaluation. More developing countries would undervalue their exchange rates if their powerful manufacturing sectors did not object to doing so.

An Institutionalist Theory of Exchange Rate Preferences

Preferences for undervalued exchange rates are likely to be influenced by a number of contextual variables. This section explains why state institutions have an important effect on whether interest groups prefer an undervalued exchange rate. I argue that two types of institutions—those relating to the structure of national labor markets and national financial markets—influence the exchange rate preferences of the manufacturing sector. My main hypothesis is that state-controlled labor and financial structures increase support for an undervalued exchange rate.

The Importance of Labor and Financial Market Institutions

There is widespread agreement among political economists that institutions matter. The more important question is which types of institutions matter and why. Most scholars of international political economy focus on formal political institutions, such as electoral rules, and suggest that institutions shape foreign economic policy because they determine how interest groups' preferences get translated into policy (see Lake 2009; Moravcsik 1997). This approach is not necessarily incorrect, but it is far too narrow. Historical institutionalists emphasize that economic policy also depends on a much broader variety of institutional structures, including "public policy institutions" (Farrell and Newman 2010, 611). Even more important, historical institutionalists point out that institutions do more than merely "aggregate" interest group preferences. Institutions also determine how interest groups formulate their policy preferences (Farrell and Newman 2010; Fioretos 2011; Thelen 1999; Thelen and Steinmo 1992). My institutionalist theory utilizes these historical institutionalist insights to explain exchange rate policy-making in the developing world.

The institutional structures of the state define the policy tools and organizational resources that are available for government policymakers (Haggard 1990; Ikenberry 1986; Katzenstein 1978; Skocpol 1985). Haggard (1990, 46) points out that state actors' policy "options are limited or expanded by the tools they have at hand." All states with independent currencies possess various policy tools that give them control over their real exchange rates. But states vary considerably when it comes to their ability to adopt certain types of microeconomic policies.

Some institutional structures provide state policymakers with an array of instruments that can be used to alter the profitability of individual firms or sectors. I refer to this type of institution as a *state-controlled system*. Other institutional arrangements leave policymakers with few instruments for targeting particular firms or industries for favorable treatment. I label such institutions non-state-controlled or *private-controlled systems* since non-state actors have substantial authority over economic outcomes.

Public policy institutions are important for exchange rate politics because they shape policymakers' ability to counter the negative effects of an undervalued exchange rate. Institutions that expand the policy instruments available to state authorities make it more likely that policymakers will implement targeted microeconomic policies that lower firms' operating costs. The manufacturing sector's costs would not increase substantially if policymakers combined real exchange rate depreciation with wage cuts, lower interest rates, or other such measures; this policy combination would increase manufacturing firms' competitiveness and sales revenue while ensuring that their costs remain low. Institutional structures that influence whether states can adopt targeted cost-reducing policies should, therefore, influence interest group preferences. Interest groups, and the manufacturing sector in particular, should be more likely to support an undervalued exchange rate when the state can render their operating costs insensitive to the exchange rate level.

I focus on the state's control over labor markets and financial markets, which are particularly important for exchange rate preferences for the following reasons. First, financial capital and labor are the two most important inputs for nearly all manufacturing businesses. Wages rates and interest rates consequently have a large impact on manufacturers' profitability and are salient concerns for this sector. Therefore, when state institutions endow policymakers with extensive control over labor and financial markets, policymakers gain powerful instruments for minimizing business costs. Second, wage rates and interest rates are closely connected to exchange rate levels. Absent countervailing actions, undervalued exchange rates increase firms' borrowing costs. Currency depreciations also intensify workers' demands for higher wage rates. A third reason to focus on the state's control over labor and finance is that this capacity varies considerably. For these reasons, variation in the state's control over labor and financial markets is a strong candidate for explaining why support for undervalued exchange rates is stronger in some countries than in others.

Institutions governing a country's labor and financial systems are strongly influenced by path dependence (Collier and Collier 1991; Hall and Soskice 2001). Early decisions about labor and financial structures and other historical factors, such as the nature and timing of a country's development and its legal system, strongly influence contemporary labor and financial systems (Amsden 2001; Beck, Demirgüc-Kunt, and Levine 2003; Botero et al. 2004; Gerschenkron 1962; La Porta, Lopez-de-Silanes, and Shleifer 2002). This does not imply that labor and financial structures are completely static. In fact, large-scale political and economic changes in the 1980s and 1990s, which included democratization, economic crises, and international political pressures, led to noticeable reductions in the state's control over labor and financial systems in a number of countries in Eastern Europe, Latin America, and sub-Saharan Africa.[21] However, rapid changes in labor and financial structures rarely occur except during periods in which a country's broader political-economic system undergoes radical change. It is unlikely that governments would drastically alter the state's control over labor and financial markets just so that they can maintain support for an undervalued exchange rate. Few policymakers or interest groups would advance radical institutional change as a solution to their concerns with prevailing exchange rate policies. When making decisions about exchange rate policy, government officials and interest groups almost always take a country's labor and financial structures for granted.

The degree of state control over financial and labor systems should, however, influence support for undervalued exchange rates. I first explain how state-controlled financial systems increase support for undervaluation and then explain why state-controlled labor systems have similar effects.

State-Controlled Financial Systems and Exchange Rate Preferences

State control of finance increases policymakers' capacity to implement two types of financial policies: targeted lending policies and forced purchases of government bonds. These policies, in turn, reduce industrialists' costs in the context of an un-

---

21. Neumayer and de Soysa (2006), Greenhill, Mosley, and Prakash (2009), and Mosley (2010) examine how these factors influenced labor systems. Boehmer, Nash, and Netter (2005), Haggard and Maxfield (1996), and Epstein (2008) show that these variables contributed to financial reform.

dervalued exchange rate. Thus, state-controlled financial structures should increase the manufacturing sector's support for an undervalued exchange rate.[22]

State-controlled financial systems are those in which state policymakers, and not private financial institutions, have the authority to determine who can borrow and lend, and on what terms. The degree of state control over the financial system depends on both formal rules and on informal decision-making procedures. With respect to formal rules, state ownership of banks is the most important issue. When the state owns the bank, it is the one that ultimately has authority to determine who receives loans and on what terms (Barth, Caprio, and Levine 2006; Beim and Calomiris 2001; La Porta, Lopez-de-Silanes, and Shleifer 2002; Mishkin 2009, 152). Official lines of authority are not everything, though: informal mechanisms of control, such as the ability of state officials to appoint and remove bank personnel, matter as well.

The degree of state control over the financial system varies substantially across the developing world. South Korea and Taiwan in the 1960s and 1970s lay on the state-controlled end of the spectrum. In both countries, the state owned most financial institutions and effortlessly controlled bank managers (Wade 1990; Woo 1991). At the other end of the continuum, in private financial systems, the state has no direct control over financial markets, and state officials do not determine who can lend or borrow money, or the terms of lending agreements between a bank and its customers. While industrialized countries such as the United States provide the clearest examples of private financial systems, some developing countries, such as Chile, Estonia, and Singapore, also approximate this ideal type. In between the ideal types, some states have partial control over their financial system: for example, in countries such as Brazil and India, private and publicly owned banks coexist (Lins 2012); in Mexico in the 1980s, the state had difficulty exerting control over nationalized banks (Maxfield 1990); and in cases such as Korea in the 1980s, state officials retained some control over managers at privatized banks (Amsden and Euh 1993).

The first reason why state-controlled banks affect exchange rate preferences is that they enable policymakers to engage in targeted lending policies. In a private financial system, firms borrow from banks at market interest rates that reflect their creditworthiness.[23] The situation is dramatically different in state-controlled

---

22. Other scholars have recognized the importance of financial structures to exchange rate policy. Henning (1994) shows that, in advanced industrialized countries, the financial sector is more supportive of an undervalued exchange rate in bank-based financial systems than in capital-market-based financial systems. Others have observed an association between financial repression and undervalued exchange rates in East Asia (Henning and Katada 2014; Lardy 2012), though the causal links between them have yet to be examined in detail.

23. In private financial systems, governments are able to impact firms' borrowing costs through interest rate policy. However, unlike in state-controlled systems, these states lack the capacity to determine which particular firms or sectors receive loans or the terms of those loan agreements.

financial systems because "ownership of banks gives government the unequivocal right to direct credit wherever it sees fit, with no pretense of a market system" (Beim and Calomiris 2001, 53). Empirical evidence confirms that state-owned banks are more likely to engage in targeted, and politically motivated, lending than their private counterparts (Bai et al. 2006; Dinç 2005; Li et al. 2008; Malesky and Taussig 2009; Micco, Panizza, and Yañez 2007; Sapienza 2004). For example, Khwaja and Mian (2005) show that state-owned banks in Pakistan give more loans to politically connected firms, but private banks in Pakistan do not evince this type of political favoritism.

Policymakers that are capable of targeting credit toward favored sectors can ensure that undervaluation does not increase industrialists' operating costs. State control of finance allows policymakers to respond to an exchange rate depreciation by increasing credit subsidies for favored firms. These credit subsidies, in turn, offset the effect of devaluation on firms' imported input costs and prevent firms' operating costs from increasing. Amsden (1989, 68) observes that "[s]ubsidies to exporters in late industrializing countries have often been seen as a necessary evil to offset the higher-than-world-price that exporters have to pay for their imported inputs as a consequence of exchange rate 'distortion' [undervaluation]." Industrialists strongly benefit from an undervalued exchange rate in state-controlled financial systems because they see their competitiveness increase without suffering from cost increases. Brazil between 2009 and 2012 illustrates this point: access to subsidized credit from Brazil's national development bank was one of the reasons the country's manufacturers strongly supported the government's efforts to prevent exchange rate appreciation (Gallagher 2014). By contrast, when policymakers cannot force banks to channel cheap credit to industry, it is more difficult for them to prevent manufacturers' costs from rising when they undervalue the exchange rate. Manufacturers should be more supportive of undervaluation when banks are state-controlled than when they are in private hands.[24]

The second reason that state-controlled banks reduce the costs of undervaluation is that policymakers often impose stringent regulations on state-owned banks. Policies such as interest rate ceilings and high reserve requirement ratios, which are often referred to as "financial repression," act as indirect taxes on financial institutions and their depositors (Giovannini and De Melo 1993; Roubini and Sala-i-Martin 1992). While these repressive financial policies have been common throughout the developing world, they have been most extreme in state-dominated financial systems because it is easier to impose these restrictions on

---

24. To be clear, I am not suggesting that state-owned banks are always used to target credit toward the manufacturing sector; this is quite unlikely when the manufacturing sector is not powerful. Rather, the argument here is that when policymakers undervalue the exchange rate, they are likely to target cheap credit toward manufacturers to win their support for undervaluation.

public banks than on private ones (Barth et al. 2006, 41; Beim and Calomiris 2001, 53; Dinç 2005, 455). Abiad, Detragiache, and Tressel (2010) show that countries with larger state-owned banking sectors make greater use of credit controls, interest rate controls, and other restrictive financial policies. Institutional structures that give the state control over the financial system facilitate repressive financial policies.

Repressive financial policies redistribute the costs of maintaining an under-valued exchange rate away from manufacturing firms and onto banks. One form of financial repression—forcing banks to purchase government bonds—is par-ticularly useful for policymakers seeking to sustain an undervalued exchange rate. As discussed, central banks sustain an undervalued exchange rate by purchasing foreign currency and selling government bonds. As the supply of these "steriliza-tion bonds" increases, central banks must pay private banks a higher interest rate to purchase these bonds, which pushes up borrowing costs for businesses (Fran-kel 1997; Reinhart and Reinhart 1998). State-owned banks offer a way around this problem. Policymakers can simply force state-owned commercial banks to buy sterilization bonds at below-market interest rates; as a result, sterilized for-eign exchange intervention will not increase domestic interest rates in state-controlled financial systems. In China, for example, the government "forc[es] its sterilization bonds down the throats of its [state-owned] banks without paying market interest rates" (Frankel 2006, 257). Since state-owned banks often pur-chase sterilization bonds at below-market rates, undervalued exchange rates should not burden industry with rising interest rates. The ability to repress state-owned banks allows policymakers to transfer the burden of undervaluation onto banks and depositors. By contrast, private banks' greater ability to resist repressive pol-icies means that undervaluation is likely to push up firms' borrowing costs in non-state-controlled financial systems.

The structure of a nation's financial system should influence firms' exchange rate level preferences. In private financial systems, undervaluation tends to push up firms' borrowing costs. In state-controlled ones, governments often reduce firms' borrowing costs when undervaluing the exchange rate. As a result, institu-tional structures that expand the state's control over the financial sector should increase the manufacturing sector's support for an undervalued exchange rate.

State-Controlled Labor Systems and Exchange Rate Preferences

State-controlled labor systems should increase industrialists' support for an un-dervalued exchange rate. The logic is similar to the case of the financial system: restrictions on labor reduce manufacturing firms' costs and increase the net ben-efits of undervaluation.

State-controlled labor systems are defined as rules and decision-making procedures that enable the state to intervene in labor markets and set wage rates. Collective labor laws, which refer to the constitutional rights and protections provided to or withheld from collective labor organizations, are the most important formal institutional device that states use to increase their control over labor. Collective labor laws address three main issues: workers' legal right to organize into labor unions; workers' rights to bargain collectively; and their right to engage in collective actions such as strikes. These collective labor rights give workers the capacity to advocate for their own economic and political interests (Anner and Caraway 2010, 167; Mosley 2010, 106).[25] Constitutional restrictions on the actions of labor unions and legal barriers to the formation of independent labor unions compromise workers' ability to shape their economic fates, and therefore expand the capacity of the state to control labor market outcomes. In addition to formal laws, the state's control over the labor system also depends on its ability to enforce the collective labor laws on the books.

While some states continue to control and restrict labor today, most developing states have signed international conventions that commit them to respect these core collective labor rights.[26] There is no shortage of historical examples of states that had extensive control over the labor system. For instance, the Chilean state in the 1970s outlawed national labor federations, denied unions' associational and bargaining rights, and forbade all collective or political activities (Drake 1996, 129). Intermediate cases also abound: for example, in the late 1960s, the Brazilian and Korean states allowed independent unions to form, but retained the right to (dis)approve all unions and extensively interfered in union operations (Domínguez 2011).

The ability to form unions gives workers the organizational capacity to lobby policymakers and helps them gain favorable labor-market outcomes. Empirical studies confirm that workers receive higher wages and benefits in countries where state laws permit them to organize (Christensen and Wibbels 2014; Morici and Schulz 2001; Rodrik 1996). Morici and Schulz (2001, 7) estimate that improvements in labor rights increase the average manufacturing worker's pay by $6,000/year.

Industrialists are less likely to support an undervalued exchange rate when workers are allowed to organize and strike. Exchange rate devaluations can be highly unattractive to manufacturing firms when labor is organized. Devaluation

---

25. Individual labor laws, which cover issues such as working conditions, minimum wages, and bans on child labor, are obviously important too, but are a separate issue.

26. For example, by the end of 2011, 150 countries ratified International Labour Organization Convention 87 on Freedom of Association (ILOLEX database).

reduces workers' real wages because it increases the costs of imports while salaries do not initially change. Workers often respond to the decline in real wages by demanding salary increases to restore their purchasing power (Cooper 1971). Take the case of Tunisia: when the International Monetary Fund (IMF) pressured the Tunisian authorities to devalue the dinar in 1964, Tunisia's union leader "decided to make his support for the devaluation policy contingent on a commensurate increase in workers' salaries, to compensate workers for the inflation that was certain to follow devaluation" (Bellin 2002, 96). When workers have rights to organize and bargain, they are more likely to succeed in raising their wages so as to restore their predevaluation purchasing power (Cooper 1971, 10). Thus, when workers are allowed to engage in collective action, devaluation might increase not just firms' foreign import and debt costs, but also their labor costs. This should make undervaluation less attractive to industrialists.

Undervalued exchange rates should be more attractive to industrialists in state-controlled labor systems. Prohibitions on labor organization reduce business costs, and these cost-savings should be especially important when the exchange rate is undervalued. When states use their control over workers to suppress business costs, industrialists will continue to have below-market costs even while the exchange rate is undervalued. In other words, a low wage bill compensates firms for high import costs and neutralizes the negative effects of an undervalued exchange rate. Labor restrictions also ensure that firms benefit from devaluation: workers are less likely to demand higher wages following a devaluation and policymakers are more likely to ignore any such demands that do arise. When states control and restrict labor, manufacturing firms should experience larger net benefits from devaluation. Consequently, institutional arrangements that enhance the state's control over labor markets should increase the manufacturing sector's support for undervaluation.

Why Institutions Influence Exchange Rates: Summary and Clarifications

The organization of labor and financial markets influences support for undervalued exchange rates. Institutional structures shape how the costs of an undervalued exchange rate get distributed across different groups. State-controlled financial systems enable policymakers to place a greater share of the burden of undervaluation onto banks and depositors. State control of the labor system makes it easier for policymakers to transfer the costs of an undervalued exchange rate onto the working class. These institutions enable policymakers to reduce industrialists' operating costs when the exchange rate is undervalued. Hence, state-controlled labor and financial systems should make industrialists more enthusiastic about an undervalued exchange rate. The main hypothesis here is the following: state control of labor and finance increases the manufacturing sector's demand for undervaluation. Consequently, these institutional structures should encourage policymakers to undervalue the exchange rate—at least in some circumstances. The precise conditions under which state-controlled labor and financial regimes promote undervalued exchange rates are the subject of the next section.

Three points of clarification are necessary before I proceed. First, it is important to explain why I do not expect state-controlled labor and financial systems to increase support for an overvalued exchange rate. I have argued that state control of labor and finance helps states minimize some of the harmful effects of undervaluation and thus increase the attractiveness of undervaluation. However, these institutions are unlikely to increase the state's ability to address the problems associated with an overvalued exchange rate. There is an important asymmetry here. Only some states can combine cost-reducing policies with an undervalued exchange rate. By contrast, most states—regardless of their institutional structures—should be able to combine competitiveness-enhancing policies with an overvalued exchange rate. It is usually quite easy for states to keep the exchange rate overvalued while also maintaining low interest rates, tax cuts, and high levels of government subsidies. These policies tend to be inflationary and thus often contribute to an appreciation of the real exchange rate. In other words, there is a natural affinity between overvaluation and monetary and fiscal policies that increase firms' short-term profitability. This affinity should be equally strong in countries with state-controlled institutions and those with private-controlled institutions.[27] Thus, state-controlled financial and labor systems are unlikely to increase manufacturers' support for an overvalued exchange rate. I expect that these institutions increase the attractiveness of undervaluation relative to the attractiveness of overvaluation, and consequently increase the probability that manufacturers lobby for an undervalued exchange rate.

Second, I am not suggesting that state-controlled labor and financial systems matter only because they alter preferences. Institutions might also affect how societal preferences get "aggregated" into policy (Lake 2009; Rogowski 1999). Restrictions on labor and finance reduce the ability of workers and banks to lobby for their interests. Since labor and finance often oppose undervaluation, state-controlled labor and financial systems may promote undervalued exchange rates

---

27. Moreover, labor and financial structures have little bearing on states' ability to use protectionist trade policies, a common instrument for helping firms cope with the problems associated with an overvalued exchange rate.

simply because they weaken these opponents of undervaluation. This "preference aggregation" mechanism is likely to influence exchange rate policy, but there are two reasons why it should be less important than the "preference formation" mechanism that my theory emphasizes.[28] First, the ways in which preferences get aggregated into policy are irrelevant if no interest groups actively support an undervalued exchange rate. The preference formation mechanism is essential because policymakers have no incentive to undervalue if no interest groups prefer undervaluation. Second, the preference formation mechanism forces scholars to recognize that institutions do more than merely determine which groups influence policy—they also have a much more profound and underappreciated effect on what interest groups want in the first place.

A third point of clarification is that labor and financial institutions are not the only variables that affect exchange rate preferences. The conditional preference theory focuses on labor and financial institutions because their effect on firms' preferences should be large, direct, and enduring. However, my causal logic suggests that any variable that affects manufacturing firms' labor and borrowing costs should influence their support for an undervalued exchange rate. Governments might use other policy instruments, such as tax cuts or energy subsidies, to reduce industrialists' costs and increase their support for undervaluation. Macroeconomic conditions are another factor that should have similar, though more transitory, effects on the manufacturing sector's exchange rate preferences. High rates of unemployment should, like state-controlled labor systems, lower industrialists' wage costs. Recessionary conditions that lead to an excess supply of capital reduce borrowing costs in a manner similar to repressive financial policies. Conversely, an overheating economy might reduce support for undervaluation to the extent that it increases wages, property prices, and other costs for firms. Preferences should respond similarly to temporary labor and financial market conditions as to labor and financial market institutions, which are more enduring.

The Domestic Political Sources of Undervalued Exchange Rates

Policymakers are likely to keep their exchange rates undervalued when powerful interest groups prefer an undervalued exchange rate. This depends, in turn, on the relative power of different interest groups and those groups' preferences. So

---

28. Chapter 2 also explains why patterns found in the cross-national data suggest that this preference aggregation explanation is incomplete at best.

TABLE 1.4.   Summary of the argument

LABOR AND FINANCIAL MARKET INSTITUTIONS	MANUFACTURING SECTOR	
	WEAK	*POWERFUL*
PRIVATELY CONTROLLED	Overvalued exchange rate	Overvalued exchange rate
	Preferences: Manufacturing sector does not prefer undervaluation	*Preferences:* Manufacturing sector does not prefer undervaluation
	Political influence: Manufacturing sector has limited influence	*Political influence:* Manufacturing sector has strong influence
STATE-CONTROLLED	Overvalued exchange rate	Undervalued exchange rate
	Preferences: Manufacturing sector prefers undervaluation	*Preferences:* Manufacturing sector prefers undervaluation
	Political influence: Manufacturing sector has limited influence	*Political influence:* Manufacturing sector has strong influence

far I have presented separate hypotheses about the determinants of interest group preferences and political influence. I now bring these two pieces of the argument together.

Exchange rates are more likely to be undervalued in countries with powerful manufacturing sectors and state-controlled labor and financial systems than in other types of developing countries. Table 1.4 summarizes the dual logics that underlie this expectation.[29] The manufacturing sector is likely to prefer an undervalued exchange rate when the state has control over labor and finance. Policymakers are likely to be responsive to the preferences of powerful manufacturing sectors. This is the only situation where industrialists have high degrees of political influence and they support an undervalued exchange rate. As a result, policymakers have strong incentives to undervalue their exchange rates.

Exchange rates are less likely to be undervalued when the manufacturing sector has few power resources because politicians do not receive sufficient political support for this policy. When the manufacturing sector is weak, policymakers are likely to overvalue the exchange rate in response to lobbying by other interest groups with more power resources, such as real estate developers, banks, or work-

---

29. For ease of exposition, table 1.4 collapses two variables, labor institutions and financial institutions, into a single dimension. When the state controls one market but not the other, my theory would expect manufacturers' preferences to fall in between cases where both or neither markets are state controlled.

ers. Policymakers are also less likely to undervalue their country's exchange rate when labor and financial markets are not controlled by the state because the manufacturing sector is less likely to prefer an undervalued exchange rate.

The conditional preference theory is not deterministic. These are not the only variables that influence exchange rate policy, and I do not expect every single country with state-controlled institutions and a powerful manufacturing sector to undervalue its exchange rate every single year. The theory proposed here does, however, suggest that exchange rates are more likely to be remain undervalued in countries with state-controlled labor and financial system and powerful manufacturing sectors than in those where one or both of these conditions is absent.

Summary and Hypotheses

This chapter developed a conditional preference theory of undervalued exchange rates. The theory maintains that policymakers are only likely to keep their exchange rates undervalued when powerful interest groups favor this outcome. Undervalued exchange rates are relatively uncommon in the developing world because few interest groups support undervalued exchange rates; even those that support undervaluation do so only some of the time.

The conditional preference theory suggests that support for undervaluation tends to be stronger in countries with powerful industrial sectors and state-controlled labor and financial systems. The main hypothesis is the following:

> *Hypothesis 1*: Exchange rates tend to be more undervalued in developing countries that combine a powerful manufacturing sector with state control of labor and finance than in other types of developing countries.

Chapter 2 tests this hypothesis using cross-national data. Establishing correlations between these variables is a necessary first step for establishing the accuracy of my argument. However, statistical association does not prove causality. Subsequent chapters also assess whether the causal mechanisms proposed in this chapter are accurate.

Two mechanisms are of particular importance: preferences and political influence. With respect to the first mechanism (preferences), I argued that the manufacturing sector is a conditional supporter of undervalued exchange rates. This is an important area in which my theory diverges from alternative interest group theories. Whereas manufacturing firms are commonly assumed to prefer undervalued exchange rates in all contexts (e.g., Frieden 1991a), I put forth the following conditional preference hypothesis:

Hypothesis 2: Manufacturing firms are more likely to prefer undervalued exchange rates when labor and finance are controlled by the state than otherwise.

Chapter 2 uses firm-level survey data from over fifty developing countries to assess this conditional preference hypothesis. The case studies in chapters 3 through 5 further test whether state-controlled labor and financial regimes increase support for undervaluation, and provide a close-up look as to why and how this occurs. According to this logic, state control of labor and finance contributes to the adoption of targeted policies that suppress industrialists' costs, which improves industrialists' opinions of undervalued exchange rates. The case studies also examine whether other factors that influence firms' cost structures, such as macroeconomic conditions, have similar effects on support for undervalued exchange rates, as my theory would expect.

Political influence is the second mechanism. The conditional preference theory argues that exchange rate policymakers are highly sensitive to the preferences of powerful manufacturing sectors, and they therefore seek to adopt policies that win them the support of large and well-organized industrial sectors.

Hypothesis 3: Manufacturing sectors have greater influence over exchange rate policy when they control more power resources.

Assessing political influence is a notoriously difficult endeavor. I use in-depth case studies of five different developing countries to evaluate whether industrialists impacted decisions about exchange rate policy. It is important to demonstrate that interest group pressures affect exchange rate policy decisions because some scholars believe that exchange rate policymakers are insulated from interest group pressures (e.g., Gowa 1988; Krasner 1978; McNamara 1998).

In conclusion, the politics of undervalued exchange rates is, in some senses, a familiar domestic interest group story. Interest groups should be just as important for exchange rate policy as they are for other economic policy issues. The theory helps dispel the notion that exchange rates are too complicated for interest groups to understand or that exchange rate policymakers are insulated from societal pressures. On the other hand, interest groups' preferences are more context-specific than most interest-based theories appreciate. It is problematic to assume—as many political economists do—that interest groups with similar internal characteristics always prefer the same policies. Only by accounting for the political influence of interest groups *and* interest groups' varying preferences can one fully comprehend how the global political economy operates.

CROSS-COUNTRY PATTERNS IN EXCHANGE RATE POLICY AND PREFERENCES

Why do some developing countries undervalue their exchange rates while others maintain overvalued exchange rates? This chapter brings two types of quantitative data to bear on this question. Both sets of statistical analyses find support for the conditional preference theory presented in chapter 1. Exchange rate policy and interest group preferences vary across developing countries in a manner that is consistent with my theoretical expectations.

The first part of this chapter analyzes a time-series cross-sectional dataset that covers a large sample of developing countries between 1975 and 2006. The data indicate that interest groups influence the exchange rate level, but in a context-dependent fashion. The results reveal that national financial market and labor market institutions influence whether the manufacturing sector promotes an undervalued exchange rate. Exchange rates tend to be most undervalued when the manufacturing sector is powerful and states have the capacity to control labor and financial markets.

The second part of the chapter investigates interest groups' preferences over exchange rate policy. The variation in preferences across countries is as striking as the variation in exchange rate outcomes. I use a cross-national survey of manufacturing firms in 1999 to determine whether and when the manufacturing sector prefers an undervalued exchange rate. These analyses also find that institutions play a role. I show that state-controlled labor and financial systems strengthen the manufacturing sector's support for an undervalued exchange rate. This finding suggests that one reason the manufacturing sector has a different effect on exchange rate outcomes in different institutional contexts is because institutions alter this sector's preferences.

Each section presents separate analyses of the effects of labor and financial institutions on exchange rate politics. I analyze these institutions separately because they are distinct institutional features that may or may not have similar effects.[1] In fact, while the data indicate that both labor and financial institutions affect exchange rate preferences and outcomes, I find that financial systems have larger and more consistent effects on exchange rate politics. In each analysis, I begin by assessing these hypotheses using simple descriptive statistics and then use regression analysis to more rigorously test these hypotheses.

The Determinants of Undervalued Exchange Rates

The Data: Overvaluation

In order to understand which political factors are associated with undervalued exchange rates, I compiled annual observations over the period 1975–2006 for all developing countries. The time period and set of countries included in the dataset were dictated by data availability and by the scope of the theory. Before presenting the findings, I describe how the main variables in the dataset are measured.

The main outcome of interest, exchange rate over/undervaluation, is defined as the difference between the actual real exchange rate and its equilibrium value. Rodrik's (2008) three-step procedure is used to construct a measure of over/undervaluation. The first step is to construct a measure of the real exchange rate. Using data from Penn World Tables (Heston et al. 2009), Rodrik operationalizes the real exchange rate as ln(XRAT/PPP), where XRAT refers to the nominal exchange rate (units of domestic currency/foreign currency) and PPP is a purchasing power parity conversion factor, also known as a GDP deflator, which measures inflation by dividing nominal GDP by real GDP. The nominal exchange rate provides an indication of the cost of foreign goods. The GDP deflator indicates the price of domestic goods. Hence, this ratio tells us the relative prices of foreign and domestic goods in a particular country and year.

The second step is to create a measure of the equilibrium real exchange rate. Chapter 1 defined the equilibrium, or market-valued, exchange rate as the real

---

1. While the two institutions are positively correlated with one another, there are many cases where they do not coincide. Quite a few states restrict labor but not finance; examples include Chile under Pinochet and Singapore under Lee Kuan Yew. Even more countries combine state-dominated financial systems with non-state-controlled labor systems, including India and Turkey.

TABLE 2.1. Summary statistics (time-series cross-sectional dataset)

VARIABLE	OBSERVATIONS	MEAN	STANDARD DEVIATION	MINIMUM	MAXIMUM
Overvaluation	4824	0.00	0.48	–5.06	2.46
Manufacturing/GDP	3686	14.24	8.35	0.29	46
State-owned banks	1845	1.92	1.15	0	3
Labor restrictions	3284	0.38	0.48	0	1

exchange rate that equalizes foreign and domestic prices, or the "purchasing power parity" exchange rate for short. Measures of the equilibrium real exchange rate need to address one complicating factor: average price levels tend to be higher, and real exchange rates more appreciated, in wealthier countries. This "Balassa-Samuelson effect" (Balassa 1964; Samuelson 1964) occurs because as economies grow wealthier, labor becomes more productive, which pushes up wages and, in turn, prices and the real exchange rate. Thus, measures of the equilibrium real exchange rate should adjust for the Balassa-Samuelson effect. To obtain the equilibrium real exchange rate, Rodrik (2008) estimates the following equation via ordinary least squares: $\text{RER}_{it} = \alpha + \beta \text{GDPPC}_{it} + f_t + u_{it}$, where GDPPC refers to real per capita GDP, f_t is a year fixed effect, and u_{it} is the error term. The equilibrium real exchange rate is defined as the fitted value obtained from this regression equation.[2] Put less technically, the equilibrium real exchange rate is the real exchange rate that one would expect on the basis of a country's level of development.

In the third and final step, overvaluation is calculated as the estimated equilibrium exchange rate minus the actual real exchange rate.[3] As shown in table 2.1, the average value of overvaluation is zero by construction, which signifies a market-valued real exchange rate. Negative values imply that the exchange rate is undervalued. Positive values signify overvaluation of the real exchange rate.

This measure of overvaluation is very useful for comparing the degree of real exchange rate over/undervaluation across countries and over time. In other words, it is well suited for determining which countries have more or less overvalued exchange rates. However, this measure is less useful for providing a precise indicator of how overvalued or undervalued a particular country's exchange rate is in a

---

2. Numerous other concepts and measures of the equilibrium real exchange rate exist, though the approach used here is probably the most common. For example, Acemoglu et al. (2003), Dollar (1992), Easterly (2001), and Johnson, Ostry, and Subramanian (2006) measure the equilibrium real exchange rate in a similar fashion. This PPP-based measure is useful because it provides a simple benchmark for the long-run equilibrium real exchange rate.

3. Rodrik (2008) instead subtracts the equilibrium rate from the actual exchange rate to construct a measure of undervaluation. I reverse his scale because this seems more intuitive.

given year. The measure assumes that the average developing country's exchange rate is at its market rate, which is probably inaccurate. As I have pointed out, it is likely that the average developing country's exchange rate is, in fact, overvalued. As a result, this variable likely understates the true degree of overvaluation for all observations. This limitation has no bearing, however, on the relative ranking of different countries. Although imperfect for estimating the degree of over/under-valuation for particular country-years, this measure is very useful for the purpose for which it is employed in this chapter: describing the relative degree of over/undervaluation across countries and over time.

The Data: The Power of the Manufacturing Sector

The first explanatory variable, the power of the manufacturing sector, is also difficult to measure. As discussed in chapter 1, three types of power resources define the power of the manufacturing sector: economic, organizational, and normative. Ideally, one could obtain data on all three types of power resources. However, it is not feasible to construct valid measures of interest groups' organizational and normative resources for large numbers of countries over thirty years' time. High-quality data is available, though, for the economic resources of the manufacturing sector. Following previous studies of exchange rate politics (Blomberg, Frieden, and Stein 2005; Frieden, Ghezzi, and Stein 2001; Frieden, Leblang, and Valev 2010; Singer 2010; Steinberg and Malhotra 2014), I use manufacturing production as a percentage of GDP to measure this sector's relative power.

Table 2.1 shows that the manufacturing sector produces 14% of GDP in the average country-year in the dataset. Developing economies vary greatly along this dimension. The manufacturing sector takes up less than 1% of GDP in some developing economies and nearly half of GDP in others.

The manufacturing sector's share of GDP provides a crude but useful indicator of its relative power. The manufacturing sector's share of the economy captures the financial resources that this sector has under its control, which is one factor that should determine its ability to influence exchange rate policy. Although this variable does not capture how well organized or prestigious this interest group is, this limitation should not be a serious one. As discussed in chapter 1, the organizational and normative resources of the manufacturing sector are likely to vary much less than this sector's economic resources. Moreover, economic resources are likely to correlate positively with other types of power resources. As countries become more industrialized, manufacturing firms tend to grow in size (Chandler 1990), which should make it easier for the manufacturing sector to overcome collective action costs and lobby (Olson 1965; Weymouth 2012). Sectors with more economic resources are also likely to be viewed as more prestigious and should have more normative resources than smaller sectors. Thus, this measure should provide at least some indication of this sector's organizational and normative power resources. On the other hand, if economic resources are not correlated with other power resources, only random measurement error would be introduced into the model; the most likely consequence of random measurement error would be to underestimate the effect of power resources on exchange rate policymaking. In short, although imperfect, this measure is useful for assessing whether certain types of power resources help the manufacturing sector obtain favorable exchange rate policies. The case studies in chapters 3 through 5 partially remedy these limitations by considering a much wider range of power resources.

The economic importance of the manufacturing sector should influence exchange rate policy, but exchange rate policy is unlikely to have a strong effect on the size of the manufacturing sector in the period under consideration. In theory, a government is capable of using exchange rate or other policies to transform its national economic structure. In reality, few countries have experienced large changes in the manufacturing sector's share of the economy in recent decades. Alice Amsden (2001) shows that the current size of countries' manufacturing sectors is overwhelmingly influenced by historical factors, particularly early differences in countries' manufacturing experiences. She demonstrates that developing countries that produced premodern handicrafts and those where migrants or colonizers imported manufacturing know-how were the only ones to develop industrial bases by the end of World War II. These early developments had a lasting impact. In those countries, a cadre of skilled managers and engineers were able to continue investing in manufacturing, and their presence made it more profitable for others to do so as well (see also Milgrom, Qian, and Roberts 1991). Manufacturing has not subsequently developed in places that lacked experience in manufacturing prior to World War II. There has been limited change in size of most countries' manufacturing sectors since the 1950s. Amsden (2001, 99–100) reports that manufacturing output per capita in 1950 explains 75% of the cross-country variation in manufacturing output per capita in 1994. "Path dependence was such that no economy emerged from the blue as an industrial competitor," Amsden (2001, 99) concludes. The power of the manufacturing sector is largely outside of contemporary policymakers' control.

The Data: State-Controlled Financial and Labor Systems

State control of the financial system is the third variable that needs to be operationalized. The state's ownership of banks provides a simple but powerful indicator of its institutional capacity to control the financial system. For reasons explained in chapter 1, state-owned banks provide states with extensive control over their financial systems. Unfortunately, precise data on the prominence of state-owned banks is scarce. The most useful data for our purposes comes from Abiad, Detragiache, and Tressel (2010). Abiad and coauthors construct an ordinal variable that covers 1975 to 2005. I reversed their ordering so that my measure of state-owned banks is as follows: 0 = less than 10% of bank sector assets are in majority-state-owned banks; 1 = 10% to 25% of bank assets are in state-owned banks; 2 = state-owned banks make up 26% to 50% of banking assets; and 3 = state-owned banks hold more than 50% of bank assets. Table 2.1 shows that the average value on this variable is just below 2, indicating that the average developing country has a moderate degree of state control over the banking system.

Ideally, one could supplement data on formal ownership of banks with information on informal mechanisms of control, such as government officials' ability to fire insubordinate bank managers. Unfortunately, it is not feasible to collect such data for large-N statistical analyses, though the case studies in chapters 3 through 5 provide "thicker" measures of state-controlled financial systems that take into account both informal decision-making procedures and formal rules and resources. For quantitative analysis, state ownership of banks is the best measure of a state-controlled financial system.

The fourth and final variable, a state-controlled labor system, is also difficult to measure. As explained in chapter 1, legal restrictions on workers' ability to unionize and strike are the most common institutional device through which states expand their control over the labor system. I use Cingranelli and Richards's (2010) data on workers' rights to construct a binary indicator of a state-controlled labor system.[4] Observations in which the "government did not allow workers to form trade unions or prohibited strikes" are coded as having labor restrictions and receive a score of one (Abouharb and Cingranelli 2007, 197). All other observations receive a score of zero.[5] The state restricts these collective labor rights in 38% of the observations in this dataset.

---

4. For these analyses, the Cingranelli-Richards dataset has two advantages over Layna Mosley's (2010) alternative measure. Although Mosley's data has the advantage of providing a much more fine-grained and continuous measure of this concept, it has more limited temporal coverage (18 versus 26 years). Second, Mosley's measure, which expands on David Kucera's (2002) study, "does a poor job of distinguishing between countries known to have superb FACB [freedom of association and collective bargaining] rights and countries known to have poor or nonexistent FACB rights" (Teitelbaum 2010, 473).

5. Following the advice of Mosley (2010, 112), I collapse two groups of countries into the nonrestrictive category: those that Cingranelli-Richards code as giving workers the freedom to unionize and collectively bargain and that do not display other problems; and those in which workers are allowed to unionize and strike but had "other problems with government respect for worker rights such as the abuse of child labor or unsafe working conditions" (Abouharb and Cingranelli 2007, 197).

The Conditional Effect of State-Controlled Financial Systems

Are undervalued exchange rates more likely in countries with state-controlled financial systems and large manufacturing sectors? As a first stab at evaluating this argument, I compare levels of overvaluation across four groups: (1) country-years where the manufacturing sector is below the average size (14.24% of GDP) and the majority of banks are privately owned; (2) those with below-average-size manufacturing sectors and where the majority of banks are state-owned; (3) those with above-average sized manufacturing sectors and where state-owned banks control less than half of the bank sector; and (4) those with large manufacturing sectors and state-dominated financial systems. Table 2.2 presents the median degree of exchange rate overvaluation for these four groups of countries.

My theory expects country-years with large manufacturing sectors and large state-owned bank sectors to have more undervalued exchange rates than those in the other three categories. This is exactly what the data show. For countries with many state-owned banks and large manufacturing sectors, the exchange rate is 24% undervalued in the typical year. This group includes data on many Asian countries, including Bangladesh, China, Pakistan, Sri Lanka, and Vietnam, but all major developing regions are represented in the lower right quadrant of table 2.2, including Burkina Faso in Africa, Belarus in Eastern Europe, Costa Rica from Latin America, and Egypt from the Middle East. In the three other groups of countries, the median exchange rate is close to its equilibrium level. The only countries that display a clear tendency toward undervalued exchange rates are those with both state-dominated financial systems and relatively large manufacturing sectors.

Figure 2.1 provides additional support for this argument. This figure shows the correlation between overvaluation and manufacturing/GDP for two different groups of countries: those with very few state-owned banks, and those where the state owns the majority of the banking sector. The horizontal axis of the figure is

TABLE 2.2. Association between state-owned banks and undervalued exchange rates

% BANK ASSETS IN STATE-OWNED BANKS	MANUFACTURING SECTOR/GDP	
	BELOW AVERAGE	*ABOVE AVERAGE*
LESS THAN 50%	0.01 (n = 217)	−0.02 (n = 730)
MORE THAN 50%	−0.02 (n = 265)	−0.24 (n = 413)

Notes: Cell entries are median levels of overvaluation for each group. All variables are described in the text.

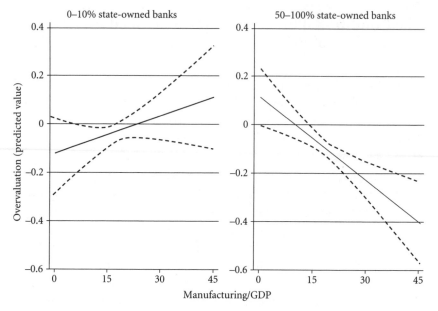

Figure 2.1. State-owned banks and undervalued exchange rates (predicted values). The solid lines indicate the predicted value of overvaluation. The dashed lines are the 95% confidence intervals. Predicted values were obtained by holding all other variables at their mean values.

the size of the manufacturing sector, measured continuously. The vertical axis is the predicted value of overvaluation. The predicted value is obtained from a linear regression model in which overvaluation is the dependent variable and the explanatory variables include manufacturing/GDP, state-owned banks, and a multiplicative interaction term between manufacturing/GDP and state-owned banks. The regression model also includes ten additional control variables to account for the fact that many factors may influence the exchange rate level.[6] The solid lines in figure 2.1 indicate the predicted level of over/undervaluation for different combinations of manufacturing/GDP and state-owned banks. The predicted level of overvaluation is the degree of overvaluation that, according to my statistical model, is most likely to occur for an observation based on the size of its manufacturing sector and its state-owned banks when the other ten control variables are held constant at their average values. The dashed lines in figure 2.1 indicate the 95% confidence intervals for these predicted values and tell us that there is a 95% probability that the true predicted value lies in between the two dashed lines.

---

6. The ten control variables are listed in table 2.7 in the chapter appendix. The appendix also provides more details on the specification of the statistical model.

My discussion focuses on the substantive results displayed in this figure because they have the most direct bearing on my conditional preference theory. Interested readers can find more information regarding the statistical model, including the full results of the model, in the appendix to this chapter.

The left-hand portion of figure 2.1 shows that there is a modest (but statistically insignificant) positive correlation between manufacturing/GDP and overvaluation for countries with private financial systems. In a private financial system, the exchange rate is predicted to be 15% undervalued in countries with no manufacturing production and 10% overvalued when the manufacturing sector is very large (and all other variables are held at their means). The data indicate that exchange rates tend to be overvalued in countries with powerful manufacturing sectors if private banks dominate their financial systems. This challenges the conventional wisdom that the manufacturing sector always pushes for an undervalued exchange rate.

The right-hand side of figure 2.1 shows that the economic resources of the manufacturing sector has the expected negative association with overvaluation when the state controls a majority of banks, and this effect is quite strong. All else equal, a one-unit increase in manufacturing/GDP leads to a decrease in overvaluation by 1.2 percentage points.[7] Exchange rates tend to be strongly undervalued in countries with large manufacturing sectors and state-owned banks. For instance, in state-controlled financial systems, the exchange rate is predicted to be 27% undervalued for countries where the manufacturing sector takes up 30% of GDP. These patterns in the data are consistent with the conditional preference theory.

The Conditional Effect of State-Controlled Labor Systems

Next, I investigate how labor institutions affect the exchange rate level. Once again, the analyses begin by comparing exchange rate outcomes across four groupings of countries. Table 2.3 shows that countries with below-average-size manufacturing sectors and states that do not restrict collective labor rights tend toward overvalued exchange rates (median = 5% overvalued). Exchange rates are even more overvalued in countries with small manufacturing sectors and state-controlled labor systems. This second group includes many African and Middle Eastern countries such as Angola, Iran, Kuwait, and Nigeria, as well as others like Myanmar and Uzbekistan. Countries with large manufacturing sectors and private labor systems tend to have mildly undervalued exchange rates, with the median country's ex-

---

7. This slope is statistically significant with a 95% confidence interval of –0.006 to –0.019.

TABLE 2.3. Association between labor restrictions and undervalued exchange rates

COLLECTIVE LABOR RIGHTS	MANUFACTURING SECTOR/GDP	
	BELOW AVERAGE	*ABOVE AVERAGE*
NOT RESTRICTED	0.05 (n = 850)	−0.08 (n = 965)
RESTRICTED	0.09 (n = 540)	−0.17 (n = 397)

Note: Cell entries are median levels of overvaluation for each group. All variables are described in the text.

change rate being 8% undervalued. Exchange rates tend to be most undervalued, with a median undervaluation of 17%, in countries with large manufacturing sectors and states that control labor.

I also used a regression model to estimate the effects of labor institutions on undervaluation. I follow the same model specification that I used when analyzing financial systems, but now use the measure of labor restrictions and its interaction with manufacturing size in place of the state-owned banking variables. Figure 2.2 presents the predicted values of overvaluation obtained from this model (the full model is in the chapter appendix). The size of the manufacturing sector has a slightly negative, but statistically insignificant, effect on overvaluation when the state does not control labor: every one-unit increase in manufacturing/GDP is associated with a 0.2% decrease in overvaluation. The size of the manufacturing sector has a larger, and statistically significant, negative effect on overvaluation when states control labor. In the latter case, every one-unit increase in the manufacturing-to-GDP ratio reduces overvaluation by 0.6%.[8]

The data indicate that large manufacturing sectors promote undervalued exchange rates when states restrict collective labor rights, but the size of the manufacturing sector has little bearing on exchange rate levels otherwise. Although labor systems appear to have a weaker effect than financial systems, the results support the hypothesis that the combination of a state-controlled labor system and a powerful manufacturing sector contributes to exchange rate undervaluation.

Overall, the patterns in exchange rate valuation across the developing world between 1976 and 2006 are consistent with the conditional preference theory. Large manufacturing sectors are associated with more undervalued exchange rates— but only in countries with state-controlled labor or financial institutions.

---

8. The 95% confidence interval for the slope is −0.001 to −0.01.

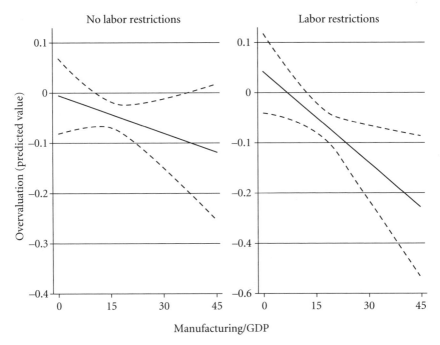

Figure 2.2. Labor restrictions and undervalued exchange rates (predicted values). The solid lines indicate the predicted value of overvaluation. The dashed lines are the 95% confidence intervals. The predicted values were obtained by holding all other variables at their mean values.

The Determinants of Exchange Rate Preferences

I have already established that labor and financial market structures influence whether a large manufacturing sector is associated with undervalued exchange rates. But why do these institutions matter? Chapter 1 argued that the preferences of the manufacturing sector are the main link in this causal chain. The next set of analyses more directly examine whether state-controlled financial and labor systems increase the manufacturing sector's support for an undervalued exchange rate.

The Data

Survey data is useful for shedding light on firms' policy preferences. A number of studies have used survey data to analyze preferences on exchange rate policy, but most of them have focused on single industrial countries, such as Germany

(Kinderman 2008), the United Kingdom (Duckenfield and Aspinwall 2010), and the United States (Knight 2010). Broz, Frieden, and Weymouth's (2008) study is an important exception. They use firm-level survey data from eighty countries, which they obtain from the *World Business Environment Survey*, conducted by the World Bank in 1999. Broz, Frieden, and Weymouth (2008) use firms' responses to the following question to measure exchange rate preferences: "How problematic is the exchange rate for the operation and growth of your business?" They created an ordered variable, labeled EXCHANGE RATE PROBLEM, which is coded as follows: 1 = no obstacle, 2 = minor obstacle, 3 = moderate obstacle, and 4 = major obstacle. Firms that report that the exchange rate is no obstacle to their business are indicating that they hold at least a minimal level of support for the country's exchange rate arrangement. Increasingly large values of this variable imply greater opposition to exchange rate policy and can be interpreted as a preference against prevailing exchange rate policies. Since this is the only large cross-national survey that asks businesses about their views about the exchange rate, I follow Broz et al. (2008) and use this variable as the dependent variable for these analyses. Table 2.4 shows that the sample average is 2.66, suggesting that the typical manufacturing firm views the exchange rate as a minor-to-moderate obstacle.

The goal of the analysis is to better understand what types of exchange rate policies are favored by manufacturing firms in developing countries. Since the objective is to understand the preferences of this single sector, manufacturing, the analysis excludes firms from other sectors.

My objective is to determine whether the manufacturing sector prefers an undervalued exchange rate, and if labor and financial institutions affect this preference. The degree of overvaluation in 1999, the year the *World Business Environment Survey* was conducted, is an explanatory variable in these analyses. If manufacturing firms prefer undervalued exchange rates, they will be more likely to report that the exchange rate is a problem when their country's exchange rate is overvalued than when it is undervalued.

Labor and financial market institutions are also used as explanatory variables in these analyses. I use the same measure of labor restrictions from the previous analysis. A different, higher-quality measure of state-owned banks is used here because more fine-grained information is available for a cross-sectional study. La Porta, Lopez-de-Silanes, and Shleifer (2002) construct a continuous measure of the share of national bank assets that are held by state-owned banks.[9] This mea-

---

9. Unfortunately, this data is only available for the year 1995. For this reason it was not used in the previous analysis. Basing their estimates on the ten largest banks in the country, Rafael La Porta et al. (2002, 269) report that the top-ten banks account for more than 75% of the banking system in almost all of the countries in their sample.

TABLE 2.4. Summary statistics (survey data)

VARIABLE	OBSERVATIONS	MEAN	STANDARD DEVIATION	MINIMUM	MAXIMUM
Exchange rate problem	2762	2.66	1.14	1.00	4.00
Overvaluation	2732	−0.15	0.42	−1.29	0.59
State-owned banks	1922	0.47	0.29	0	0.99
Labor restrictions	2692	0.17	0.38	0	1.00

sure ranges from a minimum value of zero, where no assets are in state-owned banks, to a maximum of one if the state owns the majority share of all banks. The average manufacturing firm in the dataset lives in a country where 47% of bank-sector assets are in state-owned banks (see table 2.4).

The Effect of State-Controlled Financial Systems on Preferences

Does state control of finance influence manufacturing firms' exchange rate preferences? Table 2.5 suggests that the answer is "yes." The cells indicate the proportion of manufacturing firms that report that the exchange rate is a major problem for their business. Countries are sorted into four groups depending on whether their exchange rate is overvalued or undervalued, and whether state-owned banks control the majority of banking assets.

According to table 2.5, manufacturing firms are most unhappy with exchange rate policy in countries where the rate is undervalued and few banks are state-owned. In those cases, 49% of manufacturing firms report that the exchange rate is a major problem. Far fewer firms, only 30%, view undervalued exchange rates as a major problem in state-dominated financial systems. Manufacturing firms also express little opposition to overvalued exchange rates in either type of financial system. To give an example, hardly any of the manufacturing firms surveyed by the *World Business Environment Survey* in Estonia, Lithuania, and Singapore—three countries with private financial systems that saw their real exchange rates steadily appreciate during the 1990s—viewed the exchange rate as a major problem.

Why are so many manufacturing firms unhappy about undervalued exchange rates when their state lacks control over the financial system? Part of the answer is that several countries included in the *World Business Environment Survey*, such as Indonesia and Thailand, experienced large devaluations around this time. It is not too surprising that firms often dislike major exchange rate depreciations. But

TABLE 2.5. Association between state-owned banks and exchange rate preferences

% BANK ASSETS IN STATE-OWNED BANKS	EXCHANGE RATE	
	UNDERVALUED	OVERVALUED
LESS THAN 50%	0.49 (n = 475)	0.26 (n = 571)
MORE THAN 50%	0.30 (n = 434)	0.29 (n = 442)

Note: Cell entries are proportion of firms that report that the exchange rate is a major business problem. All variables are described in the text.

this just reinforces my argument that the manufacturing sector is not nearly as happy with currency devaluations—the most common way that governments undervalue their exchange rates—as sector-based explanations suggest. It is also notable that the pattern in the data is not driven entirely by these dramatic cases of rapid devaluation. Many of the countries in this sample that have state-controlled financial systems and undervalued exchange rates also experienced large devaluations in the late 1990s. Moreover, even if countries that experienced currency crises in 1999 are excluded, firms in private financial systems remain much more opposed to undervaluation than those in state-controlled ones: 49% of manufacturing firms in the former grouping report that the exchange rate is a major problem whereas only 22% of the latter grouping express this opinion. The data indicates that manufacturing firms are far more hostile to undervalued exchange rates when the state lacks control over its financial system.

I also estimated the effect of state-controlled banks on exchange rate preferences using an ordered probit regression model. This model estimates how our explanatory variables, such as overvaluation and state-owned banks, influence the probability that a firm will respond in a particular manner on this survey question. The main three explanatory variables in this model are overvaluation, state-owned banks, and the multiplicative interaction between these two variables. This model also includes, as control variables, a number of other important firm-specific and national-level attributes that may affect firms' preferences.[10] Interested readers can find more details on these variables and the full results of these models in the chapter appendix. Figure 2.3 presents the most important findings from this regression model. The horizontal axis is the level of overvaluation.

---

10. I use the same variables that Broz et al. (2008) include in their model, plus the exchange rate regime, which is also a key variable in their study. The appendix at the end of chapter 2 shows that the results are similar when controlling for whether the country experienced a currency crisis in 1999.

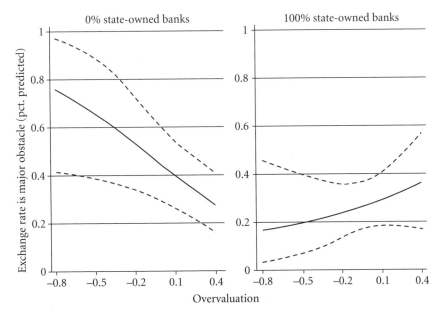

Figure 2.3. State-owned banks and exchange rate preferences (predicted probabilities). The solid lines indicate the predicted probability that a manufacturing firm reports that the exchange rate is a major business obstacle. The dashed lines are the 95% confidence intervals. All other variables were held at their mean or median values.

The vertical axis is the predicted probability that a manufacturing firm will report that the exchange rate is a major problem, as well as the confidence interval for those predicted probabilities. The predicted probabilities were calculated by fixing the control variables at their mean values (medians for dichotomous or ordered variables).[11]

The left side of figure 2.3 indicates how overvaluation affects manufacturing firms in countries with no state-owned banks. In this context, as the exchange rate becomes more overvalued, fewer firms report that the exchange rate is a major problem. When there are no state-owned banks, over three-quarters of manufacturing firms are predicted to report that the exchange rate is a major business obstacle when the exchange rate is highly undervalued (and the other variables are held at their means/medians). The model predicts that only 26% of firms report that the exchange rate is a major problem when all banks are privately owned

___

11. The predicted probabilities were generated using Clarify software (Tomz, Wittenberg, and King 2003).

and the exchange rate is highly overvalued. The results suggest that manufacturing firms prefer overvalued exchange rates in private financial systems.

The situation is starkly different in countries such as China, where states own 100% of banking assets. The positive slope in the right side of figure 2.3 indicates that, in fully state-controlled financial systems, overvalued exchange rates increase the number of manufacturing firms that view the exchange rate as a major problem.[12] The model predicts that, when there are no private banks, only 15% of manufacturing firms view highly undervalued exchange rates as a major problem whereas 35% of firms consider highly overvalued exchange rates to be a major problem. In state-controlled financial systems, manufacturing firms do not oppose undervalued exchange rates. In fact, they appear to prefer undervaluation.

The Effect of State-Controlled Labor Systems on Preferences

This final set of statistical analyses investigates how labor market institutions influence firm preferences. As before, I first compare the proportion of manufacturing firms that report that the exchange rate is a major problem across different combinations of over/undervalued exchange rates and restrictive/nonrestrictive labor laws. Table 2.6 shows that labor restrictions have similar effects to state-owned banks. In countries with no labor restrictions, few manufacturing firms view overvalued exchange rates as a major problem, but many view undervalued exchange rates as a serious problem. By contrast, when states control labor activities, the proportion of manufacturing firms that report that the exchange rate is a major problem is slightly lower in countries with undervalued exchange rates than in those with overvalued exchange rates. Manufacturing firms are happiest with the exchange rate when the state controls labor and undervalues the exchange rate: only one-fifth report that the exchange rate is a major problem in this circumstance. Cambodia, Cameroon, and China are among the countries in the dataset with state-controlled labor systems, undervalued exchange rates, and manufacturing firms that reported favorable opinions toward the exchange rate.[13]

I also used an ordered probit regression model to assess how labor institutions affect preferences. The model setup is the same as in the previous case, except that labor restrictions are used here in place of the state-owned bank variable. Figure 2.4 displays the predicted probabilities generated from this model. These results do not support my argument that labor institutions influence manufacturing firms'

---

12. The slope on the left side of figure 2.3 is statistically distinguishable from zero. The slope on the right side is not. The difference between the two slopes is statistically significant.

13. These patterns are very similar when countries that experienced currency crises in 1999 are excluded from the analysis.

TABLE 2.6. Association between labor restrictions and exchange rate preferences

COLLECTIVE LABOR RIGHTS	EXCHANGE RATE	
	UNDERVALUED	*OVERVALUED*
NOT RESTRICTED	0.45 (n = 1011)	0.25 (n = 1215)
RESTRICTED	0.20 (n = 398)	0.26 (n = 68)

Note: Cell entries are proportion of firms that report that the exchange rate is a major business problem. All variables are described in the text.

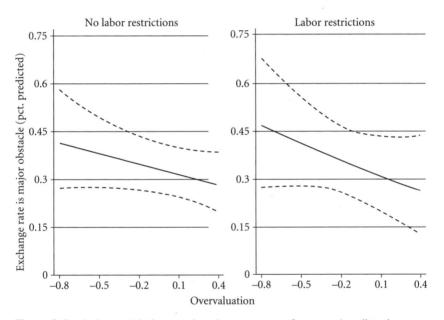

Figure 2.4. Labor restrictions and exchange rate preferences (predicted probabilities). The solid lines indicate the predicted probability that a manufacturing firm reports that the exchange rate is a major business obstacle. The dashed lines are the 95% confidence intervals. All other variables were held at their mean or median values.

preferences. In both types of labor systems, overvaluation has a negative effect on the probability that firms view the exchange rate as a major problem, but this effect is not statistically distinguishable from zero in either case.[14] Thus, while the

---

14. Contrary to theoretical expectations, the effect is slightly stronger in the case of state-controlled labor systems, but the difference between these slopes is statistically insignificant.

first, simpler analysis supports the hypothesis that state control of labor increases manufacturers' support for undervaluation, these second analyses do not find support for this hypothesis.

Conclusions

This chapter presented quantitative evidence that interest groups have strong but context-dependent effects on the exchange rate level. Using a dataset that covers a large number of developing countries for a thirty-one-year period, I showed that powerful manufacturing sectors are often—but not always—associated with more undervalued exchange rates. Institutions influence whether the manufacturing sector is a force for undervaluation. The data show that developing countries with weak manufacturing sectors rarely maintain highly undervalued exchange rates. Undervalued exchange rates are also uncommon in countries with powerful manufacturing sectors but states that lack the capacity to control labor and financial markets. Exchange rates tend to be highly undervalued in countries with large manufacturing industries and state-controlled labor systems. Undervalued exchange rates are also common when a large manufacturing sector and state-controlled financial systems coincide.

This chapter went beyond merely showing that interest groups and institutions matter. The second set of statistical analyses investigated how and why they influence exchange rate policy. The survey data showed that manufacturing sector's exchange rate preferences vary according to the nature of a country's labor and financial institutions. These analyses provide some support for the hypothesis that state-controlled labor systems increase manufacturing firms' desire for an undervalued exchange rate. The evidence strongly suggests that financial structures influence manufacturers' exchange rate preferences: the developing world's manufacturing firms strongly oppose undervalued exchange rates in private financial systems, though they prefer undervalued exchange rates in state-controlled systems.

These findings hold three important implications for our understanding of exchange rate politics. The first is the importance of interest groups. That the degree of undervaluation often depends on the size of the manufacturing sector suggests that policymakers pay close attention to the preferences of powerful interest group. Perhaps this is not surprising, but many scholars believe that monetary policymakers are highly insulated from societal pressures (Gowa 1988; Helleiner 2005; Odell 1982; Krasner 1978; McNamara 1998; Moschella 2015). These results suggest that interest groups do matter for exchange rate policy, probably no less than they do for other types of foreign economic policies.

Second, interest groups have context-dependent preferences. The country-level data show that the size of the manufacturing sector has very different effects in different contexts. The survey data provide even clearer evidence that the manufacturing sector has different preferences in different situations. These findings are at odds with prevailing interest-based theories of international political economy, which derive preferences solely from an actor's internal characteristics (see Lake 2009). Sector-based characteristics are important, but they do not determine preferences on their own. Interest groups prefer different exchange rate outcomes in different circumstances.

These results are equally inconsistent with constructivist perspectives on preferences. The evidence does corroborate constructivists' argument that exchange rate preferences are highly context-specific (e.g., Helleiner 2005, 41; McNamara 1998, 7). However, the systematic association between interest group size and exchange rate policy casts doubt on the constructivist argument that "ambiguity over the micro-level distributional effects of exchange rate[s] . . . translates into inaction on the part of domestic interest groups (McNamara 1999, 461–462). The strong association between the exchange rate level and the likelihood that firms perceive the exchange rate to be a business problem is inconsistent with the notion that "the esoteric nature of the subject of international monetary policy" produces "ignorance on the part of group leaders" (Odell 1982, 347). So, interest groups are perfectly capable of discerning their interests, and their preferences are neither constant, as sector-based explanations argue, nor incoherent, as many constructivists maintain.

Third, the data suggest that institutional structures are important, but they influence exchange rate policy for a different reason than most political economists expect. Conventional wisdom holds that institutions matter because they determine which interest groups' preferences matter most (Lake 2009; Milner 1998; Moravcsik 1997; Rogowski 1999). Two pieces of evidence presented in this chapter suggest that this conventional view is incomplete at best. First, the survey data demonstrate that preferences covary with institutions—which means that institutional structures can influence interest groups' preferences, not just whether policymakers take those preferences into account. Second, the patterns in the national-level data are more consistent with my "preference formation" mechanism than with the alternative "preference aggregation" mechanism. If institutions matter solely because they determine the political importance of private bankers and workers, as this competing explanation suggests, institutions should influence the exchange rate level irrespective of the size of the manufacturing sector. However, the data reveal that state-controlled labor and financial systems are not associated with more undervalued exchange rates when the manufacturing sector is small in size; this association only holds when the manufacturing sector is powerful (see figures 2.1 and 2.2).[15] The evidence is more consistent with historical institutionalist approaches, which posit that institutions influence preferences (e.g., Farrell and Newman 2010; Fioretos 2011; Thelen 1999), than with more conventional political economy models, which claim that institutions merely aggregate preferences.

The statistical analyses presented in this chapter help to illuminate factors that promote undervalued exchange rates and why they do. However, these quantitative datasets leave a number of questions unanswered. They do not help us make sense of why exchange rate levels correlate with the power resources of the manufacturing sector or how institutions influence exchange rate preferences. The qualitative case studies presented in the chapters 3 through 5 help fill these gaps. The case studies corroborate the findings of this chapter that interest groups and institutions profoundly influence exchange rate policy decisions.

Appendix to Chapter 2

My purpose here is to provide more detailed information about the statistical analyses presented in chapter 2. The predicted values presented in figure 2.1 and figure 2.2 were generated from a linear regression model that includes thirteen explanatory variables. This chapter has already provided a detailed description of the main explanatory variables of interest. Table 2.7 defines the control variables included in the model. Models 1 and 2 of table 2.8 present the results of the regression models that were used to generate figures 2.1 and 2.2, respectively.

All the explanatory variables in table 2.8 are lagged by one year in order to mitigate potential simultaneity or reverse causality problems. Corrections for first-order autocorrelation are included because random shocks to one country's real exchange rate are likely to persist over time, leading to serially correlated error terms. Shocks to the exchange rate are also likely to spill over to other countries, producing contemporaneously correlated errors. Moreover, panel data often exhibit panel heteroskedasticity, meaning that different countries have different error variances. I use Beck and Katz's (1995) panel-corrected standard errors because they effectively address contemporaneous correlation and panel heteroskedasticity.

---

15. If institutions solely aggregate preferences, another plausible hypothesis would be that exchange rates are most overvalued when private-controlled systems coincide with small manufacturing sectors; the balance of power should be most favorable to proponents of overvaluation in these situations. There is even less support for this hypothesis. Figures 2.1 and 2.2 suggest that the opposite is closer to the truth: when the manufacturing sector is very small, private labor and financial systems are associated with *more undervalued* exchange rates.

TABLE 2.7. Description of control variables

VARIABLE	DESCRIPTION	SOURCE
Agriculture	Value added of agricultural sector as a percentage of GDP	World Bank 2010
Services	Value added of service sector as a percentage of GDP	World Bank 2010
Imports	Imports as a percentage of GDP	World Bank 2010
Exports	Exports as a percentage of GDP	World Bank 2010
Urban population	Percentage of population living in urban areas	World Bank 2010
GDP	Logarithm of real Gross Domestic Product	World Bank 2010
Savings	Gross domestic savings as a percentage of GDP	World Bank 2010
Terms of trade	Capacity to import less export of goods and services (in constant prices)	World Bank 2010
Foreign liabilities	Foreign liabilities minus foreign assets	World Bank 2010
Democracy	21-point regime index	Marshall et al. 2009
Fixed regime	Binary indicator of whether exchange rate regime was fixed or flexible in 1999	Ilzetzki et al. 2008
State-owned firm	Binary indicator of whether firm is state-owned or not	Broz et al. 2008
Firm size	1 = firm has 0-50 employees; 2 = firm has 51–100 employees; 3 = more than 100 employees	Broz et al. 2008
GDP per capita	Logarithm of GDP per capita in home country, average for 1997–1999	Broz et al. 2008
M3/GDP	M3-to-GDP ratio in home country, average for 1997–1999	Broz et al. 2008
FDI/GDP	Foreign direct investment-to-GDP ratio in home country, average for 1997–1999	Broz et al. 2008
Currency crisis	Binary indicator of whether currency crisis occurred in year 1999; currency crisis occurs if nominal exchange rate depreciates more than 25% and change in depreciation is greater than 10%	Heston et al. 2009

In addition to the variables listed in table 2.8, models 1 and 2 include country fixed-effects (the table suppresses them for reasons of space). The fixed effects address the fact that unmeasured unit-specific attributes are likely to affect a country's average level of undervaluation. This specification, therefore, helps guard against omitted variable bias. However, fixed-effect models only identify the relationship between variables on the basis of over-time variation. Models 3 and 4 of table 2.8 reestimate these models without the country fixed effects. The results are quite similar. The only noteworthy difference is that manufacturing/GDP becomes statistically significant in model 4. The pooled (i.e., non-fixed effects) model therefore suggests that there is a negative correlation between manufacturing and

TABLE 2.8. Regression results (time-series cross-sectional data)

	(1)	(2)	(3)	(4)
Manufacturing	0.0055 [0.0043]	−0.002 [0.002]	0.00002 [0.004]	−0.0098*** [0.002]
State-owned banks	0.0837*** [0.0245]		0.0687** [0.030]	
Labor restrictions		0.048** [0.023]		0.0514** [0.023]
Manufacturing × state-owned banks	−0.0059*** [0.0012]		−0.0049*** [0.001]	
Manufacturing × labor restrictions		−0.004*** [0.001]		−0.0036*** [0.001]
Agriculture	−0.0002 [0.0032]	0.001 [0.002]	−0.0020 [0.003]	−0.0024 [0.002]
Services	0.0022 [0.0029]	0.002 [0.002]	−0.0024 [0.003]	−0.0015 [0.002]
Imports	−0.0016 [0.0014]	−0.001 [0.001]	−0.0018 [0.001]	−0.0007 [0.001]
Exports	0.0005 [0.0016]	0.0003 [0.001]	0.0008 [0.002]	0.0009 [0.001]
Urban population	−0.0008 [0.0035]	−0.004 [0.003]	0.0037*** [0.001]	0.0026** [0.001]
Foreign liabilities	1.1e-16** [4.4e-17]	1.3E-16** [5.5E-17]	8.7E-17 [6.6E-17]	8.2E-17 [8.1E-17]
Democracy	0.0041** [0.0021]	0.003 [0.002]	0.0017 [0.002]	0.0019 [0.002]
Terms of trade	−1.10E-16 [7.6E-16]	−6.3E-16 [1.5E-15]	−5.4E-16 [8.9E-16]	−9.9E-16 [1.9E-15]
GDP	−0.0647 [0.0456]	−0.002 [0.040]	0.0112 [0.017]	0.0246** [0.011]
Savings	0.0011 [0.0016]	−0.001 [0.001]	−0.0003 [0.002]	−0.0017* [0.001]
Countries	63	120	63	120
Years	31	25	31	25
Observations	1469	2138	1469	2138
R-Squared	0.38	0.48	0.04	0.03

Note: *p<.1; **p<.05; ***p<.01. Panel-corrected standard errors are in parentheses.

overvaluation when states lack control over labor. However, the interaction term remains negative and statistically significant, which indicates that the relationship between manufacturing and undervaluation is stronger when labor is restricted than when labor is not restricted.

The regression models described in the second half of this chapter included nine explanatory variables. Table 2.7 presents definitions of the control variables included in the survey-data models. Figures 2.3 and 2.4 are based on models 1

TABLE 2.9. Regression results (survey data)

	(1)	(2)	(3)	(4)
Overvaluation	−1.2034**	−0.2963	−0.9592**	−0.0837
	[0.502]	[0.233]	[0.449]	[0.341]
State-owned banks	−0.4823		−0.5411*	
	[0.297]		[0.302]	
Labor restrictions		−0.0227		−0.0480
		[0.182]		[0.193]
Overvaluation × state-owned banks	1.8308*		1.9766**	
	[0.969]		[0.981]	
Overvaluation × labor restrictions		−0.2067		−0.3704
		[0.529]		[0.595]
Fixed regime	−0.6391***	−0.6938***	−0.6296***	−0.6876***
	[0.170]	[0.168]	[0.172]	[0.177]
State-owned firm	0.0105	−0.1198	−0.0164	−0.1243
	[0.109]	[0.105]	[0.118]	[0.107]
Firm size	−0.0073	0.0394	0.0073	0.0452
	[0.045]	[0.044]	[0.044]	[0.043]
GDP per capita	0.1033	0.1706	0.1532	0.1348
	[0.176]	[0.145]	[0.179]	[0.155]
M3/GDP	−0.0004	0.0010	0.0024	0.0021
	[0.004]	[0.005]	[0.004]	[0.005]
FDI/GDP	−0.1661	−0.1068	−0.2584*	−0.1103
	[0.147]	[0.099]	[0.149]	[0.088]
Currency crisis			1.3971***	0.3604
			[0.375]	[0.326]
Observations	1616	2063	1616	2063
R-Squared	0.04	0.03	0.04	0.03

Note: *p<.1; **p<.05; ***p<.01. Clustered standard errors are in brackets.

and 2 from table 2.9, respectively. Table 2.9 presents the ordered probit coefficients. Robust standard errors that are clustered by country are in brackets. I use country-clustered standard errors because the errors of individual firms within a country may not be independent from one another.

As a robustness check, models 3 and 4 add a measure of currency crisis to the main specification. This definition of currency crisis is based on Frankel and Rose (1996). Controlling for currency crises has little bearing on the main variables of interest.

WHY CHINA UNDERVALUES ITS EXCHANGE RATE

The Domestic Politics of Currency Manipulation

Exchange rate policy has been a key ingredient in China's incredibly successful development strategy (Herrerias and Orts 2011; Rodrik 2010). The improvement in living standards in China during the past few decades has been remarkable. The average Chinese citizen was six-and-a-half times richer in 2008 than she was fifteen years earlier.[1] Even more striking, China's exports increased fifteen-fold over that time period. This rapid export-led growth would never have materialized if China's leaders did not keep their currency, the renminbi, undervalued during this period. Although the renminbi's undervaluation also has some detrimental effects on the Chinese economy, this policy has, on balance, served the country exceptionally well.

The rest of the world, however, has been far less pleased with China's undervalued exchange. There are good reasons for this hostility: Chinese undervaluation leaves foreign-based companies at a huge competitive disadvantage in global markets relative to Chinese firms.[2] Nobel Prize-winning economist Paul Krugman (2010) describes the undervaluation of the renminbi as "the most distortionary exchange rate policy any major nation has ever followed. And it's a policy that seriously damages the rest of the world." Chinese undervaluation is widely blamed for creating the "global imbalances" that contributed to the global financial crisis of 2008 (Obstfeld and Rogoff 2009; Roubini and Mihm 2010). Subse-

---

1. Data in this paragraph are from China Data Online.
2. The undervaluation of the renminbi is not entirely bad for foreign countries. It helps consumers in foreign countries purchase Chinese-made goods more cheaply, thus increasing their real wages.

quently, China's foreign critics have claimed that "China's aggressive undervaluation of its currency is providing a hugely unfair boost to its exports . . . and hindering the recovery around the world" (*New York Times* 2010). Although the U.S. government has not (yet) retaliated against China for its undervalued exchange rate, a large bipartisan majority in the U.S. House of Representatives passed a bill (HR.2378) in September 2010 that would permit tariff retaliation against currency manipulators like China. China's currency practices have been condemned by international organizations, such as the IMF, and the governments of Canada, France, and many other nations (*Associated Press* 2010; *New York Times* 2007; Chan 2010). Why has China maintained an undervalued exchange rate for most of the period since 1994, and why does it continue to do so in spite of the damage this policy inflicts on China's international reputation?

The conditional preference theory elaborated in chapter 1 answers this important question. This theory argues that the combination of a powerful manufacturing sector and state-controlled labor and financial systems contributes to an undervalued exchange rate. Politicians set exchange rate policy with the aim of pleasing powerful interest groups, and when the manufacturing sector controls substantial power resources, it has more influence than any other interest group. When states control labor and financial markets, the manufacturing sector typically favors an undervalued exchange rate because policymakers are able to unload most of the costs of undervaluation onto labor and finance. As a result, the conditional preference theory expects that policymakers face strong demands for undervalued exchange rates when the manufacturing sector is powerful and state controls labor and finance. Policymakers are more likely to keep the exchange rate undervalued as a result.

This chapter evaluates whether the conditional preference theory helps to explain exchange rate politics in China between 1993 and 2009. China's undervalued exchange rate has affected the world economy in numerous ways and is among the most contentious issues in contemporary international politics. Any understanding of the recent evolution of the international political economy is grossly incomplete without a solid grasp of the political origins of Chinese exchange rate policy.

China is also an extremely useful case for theory testing purposes. Although it is always difficult to generalize from a single country, findings are more likely to be generalizable when a country constitutes a "least likely" case for a particular theory (Bennett 2008; Eckstein 1975). Countries with high degrees of state autonomy are hard cases for interest group theories because policymakers are less likely to respond to societal pressures in these states (Kessler 1998). Due to high degrees of state autonomy in China, there is widespread skepticism that interest groups influence Chinese exchange rate policy. Most China scholars believe that

"Chinese bureaucrats [are] largely insulated from direct lobbying from societal groups" (Shih 2007, 1243). One study concluded that even though interest group theories "are generally applied to the private sector in the developed world, their direct relevance to China is limited" (Kaplan 2006, 1193). Similarly, Hongying Wang (2003, 170) acknowledges the "strong influence of interest groups" in Argentina, Japan, Germany, and France, but attributes the "lack of influence on the part of interest groups" in Chinese exchange rate policy to "the remarkable . . . resilience of state autonomy and capacity in China." In short, there is a consensus that societal interest groups do not influence China's exchange rate policy.

Contrary to this conventional wisdom, this chapter shows that interest group demands strongly influence Chinese exchange rate policy and are an important reason China keeps the renminbi undervalued. The evidence presented here demonstrates that China's powerful manufacturing sector has repeatedly lobbied the central government to undervalue the exchange rate, and this lobbying often proved decisive in convincing China's policymakers to keep their exchange rate undervalued. This chapter also shows that China's labor and financial market structures redistributed the costs of the undervalued exchange rate away from industrialists, which intensified manufacturers' demands for devaluation. The most important way that the Chinese government did so was by pushing the costs of its sterilized foreign exchange market interventions onto the country's state-owned commercial banks. China's undervalued exchange rate results from the conjunction of state-controlled labor and financial systems, which increase industrialists' support for undervaluation, and a powerful manufacturing sector, which makes policymakers more responsive to this group's preferences.

I'll begin with an overview of China's political and economic system, describing the organization of the labor and financial system and the power of the manufacturing sector. The core of the chapter examines how politics shapes exchange rate policy in China between 1993 and 2009. The third section summarizes the chapter's key findings and explains how they shed light on the relationship between domestic politics and undervalued exchange rates more broadly.

The Political Sources of Exchange Rate Policy in China

China's Political System and Policymaking Process

The Chinese Communist Party (CCP) has ruled mainland China since 1949. Political authority was extremely centralized when Mao Zedong was at the helm. Since Mao's death in 1976, China has been a "fragmented authoritarian" regime: a single-party regime with multiple lines of authority (Lieberthal and Oksenberg 1988). China remains a strong authoritarian state that is capable of violently repressing enemies—a capacity it has been willing to use at times. Notwithstanding this capacity for physical repression, Chinese leaders remain receptive to societal pressures. In fact, nongovernmental organizations and private businesses frequently provide input into policy decisions, particularly when it comes to less politically sensitive issues, such as the economy and the environment (Deng and Kennedy 2010; Kennedy 2005; Mertha 2009). This section describes how exchange rate policy gets made in China and explains why Chinese policymakers are highly responsive to societal preferences.[3]

In China, like most countries, major decisions about exchange rate policy must be approved by the country's top political elites. The most powerful individual in China is the secretary-general of the CCP, who typically serves concurrently as president of the Chinese state. In recent decades, the premier, the head of China's cabinet known as the State Council, has taken the lead in economic policymaking, exchange rate policy included. Thus, important exchange rate decisions typically require the approval of both the secretary-general and the premier. Other members of the Politburo Standing Committee (PBSC), the most powerful decision-making body in China, also play an important role in exchange rate and other economic policy decisions. Among the four to nine members on the PBSC, those with economic portfolios tend to have greater influence on exchange rate policy than those whose main responsibilities lie elsewhere, such as military affairs or minority issues. In short, while the central bank makes day-to-day decisions about the exchange rate level, the top political leaders in the PBSC are responsible for choosing the general direction of exchange rate policy.

When making decisions about exchange rate policy, China's top political elites in the PBSC consult widely. The leaders hold meetings where they receive input from various government bureaucracies, particularly the Ministry of Commerce (MOC); the People's Bank of China (PBC), the central bank; and the National Development and Reform Commission (NDRC). Exchange rate policy is also discussed at China's annual Central Economic Work Conference, where a larger set of actors, such as provincial leaders, voice their preferences. The top leadership also consults experts from the Chinese Academy of Social Sciences (CASS) and the Development Research Center of the State Council.

Since many different state actors participate in exchange rate discussions, there are various avenues through which private firms and other interest groups can inform political elites of their exchange rate preferences. Firms with ties to individual

---

3. This discussion of the policy process is based on interviews with Chinese government officials as well as Freeman and Wen (2011), Liew (2004), and Wright (2009).

politicians who sit in the PBSC can utilize such ties, for example. More commonly, interest groups use their contacts with lower-level bureaucrats and local politicians that participate in exchange rate policymaking. For example, the Zhejiang Merchants' Association, which represents the province's private investors, has regular contacts with top-level officials in Zhejiang province and beyond (Ding 2010). One survey found that a very high fraction of large private firms in China lobby the central ministries and local governments (Deng and Kennedy 2010). Private actors have an abundance of opportunities to provide input into exchange rate decisions, and they take advantage of these opportunities.

When setting exchange rate or other economic policies, China's top leaders have strong incentives to take seriously the preferences of central ministries, local governments, and other lower-level party officials. These lower-level officials sit on the Central Committee, which selects China's top leaders. China's top leaders seek to adopt policies favored by these lower-level officials in order to maintain their support and ensure that Central Committee members do not switch their allegiance to rival leaders (Shih 2008; Shirk 1993).

Local and ministerial officials advocate for policies that benefit the sectors and regions that they "represent" because this determines their ability to advance politically. These officials are more likely to win promotions and avoid demotions when their private-sector constituents are economically successful. For instance, provincial leaders in China are promoted or demoted partly based on their region's economic performance (Cheung 1998; Li and Zhou 2005). Similarly, ministers accumulate administrative merits and improve their chances of promotion when the sector that they are responsible for performs well (Shih 2008). The fact that promotions and demotions depend on *relative performance* means that politicians in China have an incentive to pay attention to the *distributional consequences* of economic policies. Political competition in China thus creates a system of "virtual representation" where politicians are encouraged to lobby for policies that benefit the industry they represent (Lampton 1992; Shirk 1993). Although undemocratic, China's political regime is responsive to the preferences of powerful societal interest groups.

China's State-Controlled Financial System

The Chinese state has near-absolute control over the financial sector. Although the state has mildly loosened its control over the financial system in the Opening and Reform era, the party still retains authority over nearly all of the nation's major financial institutions.

The communists nationalized the financial system in 1956. From 1956 to 1978, China had a "monobank system" where the PBC was the only financial institution. The PBC retains its role as the national central bank today, but it lost its commercial banking functions in the 1980s, when China created four wholly state-owned commercial banks. China's banking system grew rapidly during the past thirty years, but nonbank financial markets, such as bonds and equities, remain miniscule. Within China's bank-dominated financial system, roughly 60% of bank deposits remain in the Big Four commercial banks, which are owned and controlled by the state. The remaining 40% of deposits are held in the variety of other smaller, predominantly state-owned financial institutions that have emerged since the 1980s.[4]

Although the degree of state ownership has declined slightly in the past decade, the "government [still] owns—directly or indirectly—almost all important banks in the system" (Podpiera 2006, 3). The government gave up 100% control over the nation's major banks in the late 1990s. Private investors, including foreigners, have acquired minority ownership in many Chinese financial institutions. Unlike most countries, foreign investment in Chinese banks "has taken the form of minority shareholding with very limited management involvement" (Leigh and Podpiera 2006, 3). Chinese law stipulates that foreigners are not allowed to own more than 25% of any bank, and no single private investor is allowed more than a 20% stake; in reality, foreign investors typically own only 10% of a bank's shares (Leigh and Podpiera 2006). Although not the absolute monopoly it used to be, the state continues to have a "near monopoly in the banking sector" (Riedel et al. 2007, 170). The percentage of deposits in state-owned banks, as measured by Micco et al. (2007), declined from 100% in 2000 to 99.8% in 2003.[5]

Chinese politicians have little difficulty controlling bank behavior. Chinese financial policymakers have been extremely frank about this fact. "Commercial banking is not a sector where there is a need for 100% state ownership . . . the state can maintain absolute control . . . [with] a 75% equity interest," according to a 2000 article in the *People's Daily* by Zhou Xiaochuan, who was later promoted to central bank governor (quoted in Howson 2009, 136–137). The director of the Bank of Communications, China's fifth largest bank, concurs: since the party is "the controlling shareholder, it has the power to propose strategy arrangements for the future development of the Bank . . . . If the nation implements macroeconomic measures, [the Bank] must abide by these policies" (quoted in Howson 2009, 141). Because it is the majority owner of China's major banks, the Chinese state controls bank actions.

---

4. These institutions include joint-stock banks, development banks, and trust and investment companies.

5. Similarly, La Porta, Lopez-de-Silanes, and Shleifer (2002) report a decline in China's state-owned banks from 100% in 1975 to 99.5% in 1995. Abiad, Detragiache, and Tressel (2010) code Chinese banks as majority state-owned for all years.

Chinese policymakers use a number of instruments, both formal and informal, to control the actions of banks. Even in recent years, the Chinese government enforced limits, or quotas, on the total volume of loans that Chinese banks are allowed to issue (*The Economist* 2011). In addition to controlling the volume of lending, the State Council also dictates the interest rates that banks pay depositors and charge borrowers (Shih 2011).[6] The Chinese government also influences the actions of banks through a policy it refers to as "window guidance," a euphemism for informal pressure. The central bank regularly "summon[s] the commercial banks" to "window guidance meetings" where policymakers "convey the message of monetary policy intentions" (PBC 2003). The PBC's Quarterly Monetary Policy Report includes a section on window guidance, where the government provides clear and specific instructions to banks about how much they should be lending and to which sectors. The purpose of window guidance, according to the PBC (2010), is "strengthened coordination between credit and industrial policy."[7]

One reason that China's political elites are so successful at controlling bank behavior is that the party manages banks' personnel. Communist Party committees appoint and have the power to remove bank managers (Howson 2009; Riedel 2007, 105; Shih 2008). The state even has to approve appointments of senior managers to Minsheng Bank and Shenzen Development Bank, two non-state-owned banks (Shih 2008, 39). If bankers in China want to keep their jobs and get promoted, they must comply with politicians' directives. Chinese bankers have little ability or incentive to disobey party leaders.

The Chinese financial system has undoubtedly moved in the direction of more private ownership over the past decades, but change has occurred at a glacial pace. The state's control over banks remains almost as great as the absolute control it exerted before its market reforms. Banks in China do not respond to market signals, but to orders from their political masters.

---

6. There has been some mild loosening of interest rate controls since the early 2000s. In January 2004, banks gained the ability to charge borrowers interest rates that ranged between 0.9 and 1.3 times the benchmark rate. A few months later, the upper ceiling on lending interest rates was banished, though a ceiling on deposit interest rates and a floor on lending interest rates have remained in place. However, in practice, interest rates have hardly become much more differentiated: more than 60% of loans were at or below the benchmark rate in the fourth quarter of 2005 (Goodfriend and Prasad 2006). Zhu Min (2009, li–lii), a vice president at the Bank of China, one of the Big Four commercial banks, admits that "there is still some influence, either direct or indirect on how loans are made" and that "rates on loans are still subject to governmental guidelines."

7. The widespread belief that China's state-owned banks only lend to state-owned enterprises is quite outdated. By the mid-1990s, private enterprises received a substantial share of loans from the state-owned banks, and their share of loans steadily increased and even surpassed state-owned enterprises' share of bank loans in 2003 (see Riedel et al. 2007, 44).

China's State-Controlled Labor System

The Chinese state also has extensive control over the labor system. Workers are not allowed to unionize, strike, or engage in meaningful collective bargaining. Chinese "[w]orkers' lack of collective rights is a crucial factor that has contributed to their powerlessness" (Chen 2007, 65). Restrictive collective labor laws also augment the state's capacity to shape outcomes in the labor market.

The legal prohibition on the formation of independent labor unions is the most important mechanism by which China's state controls labor. China is one of the only countries in the world that has not signed International Labour Organization (ILO) Convention 87, which guarantees workers freedom of association rights. To be sure, many workers in China are formally members of a union. In fact, the All China Federation of Trade Unions (ACFTU) is the world's largest union federation (Nichols and Zhao 2010, 19). But a simple count of union members provides a grossly misleading indication of union strength in China because the ACFTU does not actually represent workers. China's Trade Union Law states that the ACFTU is the only legal union in the country and that the ACFTU is subordinate to the Communist Party. Thus, trade unions that lie outside of the party's control are prohibited. Attempts to subvert this law often lead to retribution, and "labor activists suffer long prison terms for attempting to organize workers outside of this official framework" (Gallagher 2005, 82). In short, no official organizations represent workers' interests in China.

The Communist Party has an expansive reach within the ACFTU (Chen 2009). Top union officials are always appointed from above. For example, the head of the ACFTU between 1993 and 2003 was a member of the PBSC. Most individual workplace unions are also headed either by party members or senior firm managers. Many of these unions are therefore "shell unions" (Chen 2009, 681). Due to top-down control of the union, the interests of union leaders are more often aligned with the party or management than with the workers they claim to represent. Survey data confirms that promoting workers' interests is not the ACFTU's main objective: 63% of union heads reported that their primary duty was to carry out party functions while only 19% reported that safeguarding worker interests was their priority (Chen 2009). For these reasons, the ACFTU is a union in name only (Taylor and Li 2007).

The second facet of collective labor rights, the right to strike, is also lacking in China. The right to strike was written into China's 1975 and 1978 constitutions, but was subsequently removed in China's 1982 constitution, which remains in force. Thus, labor strikes are in a legal limbo, neither expressly prohibited nor permitted by Chinese law (Chan and Nørlund 1998; Chen 2007). While strikes in

China have been quite common,[8] the government is able to declare strikes illegal under the Law on Demonstrations and Assemblies—an ability that the government often, though not always, exercises (Chen 2007, 73; China Labour Bulletin 2009). In short, Chinese law does not afford workers the legal right to strike.

Finally, Chinese workers have little ability to bargain collectively over their working conditions (Caraway 2009). The fact that China is one of the few countries that has not signed ILO Convention 98, which recognizes the right to collectively bargain, is instructive. Management's control over unions and their finances further hampers unions' ability to actively promote workers' interests at the collective bargaining table (Chen 2009; Gallagher 2005, 90). Instead, collective bargaining that occurs is "formalistic and ritualistic, having limited effect on labor relations" and involves collective contracts that are "implemented top-down by government agencies" (Chen 2007, 74).

The structures governing China's labor system are among the most restrictive in the world today. Chinese workers are unable to form independent unions, engage in collective bargaining, or collective actions such as strikes. Cingranelli and Richards's (2010) data indicate that China restricted collective labor rights every year between 1981 and 2006. Caraway's (2009) richer evaluation of collective labor rights in eleven Asian developing countries comes to a similar conclusion: China's collective labor laws are highly unfavorable to labor; only Burma scored lower. Overall, the rules and decision-making procedures that govern China's labor system hamper workers' capacity to promote their interests and expand the state's control over labor.

These institutional arrangements are one of the main reasons that Chinese workers are so poorly remunerated. Even though wages and benefits have increased a great deal in recent years, Chinese workers still earn far less than workers in most other countries at a similar level of development (Banister and Cook 2011; Yang et al. 2010). The state has been able to use its control of labor to contain employers' costs.

China's Powerful Manufacturing Sector

China's manufacturing sector controls many power resources, including economic resources, organizational resources, and normative resources. As a result, China's manufacturing sector should strongly influence the country's exchange rate level.

China's manufacturing sector controls a vast sum of economic resources. The manufacturing sector takes up a very large share of China economy—typically over one-third of Chinese GDP (see table 0.2), which is well over twice the size of

---

8. These strikes are never led by the ACFTU, however (China Labour Bulletin 2009).

the average in the developing world (14.2%). In 2005, China's ratio of manufacturing production to GDP was the fourth highest out of the 136 developing countries in the World Bank's (2010) database. The manufacturing sector's large share of GDP means that its economic well-being has a sizable impact on China's aggregate growth and unemployment rates. Chinese policymakers are unlikely to ignore the preferences of this economically important sector.

The organizational resources of China's manufacturing sector are also substantial. The geographic concentration of Chinese manufacturers enhances their political influence for several reasons. Most manufacturing production occurs along China's coast (Naughton 2007; Wen 2004). The six wealthy provinces of southeastern China (Guangdong, Fujian, Zhejiang, Shanghai, Jiangsu, and Shandong) account for the vast majority of China's manufacturing output, especially for high-tech products such as electronics and labor-intensive goods like textiles.[9] The southeastern provinces also produce large quantities of some capital-intensive manufacturing goods, such as metals and rubber. The northeastern provinces of Liaoning, Jilin, and Heilongjiang produce large volumes of machinery, steel, and other capital-intensive manufactures. Geographic concentration helps China's manufacturing industries overcome barriers to collective action, which should bolster their political influence (Kaplan 2006).

The manufacturing sector's close ties to key political decision makers constitute another important type of organizational resource. Two central ministries, the MOC and NDRC, represent the manufacturing sector and advocate for policies that benefit this sector (Foot and Walter 2011, 117; Freeman and Wen 2011; Wright 2009, 182–185). The MOC and the NDRC are much more powerful than other central ministries that participate in the exchange rate policymaking process. Their main opponent, the PBC, which primarily represents the banking sector, is among the lowest-ranked and least powerful ministries in China (Wright 2009, 187; *The Economist* 2013). China's manufacturing industries also have ties to powerful members of the party. Provincial leaders from China's coastal provinces have often been over-represented in party organs, such as the Central Committee, Politburo, and PBSC (Li 2005; Shirk 1993). Politicians from China's coastal provinces advocate for policies that benefit the manufacturing sector because these wealthy and powerful provinces are highly dependent on manufactured production.

In China, the manufacturing sector has long been held in high esteem. This represents an important type of "normative resource" for China's manufacturing

---

9. Shanghai is a municipality, but has the status of a province. In 2005, these six provinces accounted for 48% of China's GDP, but produced over 80% of China's clothing and shoes, electronic equipment, and textiles (China Data Online).

sector. During the Mao era, building a heavy industrial sector was economic policymakers' top priority (Naughton 2007, 115; Riedel et al. 2007, 6). There has been considerable continuity in the belief that manufacturing is China's most important sector, though the emphasis has since shifted toward higher value-added manufacturing industries, such as electronics (Gereffi 2009; Naughton 2007, 366). The "desire to propel China into a high technology future" is an issue that "unites policymakers, business leaders, and the public" (Naughton 2007, 350). The long-standing and widespread perception that the state should nurture certain segments of manufacturing provides this sector with normative resources that should help it obtain favorable economic policies.

The Economic Attributes of China's Manufacturing Sector

Although the power resources of China's manufacturing sector are quite exceptional, the economic attributes of this sector are typical in most regards. Most manufacturing goods produced in China are internationally tradable. China exports a large quantity of manufacturing goods, from T-shirts to DVD players. Chinese manufacturing firms that produce for the domestic market have had to compete against foreign producers since at least the mid-1990s when China's trade policy became relatively liberal (Naughton 2007, 388).[10] Despite much hype about China's prowess as an exporting powerhouse, its manufacturing firms only export 20% of their production, on average, which is slightly below the average for developing countries as a whole.[11] This likely reflects the fact that China has a huge internal market. Overall, manufacturing production in China is tradable but not especially export-dependent.

Reliance on imported inputs is a second similarity between the manufacturing sector in China and in other developing countries. Imported intermediate goods represent almost 50% of the value-added of China's exports (Koopman et al. 2012; Upward et al. 2013). I am not aware of systematic data on the use of imported inputs for non-exporting manufacturing firms. Domestically oriented manufacturers may be less import-dependent than exporters, but the available evidence suggests that China's manufacturing sector is heavily reliant on imported inputs. Like their counterparts elsewhere, China's manufacturing firms also depend on bank borrowing for a sizable share of their investments: 21.1% of new investment financing comes from local banks, which is close to the developing

---

10. China's capital-intensive industries face particularly stiff competition from foreign producers. China imports more capital-intensive manufactured goods than it exports (Naughton 2007, 395).

11. This figure is calculated from the World Bank Enterprise Survey (2002–2006). The average manufacturing firm in the Enterprise Survey sample exports 21.9% of its production.

world average of 20.2% (see table 1.3). Since Chinese manufacturing firms produce tradable goods using importable inputs, undervalued exchange rates simultaneously increase their costs and improve their external competitiveness. Hence, it is unlikely that manufacturers in China benefit more from an undervalued exchange rate than manufacturers in other developing countries.

One aspect of China's manufacturing sector that is somewhat unique is the relatively high percentage of firms that are owned, at least in part, by foreigners. The most likely effect of foreign ownership is to reduce the intensity of manufacturers' exchange rate preferences. Compared to domestically owned firms, the sales revenue of foreign-owned firms should be less sensitive to the host country's exchange rate level because they are likely to have production facilities in other countries (Frieden 1994, 86; Kinderman 2008; Knight 2010). Since foreign-owned companies are also less dependent on the local economy for their inputs, they should also be less sensitive to the effects of undervaluation on local input costs. Thus, foreign ownership may reduce both the benefits and costs of an undervalued exchange rate to China's manufacturing sector. However, even in China, foreign-owned firms remain a relatively small minority of the manufacturing sector. The vast majority of firms in China (76%) are wholly domestically owned. Only 7% of Chinese manufacturing firms are fully foreign-owned.[12] Because of the prevalence of mixed domestic-foreign ownership, the distinction between foreign and domestic firms is blurred in China, and the interests of most "foreign" firms overlap to a large degree with domestic firms. The case study in the second half of this chapter highlights when the preferences or political influence of foreign and domestic firms diverge, but these differences are typically minimal. Because of their broadly similar interests, I focus on the manufacturing sector as a whole.

Implications and Hypotheses

China has a state-controlled financial system, state-controlled labor system, and a powerful manufacturing sector. The conditional preference theory suggests that exchange rates are likely to be undervalued in countries that combine these three features. The solid line in figure 3.1 shows that China's exchange rate was undervalued throughout the 1993–2007 period and had an average undervaluation of 38%. Although this figure ends in 2007, more recent evaluations of China's exchange rate find that the renminbi remains undervalued (IMF 2012; Subramanian 2010; Wong and Ladler 2010). China's exchange level is consistent with the expectations of the conditional preference theory.

12. This data is from the World Bank Enterprise Survey (2002–2006). In other developing countries, 88% of manufacturing firms are fully domestic and 6% are fully foreign-owned.

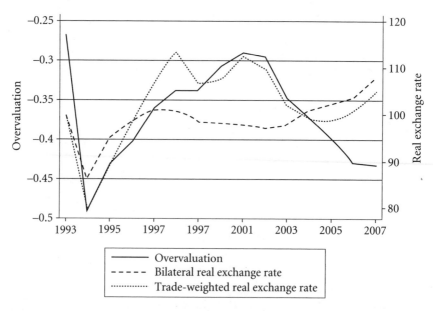

Figure 3.1. Exchange rate undervaluation in China, 1993–2007. Overvaluation is defined as the difference between the actual real exchange rate and the estimated equilibrium real exchange rate. Positive (negative) values imply an overvalued (undervalued) real exchange rate. See chapter 2 for more details. Bilateral real exchange rate is defined as the natural logarithm of the nominal exchange rate divided by the GDP deflator (Heston et al. 2009). This indicator is inverted so that higher (lower) values imply a more appreciated (depreciated) real exchange rate. Trade-weighted real exchange rate is based on Darvas 2012. Both real exchange rate variables are indexed so that 1993 equals 100.

However, this data does not tell us whether China's labor and financial structures and powerful manufacturing sector had a causal impact on Chinese exchange rate policy. To answer this crucial causal question, I will now examine, in detail, the political dynamics surrounding exchange rate policy in China. If these factors were responsible for China's undervalued exchange rate, we should be able to trace their impact through two main causal mechanisms: preferences and political influence.

The first causal mechanism is the preferences of the manufacturing sector. My theory expects that China's manufacturing sector should favor an undervalued exchange rate. The conditional preference theory also makes concrete predictions about when and why Chinese industrialists support undervaluation. I expect that China's state uses its control over labor and financial markets to suppress manufacturers' wage and interest costs, and pushes the burdens of undervalued exchange rates onto banks and workers. These actions make an undervalued exchange rate more attractive to the manufacturing sector and intensify its demands for this policy.

The theory also expects that manufacturers' support for undervaluation may vary somewhat over time. The manufacturing sector's demands for undervaluation should recede when policymakers are unable to control manufacturers' financing and labor costs. Policymakers should typically be able to lower manufacturers' costs in countries with state-controlled labor and financial systems, but they may face temporary difficulties doing so in certain contexts, such as in the face of a large external economic shock. In short, the "preference mechanism" is supported to the extent that Chinese manufacturing firms generally support undervaluation; state policymakers shield manufacturers from the negative effects of undervaluation; and the manufacturing sector's support for undervaluation wanes when policymakers are temporarily unable to shield manufacturers from the negative effects of an undervalued exchange rate.

It is also imperative to demonstrate that the manufacturing sector influenced policymakers' decisions. The "political influence mechanism" is verified only if interest groups communicate their preferences to political decision makers; policymakers are aware of interest groups' preferences; and policymakers are responsive to these preferences and evince a desire to please this interest group. Evidence that other factors, such as ideology and geopolitical interests, did not determine exchange rate policy would further bolster one's confidence that interest group pressures were important.

The Evidence: Exchange Rate Politics in China

The remainder of this chapter examines the politics of exchange rate valuation in China between 1993 and 2009. Several political and economic changes occurred at the start of this period, which make 1993 a suitable year to begin the analysis. Politically, 1993 marked the end of the "Tiananmen interlude" and the start of a new era of Chinese politics that was dominated by Jiang Zemin and Zhu Rongji (Huang 2008, 22; Naughton 2007, 100).[13] This political transition coincided with important shifts in China's economy. With the proliferation of privately owned firms and the elimination of price controls on most goods, China's economy was much more market-oriented by 1993 than it was just a few years earlier (Lieberthal 2004, 249; Riedel et al. 2007, 6–11; Tsai 2007, 53–60). This shift toward a market economy

---

13. Jiang Zemin became secretary-general during the Tiananmen crisis; he then became president in 1993. Zhu Rongji was the vice premier from 1993 to 1998, but he became "the dominant voice in policymaking in mid-1993," when Premier Li Peng suffered a heart attack and Zhu became acting premier (Naughton 2007, 100; see also Brahm 2002, 15–61; Shih 2008, 151–159).

TABLE 3.1. Exchange rate politics in China, 1993–2009

PERIOD	EXCHANGE RATE POLICY	PREFERENCES OF MANUFACTURING SECTOR	POLITICAL INFLUENCE OF MANUFACTURING SECTOR
1993–1994	Undervaluation	Undervaluation	Strong influence
1995–1996	Undervaluation	Undervaluation	Strong influence
1997–1999	Appreciation	Overvaluation	Partial influence
2000–2002	Depreciation	Indifferent/No clear position	Weak influence
2003–2006	Undervaluation	Undervaluation	Strong influence
2007	Appreciation	Indifferent/Appreciation	Partial influence
2008–2009	Undervaluation	Undervaluation	Strong influence

was officially codified in 1992 and 1993 when party and state leaders defined China as a "socialist market economy" instead of a "planned economy" for the first time (Riedel et al. 2007, 7; Tsai 2007, 67). These economic changes increased the importance of the exchange rate level. In earlier periods, before China became a full-fledged capitalist economy, the exchange rate was little more than an administrative tool that had little effect on the allocation of resources (Bell and Feng 2013, 211; Huang and Wong 1996; Interview C1). The case study, therefore, examines several exchange rate policy decisions, beginning in 1993 and continuing until 2009, the year in which my data collection ended.[14]

Table 3.1 summarizes the key political and economic features of the seven episodes covered in this chapter. For each period, table 3.1 shows the actual exchange rate outcome, the preferences of the manufacturing sector, and whether the preferences of the manufacturing sector had a strong, partial, or weak influence over exchange rate policy. Cases where the preferences of the manufacturing sector were the main driving force behind exchange rate policy are labeled as "strong influence." A "partial influence" refers to cases where the manufacturing sector's preferences were one of the main factors behind the government's exchange rate policy, but not the only one.

From Interest Group Lobbying to Exchange Rate Devaluation: 1993–1994

China's economy experienced several problems in 1993. Inflation reached 15% as a result of expansionary policies during 1992. In addition, China's multiple ex-

---

14. For a list of elite interviews conducted by the author, see the appendix.

change rate system became dysfunctional. The "official" exchange rate, which was used for most foreign trade and capital account transactions, was fixed at 5.8 renminbi/dollar and appreciated rapidly in real terms. The "swap market" exchange rate, which was used for other transactions, was highly unstable and depreciated rapidly at certain periods in 1993. A flourishing black market for dollars emerged at this time. To address these problems, the Chinese government initiated a major shift in macroeconomic strategy in 1993 and 1994. The most important consequence of these policy shifts was a substantial increase in the degree of exchange rate undervaluation.

Standard accounts suggest that Zhu Rongji and a small group of technocratic advisers initiated the 1994 foreign exchange reform because they sought to improve the efficiency of the foreign exchange market and increase the central government's ability to control the macroeconomy (Brahm 2002; Liew 2004, 28, 33; Huang and Wong 1996; Lam 1999, 372). This depiction is problematic. It understates the variety of actors who gave input into exchange rate policy. Worse, Zhu and his advisers appear to have *opposed* devaluation. This case study demonstrates that the preferences of the powerful manufacturing sector influenced the 1994 decision to undervalue the exchange rate.

In the early 1990s, Secretary-General Jiang Zemin had not yet consolidated his power. Jiang was highly reliant on Vice Premier Zhu Rongji, who had responsibility for several economic portfolios and was a crucial swing vote for Jiang in the PBSC (Shih 2008, 158). Zhu was a "finance person" who built a strong political support network within the central financial ministries (Steinfeld 1998, 48; Lam 1999, 23). Zhu initiated "16 Measures" of contractionary macroeconomic policies in mid-1993 to reduce inflation, based on the hopes that he would be promoted to premier if he solved the inflation problem (Shih 2008).

Zhu Rongji and the monetary and financial bureaucracies viewed the exchange rate as an additional instrument that they could use in their battle against inflation. As a result, they favored merging the multiple exchange rates at an appreciated level. Prominent Zhu advisers, such as Lou Jiwei and Wu Jinglian, advocated unification of the multiple exchange rate system on the grounds that it would "offer the central bank a new means of macroscopic regulation and control" and "help the country fight inflation" (Ta Kung Po 1993; Xinhua 1993b). Zhu and the PBC worried that depreciation would increase inflationary pressure and increase foreign-debt burdens (Chen 1993; Ming Pao 1993; Xinhua 1993a, 1993b). State Administration of Exchange Control officials argued publicly that the official rate of 5.7 was the appropriate value of the renminbi and considered the more depreciated swap rate to be "abnormal" (*China Daily* 1993a). In sum, Zhu and his allies favored unification, but they opposed devaluation because they feared that devaluation would further increase inflation.[15]

In this period, Jiang was actively courting China's coastal provinces. Jiang's main challengers within the PBSC, Li Ruihuan and Qiao Shi, were competing for the support of the powerful eastern provinces (Shih 2008, ch. 7). Manufacturing firms in these provinces, and their representatives in the local governments, were greatly dissatisfied with the direction of monetary and exchange rate policy in 1993. Businesses and politicians from Guangdong, Jiangsu, and other coastal provinces criticized Zhu's tightening policies for reducing their domestic business opportunities (Lam 1999, 258; Gilley 1998; Xiong 1993). Although Jiang was unable to prevent the generally restrictive stance of macroeconomic policy, he skirted Zhu's credit restrictions on several occasions to reduce opposition from these regional governments (Gilley 1998, 205; Shih 2008, 155). The manufacturing industries along China's eastern coast vocally advocated for both a unified exchange rate and an undervalued one throughout 1993. Domestic exporters and foreign investors, many of whom owned export factories, complained that regulations surrounding the multiple exchange rate system were excessively complicated and raised their administrative costs (CNA 1993; He 1993; Shao 1993).

The overvalued exchange rate was an important concern for coastal manufacturing firms. Manufacturers were concerned that high inflation in 1992–1993 led to excessive real exchange rate appreciation, and Ministry of Foreign Trade officials frequently complained about poor export performance during 1993 (*China Daily* 1993b; Chung 1993). As a result, they started to lobby for a devaluation of the renminbi. One Guangdong official argued that a "devaluation strategy" was a "good thing" because devaluation compels firms to "shift from the home market to the international market" and "every adjustment in the exchange rate has been followed by an economic leap forward" (Mai 1993). Foreign investors also favored a depreciation of the exchange rate because this would reduce the costs of domestic investment and wages in terms of their home-country currencies (He 1993). A Trade Ministry official advocated devaluing the currency from 5.8 to 7 renminbi/dollar (Wang 1993). Government officials from Taiwan, the source of much foreign investment in China, suggested that the exchange rate should be 8 renminbi/dollar (CNA 1993). In short, manufacturing industries and government officials sympathetic to their interests strongly pressured the central leadership to depreciate the exchange rate in 1993.

---

15. The financial sector in Shanghai—a key Jiang ally—did not take a clear position on the exchange rate's level but favored exchange rate unification because the national foreign exchange market was established in Shanghai (Yu 1994).

By the fall of 1993, there was agreement over the need to unify China's multiple exchange rate system, but "differences remain[ed] on the rate of exchange of the yuan when the country adopts a single rate system" (Xinhua 1993b). In the end, proponents of undervaluation prevailed. The government merged the exchange rates at a rate of 8.7—a 50% devaluation of the official exchange rate—on January 1, 1994.[16] Most contemporary Chinese observers considered this new exchange rate to be strongly undervalued (Liu 1996; Sun M. 1995; Yang 1996).

The conventional state-centric explanation, focusing on the role of autonomous technocrats, cannot explain the decision to undervalue the exchange rate. There is no evidence that the leading technocrat, Zhu Rongji, wanted to depreciate the exchange rate, and many reasons to think that Zhu opposed devaluation. The exchange rate would have been devalued much less if technocratic considerations determined currency policy.

The desire to benefit China's manufacturing industries was the central reason the exchange rate was merged at an undervalued rate. According to official government journals, enhancing external competitiveness, reversing the trade deficit, and increasing international trade were the State Council's main objectives for this policy change (Li 1995; Liu 1996; Wuhan PBC 1995). The government did not even bother to downplay the distributional effects of devaluation and publicly defended the policy based on the benefits it provided to tradable producers. Minister of Trade Wu Yi called the reform a "dream come true for her ministry" (*China Daily* 1993c). Guangdong government officials called it "very favorable to the expansion of foreign trade and exports" (Wen Pei Wo 1993). The *People's Daily* (1994), the official mouthpiece of the Communist Party, praised the policy on the grounds that "exports . . . will increase" and "foreign investors will have more profits."

Although devaluation helped the manufacturing sector, many other groups were unhappy about the devaluation. The aforementioned *People's Daily* (1994) article admitted that "common people are, individually, showing greater concerns" because devaluation pushes up prices and reduces their "purchase power." Officials from inland provinces, such as Sichuan, Guizhou, and Yunnan, also expressed their displeasure with the devaluation on the grounds that it made it costlier for them to purchase foreign imports and to pay off their foreign debts (Ming Pao 1993). The jubilation of manufacturing producers stood in sharp contrast to the discontent of workers and officials from regions dominated by nontradable industries.

The uneven implementation of the reform further attests to the political influence of tradable industries. Foreign investors "universally welcomed" the

---

16. Since the official rate was not used for all transactions the weighted average depreciation was less than 50%.

policy but expressed reservations about one aspect of the reform: the possibility of confusion and gaps in service during the transition to the new foreign exchange system (He 1993). Foreign investors actively lobbied the government to allow them to continue using the foreign-currency swap centers during the transition phase (Shirk 1994, 66). The government complied with this demand and allowed foreign-owned firms to continue trading foreign exchange on the old swap centers even though domestic firms were required to sell their foreign exchange to Chinese banks (Xinhua 1994). The Chinese government went out of its way to give coastal industries everything they wanted.

Although there is no direct evidence that the decision to undervalue the exchange rate in 1994 resulted from the political importance of the manufacturing sector, there are several reasons that, when considered in combination, suggest it was an important factor. Jiang was concerned with gaining the support of coastal provinces. Provincial politicians and economic interest groups in these provinces actively lobbied for an undervalued exchange rate while most others in the country—Zhu and the technocrats, labor, and inland provinces—seemed to oppose undervaluation. The government itself defended this policy on the grounds that it would improve external competitiveness. Implementation of this policy complied with all the demands of these producers. The exchange rate would not have been devalued as much in January 1994 if manufacturing industries did not actively lobby for devaluation or if they were less powerful.

Sustaining Undervaluation: 1995–1996

The exchange rate reform had a large effect on China's economy in 1994. Capital inflows and exports grew rapidly and the trade balance swung back into surplus. The resulting surge in foreign exchange inflows put upward pressure on the exchange rate. The central bank accumulated foreign reserves to prevent appreciation, but the renminbi gained 2.5% against the dollar over the year nonetheless. The biggest problem was inflation, which rose to 24% in 1994—the highest annual rate in China's reform era. Most Chinese economists viewed exchange rate reform and the accumulation of foreign reserves as important causes of increased inflation in 1994 (Jingji Ribao 1995). Even Zhu Rongji blamed devaluation for increasing inflation (*Kaifang* 1995).

The combination of high inflation and nominal appreciation in 1994 implied a substantial real exchange rate appreciation. Despite this considerable loss of competitiveness, Chinese manufacturing firms seemed unconcerned at first. However, by mid-1995, when the exchange rate appreciated to 8.3, much of the business community started to complain about the real exchange rate's appreciation

(Interview C1). According to one government official, the state-owned foreign trade sector was "shout[ing] loudly" that the exchange rate is no longer undervalued; they warned the government that "without a devaluation of the RMB [renminbi], second half of the year [1995] exports will suffer" (Yang 1995). Government economists sympathetic to industrial interests started publishing academic papers advocating the stabilization or depreciation of the exchange rate (Zhang 1994). The State Economic and Trade Commission published a report that argued: "If the exchange rate continues to rise, it will have a negative impact on exports . . . . We must deal with it seriously and take firm and decisive action" (Economic Information Center 1995). According to one central government official, "the central bank should strive for a rate level which promotes long-term expansion of import-export industries and maintains export-industry competitiveness" (Sun M. 1995). Liu Fei (1996) of the CASS Finance and Trade Institute echoed this view: "Exchange policy must do all possible to maintain the country's competitiveness abroad." Manufacturing industries and their political allies lobbied hard against exchange rate appreciation in mid-1995.

The industrialists were opposed by a variety of groups who felt that exchange rate and other policies were already excessively biased toward manufacturers. The central bank led this charge, arguing that "exchange rate policy . . . cannot serve to track exports to the neglect of all else" (Jing 1995). The PBC opposed undervaluation because it required the central bank to accumulate foreign reserves, which increased the money supply and contradicted the PBC and government's goal of reducing inflation. The central bank also complained that foreign exchange reserves yield low returns and hurt its balance sheet (Jing 1995; Lin 1994). Central bankers argued that the exchange rate should instead be used as an inflation-fighting tool, and the exchange rate should therefore be set at its equilibrium rate or at a slightly overvalued rate (Jing 1995; Wuhan PBC 1995). The PBC, along with its allies in the State Administration of Foreign Exchange Control (Sun L. 1995), CASS Finance Institute (Su and Lin 1995), and the Institute for World Economics and Politics (Interview C31), argued that the exchange rate must continue appreciating.

Despite these calls for continued exchange rate appreciation, government officials "decided to 'freeze' the rate at the 8.3 level" because they were "concerned that further appreciation of the currency would undermine export competitiveness" (Bottelier 2004, 6). Figure 3.2 displays the renminbi-dollar exchange rate over the 1994–1996 period, illustrating that the steady appreciation abruptly stops in June 1995, once the dollar traded for 8.3 renminbi. During the first half of this three-year period, the renminbi appreciated 4.5% but it only rose 0.02% in the latter year and a half. The slowdown in inflation meant that the rate of real

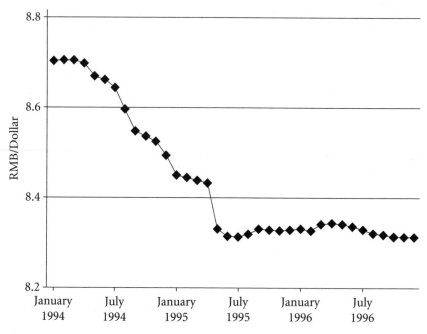

Figure 3.2. Renminbi-dollar exchange rate, 1994–1996.

exchange rate appreciation slowed from 15% in 1995 to only 5% in 1996. The government kept the exchange undervalued in 1995 in response to the manufacturing sector's forceful lobbying against appreciation.

This outcome benefited the manufacturing sector at the expense of China's state-owned banks. Sustaining an undervalued exchange rate in this period required the PBC to accumulate large volumes of foreign exchange reserves: foreign reserves increased more than 300% between 1993 and 1996 (World Bank 2010). The government used "financial repression" to ensure that reserve accumulation did not increase interest rates. The PBC controlled banks' interest rates, and while the PBC raised banks' deposit interest rates to compensate savers for higher inflation, it made sure that lending rates rose more slowly to avoid harming borrowers. The shrinking spread between deposit and lending rates squeezed the profits of banks. The government also taxed banks' profits at confiscatory rates of over 70% (Lardy 1998, 100–115, 170–172). Due to these policies, Chinese banks "lost a great amount of money" in the mid-1990s (Lardy 1998, 106). However, these measures helped keep firms' borrowing costs low. Absent these measures, which were made possible by China's state-controlled financial structures, undervaluation would have been costlier for industrialists, and they probably would have been less insistent that the government keep the renminbi undervalued. So, China combined an undervalued exchange rate with financial repression during 1995–1996, and the manufacturing sector was the main beneficiary of this policy mix.

Real Appreciation with Industrialists' Support: 1997–1999

Following the devaluation of various Asian currencies in 1997, China's exchange rate appreciated relative to that of its trading partners. In trade-weighted terms, China's real exchange rate appreciated 15% between 1996 and 1998 (see figure 3.1). Some even believe that the renminbi became slightly overvalued in this period (Naughton 1999; Sharma 2003). Despite this loss of competitiveness, China's leaders did not devalue the renminbi. Many scholars argue that the Chinese government chose not to devalue in the late 1990s because this served its foreign policy objectives, particularly the desire to improve the country's international reputation and show the world that China is a responsible state (Goldstein 2005; Kim 2006; Wang 2003). On the contrary, this analysis shows that external political considerations are neither necessary nor sufficient for explaining China's response to the Asian crisis. Rather, the Chinese government allowed the real exchange rate to appreciate because the most powerful domestic interest groups, including manufacturing industries, favored this policy.

Chinese manufacturers' demand for undervaluation was much weaker in 1998–1999 than at other times because the costs of undervaluation were far greater in this period. Although undervaluation can usually be combined with cheap and abundant credit in state-controlled financial systems, this was not possible in the context of strong capital outflows. The atypical economic conditions of the late 1990s made it harder for the government to minimize the costs of an undervalued exchange rate. This reduced manufacturers' demands for devaluation, which reduced the political incentive to undervalue the Chinese currency.

Zhu Rongji was the lead decision maker on exchange rate policy during this period.[17] Zhu and his PBC colleagues opposed devaluation because it would have harmed China's financial system. One concern was that devaluation would increase China's foreign debt burdens. Another fear was that devaluation would reduce savers' confidence in Chinese banks and lead to bank runs. A related fear was that devaluation would contribute to financial instability in Hong Kong, which started to play an important role in China's financial system in 1997. Finally, these technocrats opposed devaluation because they believed it would increase inflation.

---

17. On Zhu's role and policy priorities in this period, see Brahm (2002), Lardy (1998), Liew (2004), Moore and Yang (2001), Naughton (1999), Shih (2008), and Wang (2003).

Zhu took the lead in formulating China's response to the Asian crisis, but he "consulted widely" on exchange rate policy because the decision not to devalue required support from other political and economic elites (Liew 2004, 49). Manufacturing firms and their political patrons were among those who gave Zhu policy advice during this period. Manufacturing industries paid little attention to exchange rate policy in late 1997 when Zhu first decided to maintain the fixed exchange rate regime. However, concerns with external competitiveness grew in the first quarter of 1998 when the Japanese yen started depreciating. During the summer of 1998, the manufacturing sector started to demand that the government take a more active response to the crisis. Some even suggested devaluing the exchange rate (Liew 2004; Moore and Yang 2001). Instead of devaluing, the government adopted a variety of expansionary macroeconomic policies during the second half of 1998 to boost domestic demand. Infrastructure investment increased, interest rates were cut, and banks' reserve requirement ratio was lowered. Particular manufacturing industries also lobbied for various targeted policy measures. Steel producers, for example, successfully pressured the government to increase export tax rebates and restrict steel imports (Kennedy 2005, 85–86).

The manufacturing sector no longer lobbied for devaluation after these expansionary policies were implemented. Most manufacturing firms viewed these domestic policy remedies as more advantageous than an undervalued exchange rate. Targeted policies, such as higher export tax rebates, have similar effects on exporters as a devaluation of the currency (Broz and Frieden 2001). In fact, export tax rebates, equivalent to an export subsidy, have an important advantage over devaluation: they do not raise manufacturers' imported input costs. Moreover, the benefits of devaluation were likely to be rather small in this period. Other countries that devalued their currencies in this period saw their trade financing disrupted, which left firms in those countries unable to process exports and take advantage of their more competitive position (Love and Zaidi 2010; World Bank 2004). It is likely that devaluation would have also required China to raise interest rates, rather than lower rates as it did, to help stem the tide of capital outflows. As Chinese exporters witnessed the financial damage that devaluation wrought elsewhere, they came to realize that following this path would not be beneficial in this global economic context (Naughton 1999, 208; Interview C1). In short, since Chinese policymakers were able to implement numerous measures that increased industrialists' profits, and because undervaluation would likely have compromised manufacturers' access to cheap credit, the manufacturing sector did not favor an undervalued exchange rate in the late 1990s.

The manufacturing sector's approval of real exchange rate appreciation helps explain why Chinese leaders did not devalue the currency in the late 1990s. To be sure, the manufacturing sector was not the only actor that influenced exchange rate policy. Nevertheless, devaluation would have been much likelier if China's powerful manufacturing sector demanded devaluation. Manufacturing firms and their political allies had considerable political influence in this period. The support of the State Development and Planning Commission (SDPC), which primarily represented import-competing manufacturing industries, was crucial. The chair of the SDPC was President Jiang's main economic adviser, and he "push[ed] strongly the views of SDPC to Jiang on exchange rate policy" (Liew 2004, 28). Export tax rebates and other export-promotion policies also played a vital role in preventing coastal provincial governments and the Ministry of Trade from pushing for devaluation (Bowles and Wang 2006; Liew 2004). Had these groups all lobbied for undervaluation as aggressively as they did in 1993 and 1995, it is hard to imagine that Chinese policymakers would have deviated from their past pattern of complying with their demands.

China's policy response to the Asian crisis was aimed at winning the approval of domestic interest groups, not foreign governments. Several facts are inconsistent with the "external" explanation. First, actors with economic and financial concerns dominated the decision-making process, but the foreign policy bureaucracy played a limited role (Liew 2004, 44; Moore and Yang 2001, 206). Second, at a time when competitive devaluation was pervasive in Asia, it is unlikely that China would have received much blame for following this trend—probably much less than the condemnation it has received since 2003 for its undervalued exchange rate (as I'll discuss shortly). Third and most important, even if China's decision to keep the exchange rate fixed bolstered its image abroad, the government simultaneously adopted several foreign economic policies, such as tighter restrictions of steel imports and increased export tax rebates, that tarnished China's international image. The Chinese government was put on the defensive when the United States Department of Commerce criticized China for using the export tax rebate hikes as a "disguised way to devalue the currency" (Xinhua 1998). If concern with demonstrating China's willingness to abide by international economic norms was paramount, China would not have caved to interest group pressures to implement policies that were, quite predictably, condemned abroad.

Domestic considerations were the main driver of China's exchange rate policy in the late 1990s. In these unusually harsh economic conditions, where capital was fleeing from East Asia, Chinese authorities were unable to simultaneously keep the exchange rate undervalued and suppress manufacturers' costs. As a result, China's powerful manufacturing sector supported an overvalued exchange rate. Although manufacturers were not the only interest group that influenced Chinese exchange rate policy in the late 1990s, Zhu and Jiang were very responsive to the demands of the ministries and provinces that represented manufacturing firms. The manufacturing sector's support for overvaluation in the late 1990s helps explain why China allowed its real exchange rate to appreciate during this period.

Undervaluation Reemerges: 2000–2002

China weathered the Asian financial crisis better than most of its neighbors, but the government struggled in vain to reignite economic growth even after the region-wide crisis ended. Premier Zhu's official slogan at the time was "two prevents, one encourage"—prevent financial risk and deflation while encouraging economic growth. Although the government prevented financial collapse, it failed at its other tasks: growth remained sluggish (by Chinese standards), and the price level decreased during several of these years. Part of the problem was that a group of inflation hawks refused to loosen monetary policy (Shih 2008). The main tool used to promote growth was fiscal policy. Spending on heavy industry and on the Western provinces rose. However, even fiscal policy was not particularly expansionary, and overzealous tax collection dampened growth in 2001 (Brahm 2002, 257). Macroeconomic policy turned more expansive in 2002. Jiang encouraged increased lending and investment in 2002 to ensure that his protégés remained in power in the 16th Party Congress (Shih 2008).

There was little discussion of exchange rate policy during this period, and the renminbi remained fixed to the dollar at a rate of 8.27. Since China's inflation rate was lower than most of its trading partners, its real exchange rate depreciated in both bilateral and trade-weighted terms between 1999 and 2002 (see figure 3.1). Exchange rate depreciation occurred largely as an unintended by-product of macroeconomic policy in this period. By 2003, when power was transferred to the new president, Hu Jintao, and new premier, Wen Jiabao, the renminbi was highly undervalued again.

Manufacturers' Opposition Minimizes Appreciation: 2003–2006

Hu and Wen's factional supporters and policy preferences differed considerably from those of their predecessors. Unlike Jiang and Zhu, who were groomed in wealthy urban Shanghai, Hu, Wen, and their followers had extensive ties to poorer rural and inland regions, and they prioritized the welfare of inland provinces and the poor over that of coastal businesses (Li 2005). The new leaders wanted to rebalance the economy away from investment and exports and toward greater consumption and domestic demand (Wen 2007). The ideology of China's top decision makers was more consistent with a flexible and appreciated exchange rate than with the fixed and undervalued exchange rate that they inherited (Kaplan

2006, 1196; Wright 2009). External relations were another force promoting exchange rate appreciation. The U.S. government started to complain about the undervaluation of the renminbi in September 2003, and other members of the Group of 7 soon joined them. The market started to expect appreciation around the same time, and capital started flowing into China, putting upward market pressure on the currency.

In spite of these ideological, external political, and market-based pressures for currency appreciation, between 2003 and 2006 the Chinese government went to great lengths to keep its exchange rate undervalued. Lobbying by powerful manufacturing industries is the main reason that the Chinese government maintained an undervalued exchange rate in this period. Despite the fact that Hu, Wen, and their colleagues from inland provinces took over some top positions, leaders from the coast remained well represented in the Politburo and its Standing Committee (Li 2005, 2009). From 2003 to 2006, the provinces and central ministries that represent manufacturing were able to successfully resist their opponents' efforts to appreciate the renminbi. State control of finance increased the manufacturing sector's support for undervaluation: the government forced the state-owned banks to purchase unprofitable government securities, which helped spare the industrial sector from many of the costs of undervaluation that they would have otherwise suffered.

Starting around 2003, keeping the renminbi fixed against the dollar at its undervalued rate became a major burden for China's central bank. In particular, the PBC resumed its rapid accumulation of foreign exchange reserves. Reserves increased more than 250% from 2002 to 2006. By the end of 2006, China's foreign reserve holdings exceeded one trillion dollars in value and were equivalent to 40% of Chinese GDP (World Bank 2010).

The central bank could not sit back and passively accumulate reserves; if so, the monetary base would have ballooned and inflation would have skyrocketed. Instead, the PBC started to "sterilize" its foreign exchange operations to withdraw liquidity from the economy.[18] Two main sterilization instruments were used. First, beginning in April 2003, the PBC started selling central bank bills. This instrument consisted primarily of selling short-term debt to China's state-owned commercial banks. The PBC initially sold only small volumes of these "sterilization bonds," but bond sales steadily increased and the PBC issued about $450 billion of bonds in 2006. Second, in September 2003, the PBC began increasing the required reserve ratio, which forced banks to hold a larger quantity of deposits at the central bank. The required reserve ratio was increased only modestly at first, from 6% to 7% in September 2003, and then more aggressively in 2006, when it rose to 9%.

---

18. Zhang (2012) provides a detailed description of the PBC's sterilization operations.

The PBC, along with its allies in the commercial banks and think tanks, vigorously lobbied for an appreciation of the exchange rate throughout this period.[19] The central bank advocated a revaluation of at least 5% (Interviews C7, C22). Some CASS economists sympathetic to the PBC's concerns started pushing for a 10% revaluation of the exchange rate (Interview C33; Wang 2006; Yang 2005; Zhang 2005).

The PBC coalition opposed the undervalued exchange rate for three distinct reasons. First, central bankers frequently complained that the undervalued exchange rate was contributing to excessive growth in liquidity and exacerbating inflationary pressures. Starting in 2003, they began arguing that an exchange rate revaluation was needed to reduce the excess supply of foreign exchange and allow the central bank to combat inflation more effectively (Standard Chartered 2004; Yang 2005; Yu 2003). The central bank opposed policies that increased inflation because it is responsible for maintaining price stability. Second, the PBC opposed the undervalued exchange rate because the accumulation of foreign reserves hurt the central bank's financial well-being (Interview C32; Chin and Helleiner 2008, 95; Zhang 2005; Zhong 2004). Exchange rate policy was problematic for the PBC's balance sheet because the central bank earned a lower interest rate on its foreign exchange assets, made up primarily of U.S. Treasury securities, than they paid the holders of their sterilization bonds (Gao 2006; Zhang 2012). Third, the PBC opposed the undervalued exchange rate because of its harmful effects on the financial sector.

While sterilization was problematic for the central bank, a large share of the burden of sterilization was pushed onto China's state-owned commercial banks (Lardy 2012; Ljungwall et al. 2012; Walter and Howie 2011; Wright 2009, 228–230; Zhang 2012). "For the banks, any sterilisation whatsoever is painful," observed a report on the Chinese economy by Standard Chartered Bank (2007a). Increases in the required reserve ratio and purchases of central bank bills were both anathema to the commercial banks. The yield that the commercial banks earned on central bank bills was about 1.7% to 2.5%, far lower than the 7% to 8% interest they would earn from making loans. In fact, oftentimes no willing buyers came forth when the central bank auctioned off its bonds, and the central bank had to use "direct administrative pressure to require commercial banks to keep purchasing central bank bills" (Zhang 2012, 51). This underwriting of Chinese government bonds was "very much a political duty" of the state-owned banks (Walter and Howie 2011, 90). Increases in the required reserve ratio were equally problematic for the commercial banks because they earned a mere 1.89% inter-

---

19. Bell and Feng (2013), Freeman and Wen (2011), and Wright (2009) provide excellent descriptions of the PBC's views on exchange rate policy.

est rate on these funds. Overall, Zhang Ming (2012) estimates that sterilization reduced the profits of Chinese commercial banks by over 100 billion renminbi (about $13 billion) in 2006 alone. In short, the undervalued exchange rate gave rise to repressive financial policies that damaged China's financial sector.

The government's ability to engage in large-scale financial repression helped spare other interest groups from the harmful effects of an undervalued exchange rate that often arise. Although large-scale foreign exchange sterilization often leads to soaring interest rates (see Reinhart and Reinhart 1998; and chapter 1), this did not occur in China. For example, in the fourth quarter of 2005, almost no business paid more than 6.8% interest on a six-month loan from China's Big Four banks; the vast majority paid 5.2% or less. Firms that borrowed from China's smaller financial institutions tended to pay higher interest rates, but even they almost never paid more than 10.4% in interest (Podpiera 2006). State control over banks made it possible for the state to sustain an undervalued exchange rate while keeping borrowing costs low (Riedel et al. 2007, 177). As a result, between 2003 and 2006, China's manufacturing firms were able to enjoy the benefits of an undervalued exchange rate without the costs.

Manufacturing firms had no reason to object to undervaluation in this period where the nominal exchange rate also remained stable and firms had access to cheap credit and received export tax rebates.[20] This mixture of extremely favorable policies was a major boon to China's manufacturing sector and contributed to rapid growth in China's trade surplus after 2003. Thus, a variety of government officials with ties to the manufacturing sector strongly supported the undervalued exchange rate. Coastal provincial governments lobbied against revaluation (Interview C32). Minister of Commerce Bo Xilai was a vocal and influential opponent of revaluation in government meetings (Bell and Feng 2013, 233; Wright 2009, 183). The NDRC opposed revaluation because of concerns that it would reduce firms' external competitiveness, and because the commission worried that increased exchange rate volatility would complicate its ability to manage the macroeconomy (Wright 2009; Interview C32). Between 2003 and 2006, the manufacturing sector's allies in government lobbied China's leaders to stick with the undervalued exchange rate.

The pro-undervaluation coalition was largely successful in this period. There was absolutely no change in the renminbi-dollar exchange rate in 2003 and 2004. Since the dollar was depreciating quickly against the euro, the renminbi depreciated in trade-weighted terms, as shown in figure 3.1. In this context of real effective

---

20. The export tax rebate rate decreased in October 2003, but remained high. Exporters of machinery, electronics, and transportation equipment received a 13% export tax rebate; exporters of textiles, iron and steel, and cement received an 11% rebate (Bowles and Wang 2006, 243).

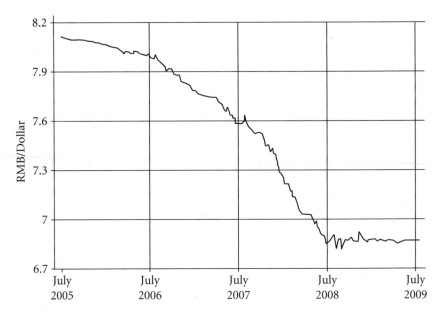

Figure 3.3. Renminbi-dollar exchange rate, 2005–2009.

depreciation and intensifying inflationary pressures, the PBC was able to eventually convince an increasing number of actors that the exchange rate must appreciate.[21] Change eventually came on July 21, 2005, when the exchange rate was revalued 2.1% and the government announced that the exchange rate regime was now a managed float based on a basket of currencies. The July 2005 revaluation was widely interpreted as a compromise between the PBC's and MOC's preferences. Many top government officials favored appreciation, but this move was delayed and the size of the revaluation minimized because of resistance from provinces and central ministries that were concerned with the performance of the country's manufacturing firms.

Despite officially moving to a more flexible regime, the actual degree of exchange rate flexibility hardly increased initially. The renminbi appreciated at a glacial pace of 1.4% against the dollar in the year after the initial revaluation (see figure 3.3). Moreover, since the dollar was falling relative to the euro, China's exchange rate hardly appreciated at all in real effective terms. Overall, despite some small moves to appreciate the exchange rate, it remained highly undervalued in 2006. According to figure 3.1, the renminbi was undervalued by 44% in 2006—the largest undervaluation since 1994.

---

21. For example, a 2004 report by the CASS and the Central Committee Research Department recommended a 3% to 4% revaluation (Interview C22). The *People's Daily* published an editorial in May 2005 calling for a 5% revaluation, which signaled a shift in elite opinion.

Contrary to popular and scholarly perceptions (e.g., Wright 2009), external pressures had little effect on China's exchange rate policy. The external pressure argument cannot explain why appreciation was so slow in coming and so limited once it did occur. The U.S. government started to put intense pressure on China to revalue in the fall of 2003, but China did not alter its exchange rate at all for another two years.[22] Moreover, revaluation in 2005 and 2006 did not come anywhere close to meeting the demands of the international community. In February 2005, two U.S. senators, Lindsey Graham and Charles Schumer, introduced a bill that demanded China make a "good faith effort to revalue its currency upward, placing it at or near its fair market value" within 180 days. Failure to do so would result in a 27.5% tariff—the estimated degree of undervaluation—on all Chinese exports to the United States.[23] However, the renminbi only appreciated by 2.4% against the dollar by the end of 2005, less than one-tenth the amount of appreciation demanded by China's critics in the U.S. Congress. If avoiding confrontation with the international community had been the principal goal of revaluation, China would have revalued much more substantially in 2005.

Chinese exchange rate policy in this period followed a domestic political logic. Opposition to appreciation from China's powerful manufacturing sector explains why revaluation was delayed for two years and why appreciation was so limited in 2005–2006. State control of the financial system also played an important role. Chinese policymakers forced the state-controlled banks to pick up the tab for the undervalued exchange rate, which made undervaluation highly appealing to China's manufacturing sector.

Manufacturers' Indifference and Faster Appreciation: 2007

Changes in economic conditions in 2007 altered the political dynamics of exchange rate policy. The Chinese economy was overheating by the second half of 2007, which made it more difficult for Chinese policymakers to keep the exchange rate undervalued while maintaining loose domestic monetary conditions. Thus, when the PBC resumed its push for revaluation in 2007, it faced little resistance from industrialists or their patrons. The lack of opposition to appreciation allowed Chinese leaders to appreciate the exchange rate rapidly in late 2007 and early 2008.

The Chinese economy boomed in 2007. Net exports increased at a breakneck pace. As a result, the central bank's foreign exchange reserves grew even more

---

22. At least ten bills opposing Chinese currency policy were introduced into the U.S. Congress in September-November 2003. These bills were: S.1586; S.1592; S.Res.219; H.Res.3058; H.Con. Res.285; H.R.3269; S.1758; H.R.3364; H.Res.414; S.Res.262.

23. This Senate bill is available at http://thomas.loc.gov/cgi-bin/query/z?c109:S.295.

rapidly than in the previous two years: 43% in 2007. The stock market entered a period of hyper-growth, in which the Shanghai Stock Exchange Composite rose more than four-fold over 2006 and 2007. The real estate market was booming, too. Overall, the Chinese economy grew by over 14% in 2007—the fastest annual growth rate in over twenty years. Inflation, however, also reached rates not seen in over a decade. Prices increased at an annualized pace of about 7% toward the end of 2007.

In response to rising prices, the central bank started to implement increasingly restrictive monetary policies in 2007. Interest rates were increased on six occasions over the course of 2007, for a total increase of 1.35% (Wright 2009). The required reserve ratio was also raised substantially, with commercial banks required to park 14.5% of their deposits at the central bank by the end of 2007, up from 9% a year earlier. Since these measures appeared insufficient to contain inflation, in October 2007 the central bank took the more radical step of imposing lending quotas on the banks (Chen 2007; Chiang 2007; Standard Chartered 2008c).

The central bank renewed its campaign for more rapid exchange rate appreciation towards the end of 2007 (Standard Chartered 2007c). "After five interest rate hikes in the first nine months of 2007 had failed to keep inflationary pressure from accelerating", explains Wright (2009, 271), "the [People's Bank of China] made a different policy proposal to the State Council: allow the yuan to appreciate at a faster rate." The central bankers and their allies stressed that appreciation was needed to reduce inflation and asset prices (Standard Chartered 2007b, 2007c). They also fretted about the harmful effects of forced bond purchases and a high required reserve ratio on China's commercial banks. Standard Chartered Bank (2008b) estimated that each percentage point increase in the required reserve ratio reduced the profits of China's banking sector by $3.4 billion per year.

Unlike the period from 2003 to 2006, there was little active lobbying against exchange rate appreciation in 2007. Some manufacturing firms were exporting so successfully that they stopped concerning themselves with exchange rate policy at the time. Many of the owners of these firms were also making additional profits from investments in China's booming real estate and stock markets. In essence, due to immensely favorable economic policies and conditions, many manufacturing firms paid little attention to the exchange rate level (Interviews C17, C23, C27, C39). The central government's main representative of export-oriented industrialists, the MOC, took its cue from these firms, and it too expressed little opposition to appreciation during 2007 (Wright 2009, 263–267).

Some segments of manufacturing, particularly the more capital-intensive firms, also became more sympathetic to the PBC's calls for appreciation in late 2007. Higher interest rates made it more expensive for these firms to borrow, and industrialists worried that further monetary tightening would lead to a slowdown in their sector (Standard Chartered 2007c). The imposition of credit quotas seems to have been an important turning point for some manufacturing firms. As a consequence of credit restrictions, state-owned banks were very reluctant to lend out funds in late 2007 and early 2008, and this became a major concern for many businesses (Chiang 2007; Lu 2008; Standard Chartered 2008b). Some manufacturing industries like steel and leather were particularly hard hit by monetary tightening because the central bank advised the commercial banks to curtail lending to these particular industries (see PBC 2007). At this point, many industries felt that inflation had to be addressed, and it was better to do so by appreciating the exchange rate than by further reducing bank lending (Interview C9). The NDRC, for example, recognized the need to reduce inflation but opposed using contractionary monetary policy, such as interest rate hikes, to do so (Wright 2009). In other words, industrialists did not want the exchange rate to appreciate, but saw appreciation as the least-bad option in this higher-inflation context.

The manufacturing sector was no longer unified in favor of undervaluation at the end of 2007 when, as a result of the overheating economy, undervaluation was no longer compatible with cheap and abundant credit. This episode reveals that difficult economic conditions can occasionally swamp the effects of institutional structures. However, this episode reinforces my argument that support for undervaluation declines when the net benefits of undervaluation fall.

The PBC's argument that appreciation should be used to slow inflation gained traction at the top of the party hierarchy. Members of the Politburo Standing Committee, including Secretary-General Hu Jintao, became convinced that inflation was the biggest threat and had to be addressed (Interview C13, C32). At the Central Economic Work Conference at the end of 2007, the top leadership announced that inflation prevention was going to be the top priority for the next year (*People's Daily* 2007). Mounting support for appreciation within the government led to a noticeable shift in exchange rate strategy. The culmination of this shift in exchange rate strategy was the PBC's November 2007 quarterly report which, for the first time, stated that appreciation would be used as a tool to reduce inflation (PBC 2007). Figure 3.3 shows that the rate of appreciation sped up considerably toward the end of 2007. During the eight months between November 2007 and June 2008, the exchange rate appreciated 8.2%—more than the total 7.9% appreciation of the previous twenty-seven months since the initial revaluation. The exchange rate was not the only tool being used to slow export growth: the government cut export tax rebates for many products in 2007, and a new labor law and stricter environmental regulations further reduced many manufacturers' profits.

The rapid exchange rate appreciation in late 2007 and early 2008 resulted from the retreat of the pro-undervaluation lobby and the intensified lobbying efforts of the central bank. Interestingly, this more rapid appreciation took place in the absence of overt pressure from the United States, indicating, once again, that China's exchange rate policy is influenced more by domestic than international pressures.[24]

Manufacturers Fight Back: The End of Revaluation, 2008

The policy of more rapid exchange rate appreciation, and the interest group preferences on which it rested, were short-lived. Although unconcerned about exchange rate appreciation in 2007, manufacturers became strongly opposed to the increasingly rapid appreciation of the renminbi in early 2008. Rather than appreciation serving as a substitute for other tightening policies, as the manufacturing sector anticipated, rapid exchange rate appreciation ended up being accompanied by several policies—including a continued tightening of monetary policy, reductions in export tax rebates, and stricter environmental restrictions—that increased manufacturers' costs (Standard Chartered 2008c; Zhang 2008). Industrialists were being battered on both ends: appreciation eroded their external competitiveness and monetary and other policies increased their operating costs. Thanks to this policy mix, in this case exchange rate appreciation did not reduce manufacturers' costs as much as it typically does. Consequently, Chinese manufacturers grew hostile to exchange rate appreciation in 2008 (Interviews C12, C17, C23, C38, C39, C41). A July 2008 survey of 170 exporters found that 41% saw exchange rate policy as the most significant problem for their business (Wright 2008, 6). The manufacturing sector reached a consensus that exchange rate appreciation was a problem that must be stopped.

Manufacturing firms, in turn, initiated a multipronged lobbying blitz. They focused much of their lobbying efforts on the governments of coastal provinces where they were concentrated. Firms discussed their problems with provincial and municipal governments and the local offices of central government agencies, and they pressed them to persuade Beijing to reduce the pace of exchange rate appreciation. The actions of private firms in Zhejiang province are instructive. The Zhejiang Merchants' Association publicly denounced revaluation on several occasions (Zhou 2010). Garment producers in Zhejiang have close ties with the Wenzhou municipal government and provincial officials and made sure that these officials were aware of their opposition to the worsening exchange rate situation

---

24. No legislation that referred to China's currency was introduced into the U.S. Congress in the second half of 2007 or the first quarter of 2008.

(Interviews C12, C39). In response to these pressures from their province's private investors, government officials in Zhejiang tried to persuade Beijing to adopt policies to help the province's ailing export-oriented businesses (Interview C12). Provincial politicians in coastal provinces pushed their case with the central government, warning the leadership that more favorable exchange rate and rebate policies were required to prevent mass bankruptcies and social unrest (Interviews C27, C32).

The MOC also stepped up its lobbying on behalf of the manufacturers, sending formal requests for slower appreciation to the State Council (Chen 2008). MOC officials requested a "helping hand" from the government during interviews with the official media (*China Daily* 2008). The MOC also encouraged researchers at government think tanks to analyze the harmful effects of appreciation and other policies (Interview C6).

The firms brought their case all the way up to the top leaders. The China National Textile and Apparel Council, for example, sent a formal request for more favorable policies to the State Council (*China Daily* 2008). One common strategy was to enlist the help of local officials to convince PBSC members to "inspect" the factories. Premier Wen Jiabao went on an inspection trip to the coastal provinces of Jiangsu, Guangdong, and Zhejiang, where he met with producers in the electronics and textile industries and heard about their difficulties (Xinhua 2008). Xi Jinping, the powerful vice president and a former party secretary of Fujian and Zhejiang provinces, expressed sympathy for the manufacturing businesses during his visit to Guangdong Province. Xi listened to firms complain about the increasing difficulties of operating a manufacturing business. In response, Xi "called for local and ministerial officials who accompanied him to implement policies to help out [these] industries" (Xu 2008)—a clear signal that Xi was in favor of more policies to help the manufacturing sector. Politicians at the top level of government with close ties to manufacturing firms keenly supported pro-industry policies.

The manufacturers' offensive worked. By the middle of July, the coalition built between manufacturing firms and their allies in the MOC and coastal provinces had gained elite patronage at the Standing Committee level. The anti-revaluation coalition overpowered their opponents: once they convinced the top leadership that appreciation must be stopped, the PBSC instructed the central bank to stop revaluation. The summary of the central bank's second quarter monetary policy committee meeting did not mention, as most previous summaries did, the use of market mechanisms in deciding the value of the renminbi (Xin 2008). One PBC official described the situation in July 2008 as follows: "PBC wants to revalue more aggressively but [is] facing so many pressures from local governments, especially from eastern areas where there are exporters" (Interview C2).[25] The exchange rate remained stable during the second half of 2008, ending the year at the same level (6.82 renminbi/dollar) as it was in the middle of July—a striking departure from the 6% appreciation during the first half of the year (see figure 3.3).

This shift in exchange rate policy was not driven by technocratic considerations or the exogenous shock of the global financial crisis. Appreciation was abandoned *prior* to the onset of the global economic crisis, at a time when Chinese exports were still growing and few exporters were worried about a lack of foreign demand. Only 14% of exporters blamed a lack of foreign demand for their problems in July 2008 (Wright 2008). Chinese exports only started to slow down in November 2008—four months after the exchange rate stopped appreciating (*The Economist* 2009). The return to a policy of undervaluation after a brief departure coincided with intense lobbying efforts on the part of Chinese manufacturing firms. Interest group pressures thus provide the most convincing explanation for China's decision to undervalue its exchange rate in 2008.

The shift in firms' exchange rate policy preferences reflected changes in the macroeconomic environment and policy mix in China. In late 2007, Chinese firms were unusually sympathetic toward an exchange rate appreciation because the Chinese economy was overheating and it became infeasible to maintain both low interest rates and an undervalued exchange rate. However, once it became clear to Chinese manufacturers that they were receiving neither an undervalued exchange rate nor cheap credit, their opinion of appreciation turned swiftly negative. And when Chinese manufacturers resumed their demands for undervaluation, Chinese political elites responded quickly.[26]

Aftermath: Continued Undervaluation between 2009 and 2012

Little changed from mid-2008 to the end of 2012. The renminbi was fixed against the dollar until June 2010. The renminbi then appreciated slowly between June 2010 and December 2012, gaining 8% against the dollar over this eighteen-month period. After appreciating only 8% in four-and-a-half years, it is hardly surprising that estimates find that the renminbi remained undervalued in 2012 (IMF 2012).

---

25. Other officials at the central bank and CASS shared this opinion (Interviews C31, C33, C40).

26. The manufacturing sector's lobbying efforts contributed to other policy shifts as well. On August 1, 2008, export tax rebates were increased. Firms also registered their strong opposition to credit quotas, which may explain why the effects of the credit quotas ended up being "mild": although the rate of growth of lending slowed down, it remained positive and some banks appear to have been exempted from these quotas (Standard Chartered 2008a, 2008b).

The cleavages over the exchange rate level were no different after 2008 than they were beforehand. The PBC continued to advocate for more rapid appreciation. The manufacturing sector and its supporters in the MOC, NDRC, and provincial governments remained opposed to appreciation (Freeman and Wen 2011; Lardy 2012, 144–153).

Chinese policymakers also continued to push the lion's share of the costs of undervaluation onto China's state-owned commercial banks. The accumulation of foreign reserves continued apace after 2008, and the PBC's reserve stockpile topped $3 trillion in 2011. To sterilize these inflows, the PBC continued to sell large volumes of sterilization bonds to the commercial banks. The required reserve ratio was raised to the unprecedented level of 21.5% in 2011. Consequently, the burden of sterilization suffered by China's commercial banks was even larger after 2009 than it was beforehand (Zhang 2012). To summarize, between 2009 and 2012, China's manufacturing sector continued to demand an undervalued exchange rate, Chinese policymakers continued to keep the renminbi undervalued, and they continued to pass most of the costs associated with undervaluation onto Chinese commercial banks.

Conclusions about Exchange Rate Politics in China

The Influence of Institutions on Preferences in China

China's manufacturing sector preferred an undervalued exchange rate throughout most of the period under consideration. According to conventional wisdom, sectors that produce tradable goods favor an undervalued exchange rate because it enhances their competitiveness in global markets. External competitiveness was certainly an important consideration for Chinese industrialists, whose output is tradable. However, tradability is not a sufficient explanation for their support for undervaluation. Many Chinese manufacturing firms rely extensively on foreign inputs and borrow from banks to finance their investments; thus, undervalued exchange rates increase many manufacturers' import and borrowing costs. In addition, as chapters 4 and 5 show, the manufacturing sector has been far less supportive of undervaluation in other countries where it shares similar attributes. Why has China's manufacturing sector championed an undervalued exchange rate?

The institutional context in China had an important effect on the manufacturing sector's exchange rate preferences. Rules and decision-making procedures placed control over the financial system in the state's hands. State control of the financial system enabled Chinese policymakers to force the country's banks to purchase sterilization bonds at below-market rates; impose extremely high reserve requirements on the banks; and implement interest rate controls that prohibited banks from charging borrowers high interest rates. These repressive financial policies prevented firms' borrowing costs from rising despite China's massive intervention in the foreign exchange market. The state's ability to shift many of the costs of undervaluation onto the state-controlled banks was an important reason why China's manufacturing sector preferred an undervalued exchange rate.

China's state-controlled labor system did not have as clear an effect on manufacturers' exchange rate preferences, though labor institutions may have been quite important nonetheless. Had labor not been controlled by the state, Chinese manufacturing firms would probably have been less enthusiastic about an undervalued exchange rate. For example, the absence of an organized labor movement left workers unable to successfully pressure the state to increase wages following the 1994 devaluation. Had wages increased after that devaluation, undervaluation would have been less beneficial for the manufacturing sector, and industrialists would probably have been less supportive of devaluation. As we will see in chapters 4 and 5, organized labor movements in Argentina and Mexico successfully pressured their governments to raise wages after exchange rate devaluations, and these postdevaluation wage hikes tempered business support for undervaluation. Although I did not find direct evidence that labor institutions influenced exchange rate politics in China, labor's limited importance in China is a marked contrast with other cases examined in this book.

Labor and financial structures are surely not the only factors that influenced Chinese firms' opinions about exchange rate policy. The Chinese state also suppressed manufacturing firms' land and energy costs (Lardy 2012, 106–115), which may have further reduced their concern with the effect of undervaluation on their business costs. Export tax rebates are another policy instrument that has played an important role in shaping firms' exchange rate preferences in China (Bowles and Wang 2006).

Although Chinese industrialists were typically supportive of undervaluation, there were two brief moments when this was not the case. China's manufacturing sector supported real exchange rate appreciation in 1998–1999 and 2007. Exceptional global economic conditions—strong capital outflows in the late 1990s and an unmanageable flood of capital inflows in 2007—made it unusually costly to keep the exchange rate undervalued during these periods. One lesson from these two cases is that institutional structures are not the only factor that shapes states' policy options; global economic forces matter, too. A second lesson from these cases is that interest groups pay attention to context when deciding which policies to support. The fact that firms switched their exchange rate preferences in response to changes in the costs and benefits of this policy lends support to the conditional preference theory, and its argument that interest groups formulate their preferences in a dynamic and context-specific manner.

The Influence of Interest Groups on Exchange Rate Policy in China

There is surprisingly little evidence that leaders' ideology or their beliefs about exchange rate policy can explain China's decision to keep its exchange rate undervalued. The economic priorities of China's top decision makers—controlling inflation in Zhu's case, and Hu and Wen's desire to reduce the economy's reliance on exports—are more consistent with an overvalued exchange rate than with an undervalued one. Nevertheless, Zhu kept the exchange rate undervalued from 1994 to 1996, and the exchange rate appreciated little during the Hu-Wen era. The limited influence that policymakers' beliefs about appropriate exchange rate policy had on exchange rate valuation decisions in China is striking. Since Chinese policymakers are relatively autonomous, this finding constitutes strong evidence against ideational theories of exchange rate politics.

There is equally little support for the argument that China manipulates its exchange rate to gain advantages in the foreign policy arena. There is no evidence that the foreign policy and security bureaucracies actively participated in debates over exchange rate policy, and no evidence suggests that Chinese policymakers favored undervalued exchange rates in order to accrue gains at the expense of China's geopolitical rivals.

External relations were also not an important cause of Chinese decisions to appreciate the exchange rate. Foreign pressures to appreciate the renminbi do not appear to have been effective. The U.S. government exerted intense pressure on China to revalue in the fall of 2003, but China did not take action. By contrast, the period with the most rapid appreciation, late 2007 and early 2008, occurred in the absence of overt pressure from the United States. This is consistent with quantitative studies, which have found that renminbi appreciation was no faster, and may have even been slower, when foreign pressure for revaluation intensified (Liu and Pauwels 2012; Ramírez 2013).

Foreign policy goals appear most relevant during the Asian financial crisis, but even in this case they were of no more than secondary importance. The fact that China simultaneously adopted some policies that won them foreigners' praise and others that brought scorn during the Asian crisis indicates that the government was willing to sacrifice the country's foreign image for other objectives.

The evidence is much more consistent with the argument that preferences of powerful interest groups determine policies toward the exchange rate level in China. Lobbying by manufacturing industries and their representatives in the Chinese political system contributed to many decisions to undervalue the exchange rate: the devaluation of 1994; the decision to slow down appreciation in 1995; the avoidance of significant appreciation between 2003 and 2006; and the return to a policy of exchange rate stability in July 2008. The only case where undervaluation did not appear to result from societal pressures was between 2000 and 2002; in that case, real exchange rate depreciation was largely an unintended consequence of tight macroeconomic policies. Even though China's autonomous state should be less responsive to interest group pressures than most other states, this chapter revealed that interest group preferences are paramount in China. The preferences of the manufacturing sector provide the most convincing explanation for why China has maintained an undervalued exchange rate since the mid-1990s.

The brief periods of exchange rate appreciation in China also follow an interest group logic. Promoting the interests of nontradable sectors was an important motivation for real exchange rate appreciation during 1997–1999 and 2007. However, since nontradable sectors consistently opposed undervaluation, their interests cannot explain the timing of shifts in China's exchange rate policy. Fluctuations in the preferences of the manufacturing sector were an important driver of temporal variations in exchange rate policy between 1993 and 2009. Manufacturing producers were tolerant, even supportive, of appreciation during the main periods of real appreciation: 1998–1999 and 2007–2008. The manufacturing sector's support for overvaluation during these periods is necessary for understanding why the Chinese government appreciated the exchange rate in these instances. Appreciation would have been even more limited in China if the manufacturers did not occasionally soften their opposition to appreciation.

This chapter highlights the key impact that interest groups have on exchange rate policy in developing countries. Previous scholarship has questioned the usefulness of interest group theories of exchange rate politics by suggesting that interest groups lack clear preferences over exchange rate policy and that exchange rate policymakers are insulated from any interest group demands that do arise (Helleiner 2005; Krasner 1978; McNamara 1998; Morrison 2015; Moschella 2015; Odell 1982). This chapter finds that neither of these critiques holds. Chinese interest groups developed clear and coherent preferences vis-à-vis the exchange rate level. Even more striking, despite the unusually high degree of state autonomy in China (Kaplan 2006, 1193; Liew and Wu 2007, 23; Shih 2007, 1243; Wang 2003, 170), Chinese exchange rate policymakers were very sensitive to interest group pressures. In this chapter, interest group theories successfully passed a "hard test."

Chinese Undervaluation in Comparative Perspective

China has maintained an undervalued exchange rate for most of the past twenty years, a period in which most developing countries overvalued their exchange rates. This outcome would have been much less likely if China did not have a powerful manufacturing sector and state-controlled labor and financial systems. State control of finance, and perhaps also the state's control of labor, increased the net benefits of an undervalued exchange rate for Chinese industrialists. Without these institutional structures, it is less likely that China's manufacturing sector would have repeatedly demanded an undervalued exchange rate. However, Chinese policymakers were only responsive to these demands because China's manufacturing sector controls substantial power resources. The combination of a powerful manufacturing sector, state-controlled labor system, and state-controlled financial system helps explains why China has maintained an undervalued exchange rate.

THE POLITICAL APPEAL OF OVERVALUATION

Industrial Interests and the Repeated Overvaluation of the Argentine Peso

Karl Marx famously wrote that history repeats itself, first as tragedy, second as farce. When it comes to exchange rate policy in Argentina, history keeps repeating itself, each time as a tragedy. Argentina's policymakers have repeatedly overvalued their exchange rate and the result has always been the same: consumers stop buying pricey Argentine goods, economic growth stalls, and eventually, when foreign currency runs out, the country plunges into a deep recession. This recurring dynamic is a major reason the average Argentine was poorer in 2002 than she was twenty-five years earlier. Why do Argentine policymakers constantly adopt exchange rate policies that inflict staggering pain on their own citizens?

Leading theories of political economy would not expect Argentina to overvalue its exchange rate. Argentina has one of the developing world's more powerful manufacturing sectors. Argentina's manufacturing sector is economically important and has maintained close relationships with most of the country's governments during the past fifty years. According to conventional wisdom, the manufacturing sector is a strong proponent of undervalued exchange rates (Frieden 1991a). Given this sector's political and economic power, most political economy theories would expect Argentina's manufacturing sector to have little difficulty convincing their government to maintain an undervalued exchange rate. Why have most Argentine governments done the exact opposite of what this powerful interest group supposedly wants?

Prevailing theories are unable to explain exchange rate overvaluation in Argentina because they misjudge the preferences of Argentina's manufacturing sector. As the conditional preference theory points out, the manufacturing sector does not always prefer an undervalued exchange rate. Undervalued exchange rates have some positive effects on the manufacturing sector—namely, increased external competitiveness. However, undervaluation also has a variety of negative effects on the manufacturing sector, which include higher imported input costs and higher borrowing costs. Chapter 1 argued that these negatives might exceed the positives in countries where labor groups and financial institutions are not controlled by the state. When policymakers have difficulty suppressing wages and interest rates, manufacturers' are likely to view an overvalued exchange rate as an attractive tool for lowering their operating costs. This helps explain why many countries with powerful manufacturing sectors and private-controlled labor and financial systems overvalue their exchange rates. In such countries, exchange rates are overvalued because of—not in spite of—the preferences of the manufacturing sector.

This chapter evaluates whether exchange rate overvaluation in Argentina follows the logic of the conditional preference theory. In the first part of the chapter, I document the Argentine state's inability to control its labor and financial systems and explain why Argentina's manufacturing sector should have high levels of influence over the country's exchange rate policies. The second half of the chapter examines the political dynamics of exchange policymaking in Argentina between 1966 and 2012.

The case study shows that Argentina's manufacturing sector has usually preferred an overvalued exchange rate to an undervalued one. There was one important exception to this general trend: between 2001 and 2005, when Argentina's economy was suffering from high degrees of excess capacity and business costs became disconnected from undervaluation as a result. The case study also shows that Argentine policymakers are strongly influenced by the demands of the manufacturing sector. Argentine governments revalued the peso when industrialists demanded, they kept the exchange rate stable when manufacturers' preferred, and devalued when asked. Argentina overvalues its exchange rate in large part because the country's powerful manufacturing sector favors this policy.

The Political Sources of Exchange Rate Policy in Argentina

Political and economic change has been the rule rather than the exception in Argentina. But despite frequent changes in Argentina's political and economic environment, the forty-seven-year period of exchange rate politics examined here also features some important and noteworthy continuities. This discussion of Argentina's political and economic system focuses on those continuities. In doing so, I inevitably gloss over some important variation across periods of time. My purpose is not to ignore or even downplay these temporal variations, but to highlight some persistent features of the Argentine political system that set this case apart from the other countries considered in this book.

Argentina's Political System and Policymaking Process

Argentina's 1853 constitution established a federal system of government and a presidential regime with a bicameral congress. This system was in place until a military coup in 1930. Between 1930 and 1983, Argentina constantly alternated between military and democratic regimes. Since 1983, Argentina has returned to a democratic system of government along the lines established in the 1853 constitution.

In Argentina, authority over economic policymaking resides primarily with the executive branch of government. Even though Argentina's political system was modeled on the U.S. Constitution, in practice Argentina's legislature is not very active in the policymaking process (Snow and Manzetti 1993, 11–13; Spiller and Tommasi 2007). Within the executive branch, it is the president and the Ministry of Economy that have the most say over the macroeconomic policy issues that most concern us here.[1]

There is little doubt that societal interest groups have ample ability to influence economic policy in Argentina. The Argentine state is weak relative to social groups (Levitsky and Murillo 2005; O'Donnell 1978; Spiller and Tommasi 2007). In the words of Samuel Huntington (1968, 84), Argentina has a "feeble state surrounded by massive social forces."

Interest groups use a variety of means to influence economic policy in Argentina. Political parties and elections are an important avenue through which business and labor groups have influenced economic policy in democratic periods. Under both democratic and military rule, Argentine interest groups have also used informal means, such as their personal connections with top decision makers, to impact policy (Schneider 2004, 2010). Interest groups in Argentina also influence government policy "through nonparty vehicles like lobbies, media pronouncements, demonstrations, urban uprisings, and labor, management, or investment strikes" (McGuire 1997, 2). Interest groups should be able to influence exchange

---

1. Although the Argentine central bank has occasionally been granted formal independence, this independence has "proved to be just ink on paper when put to the test" (Galiani, Heymann, and Tommasi 2003, 121).

rate policy in Argentina regardless of who is president, the president's partisan affiliation, or the type of political regime.

The State's Limited Control of the Financial System in Argentina

The Argentine state's control over the financial system has varied over time, but Argentina's weak state has never been able to exert effective control over this sector. Compared to many developing countries, the state's control over the financial system is quite limited in Argentina.

The Argentine economy and its financial system were liberal and market-oriented in the early twentieth century. At that time, Argentina was host to a number of foreign banks and private domestic banks organized themselves into business associations (Guillén 2001, 200; Schneider 2004, 46). Financial market development was relatively advanced in Argentina in the early 1940s (Mallon and Sourrouille 1975, 144).

Since then, the institutions governing Argentina's financial sector have changed several times. In 1946, Juan Domingo Perón substantially increased the state's powers over the financial system by requiring commercial banks to obtain permission from the central bank before making loans. This change did not last long. The military regime that overthrew Perón repealed this regulation. When the Peronists regained power again in 1973, they reimposed similar financial controls, though banks were granted more authority to channel funds this time around (Brennan and Rougier 2009, 161).[2] This second attempt to expand the state's control of the financial system was even briefer than the first one and ended when the military deregulated the financial system in 1977. State control over the financial sector was intensified again during the debt crisis of the 1980s, only to be loosened again in the 1990s. The 1990s also witnessed the privatization of many of Argentina's remaining public banks. Today, the vast majority of Argentine banks are privately owned and out of the state's control.

Although state-owned banks played an important role in the Argentine economy at certain points in time, the Argentine state was never able to fully control

---

2. For details on Perón's financial reforms in the 1940s and 1970s, see Baliño (1987), Brennan and Rougier (2009), Cortés Conde (2009), di Tella (1983, 98–101), and Dye (1955). It is often suggested that Perón "nationalized" all bank deposits, but the term is highly misleading because private and foreign banks continued to operate in Argentina. In fact, Perón left "management of most traditional lending functions to private banks" (Mallon and Sourrouille 1975, 9). The "nationalization" was, in the words of the central bank itself, a "mere fiction" (quoted in Cortés Conde 2009, 207). This system just replaced the traditional system of reserve requirements with a system of variable reserve requirements and allowed the central bank to institute reserve requirements of up to 100% (Baliño 1987, 36; di Tella 1983, 101; Dye 1955, 312).

the national financial system. At least three factors limited the state's control of finance during these periods. First, state-owned banks never achieved the complete dominance that they have elsewhere (e.g., contemporary China). State-owned banks in Argentina always had to share the stage, and thus compete, with private banks. For instance, private banks' share of loans decreased during the Peronist period of 1973–1976, but never fell below 28% (di Tella 1983, 100). Second, most of Argentina's public banks are owned by municipal and provincial governments, not the central government. For instance, even though public banks accounted for 72% of loans in 1974, only 47% of total lending originated from banks owned by the national government (di Tella 1983, 100).[3] Since the central government does not own most of Argentina's public banks, it has limited ability to control their behavior. Third, the Argentine state has not been able to institutionalize its control over central state-owned banks very effectively. As in other areas of Argentine politics, frequent changes in the ownership status of Argentine banks, constant personnel changes, and perpetual shifts in financial policy objectives prevented the Argentine state from developing effective lines of authority over the banking system (Brennan and Rougier 2009, 12; Chudnovsky and López 2007, 48; Sikkink 1991, 199). Once states retract control over banks, it is hard to quickly regain that control.

Since the 1990s, if not earlier, the state's control over the financial system went from partial to extremely limited. By 1995, state-owned banks' share of banking sector assets was down to 49% and then declined to a negligible 16% by 2003 (Micco, Panizza, and Yañez 2007). As of 2007, Argentina had sixty privately owned financial institutions, ten that were owned by provincial and municipal governments, and just two financial institutions that were owned by the national government (BCRA 2007). For the past twenty years, Argentina's financial system has been almost entirely beyond the reach of the central state.

There is no doubt that the Argentine state had a substantial presence in the financial system at certain times, but even at its peak, Argentine policymakers' control over the financial system never reached the level of absolute control obtained by many states. Due to the predominance of private banks, provincial government-owned banks, and a failure to develop effective lines of authority over central government-owned financial institutions, the state's control over the financial system in Argentina has always been circumscribed. Privatization has led to further declines in the state's ability to control the financial sector since at least the 1990s. Today, Argentine policymakers have little influence over the national financial system.

---

3. Similarly, in 1985, the central government owned just four of Argentina's thirty-five public banks (Rozenwurcel and Bleger 1998, 373).

The State's Limited Control of the Labor System in Argentina

Labor is much more powerful in Argentina than in most other nations (Collier and Collier 1991; Cook 2007; McGuire 1997; O'Donnell 1978; Ranis 1992). For most of the past century, Argentine workers have been allowed to organize into unions, bargain collectively, and strike. Argentina's organized labor movement also benefits from a highly centralized structure that consists of a single labor confederation and industry-wide collective bargaining. While some Argentine governments attempted to restrict the organizational capacity of labor, their success was never more than partial and ephemeral. Rather, "the importance of having the support of influential unions had long been understood by Argentine governments, regardless of their orientation towards labor" (Buchanan 1995 150). As with financial policy, attempts to change Argentina's labor system during the past fifty years have had only a limited effect on labor's organizational capacity. There was no time between 1966 and 2012 that Argentina's state could completely control the labor movement.

The political and organizational strength of Argentine workers has deep historical roots, going back to at least the late nineteenth century (Alexander 1962; Collier and Collier 1991; McGuire 1997; Snow and Manzetti 1993). During this period, Argentine workers unionized and created labor federations made up of various unions. By the early twentieth century, a number of labor confederations were created, including the *Confederación General del Trabajo* (CGT, or General Confederation of Labor), which remains Argentina's most powerful labor organization today. Argentine workers held their first strike in 1878, their first general strike in 1902, and signed their first collective contract in 1901.

The strength of organized labor received a large and lasting boost from Perón between 1943 and 1955.[4] When the military took power in 1943, Perón, a colonel at the time, was put in charge of labor policy, a venue he used to improve the lot of Argentine workers. In turn, workers' adulation for Perón helped propel him into the president's office in 1946. As labor minister and president, Perón passed several laws that greatly increased the organizational strength of the labor movement. The most important piece of legislation, the 1949 Law of Professional Associations, codified the right to organize and gave state-approved unions a number of important legal privileges, including the right to strike and to bargain collectively. This law prohibited more than one (official) union from forming in each industry and established the CGT as the nation's only labor confederation.

---

4. The literature on Perón's labor reforms is massive. Alexander (1962), Collier and Collier (1991), McGuire (1997), and Snow and Manzetti (1993) are some the best works on this subject.

Perón also expanded the domain of collective bargaining to new industries and shifted the locus of collective bargaining from the firm to the industry level. These actions dramatically increased the number of unionized workers and the organizational strength of labor. Perón's reforms were important not only because they "enabled the Argentine labor movement to become one of the most powerful in Latin America. More significant, this legal framework helped sustain that strength even as antilabor regimes came to power" (Cook 2007, 61).

Although de jure collective labor rights changed frequently, no government was able to gain control over the labor system. The military regime that ruled from 1966 to 1972 restricted collective labor rights, but was unable to gain de facto control over the unions or prevent labor activism. Upon regaining the presidency in 1973, Perón restored unions' formal powers. The harshest labor controls were implemented by the dictatorship of 1976–1982, but unions "survived—bent, but not broken" (Drake 1996, 149).[5] This military regime intervened in unions and the CGT, outlawed collective bargaining and strikes, and "disappeared" many union leaders. Violent repression cowed the labor movement into timidity for a short period of time, but workers continued to engage in collective action. For example, over one million workers participated in strikes in 1977, and the CGT organized four general strikes between 1979 and 1982 (Carrera 2007, 84; Collier 1999, 122). The labor movement played an important role resisting, and ultimately bringing down, the military regime (Collier 1999). The continued organizational capacity of workers in the late 1970s was as remarkable as the military's violent repression of them.

Collective legal protections for workers were restored shortly after Argentina redemocratized in 1983. The Alfonsín administration (1983–1989) restored unions' rights to participate in politics and to strike and eventually removed all restrictions on collective bargaining (Cook 2007, 66).[6] In fact, Cingranelli and Richards's (2010) data suggest that Argentina did not restrict collective labor rights at any point between 1981 and 2006 (see table 0.2). Argentine workers have benefited from the right to organize, strike, and collectively bargain for the past thirty years.

So, Argentina experienced two different labor regimes between 1966 and 2012. In thirty-three of these forty-seven years, Argentina's democratic regimes strongly protected workers' rights to organize, strike, and collectively bargain. Argentine

---

5. This description of labor-military relations in the 1976–82 period borrows from Collier (1999, 119–126), Drake (1996), McGuire (1997, 170–176), and Ranis (1992, 35–46).

6. Prior to restoring collective labor rights, Alfonsín attempted to decentralize the union structure to reduce Peronist influence, but the unions and the Peronist-controlled Senate defeated this reform attempt (see Drake 1996, 173–178; Ranis 1992, 46–65). Alfonsín's successor, Carlos Menem, reformed individual labor law to make the labor market more flexible, but he preserved unions' collective labor rights (see Cook 2007; Etchemendy 2005).

laws also enhanced the organizational leverage of the working class by creating a centralized union structure. Workers faced substantial legal barriers to organizing and striking in the fourteen years of military rule, but the laws enacted during these brief military interregnums had no more than partial success in reducing workers' ability to organize and strike. Despite their best efforts, military leaders could not erase the historical legacies of a strong union structure. Even during the military terror of the late 1970s, Argentine workers retained a greater ability to organize and strike than workers in China and Iran have today. In short, the Argentine state cedes substantial authority to autonomous labor organizations, and the state's occasional attempts to regain control over labor were largely unsuccessful.

Argentina's Powerful Manufacturing Sector

A key similarity between Argentina and China is that both countries have powerful manufacturing sectors. Argentine industrialists should be able to influence exchange rate policy because they control many economic resources, have built strong lobbying organizations, maintain extensive political connections, and are held in high esteem by the public. This section describes each of these power resources.

Argentina's manufacturing sector takes up a substantial share of the country's GDP. The manufacturing sector's share of the Argentine economy has declined over time but remains larger than most. In 2005, manufacturing was responsible for 23.2% of Argentina's GDP. Although not quite as large as in China, the relative size of Argentina's manufacturing sector ranked at the 90th percentile of all developing countries in 2005. Argentine policymakers are unlikely to ignore the preferences of a sector that controls a sizable share of the country's economic resources.

The geographic concentration of Argentina's manufacturing sector is another similarity with China. Most of Argentina's manufacturing production occurs in and around Buenos Aires. About 60% of manufacturing employment is concentrated in Buenos Aires (city and province combined), with nearly another 20% in Córdoba and Santa Fe (Sanguinetti and Martincus 2004). Furthermore, a sizable portion of Argentina's manufacturing production occurs within large diversified conglomerates known as *grupos económicos* (economic groups) (Schneider 2004). For example, Pérez Companc owns fifty-three firms in industrial sectors as diverse as electrical appliances, machinery, cement, and metals (Guillén 2001, 84).[7]

---

7. Many Argentine *grupos* are also diversified into other sectors such as services and natural resources.

This concentration within large conglomerates and a small number of geographic areas should make it easier for Argentine industrialists to act collectively and influence policy (e.g., Olson 1965; Bates 1981).

Many organizations represent and promote the interests of Argentina's manufacturing businesses.[8] The most important groups have been the *Unión Industrial Argentina* (UIA, or Argentine Industrial Union), which has historically represented the largest firms, and the *Confederación General Económica* (CGE, or General Economic Confederation), which represented small and medium-size firms.[9] Argentina also has a number of additional associations that advocate on behalf of narrower manufacturing subsectors, such as ADEFA (*Asociación de Fábricas de Automotores*, the Association of Automotive Makers), and ADIMRA (*Asociación de Industriales Metalúrgicos de la República Argentina*, the Association of Metallurgical Industries of Argentina).

Argentine manufacturing firms benefit from contacts with government officials. Owners of manufacturing firms often obtain direct access to high-level policymakers, as the following examples illustrate: Perón personally "call[ed] the owners of the factories" to discuss policy in the 1970s; members of Raúl Alfonsín's administration met regularly with the "captains of industry" during the 1980s; and UIA's president "conversed regularly with [Economy Minister] Domingo Cavallo and other ministers" in the 1990s (Schneider 2004, 179, 190, 193). Furthermore, many high-level cabinet officials were themselves previously employed at large manufacturing firms or industrial business associations. Argentina's manufacturing sector has substantial organizational resources.

Finally, throughout much of the postwar era, Argentina's manufacturing sector has been widely perceived to be the most valuable sector of the economy, a "normative power resource" that could be deployed in battles over economic policy. In Argentina during the early postwar period, there was a common "belief that industrialization was necessary for development" and "pro-industrialization policies had taken firm root in domestic consciousness" (Sikkink 1991, 32, 51). The prestige of the manufacturing sector waned somewhat between 1975 and 2001, a period in which Argentine society became more preoccupied with macroeconomic stability than with any particular sector of the economy. Developmentalist ideas, and their associated emphasis on national industrial growth, have regained prominence since the 2001 financial crisis (Grugel and Riggirozzi 2007).

---

8. Note, however, that Argentina's business associations have fewer resources than their counterparts in some other Latin American countries (Schneider 2004).

9. The CGE also included agricultural and commercial firms, but the industry confederation informally dominated the CGE, and it therefore primarily advocated for manufacturing interests. The CGE and UIA merged during the military regime of 1976–1982 (Schneider 2004, 180–182).

While the normative power resources of Argentina's manufacturing sector have fluctuated over time, ideology and public opinion have, on balance, helped rather than hindered this sector.

To summarize, the manufacturing sector should be able to influence exchange rate policy in Argentina because it controls many economic resources; is geographically concentrated; has built effective lobbying associations; has close ties with Argentine policymakers; and benefits from favorable public and elite opinion. The manufacturing sector is not the only interest group in Argentina that is capable of influencing exchange rate policy, but because of its substantial power resources, Argentina's politicians have a strong incentive to choose exchange rate policies that are favored by the manufacturing sector. As Etchemendy (2005, 73) explains, it does "not make sense for the government to confront" the country's manufacturing firms because Argentina has "relatively strong domestic players in manufacturing" with "economic resources to invest" and "institutional power . . . through the sectoral associations and the UIA." The manufacturing sector should have greater influence in Argentina than in most countries.

The Economic Attributes of Argentina's Manufacturing Sector

The economic characteristics of Argentina's manufacturing sector are much less exceptional than its political attributes. Argentina produces a variety of manufacturing goods including automobiles, machinery, metals, and textiles.[10] Before the military government liberalized international trade in the 1970s, import barriers were quite high. Trade protection in the 1960s and early 1970s significantly dampened, but did not eliminate, competition with imports.[11] However, even during this protectionist period, manufacturing products were still exportable, and therefore at least partially tradable.[12] Manufacturing in Argentina has been fully tradable since that time. Following trade liberalization in the 1970s, and

---

10. Each of these four industries accounted for about 8% to 10% of Argentina's manufacturing production in 1993. Other major manufacturing subsectors include chemicals and plastics, pulp, paper and printing, and agro-industrial production, according to data from INDEC (http://www.indec.gov.ar). These were also some of Argentina's largest manufacturing subsectors in the late 1960s (Mallon and Sourrouille 1975, 70).

11. For instance, in 1973, the net effect of a 75% overvalued exchange rate (see figure 4.1) and a roughly 100% average tariff rate (Chudnovsky and Lopez 2007, 34) was to raise import prices by about 25%. This is a substantial margin, but not large enough to eliminate import competition.

12. Mallon and Sourrouille (1975, 79) point out that the Argentine manufacturing sector was "quite export-oriented" before 1930, exporting 15% to 20% of its output; "overvaluation of the peso, however, severely curtailed industrial exporting after the war."

especially after further trade reforms in the 1990s, manufacturing firms have faced intense competition from foreign firms. During this entire period, undervaluing the exchange rate could have helped Argentina's manufacturing sector compete in export markets. Undervaluation would have also increased local firms' competitiveness vis-à-vis foreign producers in the national economy, though high import barriers may have reduced the salience of this concern before 1976. Interestingly, the evidence presented here reveals a surprising degree of continuity in this sector's exchange rate preferences before and after Argentina reduced barriers to imports.

High reliance on imported inputs is another similarity between Argentina's manufacturing sector and those in other developing countries (Chudnovsky and López 2007, 33). According to a World Bank Enterprise Survey from 2006, the average manufacturing firm in Argentina obtained 26% of its inputs from foreign sources, close but slightly below the developing world average.

Many manufacturing industries in Argentina, from automobiles to steel, are capital-intensive industries for which access to cheap credit is a major boon. Despite this need to borrow to finance new investments, Argentina's manufacturing firms have found it very difficult to obtain credit from the financial system (see table 4.2). Consequently, retained earnings have been their main source of investment finance (Schneider 2013, 43–44). These financial difficulties should make Argentina's manufacturing firms more supportive of policies that reduce their financing costs.

An undervalued exchange rate has ambiguous effects on the profitability of Argentina's manufacturing sector. Argentine manufacturers benefit from undervaluation because many of them produce tradable goods. On the other hand, undervaluation reduces their profits because it raises the costs of their imported inputs and makes it more expensive for them to borrow from local or foreign financial institutions.

Implications and Hypotheses

The conditional preference theory argues that states with limited control over labor and finance are likely to overvalue their exchange rates. The Argentine case seems to fit this prediction well. Argentina's state has rarely had the capacity to control banks or workers, and it has also tended to keep its exchange rate overvalued. Figure 4.1 shows that Argentina's exchange rate was overvalued for nearly two-thirds of the years between 1966 and 2006, with an average overvaluation of 15%. The patterns in Argentina's real exchange rate, also shown in figure 4.1, largely mirror the overvaluation measure, but this variable, which extends the data up

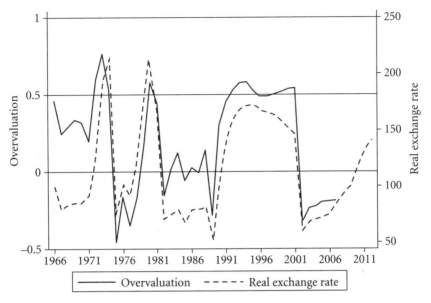

Figure 4.1.   Exchange rate overvaluation in Argentina, 1966–2012. Overvaluation is defined as the difference between the actual real exchange rate and
the estimated equilibrium real exchange rate. Positive (negative) values imply an
overvalued (undervalued) real exchange rate. See chapter 2 for more details.
Real exchange rate is defined the nominal exchange rate multiplied by the U.S.
consumer price index divided by the Argentine consumer price index. The real
exchange rate is indexed so that 1966 equals 100. This series is inverted
so that larger (smaller) values imply a more appreciated (depreciated) real
exchange rate. Data on U.S. consumer price index are from the U.S. Bureau of
Labor Statistics. Data on Argentine inflation are from World Bank 2010 for 1966
to 2006; 2007 inflation is coded as being 20% (for reasons explained in the
text); and from the Billion Prices Project for 2008 to 2012.

to 2012, shows that Argentina's real exchange rate appreciated speedily between
2006 and 2012.[13]

Although Argentina's exchange rate was undervalued for fifteen of the forty-
one years between 1966 and 2006, each period of undervaluation (1975–1978,
1982–1983, 1985–1987, 1989, 2002–2006) was short-lived. Thus, it is not the case
that Argentina has never had an undervalued exchange rate. Where Argentina

---

13. This measure of the real exchange rate is strongly correlated ($r = 0.96$) with Darvas's (2012)
trade-weighted real exchange rate measure for the 1966–2006 period for which Argentina provided
reliable inflation data.

stands apart from countries such as Bangladesh, China, and South Africa is that other countries have sustained undervalued rates for decades whereas undervaluation in Argentina tends to last no more than two or three years. A second important difference is that even Argentina's brief undervaluations were largely unwanted outcomes. Whereas China's 1994 devaluation was a conscious decision by the government to weaken the exchange rate to promote exports, the devaluations in Argentina that occurred in 1975, 1982, 1989, and 2002 only took place in the midst of wrenching currency crises and after intense efforts on the part of the government to avoid depreciation. In short, Argentine policymakers typically adopted policies that appreciated the real exchange rate, and the brief instances of undervaluation occurred largely because the government had difficulty preventing such an outcome.

The remainder of this chapter provides an in-depth look at the political dynamics surrounding exchange rate policy in Argentina to assess whether and how the country's labor and financial structures contributed to its overvalued exchange rate. To do so, I evaluate whether Argentina's institutions influenced the preferences of the manufacturing sector, and whether the manufacturing sector influenced politicians' decisions about exchange rate policy.

The case study that I'll present pays close attention to the preferences of Argentina's manufacturing sector. Conventional wisdom holds that the manufacturing sector favors undervalued exchange rates. By contrast, the conditional preference theory suggests that manufacturing firms with the characteristics of those in Argentina tend to dislike undervaluation in countries with limited labor and financial controls. If my theory is correct, we should find Argentine industrialists lobbying against an undervalued exchange rate more often than we find them lobbying in favor of one. To the extent that industrialists' preferences are influenced by institutions, two additional facts should be observed: Argentine policymakers find it nearly impossible to keep interest and wage rates below their market levels when the exchange rate is undervalued; and manufacturers object to undervaluation out of their concern that it would further increase their operating costs. In short, my theory expects that the Argentine state's inability to suppress manufacturers' wage and borrowing costs leads the country's manufacturing firms to oppose an undervalued exchange rate.

Although Argentina's manufacturing sector should typically dislike undervalued exchange rates, their exchange rate preferences are not likely to be completely constant for forty-seven years. The logic of my argument suggests that the manufacturing sector should be more supportive of an undervalued exchange rate when undervaluation has less impact on business costs. Argentine industrialists' preference for undervaluation should increase when the state's control over labor and finance increases. Their support for undervaluation should also increase when the economy is operating far below its capacity levels and business costs become less sensitive to the exchange rate level.

It is also imperative to demonstrate that the preferences of Argentina's large manufacturing sector influenced the choice of exchange rate policy. The conditional preference theory expects that exchange rate policymakers know which policies industrialists prefer, and they make substantial efforts to adopt those policies. Argentine policymakers are likely to undervalue the exchange rate if and when the manufacturing sector prefers an undervalued exchange rate. They are unlikely to undervalue the exchange rate when the manufacturing sector does not prefer an undervalued exchange rate. To be sure, political leaders do not necessarily overvalue their exchange rates solely to please manufacturers. However, the conditional preference theory expects that manufacturing firms' lack of support for undervaluation is what makes it possible for Argentine policymakers to overvalue their exchange rates.

The Evidence: Exchange Rate Politics in Argentina

This section assesses the political determinants of exchange rate valuation in Argentina between 1966 and 2012. Within this forty-seven-year period, some eras are analyzed in more detail than others. In particular, the period from 1989 to 2012 is examined more thoroughly and the analysis is based on higher-quality primary sources.[14] Although the analysis of the 1966 to 1988 period is less detailed, the case studies of this period help determine whether the dynamics of Argentine exchange rate politics are similar across a variety of different political and economic contexts. Due to the long period of time covered, it is impossible to provide a comprehensive historical account of this period. The analysis focuses instead on those historical facts that are most pertinent for evaluating the conditional preference theory.

The case study begins in June 1966, when the military, led by Juan Carlos Onganía, overthrew President Arturo Illia's government. This event marked an important turning point in Argentina's volatile history. The military government, self-described as the *Revolucíon Argentina* (Argentine Revolution), aimed for a "wholesale restructuring of the state" and a "substantial transformation" of the economy (Smith 1989, 48, 50).

Table 4.1 breaks up the 1966–2012 period into nine different episodes and summarizes some key features of each case. The table lists the actual exchange rate

---

14. A list of author interviews is available in the appendix.

TABLE 4.1. Exchange rate politics in Argentina, 1966–2012

PERIOD	EXCHANGE RATE POLICY	PREFERENCES OF MANUFACTURING SECTOR	POLITICAL INFLUENCE OF MANUFACTURING SECTOR
1966–1972	Overvaluation	Overvaluation	Partial influence
1973–1974	Overvaluation	Overvaluation	Strong influence
1975–1976	Undervaluation	Overvaluation	Weak influence
1977–1980	Appreciation/ overvaluation	Heavy industry: Overvaluation	Partial influence
		Light industry: Undervaluation	
1981–1990	Unstable	Unstable	Variable influence
1991–1998	Overvaluation	Overvaluation	Partial influence
1999–2001	Overvaluation	Undervaluation	Strong influence
2002–2005	Undervaluation	Undervaluation	Strong influence
2006–2012	Appreciation/ overvaluation	Overvaluation	Partial influence

outcome, the preferences of the manufacturing sector, and the degree to which the manufacturing sector influenced exchange rate policy. The political influence of manufacturers is deemed "strong" when their demands constitute the single most important reason behind exchange rate level decisions; "partial" when their preferences are one of several factors that influenced the real exchange rate; and "weak" if exchange rate outcomes had little to do with the manufacturing sector's preferences.

The Military's Failed Attempts at Undervaluation: 1966–1972

General Onganía's first few months in office were a difficult time.[15] The military government did not implement any major economic changes until March 1967, when Onganía filled the office of minister of economy with Adalbert Krieger Vasena, a "leading industrialist" with strong connections to large internationalized firms (Smith 1989, 74; di Tella 1983, 32). The remaining top positions in the economic bureaucracies were also given to close allies of the manufacturing sector (O'Donnell 1988, 73). Reflecting the strong representation of large industrialists in government, the growth of the manufacturing sector and that sector's ex-

---

15. This section draws on the following works: Cortés Conde (2009, 230–240), di Tella (1983, 33–48), Filippini and Olcese (1989), Mallon and Sourrouille (1975, 29–35), O'Donnell (1988), Smith (1989), and Wynia (1978, 166–200).

ports were among the Onganía regime's top priorities (Smith 1989, 74–75; Wynia 1978, 167–175).

The economic program announced by Krieger Vasena in March 1967 reflected these long-term objectives as well as Onganía's more immediate goal of reducing inflation. The centerpiece of the program was a 40% devaluation of the peso that "was intended to create an undervalued currency" (Wynia 1978, 169). Krieger Vasena (1990, 91) insisted that this was the last time that the exchange rate would be devalued and he proclaimed with "certainty that there will not be monetary overvaluation."

The manufacturing sector had a mixed reaction to this attempt at undervaluing the exchange rate. The smaller manufacturing firms in the CGE opposed devaluation and were "concern[ed] with the cost increases they assumed would accompany devaluation" (O'Donnell 1988, 86). By contrast, the larger, more capital-intensive, manufacturing firms in the UIA were "enthusiastic about the peso devaluation" (Smith 1989, 85).

UIA and the large industrialists supported undervaluation because Krieger simultaneously adopted a number of other policies that countered the negative effect of devaluation on their operating costs. Along with the devaluation, the military government imposed taxes on agricultural exports and used the revenues to provide subsidized credit to large industrialists. Major tax breaks, including a provision that allowed firms to deduct 100% of their machinery costs from their tax bill, further reduced manufacturers' costs. At this point, the government also had some success weakening and dividing the labor movement, which enabled manufacturers to impose a wage freeze—another measure that "made it easier for industrialists to control their factor costs" (Wynia 1978, 171). Some members of the manufacturing sector supported the March 1967 devaluation because undervaluation was combined with labor market controls and other policies that lowered business costs.

Despite the military's desire for undervaluation, the peso did not remain undervalued for long. Although Krieger's policies were successful in slowing down the rate of inflation, Argentine prices increased 24% in the twelve months following devaluation and another 8% the following year (O'Donnell 1988, 108). With Argentine inflation far higher than inflation in the United States and the peso-dollar exchange rate fixed, the real exchange rate appreciated swiftly. By the end of 1968, the real exchange rate was already more appreciated than it was before the March 1967 devaluation (Mallon and Sourrouille 1975, 32).

Large capital-intensive industries were the greatest beneficiary of government policy in this period. Industries such as chemicals, metals, and machinery and equipment grew rapidly from 1968 to 1969. The fixed and overvalued exchange rate, combined with reduced restrictions on international capital flows, enabled large industrial firms to borrow on international capital markets. As a result, the growing overvaluation of the peso did not concern them in the least. Instead, the UIA continued to praise Krieger Vasena's policies throughout this period and asked only for their continuation (O'Donnell 1988, 104–106, 154).

Other interest groups were equally content with Krieger Vasena's exchange rate policy, though they grew increasingly hostile to other policies he pursued. The smaller industrialists in the CGE demanded looser monetary policies and complained that excessive openness to international trade and investment was contributing to the "denationalization" of the Argentine economy. The agricultural sector, already unhappy about export taxes, became more hostile to the Onganía regime in 1968 when it implemented additional land taxes. Worker discontent over stagnant wages ultimately became the biggest problem for Krieger and Onganía. While the regime was able to successfully demobilize the unions for a brief time, strikes and demonstrations proliferated in early 1969, culminating in massive protests in Córdoba in May 1969 that came to be known as the *Cordobazo*. Krieger Vasena was forced to resign in May 1969 as a result of this humiliating failure of labor policy.

Krieger's replacement, José Dagnino Pastore, shared his predecessor's belief that an undervalued exchange rate is "more appropriate" than an overvalued one (Pastore 1990, 109). But, to the manufacturing sector's relief, Pastore made no attempts to reverse the appreciation that took place during Krieger's tenure. Instead, Pastore promised to continue Krieger's fixed exchange rate policy, and the UIA "applauded the announcement that the March 1967 [fixed exchange rate] program would be continued" (O'Donnell 1988, 180). The regime had less ability to focus its efforts solely on the interests of large industrialists in the post-*Cordobazo* context. On the contrary, the government felt compelled to issue increasingly large wage increases, which contributed to rising inflation.[16] The result was a "conspicuous overvaluation" of the peso in 1970 (O'Donnell 1988, 181; Filippini and Olcese 1989, 190; Smith 1989, 145).

This increasingly uneasy political and economic climate proved too difficult for Onganía, who was replaced by another military leader, Roberto Levingston, in 1970. Levingston's first economy minister, Carlos Moyano Llerena, shared his predecessors' belief that overvalued exchange rates are highly problematic and industrial exports are the key to successful development (Brennan and Rougier 2009, 155; Oberst 2009). To this end, Moyano Llerena largely copied Krieger Vasena's policies. In June 1970, the peso was devalued by 14%, taxes on agricultural exports were increased, and tariff rates were decreased. However, unlike in 1967,

---

16. Wages jumped nearly 10% in 1969 (Smith 1989, 144).

wages were not frozen this time—a result of the fact that labor had regained its organizational capacity to resist such a freeze.

Even though some manufacturing firms supported the large devaluation in 1967, the entire manufacturing sector condemned the much smaller devaluation in 1970. Large industrial firms "demanded a stable flow of cheap intermediate goods imports," and the UIA complained that "devaluation was 'technically inexplicable since no urgent reasons existed'" to justify this shift (Smith 1989, 166, 168). The UIA, along with others, "criticized the devaluation, calling it an 'unnecessary and suicidal' step" (O'Donnell 1988, 202). This hostility contributed to Moyano Llerena's departure from the Ministry of Economy in October 1970, just four months after he started.

The final two years of military rule were characterized by frequent changes in political leadership and economic policy. Exchange rate policy was no exception: after a brief period with a fixed exchange rate, the government shifted to a crawling peg in April 1971, and then to a dual exchange rate regime in August 1971 (see Lizondo 1989). After 1970, the top priority for the military regime was to increase its popularity to ensure a trouble-free exit from power. To this end, it sought to comply with the demands of all possible constituencies. Wages were increased to win the goodwill of the working class. Fiscal and monetary policy became more expansive to help the small industrialists in the CGE who had close relationships with cabinet officials in this period. These loose policies contributed to rising inflation in 1971–1972. Even though the peso depreciated against the dollar, this was not nearly enough to make up for the high inflation, and the real exchange rate became far more overvalued than it was beforehand (see figure 4.1, as well as Lizondo 1989). The main reason the exchange rate became overvalued in 1971–1972 was the adoption of highly expansionary macroeconomic policies that were aimed at winning support from the working class and small manufacturing and commercial firms.

In short, the military elites that took power in 1966 promised to keep the exchange rate undervalued, but then quickly broke this promise. Following an initial depreciation, the exchange rate steadily appreciated over the next five years and became highly overvalued. The military regime failed to keep the exchange rate undervalued because powerful interest groups, including the manufacturing sector, opposed devaluation and insisted on expansionary macroeconomic policies. Argentina's manufacturing sector opposed undervaluation in part because the state was unable to control labor. At the start of this period, when the military briefly had the capacity to control the working class (and adopted other cost-cutting measures), some industrialists supported an undervalued exchange rate because undervaluation did not push up their costs. As the state lost its ability to

control labor costs, the manufacturing sector's tolerance for exchange rate devaluation receded.

Small Industrialists Encourage Overvaluation: 1973–1975

Running on the Peronist ticket, Héctor Cámpora, handily won the March 1973
elections.[17] Shortly after, Juan Domingo Perón, who was personally proscribed
from contesting the March elections, dismissed Cámpora and called for new elections, which returned him to the *Casa Rosada* in October 1973. Cámpora and
Perón received enthusiastic support from organized labor and from smaller industrial firms.

Cámpora and Perón gave the CGE a "free hand over the whole of the economy" (di Tella 1983, 84). They filled most top government positions with CGE
officials and gave the position of minister of economy to José Ber Gelbard, the
"CGE's recognized leader throughout its history" (Brennan and Rougier 2009,
117). Cámpora and Perón's economic policies, which included a massively overvalued exchange rate, closely reflected the preferences of the small manufacturing firms in the CGE.

When the Peronists entered office in May 1973, they inherited a fixed exchange
rate regime, where separate exchange rates were applied to different types of transactions and all rates were already "strongly overvalued" (Sturzenegger 1991, 89).
The government's priority was reducing inflation, which was over 50% per year at
that time. However, the government did not want inflation control to come at the
expense of economic expansion because, in the words of a top administration
official, "proposals without growth would not gain support" (Leyba 1990, 130).
Thus, rather than adopting more restrictive monetary or fiscal policies, the government used incomes policy to bring down inflation. In June 1973, the government, CGE, and CGT signed a "social pact." The pact froze workers' wages following a 200-peso increase. Prices were frozen at either their initial levels or at a
reduced level. While the 1973 pact has some similarities with the March 1967
stabilization plan, a key difference was that the Peronists did not devalue the
exchange rate in 1973.

The pact was extraordinarily successful at reducing inflation. The price level
was no higher in December 1973 than it was in June of that year. Although this
was not the government's aim, Argentina's real exchange rate depreciated nearly

---

17. This section is based primarily on the following sources: Brennan and Rougier (2009, 152–
198), Cortés Conde (2009, 246–254), di Tella (1983), di Tella and Braun (1990, 18–22), Leyba (1990),
Sturzenegger (1991), and Wynia (1978, 203–227).

5% during the Peronists' first six months in office.[18] This occurred because Argentine prices increased more slowly than U.S. prices while the peso-dollar exchange rate was fixed.

The peso's real depreciation increased import costs, which resulted in the "disaffection of raw-product-consuming industrialists" (Wynia 1978, 222). Industrialists were displeased that the costs for their imported inputs increased, and the price freeze forbade them from passing any portion of these cost rises onto their customers. Firms that were heavily reliant on imported inputs started incurring losses toward the end of 1973 (di Tella 1983, 116). As a result, "pressure for revaluation of the currency began to arise. This pressure was generated by firms with fixed prices that were facing an ever higher price for their imported inputs" (Sturzenegger 1991, 99; Cortés Conde 2009, 250). Workers were equally discontent: given their fixed salaries, higher prices of imported items meant that their real wages were declining. Consequently, workers in the CGT also lobbied Perón to revalue the peso (di Tella 1983, 116).

The real depreciation of the peso was extremely short-lived. In response to these pressures, Perón revalued the exchange rate for imports in December 1973. The revaluation generated losses for the central bank, which had to pay exporters more for foreign currency than they earned from selling foreign currency to importers. However, this was considered a small price to pay for satisfying interest group demands. Demands for revaluation from firms and workers in the manufacturing sector is the main reason the real exchange rate stopped depreciating.

The peso's real appreciation accelerated in the first half of 1974. The peso-dollar rate did not change in 1974, but inflation increased substantially. The CGE, who had long advocated for expansionary macroeconomic policies, used its control over economic policy to lower interest rates and increase government spending. However, the Peronists' highly expansionary monetary and fiscal policies made it nearly impossible to prevent wages and prices from rising. Inflation started to accelerate after March 1974, when the unions convinced the government to increase wages by 30%. This action was followed by another wage increase in June 1974 and increasingly frequent adjustments afterward. The wage freeze therefore lasted less than half of the two-year period it was planned for. To mitigate the impact on business costs, Perón packaged the wage hike with an interest rate reduction. After capitulating to workers on wages, the government found it increasingly difficult to prevent prices from going up, and Argentine consumer prices rose 17% in the first half of 1974.

Since the peso-dollar rate remained fixed and Argentine inflation far exceeded U.S. inflation, the exchange rate became massively overvalued (di Tella 1983, 118;

18. Calculated based on Sturzenegger (1991, 88) and U.S. Bureau of Labor Statistics data.

Sturzenegger 1991, 101). As can be seen in figure 4.1, the real exchange rate was more appreciated in 1974 than any other year between 1966 and 2012. In sum, two policies, exchange rate revaluation and expansionary macroeconomic policies, contributed to overvaluation in 1973–1974, and both were adopted at the insistence of the manufacturing firms in the CGE.

Argentina experienced a number of economic and political shocks around mid-1974. The unexpected death of President Perón on July 1, 1974 brought Isabel Perón to the presidency. Isabel Perón's economy minister, Alfredo Gómez Morales, insisted that no change in exchange rate policy would occur: "I [Morales] reject even to consider modifying the exchange rate. A devaluation is useless, it is the last measure I will resort to" (quoted in Sturzenegger 1991, 104). Thus, the real exchange rate continued to appreciate during the second half of 1974. Shortly afterward, decreasing prices for Argentina's exports reduced foreign exchange earnings and made it increasingly difficult to sustain the overvalued peso. Despite promises to the contrary, Gómez Morales devalued the peso in February 1975. This devaluation "reduced but did not eliminate an overvaluation of the currency which had reached gross levels" (di Tella 1983, 122).

The next economy minister, Celestino Rodrigo, devalued the exchange rate more aggressively in June 1975. In response, workers demanded wage increases to prevent their real wage rates from declining. Isabel Perón initially refused to increase wages. However, when the unions responded by launching a general strike—their first against a Peronist government—the government finally caved and allowed wages to increase by 100%. The Argentine economy found itself in an unprecedented crisis: inflation reached a record 183% that year and the peso depreciated 1484% in 1975. Amid this chaos, the military overthrew the Peronist government in March 1976.

Industrialist-Banker Coalition Leads to Overvaluation: 1976–1983

Upon taking power, the *Proceso de Reorganización Nacional* (National Reorganization Process), as the military regime called itself, and its leader, Jorge Videla, staffed the economic cabinet with prominent representatives of the agricultural and industrial sectors (Frieden 1991b, 211).[19] The Ministry of Economy was placed in the hands of José Alfredo Martínez de Hoz, a former director of the UIA who previously ran the nation's largest private steel company (Lewis 1990,

---

19. The literature on this period is very extensive. Excellent sources include Calvo (1986), Cortés Conde (2009, 254–272), di Tella and Braun (1990, 22–29), Díaz-Bonilla and Schamis (2001, 76–82), Dornbusch (1989), Frieden (1991b, 206–215), Gibson (1996, 75–101), Lewis (1990, 448–475), Nogués (1986), Petrei and Tybout (1985), Schvarzer (1986), and Smith (1989, 231–266).

449; Schvarzer 1991, 224). The *Proceso*'s major economic goals were economic liberalization and reducing inflation. Martínez de Hoz and the central bank also believed that it was important to prevent the peso from becoming overvalued (see Martínez de Hoz 1967, 1990; Schvarzer 1986, 87). Nonetheless, inflation remained high and the real exchange rate quickly became overvalued. One of the main reasons the *Proceso* failed to avoid overvaluation is that large capital-intensive manufacturing firms opposed both exchange rate devaluations and anti-inflationary fiscal and financial policies.

Martínez de Hoz implemented a variety of market reforms during his first months at the Ministry of Economy. Exchange rate reforms began almost immediately: the military devalued the exchange rate 27% in April 1976 and then unified the multiple exchange rates at a single depreciated rate in December of that year. In 1976, the military regime also cut taxes on agricultural exports, reduced import barriers in some industries, froze wages, liberalized prices, and started to cut social spending. A major financial liberalization package in June 1977 freed interest rates, eliminated barriers to entry in the financial sector, and liberalized cross-border capital flows.

The military regime never succeeded in reducing inflation. Annual inflation rates exceeded 100% throughout Videla's term. Persistent fiscal deficits were a leading cause of inflation (Díaz-Bonilla and Schamis 2001, 78; Lewis 1990, 46; Nogués 1986). Even Martínez de Hoz (1990, 171) acknowledged that the "budget deficit and overexpenditure is mainly responsible for inflation." Fiscal deficits resulted from reductions in business taxes and high spending directed toward heavy industries with close ties to the military.

Financial liberalization was a second major cause of inflation. The combination of high domestic real interest rates and capital account liberalization led to large-scale inflows of capital, which inflated the money supply and exacerbated inflation (Lewis 1990, 457; Smith 1989, 237–239). This was not lost on the government: "policymakers in the central bank . . . perceived capital inflows as being inflationary" (Nogués 1986, 15). In short, the military regime's monetary and fiscal policies prevented them from succeeding in their goal of reducing inflation.

In the context of high inflation, avoiding an overvalued exchange rate would have required the authorities to consistently depreciate the peso-dollar exchange rate. During their first year in office, a dirty floating exchange rate regime and frequent devaluations prevented overvaluation. However, between the second quarter of 1977 and the fourth quarter of 1980, the rate of currency depreciation was below the rate of inflation in fourteen out of fifteen quarters (Calvo 1986, 514).

Starting in December 1978, the authorities made this slow-depreciation exchange rate policy more explicit. At that time, they began preannouncing the rate of devaluation for the following eight months. The objective of this policy, known as the *tablita*, was to lower inflation. The authorities expected that real exchange rate appreciation would force firms to cut costs and bring about a decline in the inflation rate. With inflation outpacing devaluation between 1977 and 1980, the exchange rate became "extremely overvalued" in the late 1970s (di Tella and Braun 1990, 25; Dornbusch 1989, 293; Frieden 1991b, 213; Lewis 1990, 462). The strong appreciation of the currency was a matter of "high concern" for the government (Interview A15), but the government chose this policy nonetheless because, unlike other means of lowering inflation, it did not cause a recession in the short term (Martínez de Hoz 1990).

The overvalued exchange rate was anathema to many of the business groups that supported the coup in 1976, including agricultural exporters and small labor-intensive manufacturing industries (de Palomino 1988; Frieden 1991b; Schvarzer 1986). The labor movement was also deeply hostile to the military regime, though the hostility had much more to do with the military's repression of workers than with exchange rate policy. Incredibly, even though the military outlawed strikes and used violent means to intimidate workers, labor strikes and work stoppages persisted. For example, a wave of strikes in 1977 paralyzed twenty-two sectors of the economy, and one faction of the CGT launched a fairly successful general strike in 1979 (Collier 1999, 119–126; McGuire 1997, 170–176).

However, two of the regime's closest allies, bankers and large industrialists, strongly favored overvaluation. The combination of financial liberalization with an overvalued exchange rate was a major boon to the country's financial sector. Argentine bankers intermediated huge volumes of capital inflows and were positioned at the center of an economy that was increasingly focused on financial speculation. Consequently, the financial sector became one of the military regime's most loyal supporters (Frieden 1991b, 209; Gibson 1996, 85; Pepinsky 2009, 244; Schamis 1999, 259). Overvaluation persisted in part because it benefited the financial sector.

Large capital-intensive manufacturing firms also profited tremendously in this period, and they would have not done nearly as well if the government undervalued the exchange rate. Iron and steel, metals, rubber, petrochemicals, and other heavy industries rapidly increased output in the late 1970s (Frieden 1991b, 209; Lewis 1990, 470–471; Nogués 1986; Petrei and Tybout 1985; Schamis 1999, 259; Schvarzer 1986). The government's fiscal policy was highly favorable to this group: exporters of products, such as steel and refrigerators, received fiscal incentives; sectors like iron and petrochemicals benefited from large public investments; and various heavy industrial sectors were given tax breaks for investing in poorer provinces. Martínez de Hoz (1990, 167) said, "I should have further trimmed public expenditures," but he was unable to do so because "private sectors interested in the maintenance of certain works—being the suppliers, contractors, or beneficiaries . . . put up strong pressure." Capital-intensive manufacturing firms were the prime source of the expansionary fiscal policies that contributed to inflation and therefore real exchange rate appreciation.

Large industrial firms were equally supportive of the government's financial policies, which enabled them to borrow large sums of money from abroad (Petrei and Tybout 1985). From these firms' perspective, controls on capital inflows would have been a highly unattractive means of reducing the peso's overvaluation; capital controls would have required them to borrow funds domestically at far higher interest rates. Finally, as large manufacturing firms became more dependent on foreign borrowing, devaluation became an increasingly unattractive policy option because it would have caused the value of their foreign debts to soar (Lewis 1990, 463). So, each of the policies that were responsible for the peso's overvaluation—capital account liberalization, fiscal deficits, and limited exchange rate depreciations—benefited large capital-intensive manufacturing firms. The Videla administration overvalued the peso because preventing real appreciation would have alienated the regime's powerful supporters in the manufacturing and financial sectors.

The military regime could not avoid large exchange rate depreciations forever. By early 1981, it was obvious to many observers that the overvalued peso would have to be devalued eventually. Fears of future devaluations contributed to increasingly large capital outflows and a decline in foreign reserves. With the peso under heavy selling pressure, Martínez de Hoz devalued the currency by 10% in February 1981—far above the scheduled rate. Capital flight and rapid currency depreciation continued after the scheduled transfer of power to a new military leader, Roberto Viola, in March 1981. The result was an economic crisis of unprecedented proportions. The Argentine economy was in far worse condition in 1983, when the military returned to the barracks, than when it stormed into power in 1976.

Exchange Rate Instability in a Time of Debt: 1984–1989

The October 1983 election took place in the midst of extremely trying circumstances.[20] The fiscal deficit was 11% of GDP, external debt was two-thirds of GDP, and inflation was over 300% in 1983.[21] Virtually all the presidential candidates in

---

20. For further details on this period, see Canitrot (1994), Canitrot and Junco (1993), Cortés Conde (2009, 272–291), Díaz-Bonilla and Schamis (2001, 82–85), Fernández (1991), Machinea (1990), Peralta Ramos (1992), Smith (1989, 267–297), and Smith (1990).

21. The deficit and debt data are from Machinea (1990) and inflation data are from World Bank (2010). The government's external debt grew rapidly in the early 1980s because the military regime absorbed a large share of the external debts of private firms.

the 1983 election promised to reactivate the economy with expansionary policies and adopt a crawling peg currency regime to undervalue the exchange rate (*El Cronista* 1983; *Mercado* 1983).

To many observers' surprise, Raúl Alfonsín, the Radical candidate, became the first non-Peronist to win a free election in Argentina. Alfonsín wanted to use this opportunity to create a permanent Radical electoral majority. To this end, he attempted to win over traditional Peronist constituencies, especially workers and industrialists.

Initially, the Alfonsín administration adopted a flexible exchange rate regime to keep the exchange rate undervalued, implemented expansive macroeconomic policies, and raised workers' salaries. Unfortunately, this policy mix pushed inflation above 600% in 1984. Amid rising discontent, Alfonsín's first economy minister, Bernardo Grinspun, resigned in February 1985.

Grinspun's replacement, Juan Sourrouille, adopted a different strategy to reduce inflation. In June 1985, Sourrouille unveiled the Austral Plan, which combined a fixed exchange rate with contractionary measures, such as a wage and price freeze and increased taxes. Sourrouille also attached a high priority to an undervalued exchange rate (see Mallon and Sourrouille 1975, 99–105). As a result, Sourrouille depreciated the exchange rate by more than 150% between March and June to try to prevent the exchange rate from becoming overvalued later (Canitrot and Junco 1993, 59; Cortés Conde 2009, 276; Frieden 1991b, 227; Machinea 1990). Initially, the effects were as desired: inflation fell rapidly and the exchange rate remained undervalued. The Austral Plan also paid large political dividends. Alfonsín won praise from the UIA (Smith 1990, 35). The administration's approval ratings shot up from 35% to 57% (Gibson 1996, 139), which helped the Radicals win the November 1985 congressional elections.

Support for stabilization, however, was ephemeral. As the threat of hyperinflation waned in early 1986, various actors, from industrialists to Radical politicians, started demanding more expansive policies and a loosening of price controls (Canitrot and Junco 1993; *Clarín* 1986; Machinea 1990). Moreover, in the nine months following the Austral Plan, the real exchange rate became overvalued owing to the fixed exchange rate combined with residual inflation (Canitrot and Junco 1993, 53; Canitrot 1994; Gibson 1996, 162).[22] As a result, agricultural exporters became highly critical of the overvalued exchange rate and export taxes (Smith 1990; Gibson 1996, 162). Organized labor, which never supported the Austral Plan, demanded that the government increase wages, which had fallen in real terms since June 1985. Labor unions applied incredible pressure on the govern-

---

22. The real exchange rate appreciated 10% from July 1985 to March 1986 (Fernández 1991, 128).

ment to raise their salaries and benefits, which included general strikes in August 1985, January 1986, and March 1986 (Carrera 2007).

The Alfonsín administration capitulated to these demands. According to Alfonsín's central bank governor, the administration "thought that it was impossible to try to fight against almost everybody, but that was a big mistake" (Machinea 1990, 59). In January 1986, the government increased wages and pensions to try to mollify the unions. In February, the government reduced agricultural export taxes and—to the jubilation of some industry groups—introduced new industrial promotion policies (*Tiempo* 1986; *Somos* 1986). In April 1986, the fixed exchange rate regime was abandoned in favor of a crawling peg regime in order to "provide an additional stimulus to exporters" (*La Nación* 1986).

Although many industries were pleased with the introduction of such measures, this policy mix generated major economic problems that left virtually everyone worse off in the end. Reducing export taxes and increasing subsidies to manufacturing increased the fiscal deficit considerably.[23] The higher budget deficit combined with currency depreciations quickly led to a resumption of inflation.

Macroeconomic and exchange rate policy continued to shift repeatedly throughout the remainder of Alfonsín's term. The real exchange rate experienced wild swings as a result. The adoption of a fixed exchange rate led to rapid real exchange rate appreciation in the second half of 1988. Then, between April and July 1989, the exchange rate depreciated in a rapid and out-of-control fashion as the annual inflation rate surpassed 3000%. The exchange rate was highly undervalued when Alfonsín exited office in July 1989, but this was solely the result of panicked selling of pesos amid hyperinflation, not effective government policy.

The most distinctive feature of exchange rate policy between 1984 and 1989 is the complete lack of any clear real exchange rate trend. The real exchange appreciated in even-numbered years (1984, 1986, 1988) and depreciated in odd-numbered years (1985, 1987, 1989) (see figure 4.1). Real exchange rate instability was not caused by any unique features of Alfonsín's government. Alfonsín's political and economic objectives—higher wages, industrial development, an undervalued exchange rate—were largely identical to most previous and subsequent Argentine governments (Canitrot and Junco 1993; Díaz-Bonilla and Schamis 2001). The key difference between Alfonsín and other Argentine leaders was not the existence of contradictory goals, but rather a more inhospitable economic climate that aggravated the effects of inconsistent policies.

---

23. According to Canitrot and Junco (1993), cutting export taxes cost the government fiscal revenues worth 1% of GDP. Industrial subsidies were "the largest single item in the fiscal deficit in the 1980s" (Schamis 2003, 146), responsible for over half of the deficit (Peralta Ramos 1992).

Widespread Support for Overvaluation: 1990–1998

After Carlos Menem, the Peronist candidate, won the 1989 presidential election, he implemented several failed stabilization plans. Hyperinflation continued until the passage of the Convertibility Law in April 1991. The Convertibility Law created a quasi-currency board that fixed the (re-denominated) peso to the dollar at a rate of one-to-one; established full currency convertibility; and required the central bank to maintain foreign reserves equivalent to the entire monetary base.[24] Inflation fell almost immediately, but Argentine prices still increased much faster in 1991 (172%) and 1992 (25%) than U.S. prices. As a result, the real exchange rate became highly overvalued (Baer, Elosegui, and Gallo 2002; Damill, Frenkel, and Maurizio 2007; Etchemendy 2005; Galiani, Heymann, and Tommasi 2003; Starr 1997).

The Argentine business community strongly supported the overvalued exchange rate. The banking sector was enthusiastic about the convertibility program because they benefited from overvaluation, currency stability, low inflation, and capital mobility (Baer, Elosegui, and Gallo 2002). Despite the exchange rate's overvaluation, tradable firms immediately backed Menem and his exchange rate policy. Menem won over the agricultural sector by slashing taxes on agricultural exports on the same day that the peso was tied to the dollar (Interviews A25, A26; Schamis 2003, 144). The UIA was also a "defender" of the Convertibility Law from the start (El Economista 1991b). As early as April 1991, UIA President Israel Mahler was praising the Convertibility Law on the grounds that "anchoring the exchange rate is a strong way to achieve stability" (quoted in Naselli 1991).

The UIA argued that devaluation was not the best way to address the negative effects of overvaluation. UIA's president argued that the convertibility plan "serves perfectly, what you need is to implement all the elements that are not yet in order to consolidate stability" (El Economista 1991a). In lieu of devaluation, the industrial sector asked the government to adopt other policies, such as cheaper credit and lower taxes, to improve their external competitiveness (Ambito Financiero 1991a; El Cronista 1991).

The government accepted many of these demands within a few months. In August 1991, the government signed a pact with the UIA and promised to provide industrial credit at international interest rates, increase funding for small and medium-size enterprises, reduce electricity costs, and make greater use of anti-dumping trade protection (Clarín 1991a; La Nación 1991). After winning these concessions, the UIA proclaimed that "we take the parity as given" and "devaluation makes no sense" (Clarín 1991b). According to the director of UIA's Research

---

24. Excellent summaries of the Convertibility Law and its effects can be found in Damill, Frenkel, and Maurizio (2007), Galiani, Heymann, and Tommasi (2003), Schamis (2003), and Starr (1997).

Institute, the UIA "at no point . . . worked on alternatives to Convertibility," it only "worked on alternatives within Convertibility" (quoted in Bolten 2009, 156). Manufacturing firms strongly supported the Menem administration and its overvalued exchange rate.

Menem implemented numerous other market-oriented reforms to further consolidate his political coalition (Etchemendy 2005). In particular, Menem designed these reforms so that they helped powerful constituencies better cope with the problems associated with the overvalued exchange rate. The state sold off state-owned steel and petrochemical enterprises to private domestic firms at very favorable prices, which allowed these firms to enlarge their domestic market share. Despite the overall reduction in import tariffs, trade protection remained in place for the auto, pharmaceutical, and steel sectors. The petrochemical industry was assisted by renegotiation of its debts on favorable terms. To maintain the support of organized labor, Menem maintained favorable collective labor laws that preserved unions' monopoly at the firm level as well as the centralized framework for collective bargaining. "The endurance of the convertibility system", writes Etchemendy (2005, 81), "cannot be understood without considering this matrix of payoffs that set aside the most powerful sectors in labor and industry affected by the exchange rate level."

Policymakers were more concerned about the overvalued exchange rate than tradable industries were. Economy Minister Domingo Cavallo was a former economist whose academic writings stressed the negative effects of overvalued exchange rates (Cottani, Cavallo, and Khan 1990; Cavallo and Mundlak 1982). In the words of one administration official, "Cavallo never imagined that convertibility would have been a lasting system. He didn't think that it was the sort of regime to be kept for a long time" (Interview A7). For Cavallo, convertibility was nothing more than a temporary solution to the inflation problem (Levy-Yeyati and Valenzuela 2007, 211).

Cavallo's concern with the peso's overvaluation led him to try to revise the convertibility regime early in its tenure. In October 1992, Cavallo attempted a "fiscal devaluation": he increased tariffs and export subsidies to replicate the effects of devaluation without changing the rate of currency conversion (Starr 1997, 95; *Ambito Financiero* 1992a). Cavallo's actions crushed the financial markets' confidence in the peg, leading to a speculative attack where the central bank bled foreign reserves and had to raise interest rates to defend the fixed exchange rate. This disguised attempt at devaluation failed, and the government quickly abandoned any attempt to depreciate the currency. The government chose instead to deepen convertibility. To regain investors' confidence, in November 1992 the government allowed depositors to have dollar-denominated accounts (*Ambito Financiero* 1992b). Political expediency trumped the ideals of the economy minister.

Even if the government ruled out a devaluation, there was, of course, another way that it could have depreciated the real exchange rate: contractionary macroeconomic policies. However, Menem found this option equally unappealing. In 1993, Menem turned his attention to amending the constitution to allow him to run for a second term as president, and he knew that maintaining the support of voters and organized interest groups depended on the continuation of solid economic growth (Galiani, Heymann, and Tommasi 2003; Starr 1997, 1999). Furthermore, the industrial sector and other interest groups continued to encourage the government to cut taxes, increase subsidies, and expand the quantity of low-interest loans (Starr 1999; *Panorama* 1993).

Responding to these pressures, Menem cut taxes and increased spending in late 1993, which helped turn 1993's budget surplus into a deficit in 1994. The government also reduced the banks' reserve requirements in 1993–1994, which further increased bank lending (Starr 1997; Schamis 2003). Rather than using fiscal and financial policies to reduce prices and depreciate the real exchange rate, Menem implemented "over-stimulative monetary and fiscal policies" to maximize his political support (Schamis 2003, 145). Expansionary macroeconomic policy was economically risky: it further appreciated the real exchange rate, weakened the banking system, and made the country more vulnerable to external shocks (Blustein 2005; Mussa 2002; Schamis 2003; Starr 1999). But it was politically prudent for a president concerned with maintaining the support of voters and organized interest groups.

The exchange rate regime received another strong test during the 1995 presidential election, which Menem contested after successfully amending the constitution. Speculators attacked the Argentine peso after Mexico's currency was devalued in early 1995. There was strong support throughout the political system for defending the overvalued peso. One March 1995 survey reported that 80% of Argentines opposed devaluation, while only 5% supported devaluation (15% responded "don't know") (Galiani, Heymann, and Tommasi 2003, 130–131). The UIA remained opposed to devaluation and argued that "devaluing now would be chaotic" (*Página/12* 1995). Many manufacturing firms borrowed heavily in dollars after 1991, and one of the main reasons they supported the overvalued exchange rate was that it lowered the burden of these liabilities (Bolten 2009; Schamis 2003; Woodruff 2005). Elated with Menem's economic policies, UIA expressed its support for Menem's reelection as early as 1993 (*Ambito Financiero* 1993). Similarly, many agricultural exporters preferred overvaluation because they became heavily dependent on imported inputs (Interviews A25, A26). With such a powerful coalition in favor of overvaluation, the "Menem administration did not have a single doubt" about preventing devaluation in 1995 (Interview A6). Widespread support for convertibility helped Menem win reelection in May 1995 with ease (Starr 1997).

Although the speculative attack on the currency caused the Argentine economy to go into recession in 1995, the economy recovered quickly. Political support for overvaluation remained as strong during Menem's second term as during his first. The industrialists in the UIA continued to press for "some tweaks to the Convertibility Plan without changing the actual peso-dollar parity," but emphasized that they "don't want to modify convertibility, but on the contrary, to deepen it" (*La Nación* 1996). As a result, even though Roque Fernández, Menem's minister of economy from 1996 to 1999, disliked the fixed exchange rate system, he made no efforts to depreciate the currency (Kaplan 2013, 236).

To summarize, Argentina kept its exchange rate overvalued throughout the 1990s because all the major interest groups supported this policy. This support coalition included not only nontradable sectors like banking, but also manufacturing and agriculture. Tradable firms supported overvaluation in the 1990s for several reasons. At first, these firms were fairly indifferent about the exchange rate's level, but they benefited greatly from the fixed exchange rate regime and its effects on price stability. However, the overvalued exchange rate delivered increasingly large benefits for industrial and agricultural firms in the form of lower foreign debt and input costs, which intensified their support for overvaluation. Menem also strategically manipulated economic reform measures and implemented progrowth fiscal and banking policies to mitigate the costs of overvaluation for key constituents. If the manufacturing sector had preferred undervaluation, Menem's economy ministers might have had more success reducing overvaluation.

Growing Demands for Devaluation and Convertibility's Demise: 1999–2002

Argentina's luck started to run out in 1998. Following a series of emerging-market financial crises, capital started to exit the developing world and Argentina was no exception. Argentina's export prices also started falling in the late 1990s. It was no longer possible to combine overvaluation with domestic economic growth in this more difficult global economic environment. Economic growth slowed down considerably in 1998 and the Argentine economy shrank nearly 4% in 1999. As of 1999, there was a large excess supply of labor and capital in the Argentine economy.[25]

---

25. Unemployment increased to 14.3% in 1999 (Chudnovsky and López 2007, 31). According to estimates by the Ministry of Economy (Maia and Kweitel 2003), GDP was 8.7% below potential GDP in 1999—the largest shortfall Argentina experienced between 1960 and 1999.

Opposition to overvaluation grew once the economy stopped growing and factors of production became underemployed. Although the financial sector remained an unwavering supporter of overvaluation (Baer, Elosegui, and Gallo. 2002, 79; Woodruff 2005), most other groups became ambivalent about the convertibility regime once the economy started to contract. The manufacturing sector, in particular, started becoming more supportive of devaluation in 1999 (Interviews A14, A29). In contrast to their previous defenses of convertibility, some manufacturing firms in the UIA now pledged only "conditional support" for the fixed exchange rate (*La Nación* 1999). In August 1999, the head of Techint, a conglomerate focused on steel production, became the first prominent businessman to publicly criticize convertibility (Etchemendy 2005, 83). By the time of the October 1999 presidential election, many within UIA were privately suggesting that the next government should devalue the currency (Montenegro 1999). As a result of the deepening recession, manufacturing firms increasingly believed that regaining profitability would only be possible with a change in exchange rate policy (Bolten 2009, 159). In 1999, manufacturers did not present a clear or unified preference with respect to the exchange rate level. Their ambivalence in 1999 was a marked contrast from their earlier pro-overvaluation stance. This preference shift reflected the emergence of a new macroeconomic environment characterized by underemployment of labor and capital.

After winning the October 1999 presidential election, Fernando de la Rúa of the *Alianza* (a coalition between the Radicals and a second political party, FREPASO), had little success reversing overvaluation. The new administration subscribed to neo-Keynesian ideas and viewed overvaluation a serious problem (Interview A3). De la Rúa plucked José Luis Machinea from the UIA to become his minister of economy, an illustration of the emphasis this government placed on the interests of manufacturing.

As de la Rúa and his team prepared for their December 1999 inauguration, top *Alianza* officials studied possibilities for devaluation. Despite their acute awareness that keeping the exchange rate overvalued was not optimal for Argentina's long-run development, they decided against devaluation because they believed that devaluation would plunge the Argentine economy into a terrible economic crisis (Interview A28). Their decision to stick with the overvalued exchange rate is hardly surprising: at this point in time no major interest groups were making overt demands for devaluation while others still strongly favored the status quo.

The *Alianza* instead opted for deflationary macroeconomic policies. In their first year in office, they raised taxes, cut spending, and lowered public employees' wages. They hoped that these measures would restore confidence, or that commodity prices would recover, and that this would enable them to return to progrowth policies (Interview A20). The government was playing for time.

Contractionary macroeconomic policies contributed to price deflation and led to a slight depreciation of the real exchange rate. But, unfortunately, these policies also contributed to further economic contraction. GDP fell and unemployment rose again in 2000. In response to these economic troubles, Machinea resigned from the Ministry of Economy in March 2001.

Subsequently, things took a turn for the worse. Machinea's replacement, Ricardo López Murphy, lasted a mere two weeks as economy minister. Next, de la Rúa brought Domingo Cavallo back to the post, hoping that the "Father of Convertibility" would be able to regain the confidence of the markets and win interest groups' support. Cavallo experimented with a variety of heterodox and expansive measures. He removed limits on the central bank's ability to inject liquidity, a basic element of the currency board. Reminiscent of his efforts in 1992, Cavallo attempted to devalue while maintaining the convertibility system by imposing import taxes and export subsidies. He also tried moving to a basket peg. These measures just made the population even more skeptical that the peso-dollar parity could be sustained. In anticipation of an eventual devaluation, capital took flight.

On December 1, 2001, the government had to take some radical measures to prevent devaluation. A deposit freeze prohibited individuals from withdrawing more than $250 a week from their bank. Stringent capital controls banned the transfer of funds outside of the country. Amid protests and riots, de la Rúa resigned on December 20.

It was only after the implementation of exchange controls that the UIA officially adopted a stance in favor of devaluation. On December 21, the UIA announced a proposal that called for devaluation along with the "pesification" of debts at the original one-to-one exchange rate (Bolten 2009, 159; Calvo 2008, 18). In other words, the industrialists wanted a more depreciated exchange rate to be used for international trade purposes, but they wanted to be able to transfer their dollar debts into pesos at the old overvalued rate. They wanted the best of both worlds.

While the UIA was unleashing its proposal, the Argentine Congress selected Peronist Adolfo Rodríguez Saá to serve as the next Argentine President. Rodríguez Saá declared a default on the government's external debts, but he chose to keep the peso-dollar exchange rate intact. On January 1, 2002, Rodríguez Saá was replaced by another Peronist, Eduardo Duhalde. Duhalde, in turn, appointed UIA President José de Mendiguren to head the new Ministry of Production. On January 6, Duhalde instructed Congress to repeal the Convertibility Law. It was replaced by a dual exchange rate regime that used a fixed rate of 1.4 pesos per dollar for trade transactions and a freely floating rate, which quickly depreciated below 1.4, for other transactions. The legislation passed on January 6 also allowed firms or individuals to convert up to $100,000 of their dollar debts into pesos at the previous one-to-one exchange rate instead of the more depreciated exchange rates prevailing at the time. Sixteen days after the UIA proposed a shift in exchange rate policy, the government enacted their plan in almost its entirety.

Incredibly, the UIA complained that Duhalde's policies did not go far enough. They insisted on "total pesification" with no limits on the amount of dollar debt that can be transferred into pesos at the original exchange rate (*La Nación* 2002; Calvo 2008, 25). This continued lobbying paid off. On February 3, the government allowed firms to convert their entire stocks of dollar debts into pesos at par value.[26] Depositors received less favorable treatment: dollar deposits were converted into pesos at a rate of 1.4 pesos per dollar, which was better than the prevailing floating exchange rate, but still imposed a 40% loss in the value of their savings. Instead of leaving the banks on the hook for this difference, the government compensated the banks for this gap. The result was very costly for the state and, ultimately, Argentine taxpayers (Chudnovsky and López 2007, 152). But, for industrial firms, packaging devaluation with pesification was, to quote the president of *Banco Hipotecario* (Mortgage Bank) at the time, "basically paradise" (Interview A9). This policy combination, which improved external competitiveness without increasing firms' foreign-debt burdens, significantly increased the profits of many of Argentina's largest manufacturing firms (Bolten 2009; Calomiris 2007; Calvo 2008).

In light of the benefits that devaluation-cum-pesification delivered to Argentina's manufacturing sector, it is striking that it took more than a decade, including several years of economic contraction, before manufacturers advocated for this outcome. A likely reason for their delay in pushing for pesification is that this policy was not likely to be implemented during "normal" times. Since Argentina's state had little control over the financial system, pesification was hardly imaginable before the financial system was in a severe crisis. By contrast, as we will see in chapter 5, Korea adopted a similar mix of devaluation with debt relief in the early 1970s in far less drastic conditions. If Argentina's state controlled the financial system, wiping away firms' debts would have been more feasible in noncrisis conditions and interest groups may not have waited so long to lobby for devaluation with pesification. This episode illustrates how, absent extraordinary economic circumstances, non-state-controlled financial systems make it difficult for states to compensate manufacturers for the costs of devaluation, which, in turn, reduces support for undervaluation.

Another reason the 2002 devaluation was so beneficial for the manufacturing sector was that it contributed to an unusually large decline in real wages. Following the unification of the foreign exchange market in February 2002, the peso's

---

26. For a detailed chronology of events in this period, see Calvo (2008).

value plummeted as low as 3.8 pesos/dollar in June. This 74% depreciation substantially increased the costs of imports and other goods. And yet, remarkably,
salaries hardly increased at all in 2002 (Kritz 2002; McKenzie 2004). Exceptionally high unemployment on the eve of the 2002 devaluation reduced workers' wage
demands. As a result, nominal wages were far less responsive to price rises than
they typically are in Argentina (Damill, Frenkel, and Maurizio 2007, 74; Damill,
Frenkel, and Maurizio 2011, 26; Etchemendy and Garay 2011, 304; Levy-Yeyati
and Valenzuela 2007, 207). By lowering wages, the 2002 devaluation made businesses more profitable than they would have otherwise been. Even though the 2002
devaluation led to an unprecedented 11% economic contraction, the costs of this
devaluation were minimal for many manufacturing firms because they saw neither their foreign debt burdens nor their labor costs increase.

The preferences of the manufacturing sector strongly influenced Argentina's
exchange rate policy in early 2002. In the words of one prominent Argentine economist, the Duhalde government was "completely taken, in terms of economic policy, by the industrial lobby" (Interview A7). Annika Bolten (2009, 160) echoes
this view: the "dramatic shift in exchange rate regime was thus the direct result
of industrial interests' involvement." The most unique aspect of the 2002 devaluation was not the political influence of the manufacturing sector; it was the fact
that manufacturers were lobbying in favor of devaluation, rather than against it.
Argentine manufacturing firms were more supportive of undervaluation in 2002
than in previous periods because of high unemployment of labor and underuti-
lization of capital. These conditions made devaluation less costly for these firms
than is usually the case.

The Temporary Success of Undervaluation: 2003–2005

Campaigning on his Peronist Party's traditional center-left platform, Néstor Kirchner won the April 2003 presidential elections with 22% of the vote. Since Kirchner started off in a relatively weak political position, he felt it necessary to expand
his support coalition. Kirchner actively courted the support of two of Argentina's
most powerful social groups: organized labor and domestic industry (Etchemendy
and Garay 2011; Richardson 2009). When Kirchner took office, he benefited from
favorable economic conditions, which included a highly undervalued exchange
rate and an economy that was already recovering from its previous crisis yet still
operating far below its capacity level.

At the start of his tenure, Kirchner faced a choice between two competing economic programs. Central bank governor Alfonso Prat-Gay advocated appreciating the exchange rate and adopting an inflation-targeting regime. Roberto Lavagna
and his team at the Ministry of Economy instead recommended maintaining a

more depreciated exchange rate. Kirchner opted to follow Lavagna's preferred approach, and the maintenance of a stable and undervalued exchange rate became one of the Kirchner government's central objectives from the beginning of his tenure.[27]

To limit the appreciation of the peso, the central bank accumulated foreign reserves at a rapid clip. The central bank also sold growing volumes of short- and medium-term bonds to "sterilize" its reserve purchases and ensure that reserve accumulation was not inflationary. In June 2005, the Kirchner government implemented controls on capital inflows to help prevent real exchange rate appreciation. These policies succeeded in keeping the nominal exchange rate stable, and the real exchange rate undervalued, between 2003 and 2005 (see Damill, Frenkel, and Maurizio 2007; Frenkel and Rapetti 2006).

The manufacturing sector's strong support for an undervalued exchange rate in the early 2000s was an important reason why Kirchner opted for this policy. During the election campaign, when the peso appreciated to 3.1 pesos per dollar, the UIA firms made clear that this was too strong for them and advocated an exchange rate closer to 3.5 (Burgueño 2003). After Kirchner was elected, the UIA continued to express support for an undervalued exchange rate (Interview A27; Cufré 2003; *Ambito Financiero* 2005a). Associations that represented individual manufacturing subsectors, such as automobiles, metals, and textiles, were equally enthusiastic about the maintenance of a competitive exchange rate (Interview A29; *Ambito Financiero* 2005b; Bergaglio 2005; Riggi 2004). To the extent that industrialists complained about exchange rate policy, it was because the exchange rate should be even more undervalued. For example, even though the exchange rate of 2.8 pesos per dollar in July 2005 was substantially undervalued, industrial firms lobbied for an exchange rate of 3 pesos per dollar (Martín 2005). The manufacturing sector expressed a clear preference for an undervalued exchange rate during the first years of Kirchner's term, and the maintenance of an undervalued exchange rate was "crucial and necessary in order to maintain the UIA-Kirchner/Lavagna coalition" (*Ambito Financiero* 2005a).

Organized labor was a second group that strongly supported Néstor Kirchner's government (Etchemendy and Collier 2007; Etchemendy and Garay 2011; Tomada and Novick 2007; Richardson 2009). Since undervalued exchange rates reduce real wages, workers do not typically favor policy programs that are based around an undervalued exchange rate. However, due to the persistence of high unemployment, the government was able to keep the exchange rate undervalued

---

27. The debate between Lavagna and Prat-Gay is discussed in *Bloomberg* (2003) and Levy–Yeyati and Valenzuela (2007, 224–226). Damill, Frenkel, and Maurizio (2007), Frenkel and Rapetti (2006), and Richardson (2009) discuss the centrality of a competitive exchange rate to Kirchner's economic model.

and increase real wages at the same time. The Kirchner government increased the minimum wage from $200 in 2003 to $800 in 2006—a rate of increase that was far above inflation (Tomada and Novick 2007, 34). Kirchner also used taxes on agricultural exports to increase workers' real wages: these taxes reduced food prices and the government used these revenues to subsidize consumption of energy and transportation. These actions, part of Kirchner's strategy of "export-oriented populism" (Richardson 2009), successfully mitigated labor opposition to the undervalued exchange rate.

A number of nontradable industries supported Kirchner. Construction firms expressed little concern that the undervalued exchange rate increased their imported input costs. "We are pampered by Kirchner" thanks to Keynesian fiscal policies and an expansion of public works, boasted the construction sector's main lobby group (Candelaresi 2003a, 2003b). Similarly, bankers and nontradable firms were unconcerned about the undervalued exchange rate because the domestic economy was growing rapidly, and they were able to increase loans and sales to tradable-sector firms (Interview A16; Meaños 2005). Kirchner's strongest opponent was the agricultural export sector, which longed for the extremely stable exchange rate of the 1990s and intensely disliked export taxes (Interviews A25, A26).

Kirchner accomplished a remarkable mix of outcomes during his first years in office: the exchange rate remained stable (in nominal terms) and undervalued (in real terms) at a time when the government also maintained high levels of spending and increased workers' real wages. This combination of policies is rife with tensions that previous Argentine governments have not been able to reconcile. Onganía, Perón, and Videla tried similar macroeconomic policy packages, but their expansionary fiscal policies increased inflation and contributed to an appreciation of the real exchange rate.

Kirchner's exceptional ability to sustain this policy mix was strongly affected by one factor that was entirely out of his control: large excess capacity in the Argentine economy. The Argentine economy was still producing below its capacity in 2004, and it only reached its full capacity levels around 2005.[28] Idle capacity meant that expansive macroeconomic policies increased production but had little effect on the price level (Interview A4). Underemployment of labor and capital made it feasible to maintain the normally impossible combination of undervaluation, expansionary macroeconomic policies, and a stable exchange rate. According to one government official, these unusual economic conditions "allowed inconsistent policies to survive for a longer time than [would be possible] in other instances" (Interview A23).

---

28. Rodríguez (2007) estimates that GDP was 3.6% below potential GDP in 2004 and 1.7% above its capacity in 2005.

Unusual economic conditions during Kirchner's first years in office lowered the costs of keeping the exchange rate undervalued. These exceptionally low costs explain why Argentina's manufacturers were much more amenable to undervaluation than they normally are. It is unlikely that Kirchner would have undervalued the exchange rate during his first years in office had industrialists not supported undervaluation.

History Repeats Itself: Real Appreciation Since 2006

The tensions in Kirchner's economic program started to emerge toward the end of 2005. After several years of solid growth, aggregate production started to reach its capacity levels.[29] Moreover, with an eye toward the October 2005 legislative elections, Kirchner used fiscal policy to further increase growth, and the fiscal surplus fell from 3% of GDP in October 2004 to less than 1.5% in October 2005.[30] These changes pushed inflation above 10% in the second half of 2005.

Minister of Economy Roberto Lavagna and his advisers were worried. They believed that reducing inflation and preventing an appreciation of the real exchange rate ought to be the government's top priorities. The Lavagna team also believed that increasing the fiscal surplus was the best means for achieving these goals (Interviews A18, A19, A23, A28). A *Proposal for the Post-Electoral Economic Agenda,* written in October 2005 by the sub-secretary of economic programming, Sebastian Katz, illustrates the Lavagna team's thinking. After diagnosing "the closure of the output gap" and the "markedly expansive bias" of macroeconomic policies as among the main causes of rising inflation, Katz proposed that the government increase the fiscal surplus and establish a counter-cyclical fiscal stabilization fund.[31] Lavagna publicly proposed these measures later that month (Rebossio 2005).

Lacking in private-sector support, Lavagna's proposed shift in fiscal policy came to naught. In November 2005, it was clear to Lavagna that Kirchner and his backers had little tolerance for fiscal retrenchment, so he decided to step down. Although there was a modest improvement in the fiscal balance after the October 2005 elections, fiscal policy remained expansionary until late 2008 (Damill, Frenkel, and Maurizio 2011, 35–36). The resulting high growth, averaging over 8% per year between 2005 and 2008, helped Kirchner's spouse, Cristina Fernández de Kirchner, win the October 2007 presidential election. However, as Lavagna prophesied, the continuation of expansionary fiscal policies resulted in increas-

---

29. See previous footnote.
30. This figure is from the Inter-American Development Bank Latin Macro Watch Database.
31. Quotes are from a copy of the proposal obtained from Sebastian Katz.

ingly high rates of inflation. Prices are estimated to have increased by 20% to 25% in both 2007 and 2008.[32]

Although the peso started to depreciate a little faster against the dollar—it depreciated 10% in 2008—the combination of a relatively stable exchange rate with rising inflation caused the real exchange rate to appreciate 23% over 2007–2008 (see figure 4.1). This real appreciation occurred in spite of the fact that Néstor and Cristina Kirchner, and all four economy ministers in office between 2007 and 2008, continued to stress the importance of maintaining a competitive real exchange rate.[33] This rhetoric notwithstanding, the peso was no longer much, if at all, below its equilibrium value.[34]

The preferences of labor and industry contributed to real appreciation in 2007–2008. Organized labor demanded that the government maintain expansionary macroeconomic policies in order to maintain high real wage and employment rates. Labor also opposed devaluation on the grounds that it would reduce workers' real wages (Interview A17; Etchemendy and Collier 2007; Etchemendy and Garay 2011).

The manufacturing sector's support for undervaluation also started to wane in this period. As noted previously, manufacturers favored inflationary fiscal policies, which contributed to real appreciation. They also became less tolerant of exchange rate depreciation at the very time that it became essential for preventing overvaluation. Toward the end of 2008, after two years of rapid real appreciation, manufacturers did not ask for a large devaluation, but claimed instead that "an exchange rate *a little higher* would be better" (Olivera 2008; emphasis added). UIA economist Sergio Woyecheszen was more specific: in October 2008, on a day in which a dollar traded for 3.25 pesos, he suggested that an exchange rate of 3.4 or 3.5 would be good, but the UIA would not want the exchange rate to be at 4 or 5 pesos per dollar because this would be inflationary and increase firms' costs too much (Interview A27). The UIA was therefore asking for the same peso-dollar rate in October 2008 that the manufacturers favored in February 2003; given years

32. The government forced the national statistical agency, INDEC (*Instituto Nacional de Estadística y Censos*), to alter the computation of the consumer price index in 2007 to avoid the appearance of high inflation. Despite government claims that inflation was only 9% in 2007, most private estimates put inflation at more than twice that level (Barrionuevo 2007; *The Economist* 2007; Damill, Frenkel, and Maurizio 2011, 30–32).

33. The views of Felisa Miceli, economy minister from November 2005 to July 2007, and her replacement, Miguel Peirano, are discussed in *La Nación* (2007a) and Rebossio (2007), respectively. On Cristina Kirchner's support for a competitive real exchange rate, see Rebossio (2008). Within days of entering office, Cristina's first economy minister, Martín Lousteau, pledged to maintain a competitive exchange rate (*La Nación* 2007b), as did his successor, Carlos Fernández (*La Nación* 2008).

34. In anonymous interviews during the fall of 2008, central bank and Ministry of Economy officials agreed that the real exchange rate was close to its market rate. Industrial groups (Interview A13) such as the UIA (Kanenguiser 2009) echoed this view.

of price increases, this implies that they wanted a much less undervalued rate in 2008 than they did in 2003. Similarly, ADIMRA wanted the government to maintain a competitive exchange rate, but it didn't think it was wise to devalue too much because this would increase inflation (Interview A29). In 2008, the manufacturing sector favored expansionary macroeconomic policy and no more than small devaluations of the exchange rate—a policy mix that appreciated the real exchange rate.

The manufacturing sector started to downplay the importance of an undervalued exchange rate around 2009. The UIA now argued that changes in the economy since 2003 created the need for a "new approach" to economic policy (Coatz 2009). For instance, a 2010 editorial written by UIA's chief economist suggested that even though "a competitive real exchange rate was and remains a very important boost to production," "development planning" was now the "more important" issue (Coatz 2010).

Not only did exchange rate policy become a less salient issue for the manufacturers after 2009, but their preferences also continued to shift in an anti-undervaluation direction. In 2009, the UIA implored the government to do more to prevent capital outflows, which, in the UIA's view, was responsible for excessive downward pressure on the currency (Coatz et al. 2009; Coatz and Zack 2009). When discussing exchange rate policy in 2010, José de Mendiguren, back in the UIA after his time in the Duhalde administration, emphasized the negative effects of devaluation on imported input costs and claimed that an undervalued exchange rate "is useless" if inflation erodes competitiveness (*La Nación* 2010). Since then, de Mendiguren has suggested that the UIA does not favor devaluation (*La Nación* 2011). When asked, in a 2013 interview, whether the government should devalue, de Mendiguren was emphatic: "I think that is nonsense" (Sehinkman 2013). Industrialists' hostility to devaluation was back in full force between 2009 and 2013.

Increased support for overvaluation was a result of the economy reaching and then surpassing its capacity. With the economy again operating at full capacity, businesses regained their usual preoccupation with the cost side of their business. Interest rates were much higher than they used to be—the interest rate on ninety-day government bonds increased from an average of 6% in 2005 to 11.8% in 2010—and real wage levels increased 65% between 2005 and 2010.[35] As shown in table 4.2, most Argentine manufacturing firms were concerned with access to finance and labor regulations, two factors that affect the cost side of their business, in 2010. Argentine firms were more concerned with these cost-related issues in 2010 than they were in 2006, when there was more slack in the economy.

---

35. These figures were calculated using data from Argentina's central bank and from the Inter-American Development Bank's Latin Macro Watch database, respectively.

TABLE 4.2. Obstacles to business in Argentina

	ACCESS TO FINANCE	LABOR REGULATIONS
Argentina, 2006	0.81	0.91
	(n = 726)	(n = 740)
Argentina, 2010	0.86	0.93
	(n = 780)	(n = 790)
China, 2012	0.67	0.46
	(n = 3452)	(n = 3463)
Other Countries, 2006–2013	0.71	0.56
	(n = 36730)	(n = 38015)

Note: Data are from the World Bank Enterprise Survey (2006–2013). Column 1 presents the proportion of manufacturing firms that report that access to finance is an obstacle to business. Column 2 presents the proportion of manufacturing firms that report that labor regulations are an obstacle to business.

Table 4.2 also shows that finance and labor issues were more salient for Argentine firms than for their counterparts in other developing countries, and China in particular.

After 2006, as manufacturers became increasingly worried about rising costs, they stopped pushing for an undervalued exchange rate. One journalist compared UIA's position on exchange rate policy in 2011 with its earlier stand as follows: "Far from previous UIA meetings, in which many clung to the dollar [exchange rate] as the salvation for their companies, this time their statements focused on microeconomic corrections related to cost reduction, such as logistical difficulties, lack of funding, and high labor litigation" (Galak 2011). Likewise, when the UIA president met with President Kirchner in early 2013, he chose to discuss tax and labor policy instead of exchange rate policy (Sehinkman 2013).

Whereas manufacturers' views on devaluation changed quite dramatically between 2003 and 2013, their preference for an expansionary fiscal policy persisted. The UIA continued to argue that it was inappropriate to use fiscal policy to reduce inflation and kept lobbying Cristina Kirchner's administration to use fiscal policy to sustain high demand (Coatz 2011; Coatz and Woyecheszen 2013).

Macroeconomic and exchange rate policies between 2010 and 2012 mirrored the preferences of the manufacturing sector. The government's fiscal position deteriorated steadily, from a small surplus toward the end of 2010 to a deficit of more than 2.5% by the end of 2012. Expansionary fiscal policies helped sustain high rates of economic growth in 2010 and 2011. However, this came at the expense of 25% average annual inflation rates in this period. By contrast, the peso's depreciation against the dollar averaged only 9% per year between 2010 and 2012.

Since inflation outpaced depreciation by a substantial margin, the real exchange rate appreciated 43% between 2010 and 2012—far more rapidly than Cristina Kirchner's first years in office. Figure 4.1 shows that the real exchange rate was even more appreciated in 2012 than it was in 1991. In May 2013, a dollar traded for more than ten pesos on the black market, 70% above the official price at the time and a clear indicator that Argentine investors think the peso is grossly overvalued (*Ambito Financiero* 2013).

Similarly to previous periods, the overvalued exchange rate started to take its toll on Argentina's economy in 2013. In anticipation of an eventual devaluation, capital flight intensified. Capital outflows reduced the central bank's reserves and made it increasingly difficult for the government to prevent devaluation. By January 2014, the peso started to rapidly lose its value—it depreciated a full 20% in the week of January 20 to 24. As per usual, the currency crisis of 2013–2014 coincided with a dramatic slowdown in the rate of economic growth.

So, the manufacturing sector supported large devaluations in the early 2000s, preferred small devaluations in 2007–2008, and then opposed devaluation altogether after 2009. This shift in preferences reflected the steadily rising costs of devaluation. Before 2005, when the economy was operating below its capacity, manufacturing firms favored devaluation because devaluation had little effect on wages or other business costs. But, as the economy reached and then surpassed its full capacity level, currency depreciations had increasingly large effects on businesses' costs. Changing economic conditions reduced the net benefits of undervaluation, causing manufacturing firms to stop supporting this policy. The manufacturing sector, however, continued to demand expansionary fiscal policies. The real exchange rate appreciated rapidly between 2006 and 2012 because the Kirchners maintained inflationary fiscal policies and a stable exchange rate. One of the main reasons that they adopted these policies was because Argentina's powerful industrialists lobbied for them.

Conclusions about Exchange Rate Politics in Argentina
The Influence of Institutions on Preferences in Argentina

Argentina's manufacturing sector preferred an overvalued exchange rate to an undervalued one for the vast majority of the 1966–2012 period. Argentine industrialists registered their opposition to devaluing the currency from 1969 to 1971, 1977 to 1980, 1991 to 1998, and 2008 to 2012. In 1973, Argentina's manufacturing firms even pressed the government to revalue the currency. The manufacturing sector also continuously opposed using deflationary macroeconomic policies to depreciate the real exchange rate.

Why does Argentina's manufacturing sector usually oppose an undervalued exchange rate? This opposition to undervalued exchange rates stands in contrast to dominant theories of political economy, which assert that tradable industries such as manufacturing prefer an undervalued exchange rate in order to increase their external competitiveness. Argentina's manufacturing firms recognized this benefit of undervaluation, but considered the costs to be larger. In the early 1970s and 2000s, the manufacturing sector preferred an overvalued exchange rate because it lowered their imported input costs. They favored overvaluation in the late 1970s and 1990s to reduce their foreign debt burdens. Argentina's manufacturing sector has tended to oppose undervalued exchange rates because this policy increases their operating costs.

The state's limited control over labor and financial markets intensified manufacturing firms' preoccupation with the costs of undervaluation. The manufacturing sector would almost certainly have been more supportive of an undervalued exchange rate if the Argentine state had the capacity to control firms' labor costs. The strength of organized labor helps explain why Argentina's manufacturing sector was less supportive of devaluation than their counterparts in China. Compare, for example, Argentina's 1975 devaluation with China's 1994 devaluation. Following a large devaluation in June 1975, organized labor demanded salary increases in order to ensure that workers' real wages did not fall. After launching a general strike, Isabel Perón awarded them large wage increases. As a result, Argentina's manufacturing firms saw both their import costs and their wage bills spike in 1975. By contrast, chapter 3 showed that Chinese workers, who lack the organizational capacity for collective action, were unable to prevent their real wages from falling after the 1994 devaluation; hence, devaluation had a smaller effect on firms' costs in this case. Devaluation would have been less problematic for manufacturers if Argentina had a state-controlled labor system.

Argentina's private-controlled financial system also made undervaluation less attractive to the manufacturing sector. A comparison of sterilization costs in Argentina and China between 2003 and 2012 is instructive. During this period, both countries' central banks accumulated foreign reserves and sold "sterilization bonds" to limit exchange rate appreciation. However, even though China's foreign exchange market interventions were far larger, in absolute terms and relative to the size of the economy, the costs of sterilization were far lower in China than Argentina. During the 2003–2012 period, the Argentine central bank paid an average annual interest rate of 11% on its ninety-day central bank bills and paid bondholders as much as 23% interest at one point.[36] The People's Bank of China forced the country's state-owned banks to purchase its ninety-day bills at very

---

36. These figures are based on data from the central bank's website (http://www.bcra.gov.ar).

low rates in the range of 1 to 4% (Zhang 2012). This has important effects on manufacturing firms' borrowing costs, which rise when interest rates on government bonds increase. These institutional and policy differences help make sense of why far more Argentine manufacturers than Chinese manufacturers have difficulties obtaining access to credit (see table 4.2). Rules and decision-making procedures that limited the state's control of the financial system raised the costs of an undervalued exchange rate for businesses in Argentina.

While the manufacturing sector favored an overvalued exchange rate for most of the 1966–2012 period, there were some important yet brief moments when they favored an undervalued exchange rate. The manufacturing sector strongly preferred an undervalued exchange rate between 2001 and 2005 and some, though not all, manufacturing firms supported devaluation in 1967. Preferences were different in these periods because the costs of undervaluation were unusually low at these times. The 2002 devaluation had little effect on wages and costs because it was preceded by immense unemployment, which rendered firms' costs less responsive to undervaluation. Moreover, the extreme circumstances of a financial crisis in 2002 permitted the government to adopt financial policies that prevented industrialists' foreign debts from increasing. The story is similar with the March 1967 devaluation: the then-newly installed military government was temporarily able to control labor and froze wages to reduce the costs of devaluation. These two periods featured a set of unusual economic and political conditions that weakened the effect of undervaluation on businesses' costs. These transitory conditions served the same function that state-controlled institutions served in China: they reduced the costs of undervaluation. The only difference was that their effects were extremely short-lived in Argentina. These episodes provide further evidence that state-controlled labor and financial systems increase the manufacturing sector's support for undervaluation.

The Influence of Interest Groups on Exchange Rate Policy in Argentina

Argentine policymakers usually favored undervalued exchange rates but, time and again, failed to keep the exchange rate undervalued. Krieger Vasena and Pastore in the 1960s, Martínez de Hoz in the 1970s, Sourrouille from 1985 to 1986, Cavallo in the 1990s, de la Rúa at the turn of the century, and the Kirchners since 2006— none of these policymakers succeeded in their pursuit of undervalued exchange rates. This pattern discredits the argument that policymakers' beliefs about undervalued exchange rates can explain their policy decisions. The fact that right-wing conservative governments, such as Menem and Videla, populists on the left like Perón and Cristina Kirchner, and pragmatic centrists, such as de la Rúa, all overvalued the peso casts further doubt on the claim that ideology influences exchange rate policy.

External political factors also had little effect on Argentine exchange rate policy. Many believe that the IMF exerts an undue influence on Argentina's economic policies. This, however, has not been the case at all—at least with respect to Argentina's exchange rate policy. The IMF had little effect on Argentina's exchange rate or other policies in the 1990s, when Argentina continually borrowed from the fund and the IMF's influence over Argentina was probably at its peak (Mussa 2002). Far from pushing Argentina to overvalue the exchange rate, the IMF staff was skeptical of the convertibility regime and worried about the peso's overvaluation in the early 1990s (Blustein 2005, 14–15; Independent Evaluation Office 2004, 17). As Paul Blustein (2005, 199) recounts, "the remarkable characteristic of relations between the IMF and Argentina during much of this period [1990s] is the extent to which Argentine officials were leading the Fund around by the nose, in everything from the initiation of convertibility in 1991 to the announcement of the zero-deficit policy in 2001." There is little evidence that the IMF or other external political forces are to blame for the perpetual overvaluation of the Argentine peso.

Another explanation for Argentine overvaluation focuses on the country's dependence on exports of beef and wheat. According to this theory, Argentine policymakers overvalued the exchange rate to reduce food exports and lower the cost of food to workers (O'Donnell 1978; Richardson 2009). Neal Richardson (2009) also argues that the shift away from food exports and toward greater reliance on exports of soy, which is not consumed in large quantities by Argentine workers, explains why Kirchner undervalued the peso. However, this change in the nature of Argentina's commodity exports cannot explain why Argentina's real exchange rate rapidly appreciated after 2006. Moreover, as chapter 5 shows, oil exporters like Iran and Mexico frequently overvalue their exchange rates. Reliance on food exports has not been the driving force behind overvaluation in Argentina.

The preferences of powerful interest groups had a much larger effect on Argentine exchange rate policy than policymakers' ideas, external pressures, or dependence on food exports. The manufacturing sector's preferences were an especially important driver of overvaluation. Manufacturing firms lobbied the government to keep the peso overvalued during each of the five main episodes of appreciation/overvaluation examined in this chapter: 1967–1972, 1973–1974, 1977–1980, 1991–2001, and 2006–2012. And in all five cases, policymakers were very sensitive to this sector's demands. Argentine policymakers' desire to satisfy the manufacturing sector was rarely the sole reason that they overvalued the exchange rate. In all five cases, however, overvaluation would have been less likely if Argentine industrialists opposed this outcome.

The only period that Argentine manufacturers favored an undervalued exchange rate, 2001–2005, provides additional evidence of this group's strong influence. After being overvalued for over a decade, the peso was devalued not years or weeks, but days after the UIA proposed devaluation. This devaluation was also designed in a manner that minimized any harm to the manufacturing sector. Furthermore, the Kirchner administration sustained the undervalued exchange rate from 2003 to about 2007 during a period in which the manufacturing sector continued supporting undervaluation. Argentine policymakers undervalued the exchange rate when the manufacturing sector preferred an undervalued exchange rate. The manufacturing sector's opposition to an undervalued exchange rate is one of the most important reasons that Argentina has rarely kept its exchange rate undervalued.

Argentine Overvaluation in Comparative Perspective

Argentina's manufacturing sector is large, highly organized, and has had close contacts with nearly every government over the past fifty years. When industrialists speak, Argentina's exchange rate policymakers listen. Industrialists' opposition to exchange rate devaluation has discouraged Argentine policymakers from keeping their exchange rate undervalued. The exchange rate preferences of Argentina's manufacturing sector were influenced by the state's inability to control the labor and financial system. Because of these institutional arrangements, undervalued exchange rates tend to substantially increase not only firms' import costs, but also their salary expenses and borrowing costs. Institutions that curtail some of the state's policymaking capacities, in combination with a powerful manufacturing sector, tend to produce a strong pro-overvaluation coalition in Argentina, making it difficult for Argentine policymakers to resist this perilous policy.

INTERESTS, INSTITUTIONS, AND EXCHANGE RATES IN SOUTH KOREA, MEXICO, AND IRAN

The evidence provided in earlier chapters suggests that institutions influence interest groups' exchange rate preferences, and powerful interest groups, in turn, influence government decisions about exchange rate policy. This chapter further investigates the impact of interests and institutions on exchange rate policy with case studies of South Korea, Mexico, and Iran. These three countries are all important in their own right. Here, they are examined side by side because each has a distinct combination of institutions and interests. This chapter shows that each of these countries' exchange rate politics follows a unique trajectory at least in part as a result of their differing domestic political arrangements.

Park Chung Hee ruled South Korea from 1961 to 1979. Throughout this period, the state controlled the country's labor and financial systems and the manufacturing sector was powerful. In these ways, South Korea was very similar to the case examined in chapter 3: contemporary China. However, these two cases are dissimilar in many other respects: the global political and economic system that Korea confronted between 1961 and 1979 could hardly be more different from the one that China faced between 1993 and 2009; South Korea was ruled by a military dictatorship, China by a single-party regime; and Korea's economy in 1961 was one-twentieth as large as China's economy in 1993. Despite these and other differences, exchange rate politics in Park's South Korea and in contemporary China have much in common with one another. The Korean state used its control over financial and labor markets to suppress manufacturing firms' costs. As a result, Korea's manufacturing sector preferred an undervalued exchange rate for large portions of this period. The evidence also suggests that the preferences of Korea's powerful manufacturing encouraged President Park to undervalue Korea's exchange rate.

Exchange rate politics in Mexico is much more similar to a different case encountered in chapter 4: Argentina. In Mexico, as in Argentina, financial and labor institutions were beyond the control of the state and the manufacturing sector was powerful. Mexican industrialists consistently opposed an undervalued exchange rate, and their preferences had considerable influence on their country's exchange rate policy. Manufacturers' opposition to devaluation is a major reason Mexico maintained an overvalued exchange rate for most of the twenty-five-year period examined in this chapter. The similarities between Mexico and Argentina are especially noteworthy in light of the striking differences between the two countries' economic structures (Mexico is an oil exporter, Argentina is not), political regimes (Mexico, unlike Argentina, had a stable single-party regime during the period under consideration), and foreign relations (Mexico is much more closely allied to the United States).

The third section of this chapter examines exchange rate politics in Iran between 1953 and 1997. Iran's labor and financial institutions are similar to those seen in the case studies of China and Korea. However, the manufacturing sector in Iran has far fewer power resources than it does in China, Argentina, Korea, or Mexico. Although Iran's 1979 revolution led to profound changes in the country's political economy, both pre- and postrevolutionary Iran are characterized by state-controlled labor and financial systems and a weak manufacturing sector. As in other countries with state-controlled institutions, Iran's manufacturing sector preferred an undervalued exchange rate both before and after 1979. However, for large portions of this forty-five-year period, Iranian policymakers could hardly have cared less about the preferences of Iranian industrialists. Iran's politicians were often much more concerned with the interests of the country's large and well-organized service sector. Iran overvalued its exchange rate in order to benefit the country's powerful service sector. The case study of Iran suggests that industrialists with few power resources are less likely to influence exchange rate policy.

These case studies suggest that the preferences of powerful interest groups impact whether exchange rates are undervalued. Policymakers in all three countries sought to maintain the exchange rate at a level favored by powerful sectors. The evidence presented in this chapter also supports my argument that labor and financial market institutions influence whether the manufacturing sector prefers an undervalued exchange rate. The case studies of Korea, Mexico, and Iran demonstrate that the mixture of interest groups and institutions influences whether a country maintains an undervalued exchange rate.

The Politics of Undervaluation in South Korea, 1961–1979

The Political Sources of Exchange Rate Policy in South Korea

On May 16, 1961, the military, led by Park Chung Hee, seized control of the state in South Korea. Park radically restructured the state's relations with the financial sector.[1] The banking system was nationalized in 1961, and the central bank was brought under the direct control of the executive branch in 1962. These institutional changes resulted in a state-controlled financial system. The Park government controlled the appointments of all bank officers and interfered in all aspects of commercial bank operations. Accordingly, banks in Korea were unable to make loans according to economic criteria, such as profits. Instead, Korean bankers adopted the political goals of their masters, for this was the only way they were able to keep their jobs or win promotions.

Unions proliferated and became more militant during the latter half of the 1950s (Deyo 1989, 120; Vu 2010), but Park Chung Hee quickly reversed this trend.[2] The state expanded its control over labor during Park's presidency. In August 1961, Park created a government-supported labor federation, the Federation of Korean Trade Unions (FKTU), and required all union locals to join this federation. This centralized federation helped the state control the labor movement. The FKTU was primarily used as a vehicle for controlling and taming labor, not for promoting workers' interests. A major amendment to the labor law, passed in 1963, expanded state intervention in the internal operations of unions. A new law in 1971 further limited workers' rights to collective bargaining and collective action. The Korean Central Intelligence Agency also intensified its surveillance and intimidation of union leaders in the 1970s. In essence, Park Chung Hee quickly built an institutional apparatus that gave the state strong control over the labor system.

Korea's manufacturing sector wielded tremendous power resources during the Park era. Even though South Korea was quite poor in 1960, the country already had one of the developing world's largest manufacturing sectors. Korea experienced rapid industrialization during the period of Japanese colonialism, 1910–1945 (Amsden 2001, 101–105; Kohli 2004, 48–56). By "1945 Korea had an industrial infrastructure that . . . was among the best developed in the Third World"

---

1. For more details on Korea's financial system during the Park era, see Choi (1993), Cole and Park (1983), Park (1991), and Woo (1991).

2. This paragraph is based primarily on Choi (1989), Deyo (1989), Ogle (1990), Kim (1997, 120–123), and Kohli (2004, 98–101).

(Cumings 1984, 13). While most heavy industries were located in what became North Korea, the South was home to nearly half of all industrial production, including most of the factories producing light manufacturing goods, such as textiles, machinery, and metals (Amsden 2001, 104; Kohli 2004, 54–55). The South Korean manufacturing sector suffered major setbacks during the period of Japanese decolonization and the Korean War (1945–1953), but South Korea's manufacturing sector grew rapidly again between 1953 and 1958 (Amsden 1989, 41; Woo 1991, 59). By the early 1960s, Korean manufacturing production was 13.8% of GDP (Mason et al. 1980, 100). Korea's manufacturing sector was in the upper-third of all developing countries at this time.[3]

Korea's manufacturing sector was also highly concentrated, which boosted its organizational power resources. The Japanese colonial government encouraged the formation of large-scale enterprises (Amsden 2001, 103; Kim 1997, 90–91; Kohli 2004, 54). The 1950s witnessed a further increase in the size of industrial enterprises when Korean indigenous entrepreneurs took over plants that were previously controlled by the Japanese (Amsden 1989, 39; Kohli 2004, 76). It was during the 1950s that many of Korea's infamous chaebol—large family-controlled business conglomerates—were born (Kim 1997, 125–126). Korea's industrialists were well positioned to influence the military regime that emerged in 1961.

Initially, Park did not plan on allying with the manufacturing sector. Immediately after coming into power, he imprisoned a number of prominent business leaders for illicit and corrupt activities. Despite his initial dislike of this group, Park quickly came to realize that antagonizing industrialists did not serve his political interests. America's ambassador to Korea met with Park to explain that maintaining bad relations with industrialists would have disastrous economic consequences (B. Kim 2011, 95). The leader of Samsung echoed this view and encouraged Park to cooperate with the industrialists (Kim and Park 2011, 274). Their cases were convincing. Park quickly came to realize that the best way for him to grow the economy was to join forces with the large business groups (Clifford 1994, 40; Kim 1997, 117–119; Kohli 2004, 96). Accordingly, Park quickly did a U-turn and formed an enduring alliance with the chaebol (Haggard 1990, 72; Woo 1991, 84).

The nation's leading industrialists had regularized access to the regime's top decision makers, including President Park himself. Korean industrialists created a number of business associations, such as the Federation of Korean Industries and the Korean Traders Association, which lobbied for favorable policies. These associations maintained close relations with the Ministry of Commerce and In-

---

3. Of the fifty countries that have data on the manufacturing/GDP ratio for 1965 in *World Development Indicators*, Korea's was the sixteenth largest—with 1965 being the earliest year that this database includes data for Korea on this variable.

dustry (Haggard 1990, 70). Korean industrialists also had regular opportunities to discuss economic policy with top state officials. For example, the monthly Export Promotion meetings that were chaired by President Park "increased the exposure of the president to special pleading by business groups" (Brown 1973, 145). Extensive personal ties also developed between individual industrialists and state leaders. For instance, the leaders of Hyundai and Daewoo, two of Korea's largest chaebols, became close personal friends of Park (Kohli 2004, 97). At least by their own perception, Korean business leaders had a very strong influence on economic policy in the 1960s and 1970s.[4]

As is typical for developing countries, Korea's manufacturing sector had mixed interests regarding the exchange rate level. Korean manufacturing was tradable, and a sizable share of manufactured production was exported. In 1968, for example, exports accounted for 37% of the value-added of the manufacturing sector (Cole and Lyman 1971, 154). Although import barriers were high for consumer goods, these were precisely the goods that faced competition in foreign export markets; producers of intermediate manufactured goods were much less protected and had to compete with foreign producers for domestic market share (Cho 1994, 153). Korea's manufacturing sector was also heavily reliant on imported inputs. Data from the 1960s and early 1970s indicates that imported inputs accounted for about 25% of total manufactured production (Cole and Lyman 1971, 157; Frank, Kim, and Westphal 1975, 82). Finally, Korea's manufacturing sector was highly indebted, as evidenced by a loan-to-value added ratio close to two during the Park era (Amsden 1989, 86–87; Hong and Park 1986, 169). Domestic banks were the leading source of these loans, but Korean firms also borrowed heavily from abroad; foreign borrowing even surpassed domestic bank borrowing between 1966 and 1971 (Amsden and Euh 1993, 381). As producers of tradable goods that are highly reliant on imported inputs and domestic and foreign borrowing, an undervalued exchange rate benefited Korea's manufacturing sector in some ways but harmed it in other ways.

To summarize, Park Chung Hee's eighteen-year rule featured state-controlled labor and financial systems and a powerful manufacturing sector. The conditional preference theory expects Korea's manufacturing sector to prefer an undervalued exchange rate, for them to have considerable influence on exchange rate policy, and for Korean policymakers to keep the exchange rate undervalued as a result.

The case study covers the entire period in which Park ruled Korea. The coup that brought Park to power is a useful time to begin the analysis. Not only was this a major political turning point for Korea, but it also marked an important

---

4. A survey of Korean businesses found that 43% believed that they sometimes influenced policy and 27% believed that they frequently influenced policy (Jones and Sakong 1980, 73).

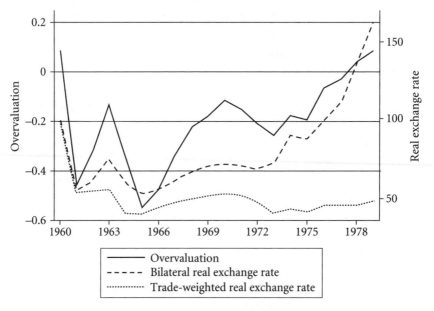

Figure 5.1. Exchange rate undervaluation in South Korea, 1960–1979. Overvaluation is defined as the difference between the actual real exchange rate and the estimated equilibrium real exchange rate. Positive (negative) values imply an overvalued (undervalued) real exchange rate. See chapter 2 for more details. Bilateral real exchange rate is defined as the natural logarithm of the nominal exchange rate divided by the GDP deflator (Heston et al. 2009). This indicator is inverted so that higher (lower) values imply a more appreciated (depreciated) real exchange rate. Trade-weighted real exchange rate is based on Darvas (2012). Both real exchange rate variables are indexed so that 1960 equals 100.

change in the country's labor and financial system. The case study ends with President Park's assassination in 1979, another event of immense consequence for South Korean politics and economics.

Figure 5.1 shows that the exchange rate was undervalued by 23% on average between 1961 and 1979. The Korean won is estimated to be undervalued for all but two years, 1978 and 1979. Although the real exchange rate appreciated sharply vis-à-vis the U.S. dollar after 1973, figure 5.1 shows that, during this period, Korea's real exchange rate appreciated hardly at all on a trade-weighted basis. Thus, the overvaluation measure may exaggerate the true extent of overvaluation in 1978 and 1979. Overall, Korea's exchange rate had a strong tendency toward undervaluation during Park Chung Hee's rule. The next sections demonstrate that Korea's state-controlled institutions and its powerful manufacturing sector contributed to this outcome.

The Shift to an Undervalued Exchange Rate: 1961–1965

In January and February 1961, Korea's exchange rate was devalued from 65 to 130 won per dollar.[5] As a result, the exchange rate was undervalued when the military took over in May of that year. Park initially kept the official exchange rate fixed against the dollar and implemented highly expansionary fiscal policies to increase economic growth. The government's budget deficits, financed by money printing, drove up inflation and, in the context of a fixed exchange rate, led to a sizable appreciation of the real exchange rate in 1962 and 1963. According to the estimates presented in figure 5.1, the exchange rate went from 48% undervalued in 1961 to only 14% undervalued in 1963.

The strengthening of the won reduced export growth. Around the same time, foreign aid to South Korea started declining. A bad harvest in 1962 required Korea to import more grain than is typical. This confluence of factors generated a sharp decline in Korea's foreign reserves. By late 1963, shortages of foreign currency created dire problems for the Korean economy. Plants could not get the imported raw materials they needed, and investment and construction projects had to be postponed. Something had to be done to deal with the impending foreign exchange crisis.

Park received no shortage of advice on how to solve the foreign exchange crisis. Leaders of some large chaebols, such as Chonusa and Samsung, encouraged Park to adopt a strategy of export promotion (Clifford 1994, 54; Kim and Park 2011, 277). The U.S. government also encouraged Park to devalue the exchange rate in order to promote exports (Collins and Park 1989, 186; Haggard, Kim, and Moon 1991, 864; Woo 1991, 78). Export promotion was not something that Park gave much thought to at the start of his term (Clifford 1994, 54; Kohli 2004, 116). But, when Korea was in dire need of foreign currency, Park decided that increasing exports was the surest solution to this problem (C. Kim 2011, 129–130). As of early 1964, the Park administration had decided that export promotion was its "foremost task" (Han 1964a).

It was in this context that Park made his first major move in exchange rate policy. On May 3, 1964, the exchange rate was devalued from 130 to 255 won/dollar, a rate at which it was kept for most of the next year. According to the president, the aim of the devaluation was to create a "realistic" (i.e., non-overvalued) exchange rate and, in turn, increase net exports (Han 1964b). This almost 100%

---

5. This section relies on Brown (1973, 131–154), Clifford (1994, 45–66), Cole and Lyman (1971), Frank, Kim, and Westphal (1975, 42–55), Haggard (1990, 61–75), Haggard, Kim, and Moon (1991), and K. S. Kim (1991).

devaluation substantially increased the degree of undervaluation of the Korean won.[6]

Most interest groups, tradable firms included, opposed this initial devaluation. Farmers opposed devaluation because it increased their fertilizer prices (Cole and Lyman 1971, 87). Similarly, many manufacturers opposed devaluation because it increased the costs of their imported inputs (Brown 1973, 138; Han 1964b, 1965; Haggard, Kim, and Moon 1991, 864; K. S. Kim 1991, 106). For example, textile firms worried that devaluation made imports of cotton, one of their main inputs, more expensive (Amsden 1989, 67). Although some large manufacturing firms supported devaluation (Haggard, Kim, and Moon 1991, 859), they were in the minority at this early stage.

The government was in a bind. It realized that an undervalued exchange rate would promote exports and generate foreign currency. But it also needed political support for its undervalued exchange rate. To this end, shortly after the May 1964 devaluation, the Park administration started to implement an array of policies that reduced industrialists' costs. In February 1965, the government lowered the interest rate on loans to exporters from 8% to 6.5%. The size of this credit subsidy grew even larger in September of that year, when the government raised interest rates for non-exporters from 16% to 26% but kept the rate for exporters at 6.5%. The government also gave exporters a variety of new tax breaks in 1965, which included duty-free imports of capital equipment and more favorable schedules for depreciating the value of their plants and equipment. Thus, although devaluation pushed up manufacturers' costs, these targeted measures "were more than offsetting compensations" (Cole and Lyman 1971, 190).

The combination of an undervalued exchange rate with targeted assistance to manufacturing exporters started to pay dividends in no time. During the second half of 1964, this policy mix caused manufactured exports to grow rapidly and the trade balance to improve (Amsden 1989, 67; Kohli 2004, 119). However, these effects started to wear off in early 1965. Although tight monetary and fiscal policies helped contain inflation, Korean prices were still increasing more quickly than U.S. prices. The resultant appreciation of the real exchange rate started to dampen the growth of exports.

On March 22, 1965, the government responded by devaluing the won from 255 to 260. The won continued depreciating against the dollar over the next six months. By August 1965, the exchange rate depreciated about 6% against the dol-

---

6. There is some dispute as to whether the exchange rate was highly undervalued at this time or only moderately undervalued, but there is little disagreement that it was, in fact, undervalued at the time. K. S. Kim (1991, 105) suggests that the new exchange rate "was considered by many to have undervalued the won slightly." By contrast, figure 5.1 suggests that the won was undervalued by a rather considerable 37% in 1964.

lar. The purpose of these additional devaluations was to "improve the balance of payments position by always maintaining a realistic exchange rate" (Han 1965).

Unlike the 1964 devaluation, the manufacturing sector did not oppose devaluation from March to August 1965. This time, far from condemning this action, the manufacturers "expressed hopes that the floating rate (more precisely, the resultant devaluation) will help to increase exports during 1965" (Han 1965). Manufacturers were receptive to devaluation in 1965, after they gained access to duty-free imports, cheap credit, and other tax breaks.

Interest group demands were not the main driving force behind Korea's initial devaluation in 1964. However, the manufacturing sector's support for undervaluation in 1965 encouraged the government to keep the exchange rate undervalued. The manufacturing sector preferred undervaluation in 1965 because the government used credit subsidies and various other targeted policies to reduce their costs. These credit subsidies were only feasible because of the state-controlled financial system. State control of finance and the manufacturers' burgeoning support for an undervalued exchange rate in 1965 laid the foundations for Korea's spectacular export-led growth.

Korea Sustains an Undervalued Exchange Rate: 1966–1970

The Park regime kept the won undervalued over the next half decade. The manufacturing sector's demands for undervaluation were an important reason why. Many manufacturing firms favored an undervalued exchange rate because the government used labor and financial controls to keep their costs low.

The won was kept very stable against the dollar at an undervalued rate throughout 1966 and 1967. Doing so was not easy. Foreign exchange was pouring into Korea because of rapid export growth and large inflows of foreign capital. To keep the exchange rate stable, the Korean authorities intervened in the foreign exchange market by purchasing foreign reserves. Their reserve holdings climbed steadily from $140 million in 1965 to $350 million in 1967 (World Bank 2010). It was also necessary to ensure that this massive increase in liquidity did not give rise to inflation, which would have eroded the won's undervaluation. The Park regime was also remarkably successful at containing inflation. But the tools they used to do so were anathema for the state-owned banks, depositors, small business, and labor.

The largest burden of sustaining an undervalued exchange rate in the late 1960s fell upon Korea's state-owned commercial banks.[7] To confront the large

---

7. For more details on financial policy in this period, see Brown (1973), Cole and Park (1983), Hong and Park (1986), K. S. Kim (1991), Park (1991), and Woo (1991, 97–110).

expansion of liquidity, the government intensified restrictions over the financial system. The required reserve ratio, the fraction of deposits that banks must hold in reserve rather than lend, was raised to astronomical levels: in February 1966, the required reserve ratio on demand deposits was raised to 35%, and it stayed there for the next three years. From October 1966 to March 1967, the marginal reserve requirement was even higher, at 50%. High reserve requirements reduced the profitability of banks because the interest that they received on these reserves (3% to 15%) was lower than the rate banks earned from making loans (up to 26%). Another way the government mopped up the excess liquidity was by forcing banks to purchase central bank bonds. These bonds, which earned a maximum interest rate of 10%, were very unattractive for the banks given that inflation averaged 12% between 1965 and 1970. Since banks would not purchase these securities voluntarily, "sales of these bonds were allocated among the banks in specified amounts in an administrative fashion" (Cole and Park 1983, 243). Starting in March 1967, banks were also forced to deposit some of their funds at a stabilization account at the central bank, a move intended to limit their ability to lend. These "repressive" financial policies prevented inflation from spiraling out of control and enabled the exchange rate to remain undervalued. Doing so, however, inflicted serious pain on the financial sector.

Financial repression was also problematic for many firms. As noted earlier, the maximum interest rate for bank loans was raised from 16% to 26% in 1965. Things got worse in 1968 when the state imposed ceilings on the total volume of lending, which meant that many firms were unable to borrow funds at all. These tight financial policies did not impact preferred borrowers—namely, large exporters in the manufacturing sector. But, nonmanufacturing firms and smaller manufacturing firms were unable to obtain affordable credit in the late 1960s.

Labor policy was also utilized to help sustain an undervalued exchange rate. The state-controlled labor regime ensured that businesses could pay their employees low wages. Slow wage growth reduced inflation, which helped sustain an undervalued exchange rate (Park 1991, 77). As a further boon for businesses, the state resorted to indirect taxation of wage income as a substitute for raising corporate taxes (Woo 1991, 159, 171). The government's cheap labor policy made it easier for Korean industrialists to successfully adapt to the new export-led development model (Kohli 2004, 98; Deyo 1989, 24; Haggard 1990, 63).

The largest and most powerful manufacturing firms could hardly have imagined a more favorable mix of policies. Exporters of manufacturing goods were guaranteed loans at the "gift rate" of 6.5%, which was below the rate of inflation and far lower than the rates available to most other firms (Hwang 1967). The government also guaranteed foreign loans for manufactured exporters. Interest rate subsidies for export-oriented industrialists were equivalent to 3% of total exports in 1965 (Frank, Kim, and Westphal 1975, 63). Repressive labor policies further lowered costs for industrial firms. The mixture of an undervalued exchange rate, labor repression, and financial repression improved the external competitiveness of manufacturers while keeping their costs down. The result was a near doubling of exports between 1965 and 1967.

These benefits led many manufacturing firms to demand a further depreciation of the exchange rate in 1967. As shown in figure 5.1, Korea's real exchange rate appreciated modestly in 1966 and 1967. The manufacturing sector wanted real appreciation to stop. According to Gilbert Brown (1973,176), many manufacturing firms were "urging further devaluation" of the exchange rate in 1967. Kwang Suk Kim (1991, 108) echoes this view: "most exporters were urging more rapid depreciation."

In December 1967, the Park government responded to these demands by shifting from a fixed exchange rate system to a crawling peg regime that steadily depreciated the won. The won depreciated about 16% against the dollar over the next three years. As a result, the real exchange rate was very stable between 1968 and 1970 (see figure 5.1). To sustain the undervalued exchange rate, the government continued accumulating foreign reserves and repressing labor and finance.

Many Korean industrialists favored an undervalued exchange rate between 1966 and 1970. What was there for them not to like? The undervalued exchange rate increased their external competitiveness, but domestic labor and financial controls kept their production costs low. The fact that manufacturing production grew at an average annual rate of 29% and exports grew at an average annual rate of 37% between 1965 and 1970 (World Bank 2010) gives a sense of how much the manufacturing sector benefited from Park's economic policies. By contrast, currency appreciation would have benefited most other interest groups: it would have boosted workers' real wages, enabled a loosening of administrative controls over banks, and helped nonpreferred firms obtain credit. President Park would have been less inclined to keep the won undervalued if the manufacturing sector also opposed this policy.

From Devaluation to Decree: 1971–1973

Korea's export-led growth model became strained in the early 1970s. Rapid increases in credit increased inflation to 16% in 1970. With prices rising more quickly than the currency was depreciating, the real exchange rate became almost as appreciated in 1970 as it was in 1963. The International Monetary Fund stepped in and encouraged Korea to follow more orthodox policies. The IMF suggested the government abandon export subsidies and devalue the exchange rate. Although Park refused to cut export subsidies, he was receptive to the IMF's exchange rate advice.

The Park administration devalued the won by 12% in July 1971. The exchange rate was then stabilized for the remainder of the year, but devalued an additional 8% against the dollar between December 1971 and July 1972. As can be seen in figure 5.1, this devaluation, coupled with the dollar's depreciation against other currencies, led to a depreciation of Korea's trade-weighted real exchange rate in the early 1970s.

Exchange rate depreciation caused many industrialists to "howl in pain" (Clifford 1994, 103). Many of Korea's large manufacturing firms had accumulated massive volumes of foreign debt in the preceding years, and the devaluation made it difficult for them to repay these debts (Frank, Kim, and Westphal 1975, 57; K. S. Kim 1991, 164; C. Kim 2011, 322; Woo 1991, 110). Firms, in desperate need of short-term funds, turned increasingly to informal, and often illegal, domestic lenders, known as the "curb market," for emergency loans. Curb market borrowing was far from an attractive alternative, however: interest rates were as high as 50% to 60% (Cole and Park 1983). In the aftermath of these devaluations, the chaebol were in serious financial trouble.

The industrialists did not take this lying down. The Federation of Korean Industrialists, which represents the large chaebols, demanded help. Although an exchange rate revaluation would have alleviated their financial problems, they did not ask the government to appreciate the won. Instead, when the Federation's chairman, Kim Yong-wan, met with President Park in June 1972, he demanded extra doses of targeted financial and fiscal relief. Specifically, Kim urged the president to nullify the high-interest curb market loan contracts, lower interest rates at the state-owned banks, and reduce corporate tax rates (B. Kim 2011; C. Kim 2011, 323–324; Kim and Park 2011; Woo 1991, 111). Kim Yong-wan "was adamant that every company in Korea would go bankrupt if something was not done to help them" (C. Kim 2011, 325).

The chaebols' warning made quite the impression on the Park administration. According to President Park's chief of staff,

> Kim [Yong-wan]'s warning of a pending economic crisis, lest the government intervene, weighed on the President's mind. It too weighed on my mind that night . . . . It was clear that if the government did not address the situation, a serious financial or industrial crisis would ensue. The financial or industrial crisis would create a chain reaction of bankruptcies of other companies and mass unemployment, seriously affecting the national economy. (C. Kim 2011, 325–326)

The Federation of Korean Industrialists was able to convince the government that all hell would break loose if political decision makers did not follow their policy prescriptions.

The industrialists' lobbying campaign worked. On August 3, 1972, President Park signed an emergency decree into law that mirrored the chaebols' demands. The government nullified all loan agreements between firms and curb market lenders. The maturity on curb market loans was extended to five years after a three-year moratorium on interest and principal payments, and interest rates were reduced to a maximum of 16% per annum. The government reduced the state-owned banks' lending rate from 19% to 15.5%. An industrial rationalization fund, which provided long-term, low-interest loans to priority sectors, was created. Corporate tax rates were reduced. The government also reduced the rate of increase of public employees' wages (Amsden 1989, 96; Cole and Park 1983, 160–163; Haggard 1994a, 32; Kohli 2004, 109; C. Kim 2011, 332–333; W. S. Kim 1991; Woo 1991, 113–115).

The decree transformed the mood in the manufacturing sector from severe despair to "great jubilation" (Ogle 1990, 43). Thanks to the decree, the large chaebols were profitable again (Cole and Park 1983, 167; Kim 1997; Woo 1991, 114). In 1973, exports increased by an astounding 73% (Amsden 1989, 96), and GDP grew an impressive 12% (World Bank 2010). Devaluation with financial repression provided windfall gains to Korea's large indebted manufacturing firms.

Not everyone was pleased with this policy package. As with Park's previous economic policies, this one proved of little use for the country's smaller firms (Kim 1997, 149; Woo 1991, 113). The biggest losers, however, were financial institutions and a "hapless stratum in society . . . the small savers," who earned low interest rates on their savings (Cole and Park 1983, 165; Choi 1993, 31; Kohli 2004, 109; Woo 1991, 113). Opposition groups accurately depicted these policies as nothing but a transfer of wealth to the chaebol (B. Kim 2011, 219–220; Kim and Park 2011, 285).

The Emergency Decree of 1972 was an extraordinary event. "There are not many countries . . . that simply erase the assets of nonbank savers with a presidential decree" (Clifford 1994, 104; see also C. Kim 2011, 331; Cole and Park 1983, 159). Kohli (2004, 109) correctly observes that these "adjustments clearly could not have been made without public control of credit." By making the decree possible, Korea's state-controlled financial structures had the important effect of convincing the manufacturing sector to support the undervalued exchange rate— support that made it more politically feasible to keep the exchange rate undervalued.

Industrialists Demand Devaluation: 1974–1979

The October 1973 oil crisis brought Korea's rapid export-led growth to a grinding halt.[8] The quadrupling of international oil prices could hardly have arrived

---

8. This section borrows heavily from Collins and Park (1989), Cooper (1994), Haggard (1994a, 1994b), W. S. Kim (1991), and Woo (1991, 118–175).

at a worse time for the Korean government. Earlier that year, the Park administration started to promote the development of heavy manufacturing industries such as steel and shipbuilding—industries that are also very energy-intensive.

President Park was adamant that the oil crisis would not reduce economic growth. To keep the economy humming, the government adopted expansionary fiscal policies. Korea also borrowed increasingly large amounts of funds from abroad to cover the costs of the country's increasingly expensive imports. The oil price rise and expansionary policies led to a sharp jump in the inflation rate, and with the exchange rate still fixed, Korea's real exchange rate appreciated as well. As a result, 1974 was the only year during Park's tenure that exports fell.

Concerned about losing their competitive edge, throughout the second half of 1974 manufacturing firms lobbied the government to devalue the exchange rate (*Far Eastern Economic Review* 1974; Haggard 1994a, 39). Their demands were satisfied in December 1974 and January 1975, when the exchange rate was devalued 21%. The devaluation was accompanied by a wide array of new supports for exporters of manufactured goods, including tax deferments and further cuts in interest rates. Most important, private firms whose dollar loans were maturing within the next three years were granted special domestic loans to compensate them for the rise in their foreign debt burdens. The government hoped that combining devaluation with increased financial assistance for manufacturing firms would reignite export-led growth (*Far Eastern Economic Review* 1974; Haggard 1994a, 35–41).

The Korean authorities kept their exchange rate fixed at 484 won per dollar from January 1975 onward. The government continued to channel large volumes of cheap credit to the manufacturing sector and to heavy industry in particular. As a result of rapid credit growth, inflation averaged 15% between 1975 and 1978. This situation, of course, meant that the won appreciated against the dollar in real terms. The estimates presented in figure 5.1 suggest that the exchange rate was about 3% overvalued by 1978. However, this figure may exaggerate the degree of overvaluation in this period. Since the dollar depreciated sharply against the Japanese yen and other currencies, the won's trade-weighted real exchange rate remained competitive between 1976 and 1978. Figure 5.1 shows that the bilateral won-dollar real exchange rate appreciated rapidly in this period, but the trade-weighted real exchange rate was very stable. By that measure, Korea's exchange rate was more undervalued in 1978 than it was in 1963. Due to the won's previous devaluation, the dollar's depreciation against the yen, and the recovery in world demand, export growth remained strong between 1975 and 1978 (Collins and Park 1989). Rapid export growth and the won's depreciation against the yen reduced private-sector demands for devaluation through 1978 (Cooper 1994, 273).

Debates about macroeconomic and exchange rate policy heated up in 1979. Hyun-Hwack Shin, a longtime advocate of macroeconomic stabilization, was elevated to the posts of economic planning minister and deputy prime minister in late 1978. Shin and his allies in the Ministry of Finance believed that inflation was Korea's most serious economic problem, and they urged President Park to adopt more restrictive macroeconomic policies. These technocrats opposed devaluation out of concern that it would exacerbate inflation. The Ministry of Commerce and Industry, however, started to worry that inflation in Korea and the depreciation of the Japanese yen were reducing the external competitiveness of their allies in the manufacturing sector. They proposed the very opposite policy mix: devaluation with lower interest rates (Haggard 1994b, 64–69).

These high-level disagreements produced sharp swings in macroeconomic policy. In April 1979, Shin adopted a stabilization plan that involved spending cuts and a credit squeeze. Then, in June 1979, when Shin was traveling abroad, the government restored preferential credit policies (Haggard 1994b, 66–67). On October 26, 1979, the head of the Korean Central Intelligence Agency assassinated Park Chung Hee. In January 1980, the transitional government adopted the devaluation that the manufacturing sector coveted. Then, in April 1981, President Chun Doo Hwan started to privatize the nation's banks. Slowly but surely, Korea started to dismantle the state-controlled institutions that underpinned the country's export-oriented exchange rate policies.

Summary of the Korean Case

Between 1961 and 1979, South Korea had state-controlled labor and financial systems and a powerful manufacturing sector. The conditional preference theory would expect Korea to undervalue its exchange rate in this period. This case study showed that Korea did, indeed, keep its exchange rate undervalued for nearly this entire period.

The Korean case also shows that institutions influence preferences. Between 1965 and 1970 and from 1974 to 1979, many Korean manufacturing firms lobbied for an undervalued exchange rate. They preferred undervaluation in large part because Korean policymakers used labor and financial controls to absolve manufacturers of most of the costs otherwise associated with an undervalued exchange rate. The 1971–1972 period provides an even clearer illustration of how state-controlled institutions increase manufacturers' support for undervaluation: Korean industrialists initially opposed devaluation, but the August 1972 decree, which reduced industrialists' borrowing costs, completely addressed their concerns about the undervalued exchange rate. The manufacturing sector would have been less supportive of undervaluation if Korea's labor and financial systems were outside the state's control.

The preferences of Korea's powerful manufacturing sector strongly influenced President Park's exchange rate policies. Although Park's initial currency devaluation in 1964 was not principally driven by interest group demands, it would have been nearly impossible for the government to sustain an undervalued exchange rate over the next dozen years without the manufacturing sector's support. The manufacturing sector warmly welcomed devaluation in 1965 and supported undervaluation in 1972 and 1973, after the government addressed some of its concerns. The manufacturing sector also lobbied for devaluations in 1969, 1974, and 1979, and in each case the government devalued the exchange rate within the next year. Given that virtually every other interest group opposed Park's financial policies, it is unlikely that the won would have remained undervalued if Korea's large, concentrated, and politically connected industrial conglomerates opposed undervaluation. State-controlled labor and financial structures and a powerful manufacturing sector both contributed to the undervaluation of the won.

The Politics of Overvaluation in Mexico, 1970–1994

The Political Sources of Exchange Rate Policy in Mexico

Mexico's 1917 constitution, signed in the aftermath of the Mexican Revolution of 1910, created a presidential system of government that concentrated decision-making authority in the executive branch of government.[9] Throughout the period under investigation, Mexico had a single-party dictatorship whereby the Institutional Revolutionary Party (*Partido Revolucionario Institucional*, PRI) used highly compromised elections and patronage to retain control of the government. Each Mexican president served a single six-year term due to a prohibition on reelection.

Mexico has strong, independent labor organizations that operate outside the state's control.[10] The 1910 revolution generated a highly organized working class with close links to the ruling party, a feature that has persisted to this day (Collier and Collier 1991). Mexico's constitution treats workers' right to organize as one of the natural rights of man; protects the right to strike; and permits

---

9. Lehoucq et al. (2008) provide a useful overview of the Mexican political system.

10. See Cook (2007), Collier and Collier (1991), and Schlagheck (1977) for more details on Mexico's labor system.

both plant- and sector-wide collective bargaining. Collective labor law has changed little since 1917, though subsequent legal changes have, if anything, further strengthened constitutional protections on organized labor. These legal protections helped labor unions develop into one of the most powerful political actors in the Mexican political system. Most Mexican unions, and about 70% of unionized workers, are associated with the dominant national labor confederation, the Confederation of Mexican Workers (*Confederación de Trabajadores de México*, CTM). The CTM has strong ties to the PRI.[11] Although there are some constraints and limitations on Mexican unions,[12] they maintain a politically advantaged position thanks to favorable laws, strong organization, and a close affiliation with the ruling party.

The state's control over the financial system has varied somewhat over time, but it has typically been limited. In the aftermath of the revolution, the Mexican state promoted the development of private banks and formed a political alliance with the banking community (Maxfield 1990; Hamilton 1982). The government also created some public banks in this period, but they accounted for less than half of financial resources by the latter half of 1960s (Maxfield 1990, 66). State-owned banks continued to decline in importance and accounted for less than 10% of bank assets in the late 1970s (Abiad, Detragiache, and Tressel 2010). "Private bankers did not consider them [state banks] a threat" because the state-owned banks did not accept deposits from the public and manufacturing firms did not rely on state banks for funding (Maxfield 1990, 63, 181; Minushkin 2002, 918). Mexican bankers were also organized into the powerful *Asociación de Bancos de México*, or ABM (Camp 1989, ch. 6; Schneider 2004, ch. 3; Maxfield 1990; Story 1986, 119–122; Minushkin 2002). It was typically the government that "needed the support of the *banqueros*," not the other way around (Minushkin 2002, 918).[13]

President López Portillo nationalized Mexico's banks in the midst of a financial crisis in 1982, which altered the relationship between the state and financiers, but considerably less than one might expect.[14] The main goal of the nationalization was to rescue the financial system from bankruptcy, not to increase the state's

---

11. Mexican labor unions retained autonomy from the state, and the state's capacity to intervene in internal union affairs has generally been limited (Collier and Collier 1991, 584–586).

12. For example, there are restrictions on unionization in the public sector and financial sector.

13. The government regulated private banks until the 1980s, but its regulations were never intense. The government avoided negative real interest rates to ensure that banks remained profitable (Kessler 1999, 36). Credit controls that were implemented were never effective because, to quote a Mexican minister of trade and industry, they "depend[ed] on the ethics of commercial banks" (quoted in Maxfield 1990, 71).

14. Most scholars emphasize continuity rather than change in state-bank relations in this period (e.g., Auerbach 2001; Kessler 1999; Maxfield 1990; Minushkin 2002).

control over the financial system (Auerbach 2001, 29; Maxfield 1990, 142). The "nationalization decree did not . . . increase state control over investment patterns through credit allocation or improve the state's financial position" because the state had neither the desire nor the ability to subordinate the financial sector in these ways (Maxfield 1990, 143). This period of nationalization was also extremely short lived. Privatization resumed in 1983, just months after the nationalization. By the late 1980s, the financial sector was deregulated, with credit controls fully banished and reserve requirements reduced. Between July 1991 and July 1992, the government sold off eighteen state-owned banks, and the state-owned banks' share of bank assets fell below 25%.[15] Throughout the 1980s, the state's control over the financial system remained limited, and Mexico officially returned to a private financial system by the early 1990s.

In addition to powerful organized labor and financial sectors, Mexico also has a powerful manufacturing sector. Mexico's industrial sector was an important supporter and beneficiary of the 1910 revolution (Story 1986, 3). Manufacturing production doubled in the thirty years following the revolution (1910–1940) and doubled again in the 1940s (Carrillo Arronte 1987). By 1970, the manufacturing sector contributed 23% of GDP and has remained close to that level since. The manufacturing sector controls a large share of Mexico's economic resources.

The Mexican manufacturing sector also has impressive organizational resources. Manufacturing production is highly concentrated geographically, with most production occurring in Guadalajara, Mexico City, and Monterrey. Industrial output is also concentrated in a relatively small number of firms.[16] This concentration should help Mexican industrialists overcome their collective action costs and lobby for favorable economic policies. Manufacturing firms have formed a medley of lobbying groups that include both compulsory corporatist-style organizations and those based on voluntary membership.[17] Many of these lobby groups have extraordinary access to top officials in the Mexican government, and policymakers frequently consult these groups before changing economic policy. Because of the important voice that business associations have over the selection of cabinet officials, and even PRI presidential candidates, "ambitious officials will, as they contemplate future promotions, court business support and be more at-

---

15. Abiad, Detragiache, and Tressel (2010) report that state-owned banks' share is either below 10% or between 10% and 25% for the 1991–2006 period. Micco, Panizza, and Yañez (2007) report a range of zero to 24% for 1995–2003.

16. In 1980, fewer than 3% of firms were responsible for 77% of the value-added in industry (Story 1986, 29).

17. Schneider (2004), Camp (1989) and Story (1986) provide excellent descriptions of business-government relations in Mexico.

tentive to their views on policy" (Schneider 2004, 72).[18] Although they are not the only influential group in the Mexican political system, the manufacturing sector is second to none. Mexican policymakers have strong incentives to adopt exchange rate policies favored by the manufacturing sector.

The exchange rate preferences of the manufacturing sector are influenced by their tradability as well as their high reliance on imported inputs and debt. First, Mexican manufacturing products were at least partially tradable throughout the 1970–1994 period. Although Mexico's manufacturing sector did not export a large share of its production for most of this period, this was largely due to exchange rate overvaluation (Balassa 1983, 803–805; Story 1986, 37). The manufacturing sector has also been exposed to competition in the home market since at least 1986, when Mexico joined the General Agreement on Tariffs and Trade and liberalized trade. Even before 1986, Mexico's import barriers were lower than most developing countries, and trade was relatively free for intermediate goods and traditional consumer goods such as textiles (Aspe 1993, 150–152; Frieden 1991b, 193; Reynolds 1978, 1009). Overall, consumer durable manufacturing was partially tradable before 1986 and fully tradable after; the rest of Mexico's manufacturing sector had high levels of tradability throughout the period under consideration. Second, Mexico's manufacturing sector is highly reliant on imported inputs into production (Kessler 1999, 105; Maxfield 1990, 109–113; Story 1986, 29). One survey in 1980 found that 47.5% of industrial firms purchased raw materials from abroad (Story 1986, 114). Third, Mexican manufacturers borrow from domestic and international banks to finance their investments. The industrial sector is the largest recipient of private commercial bank loans (Maxfield 1990, 106). Moreover, a large share of their debt is denominated in foreign currency (Frieden 1991b, 190–194; Kessler 1999, 112; Maxfield 1990, 104; Story 1986, 114). Because of these attributes, an undervalued exchange rate should have a mixture of positive and negative effects on Mexico's manufacturing sector.

To summarize, Mexico has privately controlled labor and financial systems and a manufacturing sector that controls a plethora of power resources. The conditional preference theory therefore anticipates that Mexican manufacturing firms do not usually favor undervalued exchange rates, and that this preference discourages Mexican policymakers from undervaluing the peso.

We now turn to twenty-five years of Mexican political history to test these hypotheses. The analyses cover four presidential administrations, from Luis Echeverría's inauguration in 1970 through the end of the administration of Carlos

---

18. According to survey data, Mexican industrialists believe that they are able to influence government policy (Camp 1989, ch. 6; Story 1986, 119–122).

Salinas in 1994. Echeverría's presidency is a suitable time to start the case study because his administration inaugurated a new development strategy known as "shared development." This shift was a response to the perceived failings of the PRI's previous "stabilizing development" model. The so-called stabilizing development model contributed to rising social unrest, which culminated in violent confrontations between protestors and the state in 1968.[19] The violence in October 1968 was a "watershed in Mexican politics" (Camp 1989, 24), which convinced Echeverría to shift development models. The case study ends with another period of political and economic change: a financial crisis that coincided with the end of Salinas's six-year term.

Figure 5.2 presents data on the degree of overvaluation in Mexico during this period. According to this measure, Mexico's exchange rate was 2.5% undervalued on average between 1970 and 1994. In this case, the average does not provide an accurate indication of Mexico's exchange rate level in the "typical" year. Mexico's exchange rate was highly undervalued on two occasions: during the 1976–1977 financial crisis and throughout the debt crisis of 1982–1989. The average undervaluation during those ten years was 19%. I will show that the depreciations of 1976–1977 and 1982–1983 occurred in spite of concerted attempts by policymakers to avoid this outcome, and the government felt it had little choice but to undervalue the peso after 1983, when it was in default on its foreign debts. During the remaining fifteen years, Mexico's exchange rate had a strong tendency toward overvaluation, and was 9% overvalued on average. In fact, this measure probably understates the degree of overvaluation in some of these periods: it is likely that Mexico's exchange rate was overvalued throughout the 1970–1975 period and became overvalued again shortly thereafter.

Mexico's real exchange rate displayed a strong and persistent tendency to appreciate during this period. As can be seen in figure 5.2, the real exchange rate rapidly appreciated in 1972–1975, 1977–1981, and 1987–1993. In the median year during this sample period, Mexico's real exchange rate appreciated 11%.[20]

Overall, between 1970 and 1994, Mexico's frequent overvaluations could hardly look more different from China's long-standing undervaluation or the constant undervaluation of South Korea's won between 1961 and 1977. Although Mexico's exchange rate was not as overvalued as Argentina's, its frequent real exchange rate appreciations closely resemble what we observed in Argentina in chapter 4. Indeed, during three of the four presidential administrations, the real exchange rate steadily appreciated and became overvalued. Mexico's exchange rate displayed

19. For more information on the stabilizing development model, see Balassa (1983), Buffie and Krause (1989), Reynolds (1978), and Solís (1981, 1–38).

20. The pattern looks very similar using Darvas's (2012) trade-weighted measure of the real exchange rate, which has a 0.92 correlation with the real exchange rate series from figure 5.2.

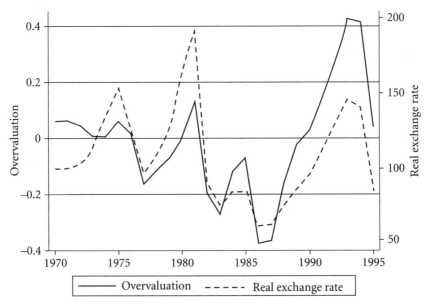

Figure 5.2. Exchange rate overvaluation in Mexico, 1970–1995. Overvaluation is defined as the difference between the actual real exchange rate and the estimated equilibrium real exchange rate. Positive (negative) values imply an overvalued (undervalued) real exchange rate. See chapter 2 for more details. Real exchange rate is defined as the natural logarithm of the nominal exchange rate divided by the GDP deflator (Heston et al. 2009). This indicator is inverted so that higher (lower) values imply a more appreciated (depreciated) real exchange rate. It is indexed so that 1970 equals 100.

a strong tendency toward overvaluation during the twenty-five years covered in this case study.

"Shared Development" with an Overvalued Exchange Rate: 1970–1976

When Luis Echeverría became the president of Mexico on December 1, 1970, the peso had been fixed against the dollar at a rate of 12.5-to-1 since 1954.[21] Over that sixteen-year period, Mexico's real exchange rate appreciated 42% because inflation, though low, exceeded U.S. inflation rates. By the time Echeverria entered

---

21. This section borrows from the following sources: Bazdresch and Levy (1991), Frieden (1991b, 196–197), Heath (1999, 18–20), Kessler (1999, 17–29), Maxfield (1990, 59–94), Ortiz and Solís (1979), Schlagheck (1977), Solís (1981), and Thompson (1979, 189–209).

office, the peso was mildly overvalued.[22] Overvaluation had already contributed to a burgeoning trade deficit and rising underemployment prior to 1970 (Reynolds 1978; Solís 1981).

Following destabilizing protests in 1968, Echeverría and the PRI were concerned that social unrest threatened their rule. Echeverría proposed a program of "shared development" to try and mitigate this potential threat. The program aimed to continue his predecessors' efforts to promote growth and industrialization—that is, "development"—but also sought to promote a more equitable income distribution—the "shared" part. Echeverría, therefore, sought to reach out to previously marginalized groups while continuing to receive support from industrialists. The president solicited industrialists' input both during and after his presidential campaign, and he was especially interested in assisting this sector's smaller, domestically oriented firms (Solís 1981, 41).

Early in Echeverría's term, a vigorous debate over exchange rate policy emerged within the government. When America devalued the dollar vis-à-vis gold in August 1971, a group of officials, led by Leopoldo Solís, the head of the Economic Programming Directorate of the Secretariat of the Presidency, argued that Mexico should devalue, too.[23] Solís claimed that devaluation was necessary because the peso was overvalued, and overvaluation was creating problems, such as trade deficits, that would only worsen over time. He argued that devaluation would improve the trade balance as well as the state's fiscal position because it would allow the government to increase taxes on tradable businesses. Moreover, Solís claimed that the timing was ideal: his internal memo proposed that the government tell the public that "it is the dollar's instability and U.S. inflation that make the measure imperative. The government would thus avoid paying the internal political price of unilateral devaluation, which will occur in the future if our balance of payments is not improved (but then we would not be able to blame anyone)" (quoted in Solís 1981, 59). Mexico's finance minister and central bank disagreed. They argued that the fixed and overvalued exchange rate should continue because it provides important benefits, such as helping maintain price stability.

Solís and the proponents of undervaluation were unable to convince Echeverría. Echeverría feared that devaluation would lead to labor unrest, just as it did when Mexico devalued in 1954 (Solís 1981, 40). In addition, a survey conducted by the Echeverría government revealed strong business support for the fixed exchange rate: they found that "the interviewed entrepreneurs share the opinion that private investment . . . has been stimulated in the last decade by the . . . [m]aintenance of

---

22. Figure 5.2 suggests the exchange rate was 5% overvalued. Many observers agree that Mexico's exchange rate was modestly overvalued as of 1970 (Balassa 1983, 800; Reynolds 1978, 1009; Solís 1981, 26–30; Thompson 1979, 93).

23. Solís provides a detailed, if biased, account of this debate in his 1981 book (pp. 57–62).

exchange parity" (Solís 1981, 207). The president decided against devaluation because his coalition of manufacturing businesses and workers opposed this option.

Initially, Echeverría's macroeconomic policies were relatively conservative, but fiscal and monetary policies shifted in a decidedly expansionary direction in 1972. To finance higher spending on health, education, and other social policies, the Echeverría administration attempted to raise taxes in late 1972. But the unified opposition of business groups—including those representing manufacturing firms—convinced the government to back down. An increasing budget deficit and lower interest rates caused inflation to reach double-digits by 1973. It also led to an intensification of demands from labor unions to increase their salaries. The CTM demanded 20% wage increases, and a full 20% wage increase was granted after a weeklong strike in September 1973. Labor unions used similar tactics again in 1974 and won another wage increase that averaged 22%. The result was a substantial improvement in workers' real wages but also a wage-price spiral that caused inflation to increase to 23% in 1974 (Kessler 1999, 36; Schlagheck 1977, 60–64; Solís 1981, 80).

The real exchange rate, already overvalued at the start of Echeverría's term, appreciated an additional 25% in 1973 and 1974 as a result of inflationary policies combined with a fixed exchange rate (see figure 5.2). Although figure 5.2 concurs that the exchange rate was overvalued in 1975, it fails to capture what most observers consider to be a rapidly increasing degree of overvaluation.[24] There is widespread agreement among experts on the Mexican economy that the peso became highly overvalued in the latter part of Echeverría's term (Balassa 1983, 803; Bazdresch and Levy 1991, 242; Buffie and Krause 1989, 146; Dornbusch 1988, 250; Heath 1999, 19; Maxfield 1990, 75; Reynolds 1978, 1014; Thompson 1979, 189).

Inflation and exchange rate overvaluation were taking a serious toll on the Mexican economy by 1975. For instance, due to rapid import growth, the trade deficit doubled in size between 1971 and 1974. In response, a stabilization plan was implemented in 1975, which helped bring inflation down to 15%. Nevertheless, the plan lacked the stringency needed to effectively tackle the economy's problems. The government also undertook an "aggressive trade improvement campaign" to improve the trade balance: import duties were raised to curb imports and taxes on exports were reduced (Schlagheck 1977, 48; Solís 1981, 46). But one

---

24. The overvaluation measure presented in figure 5.2 misses this increased overvaluation because large numbers of countries had overvalued exchange rates in this period, a dynamic that creates the false impression that Mexico's currency was not becoming increasingly overvalued. Due to the use of year fixed-effects in the construction of the overvaluation measure, the average degree of over/undervaluation in the developing world is zero for *each year*. If overvaluation were measured in the same way except without year fixed-effects, Mexico's exchange rate would be estimated to be 23% overvalued in 1974.

effective tool of export promotion—exchange rate devaluation—was conspicuously absent from this package.

As the peso grew more overvalued, capital flight mounted and the central bank started to bleed reserves. By the middle of 1976, reserves were almost completely depleted. In September 1976, the government had little choice but to devalue the peso for the first time in twenty-two years. The peso depreciated by more than 60% in that month.

Echeverría "refused to take any needed actions to complement the devaluation" and instead "he allowed for wage settlements with gains in excess of 20 per cent" (Thompson 1979, 207; Collier and Collier 1991, 592; Schlagheck 1977, 64). The devaluation alone would have been painful enough for businesses that saw their imported input costs and foreign debt burdens increase. The wage increase poured salt in their wounds by further adding to their expenses and increasing inflation more generally (Ortiz and Solís 1979; Schlagheck 1977, 67). James Schlagheck (1977, 67) describes the effect on Mexico's automobile industry: the devaluation "sent the cost of imported inputs, including auto parts, soaring . . . . The result was that auto companies' costs rose immediately—and then rose further as labor tried to catch up with higher wages." By the time his *sexenio* ended in November 1976, the entire manufacturing sector opposed Echeverría and his policies (Camp 1989, 162; Story 1986, 97, 152).[25]

This case illustrates why the manufacturing sector is unlikely to prefer an undervalued exchange rate in non-state-controlled labor systems. Most manufacturers supported the fixed and overvalued exchange rate that prevailed during Echeverría's term. By contrast, the manufacturing sector opposed the 1976 devaluation. Labor market institutions were partly responsible for manufacturers' opposition to undervaluation: the 1976 devaluation was especially costly for industrialists because it was accompanied by wage increases. These wage increases would have been less likely if the Mexican state controlled labor.

This case also supports my argument that the preferences of powerful manufacturing sectors influence exchange rate policy. Manufacturing firms were among the main interest groups whose opposition discouraged Echeverría from devaluing during his first five years as president. The manufacturing sector also helped prevent taxes from increasing, which contributed indirectly to overvaluation as well because it increased the budget deficit and, in turn, inflation. The manufacturing sector's preferences cannot fully explain why the exchange rate became overvalued; much of the overvaluation in this period was driven by high spending policies, which Echeverría adopted in order to improve income distribution and minimize social unrest. But, if manufacturers were less hostile to devaluation or

---

25. For most of the 1970–1975 period, smaller manufacturing firms strongly supported Echeverría.

contractionary fiscal policies, the real exchange rate would probably not have appreciated as rapidly during Echeverría's tenure.

The Alliance for Production and Against Devaluation: 1977–1982

Mexico was in crisis mode when José López Portillo assumed the presidency on December 1, 1976.[26] López Portillo inherited an undervalued exchange rate and an economic stabilization plan established as part of an IMF agreement. He was a technocrat who lacked a strong political base of his own (Story 1986, 151). Moreover, political tensions were high. Rumors of a military coup circulated.

López Portillo's first priority was to repair relations with the business community. In his inaugural address, the president invited business and labor to join the government in an "alliance for production." This initial charm offensive worked, especially with the larger firms. Business groups, including the peak industrial association (CONCAMIN) and the chamber of commerce (CONCANACO), strongly supported López Portillo (Camp 1989, 27; Escobar Toledo 1987, 66; Schneider 2004, 84).

The peso was finally stabilized against the dollar starting around March 1977. The Mexican government decided to fix to the dollar to reestablish monetary stability. The new exchange rate regime was slightly more flexible than before, with the peso allowed to depreciate against the dollar by a small fraction each day. The amount of depreciation was tiny though: depreciation totaled 0.2% over the next twelve months. López Portillo also adopted restrictive monetary and fiscal policies in his first year in office. He also convinced labor to exercise restraint, and workers' wages rose more slowly than inflation in 1977 and 1978 (Collier and Collier 1991, 592). The trade balance dramatically improved as a result.

The massive increase in international oil prices in 1978–1979 had a major impact on Mexico, which had started producing large volumes of oil in the preceding years. This led to a vigorous debate over whether Mexico should save or spend its oil revenues. Proponents of spending, which included CONCAMIN, CONCANACO, and the labor unions, easily carried the day, and fiscal restraint was recklessly abandoned. Incredibly, government spending increased even faster than government revenues. The government started borrowing large amounts from abroad to finance the ballooning budget deficit. Consequently, inflation accelerated from its nadir of 17.5% in 1978 to 26% in 1980.

---

26. The main sources for this section are Bazdresch and Levy (1991, 246–252), Escobar Toledo (1987), Frieden (1991b, 190–199, 217–220), Heath (1999, 20–22), Kessler (1999, 29–35), Lustig (1992, 20–27), Maxfield (1990), Ortiz and Solís (1979), and Story (1986).

Since the exchange rate depreciated far slower than inflation—depreciation averaged 0.06% per month during the period from 1978 to 1980—the real exchange rate appreciated rapidly. The real exchange rate appreciated 99.8% between 1977 and 1981. There is some debate as to when exactly the peso became overvalued. Figure 5.2 suggests overvaluation did not occur until 1981, though the biases in this measure, which were discussed in chapter 2, suggest that the peso was probably overvalued earlier than that. At the other extreme, some observers considered the peso to be overvalued as early as 1978 (Maxfield 1990, 129). Though the precise timing of overvaluation is hard to pinpoint, most experts agree that the peso had become "badly overvalued" by the early 1980s (Kaufman, Bazdresch, and Heredia 1994, 365).[27]

López Portillo's mixture of a fixed-overvalued exchange rate with expansionary macroeconomic policies had few detractors—at least in the short term. The three most important constituencies in the PRI—labor, finance, and manufacturing— all benefited from this policy mix. Workers were satisfied because high spending boosted employment and the overvalued exchange rate increased their purchasing power (Bazdresch and Levy 1991, 252). Mexican banks profited handsomely from their ability to intermediate large volumes of funds between foreign and domestic financial markets (Frieden 1991b, 198; Maxfield 1990, 100–101). Finally, industry "was pleased by an overvalued exchange rate and the sizable profits that could be made in the domestic market" (Bazdresch and Levy 1991, 253). This was particularly true of large firms producing heavy industrial goods. For example, while manufacturing production grew 38% between 1978 and 1981, consumer durable production increased 69% (Frieden 1991b, 197). One of the reasons that large capital-intensive industrialists were so content with the peso's overvaluation is that it gave them access to cheap international borrowing—a privilege they made extensive use of. Fiscal policy also targeted these firms for special treatment, and they benefited from tax credits, subsidies on input costs, and government purchase orders. A survey of industrialists in the early 1980s found widespread enthusiasm for López Portillo, with 64% of firms responding that they were satisfied with his policies (Story 1986, 123).

Nevertheless, a small number of economists and technocrats advocated changing exchange rate policy. In 1979, two central bank officials published an article

---

27. Bazdresch and Levy (1991, 250–253), Dornbusch (1988, 244), Heath (1999, 20), Kessler (1999, 33), Story (1986, 37), Pepinsky (2009, 252), and Zamora (1984, 102) all concur that the exchange rate was overvalued during López Portillo's term, though they do not specify particular dates. Lustig (1992, 151) reports an estimate of 25% overvaluation in 1980. Buffie and Krause (1989, 166) assert that "the peso was heavily overvalued between 1979 and 1981." Balassa (1983, 807) suggests that prior to devaluation in 1982, there was a "long-standing overvaluation of the peso," indicating that he believed the peso became overvalued well before 1981.

in which they warned of the "risk of overvaluation" and "insist[ed] on the importance of avoiding an overvalued exchange rate and its depressing effect on employment and economic activity" (Ortiz and Solís 1979, 539, 541). These officials went on to propose depreciating the exchange rate under a crawling peg regime "to insure the correct valuation of the exchange rate" (Ortiz and Solís 1979, 540). In 1980, the influential economist Bela Balassa told government officials that they "need . . . to accept exchange rate changes for the sake of improving the competitiveness of the non-oil sector" (quoted in Balassa 1983, 806). The finance minister and central bank's director also tried to convince the president to devalue in 1980. They were opposed by the Ministry of National Patrimony and Industrial Development, charged with the well-being of the manufacturing sector, and Miguel de la Madrid, a politically ambitious minister of budget and planning (Maxfield 1990, 129). The opponents of devaluation carried the day in 1980, just as they did in 1971.

Mexico's economy became more strained in 1981. Falling oil prices led to a reduction in government revenues. Rising U.S. interest rates made foreign borrowing more expensive. This had remarkably little effect on macroeconomic policy at first. In 1981, the government continued to increase foreign borrowing, mostly at short maturities and at variable interest rates. Manufacturers started to become more concerned about the economy's lack of external competitiveness. The peak industrial association (CONCAMIN) and the association that represents small manufacturing firms (CANACINTRA) lobbied the government to promote manufactured exports. The López Portillo administration responded by raising tariffs, creating export promotion committees, and announcing a credit fund to support exporters (Story 1986, 159; Bazdresch and Levy 1991).

In the absence of societal demands for changing exchange rate policy, the government, once again, decided against devaluation in 1981. Instead López Portillo gave a speech toward the end of the year in which he promised to defend the peso "like a dog" (Kessler 1999, 34). López Portillo did, however, let the peso start to crawl more rapidly, and the exchange rate depreciated by 11% during that year. But with inflation over 25%, the real exchange rate continued to appreciate. The peso was far more overvalued in 1981 than it was during Echeverría's tenure (see figure 5.2).

Capital flight continued and the central bank's coffers were nearly empty in early 1982. With no reserves left to defend the currency, the exchange rate devalued rapidly in February and March of 1982. The aftermath of the February 1982 devaluation followed the playbook of the 1976 devaluation. Labor unions insisted on wage increases to restore their purchasing power, and "instead of following up [the devaluation] with an orthodox adjustment program, the government announced an emergency salary increase in March, which increased the government's payroll and exacerbated inflationary expectations" (Heath 1999, 22; Lustig 1992, 25). The devaluation also "devastated the private sector" (Kessler 1999, 65; Zamora 1984). Devaluation made it much harder for manufacturing firms to service their sizable foreign debts and to purchase imported inputs. Perhaps their biggest complaint, however, was the 30% wage increase that accompanied the devaluation (Story 1986, 30, 160).

The government was able to limit the exchange rate's depreciation over the next few months, but then in August 1982 the exchange rate devalued another 60% and a dual exchange rate system was introduced. That same month, the Mexican government declared that it was suspending its payments on its foreign debts. This was followed by an even more shocking act on September 1: nationalization of the banking system. While some smaller firms that had difficulty obtaining credit were happy with bank nationalization, most manufacturing firms were furious with López Portillo's financial policies in 1982. López Portillo left office as unpopular as his predecessor.

In short, López Portillo's macroeconomic policies were "an attempt to 'please all'" (Bazdresch and Levy 1991, 252). Real exchange rate appreciation was one policy that pleased many interest groups, including the manufacturing sector. Opposition to undervaluation from large manufacturing firms helps explain why the peso became overvalued in this period.

Exchange Rate Policy during the Debt Crisis: 1983–1986

When Miguel de la Madrid became President in December 1982 he faced many of the same challenges that López Portillo faced six years earlier.[28] The scale of these problems was much more severe this time, however. In 1976, the peso depreciated 62% and consumer price inflation was 16%. In 1982, the peso depreciated over 200% and inflation was 59%. The international economic environment was also far less benign in 1982, as Mexico faced declining prices for its oil exports and was in default on its foreign debts.

The intense economic constraints of the debt crisis influenced de la Madrid's exchange rate policies. Because of the country's reliance on global capital markets, "Mexico needed to maintain good relations with the U.S. and the American financial community" (Aggarwal 1996, 337). In this situation, staying in good standing with Mexico's external creditors left de la Madrid little choice but to keep the exchange rate weak to increase non-oil exports and earn foreign currency

---

28. This section borrows from Aspe (1993), Flores Quiroga (2001), Heath (1999, 20–30), Kessler (1999, 49–78), Lustig (1992), Minushkin (2002), Schamis (1999, 252–254), Story (1986), and Ten Kate (1992).

(Dornbusch 1997, 127; Lustig 1992, 45–46). Although domestic political interests may not have been the primary driver of Mexico's undervalued exchange rate
in this period, the way that this policy was implemented reflected the preferences
of Mexican manufacturing firms.

Restoring a good relationship with business was de la Madrid's top political
priority. In this regard, de la Madrid started off on a positive note. In his previous role as budget and planning minister, he defended industrialists' interests; his
previous opposition to devaluation provides one example. Now, as Mexico's president, de la Madrid sought to solidify his relationship with business, particularly
finance and large manufacturing firms, two powerful actors that had grown dis-
illusioned with the PRI (Kessler 1999, 52; Minushkin 2002; Schamis 1999, 253).

The new president's initial economic priorities were to reduce inflation and
maintain a "realistic exchange rate" in order to promote exports (Story 1986, 162–
163). To this end, he implemented fiscal austerity and further exchange rate depreciations. These actions succeeded in depreciating the real exchange rate during his first year in office, and the undervalued exchange rate helped manufactured
exports recover.

As part of his coalition-building strategy, fiscal and exchange rate policies were
designed to ensure that the burden of fiscal austerity and undervaluation did not
fall on de la Madrid's big business allies. Spending cuts throughout his term were
focused on social spending (Kessler 1999, 53). To blunt the negative impact of
the undervalued exchange rate, in April 1983, the government launched a program called Ficorca that allowed private firms to pay off their foreign debts at a
more appreciated exchange rate than the one prevailing at the time.[29] The de la
Madrid administration, therefore, ensured that the undervalued exchange rate did
not increase large companies' foreign debt burdens. Although devaluation initially made private firms' debts "unbearably burdensome," Ficorca and other debt
relief programs made these burdens more bearable (Zamora 1984, 134). During
this period, the "weak peso increased foreign sales but also increased real foreign
debt. As long as Ficorca protected the largest firms from surges in foreign-
denominated debt obligations, they benefited from the floating exchange rate"
(Kessler 1999, 66). The selective nature of fiscal and exchange rate policy in
Mexico in the 1980s was aimed at maintaining the support of powerful interest
groups, and no group received more assistance than indebted manufacturing
firms (Kessler 1999, 53).

Even with these targeted compensations, sustaining the undervalued exchange
rate was politically difficult. The deep economic contraction—per capita income

---

29. Ficorca was a complicated program that involved a variety of different arrangements for different firms. Zamora (1984) provides a detailed description.

fell more than 8% in 1983—made it difficult to stick with tight fiscal policies. Feeling pressure to promote growth in 1984, de la Madrid adopted more expansionary fiscal policy (Camp 1989, 31). He also slowed the rate of depreciation to prevent inflation from increasing. Thus, the real exchange rate appreciated 14% in 1984 and 1985, wiping away much of the competitive advantage accrued in 1983 (when the real exchange depreciated 18%).

The Mexican economy experienced another set of negative shocks in 1985–1986. In September 1985, an earthquake inflicted serious damage on Mexico City. The IMF decided to stop disbursing loans to Mexico around the same time. Next, in 1986, a sharp decline in international oil prices left Mexico short of foreign-currency revenues and "forced the government to increase the peso's controlled devaluation" (Minushkin 2002, 931). Thus, in a seesaw-like fashion, the real exchange rate resumed its depreciation in 1986. This post-1985 shift in exchange rate policy was accompanied by additional measures of trade liberalization and financial liberalization to build support among export-oriented manufacturers and the financial sector, respectively (Ten Kate 1992; Kessler 1999; Minushkin 2002; Schamis 1999).

De la Madrid adopted very different exchange rate policies from the other three Mexican presidents considered in this chapter. Between 1982 and 1986, exchange rate policy shifted more frequently and lacked the steady trend of real appreciation that occurred under Echeverría, López Portillo, and Salinas. Mexico's dire need to generate export revenues in the midst of the debt crisis goes a long way toward explaining why de la Madrid undervalued the peso. However, undervaluation also required support from powerful interest groups, which de la Madrid gained by providing targeted financial assistance. These actions support my argument that state intervention in domestic financial markets increases support for undervaluation. On the other hand, the conditional preference theory posits that states, such as Mexico, that lack extensive control over the financial sector have difficulty maintaining these types of interventionist policies. One lesson of this case is that extreme economic conditions—in this case, a debt crisis—can enable policymakers to temporarily adopt financial policies that are not feasible in more normal circumstances.

The Domestic Politics of Overvaluation and the Tequila Crisis: 1987–1994

The Mexican economy remained troubled in 1987. Inflation accelerated throughout the year and the peso-dollar exchange rate continued to depreciate. Starting in July 1987, major business leaders discussed options for stabilizing the economy, and tripartite negotiations were held between the government, business, and labor.

The end result of these negotiations was the Pact for Economic Solidarity, signed by these three parties in December 1987.[30] The pact included a devaluation of nearly 20% that was followed by fixing the peso-dollar exchange rate in February 1988. Thanks to depreciation over the previous five years, the peso was considerably undervalued by the end of 1987 (see figure 5.2). To compensate for devaluation, workers received an immediate wage increase of 15% and another 20% increase on January 1, 1988, which was followed by a wage freeze in most sectors. Business pledged to freeze prices. The government committed to continue cutting expenditures and liberalizing international trade.

The Pact for Economic Solidarity was successful in reducing inflation. Inflation, which topped 100% in 1988, fell to 27% by 1989. However, with inflation still far above international levels, the 1987 pact contributed to a substantial appreciation of the real exchange rate. In January 1988, a number of major business associations complained about the real exchange rate's appreciation. However, these complaints ceased almost entirely after February, when the peso became fully fixed against the dollar and other follow-up agreements were concluded (Kaufman, Bazdresch, and Heredia 1994, 391–392).

During 1988, attention shifted to the impending presidential election. After consulting with business groups, de la Madrid selected Carlos Salinas to succeed him as the PRI candidate (Schneider 2004, 79). Salinas won the 1988 election, but hard economic times strengthened the opposition, and this election was more difficult for the PRI than previous contests (Heath 1999, 29–30; Kessler 1999, 82–83).

Salinas sought to continue to liberalize and stabilize the Mexican economy. The president recognized that doing so required the construction of a new center-right coalition. Salinas courted two groups in particular: large manufacturing firms, particularly export-oriented factories in Northern Mexico; and the private financial sector (Dresser 1997; Kessler 1999, 84–86; Minushkin 2002; Schamis 1999). As part of his effort to win over big business, Salinas asked a former president of the *Consejo Coordinador Empresarial* (CCE), an association whose members include large firms and other business groups (e.g., CONCANACO and CONCAMIN), to become his adviser. Top administration officials also held monthly meetings with CCE leaders (Schamis 1999, 255; Schneider 2004, 85).

By the time of Salinas's inauguration in December 1988, the exchange rate was still undervalued, but not by much (see figure 5.2). Although inflation steadily decreased over this period, inflation remained in the double-digits throughout 1989–1992. Salinas sought to strike a better balance between fighting inflation and preserving the economy's external competitiveness. To this end, in January 1989, he

---

30. Aspe (1993, 23–54), Kaufman, Bazdresch, and Heredia (1994), and Lustig (1992, 50–54) describe the pact in detail.

adopted a crawling peg regime that depreciated the peso by up to one peso per day. In January 1990, the crawling band was narrowed to 80 centavos (cents)/day. By the end of 1991, the band decreased to 20 cents/day (Aspe 1993, 25–26). The nominal exchange rate depreciated by 14% during 1990, 7% in 1991, and 2.5% in 1992. Thus, exchange rate depreciations reduced the pace of real appreciation, but were too small to stop it altogether. By 1992, the peso had become highly overvalued.[31]

Large foreign capital inflows were required to cover the current account deficit. These capital inflows came primarily in the form of short-term investments, with investors attracted by Mexico's high interest rates and recent capital account liberalization. These inflows had a dark side, however: they put additional upward pressure on the exchange rate. So, a stable nominal exchange rate and financial liberalization contributed to a substantial real exchange rate appreciation in the early 1990s.

A debate over exchange rate policy erupted in 1992 when the problem of overvaluation became increasingly apparent. A number of external actors raised concerns that the overvalued exchange rate, trade deficit, and heavy reliance on volatile international capital flows were making the Mexican economy susceptible to a balance-of-payments crisis. Renowned MIT economist Rudiger Dornbusch wrote in 1992 that "the current problem of the Mexican economy is the overvalued exchange rate"; thus, Dornbusch advocated increasing the rate of devaluation to 1.2 pesos/day (Edwards 1997, 107; Flores Quiroga 2001). The World Bank also counseled Mexico to depreciate the peso more rapidly in 1992 (Burki 1997, 249–250; Edwards 1997, 107).

The Salinas administration debated devaluing the exchange rate in the spring of 1993, but decided against doing so (Dornbusch 1997, 131). Government officials presented a variety of dubious arguments to defend this decision, which included denying that the exchange rate was overvalued and arguing that market reforms would soon make Mexican firms more productive and allow them to narrow the trade deficit.[32] Another argument that the government made in defense of its policies was that social groups did not find the overvalued exchange rate problematic (Gil-Díaz and Carstens 1997). In fact, opposition to depreciation from powerful interest groups was almost certainly the main reason that Mexican policymakers chose to ignore outsiders' advice to devalue the peso.

---

31. According to figure 5.2, the exchange rate was 26% overvalued in 1992. Dornbusch (1997, 127), Dresser (1997, 65), Edwards (1997, 97), Heath (1999: 37), Kessler (1999, 109–110), Naím (1997, 299), Pepinsky (2009, 259), and Ramírez de la O (1996, 14) all describe the peso as overvalued in the early 1990s. The sizable trade deficit, equal to 5% of GDP, in 1992 (World Bank 2010), is further evidence of overvaluation.

32. Aspe (1993) and Gil-Díaz and Carstens (1997) present some of these official views. Burki (1997), Dornbusch (1997), and Edwards (1997) effectively critique the government's arguments.

Almost all of PRI's main constituents supported the overvalued exchange rate. As Kessler (1999, 111) explains:

> The primary reason for Salinas's apparently deliberate strategy to over-value the peso was that virtually all of the domestic interests that exercised influence over the PRI's political future were united, either implicitly or explicitly, in their support of the status quo. For bankers and large industrialists, the middle class, and workers, Mexico's crawling peg provided important economic benefits. Searching for a way to satisfy such disparate groups, the ruling party found itself under intense pressure to maintain an increasingly unsustainable 'please all' exchange rate policy. What is remarkable about overvaluation is that it had virtually no detractors.[33]

Each group preferred an overvalued exchange rate for a different reason. Workers preferred overvaluation because it increased their real wages. The financial sector opposed devaluation because it would have increased their foreign debt burdens and because they viewed the stable exchange rate as essential for price stability.

The manufacturing sector joined these groups in supporting the overvalued exchange rate for three main reasons.[34] First, overvaluation reduced manufacturers' imported input costs. "Even those industrial interests that might have been expected to gain competitiveness through a devaluation supported the peg. Because so much of the value-added in Mexican manufacturing came from foreign inputs, a weakened peso would result in higher production costs" (Kessler 1999, 112). Second, many manufacturing firms opposed devaluation because it would increase their foreign debt burdens. Finally, the exchange rate's stability was also beneficial to manufacturing firms, and they "routinely argued that the benefits of maintaining confidence and a stable currency outweighed the dangers of overvaluation" (Kessler 1999, 112). Manufacturers recognized that overvaluation was harming their competitiveness, but they insisted that devaluation would create worse problems than it would solve. The preferences of Mexico's powerful manufacturing sector was a major reason that Salinas chose not to devalue the exchange rate. This refusal to devalue caused the peso to continue its real appreciation (see figure 5.2).

The political and economic environment took an abrupt turn for the worse in early 1994. On January 1, 1994, the day that the North American Free Trade Agreement came into effect, the Zapatistas initiated an uprising in the Mexican

---

33. Dresser (1997), Flores Quiroga (2001), Ramírez de la O (1996), and Schamis (1999) also suggest that interest group preferences were one of the main causes of overvaluation.

34. This paragraph draws heavily from Kessler (1999, 111–113).

state of Chiapas. In February, the United States Federal Reserve started to increase interest rates. Next, the PRI's presidential candidate, Luis Donaldo Colosio, was assassinated on March 23, which was followed by the assassination of the PRI's secretary general in September. Attracted by higher interest rates abroad and scared of political instability in Mexico, capital took flight.

The impending presidential election also raised the political stakes of exchange rate policy. Salinas was "eager to finish his term in a blaze of glory" to protect his political legacy and help him secure the job that he coveted next: the director-general of the World Trade Organization (Smith 1997, 40). Salinas's finance minister, Pedro Aspe, had his own political motivations: he wanted to stay on as finance minister in the next administration and had presidential ambitions of his own. Both Aspe and Salinas knew that the strong peso was very popular among key PRI constituencies and that devaluation would compromise their chances of achieving their political objectives (Dresser 1997; Heath 1999; Smith 1997). The Salinas administration also did not want to raise interest rates, which could have helped attract capital back into Mexico and stave off devaluation, because higher borrowing costs "would threaten relations with the PRI's allies in the business community and labor" (Frieden 1997, 90).

Salinas chose instead to loosen monetary policy to kick-start economic growth.[35] The central bank chose to sterilize the capital outflow, meaning that it issued more local credit to counteract the exit of foreign capital. Thus, the money supply increased in this period, and interest rates on Mexican treasury securities (*Cetes*) fell. To limit the capital outflow, Mexico also changed the composition of the money supply by issuing dollar-linked debts; these *Tesobonos* transferred the risk of devaluation from investors to the government. Expansionary monetary policy achieved its goal over the short run: in spite of the unfavorable shocks, economic growth actually increased in the second quarter of the year (Heath 1999, 39), and the PRI's candidate, Ernesto Zedillo, won the August 1994 election.

Debate over devaluation resurfaced between the August 1994 election and Zedillo's inauguration on December 1. In October, some members of the U.S. Federal Reserve Board recommended taking the opportunity to alter the exchange rate regime in order to reduce the peso's overvaluation (Edwards 1997, 115). In a private meeting on November 20, President-elect Zedillo and his advisers pleaded with Salinas, Aspe, and other top officials to devalue the currency. But the Salinas team refused to devalue, and business and labor leaders applauded this decision (Edwards 1997, 117; Smith 1997, 44; Ramírez de la O 1996, 12). A 1994 sur-

---

35. See Edwards and Naím (1997), Flores Quiroga (2001), Heath (1999, 32–43), and Ramírez de la O (1996) for more details on Mexican economic policy in 1994.

vey provides further evidence that interest group support for devaluation was virtually nonexistent: 80% of firms opposed further depreciation of the exchange rate, and although 20% believed that depreciation should be increased, not a single surveyed firm said that a large devaluation was warranted (Gil-Díaz and Carstens 1997, 171). All sectors of Mexican business opposed exchange rate devaluation.

On December 2, 1994, the day after he moved into the presidential palace, Zedillo pledged to continue his predecessor's exchange rate policy, despite his earlier hushed request for devaluation (Smith 1997, 32). Unfortunately, Mexico was quickly losing its ability to sustain the overvalued exchange rate. By the time Zedillo entered office, foreign reserves were at a "dangerously low" level of $12.5 billion—a mere fraction of the $27 billion in short-term public debt at the time (Edwards 1997, 118, 116). Zedillo made a bad situation worse on December 9, with the release of his 1995 budget that ignored the economy's underlying vulnerabilities and proposed no changes to exchange rate or fiscal policy. The budget release exacerbated capital flight and drained an additional $1 billion of reserves within a week (Heath 1999, 44–45).

With his back up against the wall, on December 21, Zedillo finally widened the exchange rate band, and the peso depreciated 15%. The peso came under massive selling pressure, and with the government no longer able to contain the damage, the peso began floating on December 22. The peso depreciated nearly 100% over the next three months. The predictions made by Dornbusch and other economists in 1992 were prescient: the overvalued peso ended up plunging Mexico into a painful currency and banking crisis in 1994–1995.[36]

With the benefit of hindsight, it is obvious that an "earlier and large-scale devaluation would have been a much wiser course" than "squander[ing] the nation's resources in an ultimately unsuccessful effort to sustain the value of the currency" (Smith 1997, 39). Why did Mexican policymakers allow their exchange rate to become overvalued in the 1990s, and why did they fail to correct overvaluation earlier? Salinas overvalued the exchange rate because the most powerful interest groups in Mexico favored this policy. One such group was the manufacturing sector: although manufacturers opposed real exchange rate appreciation in January 1988, they were die-hard supporters of a strong peso for the next six years. It is likely that the peso would have been less overvalued in the early 1990s if Mexico's powerful manufacturing sector preferred a more undervalued exchange rate.

---

36. Dornbusch (1997) forcefully argues that overvaluation was the most important cause of the crisis. Many others view overvaluation as one of the most important causes (Edwards 1997; Flores Quiroga 2001), though central bankers Gil-Díaz and Carstens (1997) disagree.

Summary of the Mexican Case

The conditional preference theory argues that exchange rates tend to be overvalued in countries like Mexico that combine a powerful manufacturing sectors with non-state-controlled institutions. Overvaluation is likely in such countries because manufacturers are politically influential and they tend to dislike undervaluation. These expectations are largely borne out in the Mexican case. First, in three of the four periods examined in this case study, Mexico's real exchange rate rapidly appreciated and became overvalued. The only exception was 1982 to 1989, a period in which Mexico was in a severe debt crisis and faced strong pressures to earn foreign currency to resolve this crisis.

The Mexican case is also consistent with my hypothesis that private-controlled labor and financial systems reduce industrialists' support for an undervalued exchange rate. As expected, when policymakers considered devaluing the peso in 1971, 1979–1980, and 1992–1994, the manufacturing sector registered their opposition each time. Furthermore, industrialists complained about each of the major devaluations that occurred during the period investigated here (1976, 1982, 1994). Manufacturers preferred an overvalued currency to lower the costs of their foreign imports and external debts.

The evidence suggests that private-controlled labor institutions had a causal impact on Mexican industrialists' exchange rate preferences. Labor unions demanded, and won, wage increases following most exchange rate devaluations. These wage hikes further increased business expenses during these devaluation episodes and were one of the main reasons manufacturing firms disapproved of the devaluations of 1976 and 1982. The structure of the financial system did not have as clear an impact on manufacturers' preferences. However, in the mid-1980s, the government had considerable, but temporary, success using interventionist financial policies to reduce opposition to undervaluation. The fact that manufacturers were more tolerant of devaluation in that period than other times suggests that Mexico's private-controlled financial system probably increased their support for overvaluation.

Finally, the preferences of the manufacturing sector influenced Mexico's policymakers. Manufacturers were not solely responsible for this outcome. However, every Mexican president between 1970 and 1994 tried to win the support of the manufacturing sector, or at least some segments within this sector. Given the priority that most Mexican leaders placed on the manufacturing sector, it is likely that the peso would have been more undervalued if Mexican industrialists favored an undervalued exchange rate. The preferences of Mexico's powerful manufacturing sector contributed to overvaluation.

The Politics of Overvaluation in Iran, 1953–1997

The Political Sources of Exchange Rate Policy in Prerevolutionary Iran

This case study begins in 1953, when Iran's constitutional monarch, Mohammad Reza Shah Pahlavi, deposed the democratically elected government to become the effective ruler of Iran. The new regime quickly demolished Iran's independent labor movement (Abrahamian 1982, 230–231; Bayat 1987; Ladjevardi 1985; Moghadam 1996; Pfeifer 2006, 126–127; Rahnema 1992). Iran's main union federation, which was affiliated with the Tudeh (Communist) Party, was disbanded and many of its leaders were arrested. Strikes were prohibited, and collective bargaining was nonexistent. The 1959 Labor Law allowed unions to form, but all unions were kept under the regime's tight control. The permitted unions did not promote workers' interests because union elections were rigged by the state and the secret police controlled many top union positions. "Small wonder, then," Moghadam (1996, 78) retorts, "that most workers were hostile to the syndicates." In brief, the Shah "decisively crushed" the Iranian labor movement (Bayat 1987, 57).

Under the Shah, the state's control over the financial system was nearly as great as its control over labor. Even before the coup, four of Iran's six banks were government-owned. The creation of two development banks in the 1950s, the Industrial Credit Bank and the Industrial and Mining Development Bank of Iran, further increased the state's role in the financial system.[37] These two development banks were the source of most loans to the manufacturing sector; for instance, they originated over 90% of all industrial loans in 1976 (Amid and Hadjikhani 2005, 25; Karshenas 1990, 98–100). Mazaheri (2008, 590) reports that 72% of bank assets were in state-owned banks, another 27% were in mixed public-private banks, and only 1% were in fully private-owned banks.[38] "[D]ue to its overwhelming control of these assets, the Iranian state was able to unilaterally determine the policies and patterns of credit allocation," concludes Mazaheri (2008, 590). The state controlled most of the country's financial institutions during the Shah's reign (Keshavarzian 2007, 86; Salehi-Isfahani 1989, 374).

Although Iran's labor and financial structures are similar to some of this book's other cases, the power resources of Iran's manufacturing sector could hardly be more different from those cases. Consider first this sector's economic resources.

---

37. The former was fully state-owned and the latter was a joint stock company in which the state and World Bank were the main owners.

38. Gwartney and Lawson (2009) suggest that over 90% of bank deposits were in state-owned banks. According to La Porta, Lopez-de-Silanes, and Shleifer. (2002), 89% of assets were in state-owned banks in 1975.

In 1965, the earliest year with data from the World Bank (2010), Iran's manufacturing sector produced 8.5% of the country's GDP. Iran's manufacturing sector was far smaller than the agricultural sector (27.5% of GDP in 1965) and the service sector, whose share of GDP of 42.5% in 1965 made it far and away the country's most economically important industry (Katouzian 1981, 257–286). At the start of this period, the oil industry played a relatively minor role in the economy, though it grew substantially over time (Katouzian 1981, 257). Although the manufacturing sector experienced tremendous growth during the Shah's tenure, its overall contribution to GDP remained small (7.2% in 1978), especially when compared to the still-dominant service sector (whose share of GDP was 46% in 1978).

Iran's service sector also had more organizational resources than the manufacturing sector. The Iranian service sector, including the country's merchants, shopkeepers, retailers, and wholesalers, is centered in the nation's bazaars. The bazaars are centralized marketplaces that are composed mostly of nontradable industries, though they do include some small-scale tradable industries like carpet production (Parsa 1995, 811; Shambayati 1994; Keshavarzian 2007). The Tehran Grand Bazaar alone contains 20,000 to 30,000 commercial units, employs 40,000 to 50,000 employees, and controls two-thirds of country's domestic wholesale trade (Keshavarzian 2007, 6, 43). The locational concentration of firms within the bazaar gives them a "strong capacity for collective action" and is an important reason that the bazaaris are so powerful politically (Parsa 1995, 812). Dense trade networks between bazaaris from different towns link members of this community and enhance their political solidarity (Mazaheri 2006, 403). These are among the many reasons the Iranian bazaar has been a pivotal actor in most of the country's political conflicts (Mazaheri 2006; Parsa 1995).

Ideology was the manufacturing sector's greatest power resource. The Shah, like many other leaders in the developing world, believed that development required industrialization (Amuzegar 1991, 171; Clawson and Rubin 2005, 76; Nasr 2000, 106). He wanted Iran to follow in the footsteps of Japan. To this end, he created a Ministry of Economy in the mold of Japan's infamous Ministry of International Trade and Industry (Nasr 2000). This ministry and its chief, Alinaghi Alikhani, advocated on behalf of private industrialists in the 1960s (Milani 2008, 60; Nasr 2000), which bolstered this sector's organizational resources. Despite these normative power resources and ties to some policymakers, Iran's manufacturing sector had far fewer economic and organizational resources than the service sector. Overall, the power resources of Iran's manufacturing sector fell on the low end of the spectrum.

Although the power resources of the country's manufacturing sector are far more limited than the other cases considered in this book, their production profile is quite typical. Manufacturers in Iran produce an array of goods, from labor-intensive goods such as textiles and carpets to capital-intensive ones like metal, cement, and motor vehicles (Amid and Hadjikhani 2005, 57; Katouzian 1981, 281). Iranian manufactured goods are also exportable, and though the overvalued exchange rate often made it difficult for them to export, Iranian industrialists had some success exporting at certain times, especially following exchange rate depreciations (Amid and Hadjikhani 2005, 24, 54–57, 77; Behdad 1988, 4; Katouzian 1981, 326; Lautenschlager 1986, 43; Mazaheri 2008, 590). Trade protection often reduced competition with foreign producers, but many manufacturing industries received limited protection and faced steep import competition at times (Amid and Hadjikhani 2005, 24; Behdad 1988, 12; Mazaheri 2008, 590; Salehi-Isfahani 1989, 370). "[H]eavy reliance upon imported inputs" is another "important feature of Iranian industrialization" that is common to the developing world (Assadi 1990, 36; Amid and Hadjikhani 2005, 28, 67; Behdad 1988; Katouzian 1981, 324; Pesaran 1992, 109; Salehi-Isfahani 1989, 372). Finally, Iran's manufacturing sector was heavily dependent on borrowing. The industrial sector was the largest recipient of credit in the 1970s, and though its share of bank loans declined after the revolution, it still received about one-third of all loans (Salehi-Isfahani 1989, 369; Valibeigi 1992, 64). Since Iranian industrialists produce tradable goods and depend on imported inputs and debt, undervaluation should help them compete against foreign producers but also increase their operating costs.

Iran's mixture of domestic political arrangements differs from the four other cases in this book. Since Iran's state has extensive control over labor and financial markets, my theory anticipates that Iranian industrialists should prefer an undervalued exchange rate. However, since Iran's manufacturing sector has fewer power resources than in most developing countries—including China, Argentina, Korea, and Mexico—its influence over exchange rate policy should be more limited. Instead, the preferences of Iran's powerful service sector should have a greater effect on Iranian exchange rate policy. Given the service industry's preference for an overvalued exchange rate, my theory expects Iran's exchange rate to tend toward overvaluation.

Real Appreciation to Court the Bazaar: 1953–1959

The Shah was in a tenuous political position at the start of his tenure. The population viewed him as a weak and illegitimate leader (Clawson and Rubin 2005, 69). The Iranian Parliament, though not democratically elected, had real powers and many of its members were no fans of the Shah (Katouzian 1981, 197). The bazaaris longed for ousted Prime Minister Mossadegh and frequently closed their shops to protest the new regime (Parsa 1995, 812). Seeking to consolidate his power, throughout the 1950s the Shah adopted a conciliatory posture toward the bazaaris, wealthy landowners, and other powerful conservative interests. His goal was to gain their support (Clawson and Rubin 2005, 71; Karshenas 1990, 89; Smith 2007, 70–71).

Macroeconomic and exchange rate policies in the 1950s reflected the interests of this conservative political coalition.[39] Fiscal and credit policies were highly expansionary. The Shah's first Five-Year Development Plan, covering the period 1955–1962, prioritized infrastructure spending, with agriculture the second priority, and the needs of industry third. Although inflation remained low at first, it started to creep up from 1957 onwards. The Shah also reduced import barriers.

An important shift in exchange rate policy took place in the mid-1950s.[40] The Shah inherited a multiple exchange rate system. Initially, an appreciated "official" rate of 32.5 rials/dollar applied to oil exports and certain imported goods, but most of the transactions that affected private-sector traders took place at the more depreciated exchange rate of 90.5. The Shah's government started to gradually revalue the latter exchange rate. It was appreciated from 90.5 to 84.5 in 1954, and then to 76.5 in 1955. This was equivalent to a 15% appreciation in nominal terms. Because Iranian prices were increasing much faster than U.S. prices, the real exchange rate appreciated substantially more than that. Thus, the exchange rate used by most private actors appreciated, improving the purchasing power of consumers and importers. The government then unified the two exchange rates at 76 rials/ dollar. Although this meant that the official rate was devalued, the main effect of devaluing this exchange rate was to increase the government's oil revenues because each dollar of oil was exchanged for more rials. This situation ultimately benefited the private sector, too: the government used these additional revenues to provide more loans to them. Over the course of the 1950s, rising inflation and nominal exchange rate appreciation generated a "noticeable revaluation of the real exchange rate" (Karshenas 1990, 117). Figure 5.3 shows that the exchange rate was as overvalued as 55% in the late 1950s.

These policies reflected a domestic political logic. Numerous groups benefited from the mixture of exchange rate revaluation, expansive fiscal and monetary policies, and liberal trade policies. None, however, benefited as much as the bazaaris. Expansionary policies increased consumption, causing people to purchase more goods from the bazaar. Housing in particular experienced a boom. Bazaaris profited handsomely from speculating on urban land. Finally, trade and exchange rate policies, which made imports more affordable, encouraged middle-class consumers to purchase imported consumer goods from the bazaar (Katouzian 1981, 202– 208; Looney 1982, 12–14; Smith 2007, 101). According to Karshenas (1990, 89), the "revaluation of the rial . . . and the gradual removal of trade restrictions and import quotas . . . largely benefited the bazaar merchants." Karshenas (1990, 3)

---

39. The summary of policies in this period is based on Abrahamian (1982, 419–422), Katouzian (1981, 202–208), Karshenas (1990, 88–131), and Looney (1982, 12–14).

40. This paragraph draws heavily from Karshenas's (1990, 98–127) detailed analysis.

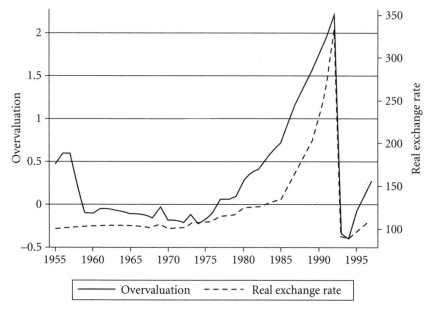

Figure 5.3. Exchange rate overvaluation in Iran, 1955–1997. Overvaluation is defined as the difference between the actual real exchange rate and the estimated equilibrium real exchange rate. Positive (negative) values imply an overvalued (undervalued) real exchange rate. See chapter 2 for more details. Real exchange rate is defined as the natural logarithm of the nominal exchange rate divided by the GDP deflator (Heston et al. 2009). This indicator is inverted so that higher (lower) values imply a more appreciated (depreciated) real exchange rate. It is indexed so that 1955 equals 100.

suggests that exchange rate appreciation and these other policies "were highly rewarding to the traditional ruling coalition—namely, the merchant bourgeoisie of the bazaar and the landlords—who in turn provided the social support which was crucial for the maintenance of the regime."

The Shah's Risky Gamble with Undervaluation: 1960–1978

The boom of the 1950s came to a crashing halt toward the end of the decade.[41] Rapid economic growth turned into inflationary overheating. The import boom

---

41. This section borrows from the following sources: Abrahamian (1982), Clawson and Rubin (2005, 71–85), Karshenas (1990), Katouzian (1981), Keshavarzian (2007), Looney (1982), Mazaheri (2008), Pesaran (1982), Salehi-Isfahani (1989), and Smith (2007, 100–119).

became an increasingly unsustainable balance-of-payments deficit, and Iran started hemorrhaging foreign reserves. The Shah turned to the United States and the IMF for help, which they provided in return for the standard set of belt-tightening measures: higher interest rates, lower public spending, and restrictions on imports. Iran's economy fell into recession in the early 1960s as a result. Service industries, such as construction and domestic trade, were particularly damaged by the credit restrictions and import controls. By contrast, the manufacturing sector managed to continue growing throughout the early 1960s.

The brief recession in the early 1960s marked an important turning point in the Shah's political coalition. The Shah was fed up with kowtowing to conservative forces and decided it was time to take the Iranian political economy in a new direction. During the early 1960s "the shah changed the fabric of Iran's ruling elite and forcefully retired nearly every member of the aristocracy that had, for centuries, dominated Iranian politics" (Milani 2008, 57). For example, in May 1961, he dissolved the newly elected parliament, which had been dominated by conservative landlords (Abrahamian 1982, 423). Then the Shah permitted only a small group of "soulless puppets," which he handpicked himself, to contest the 1963 parliamentary elections (Katouzian 1981, 235). The Shah also announced a six-point policy program known as the "White Revolution" whose centerpiece—land reform—was accurately viewed by the clergy and other landlords as an existential threat. These political and institutional changes laid the groundwork for a shift in economic strategy. The Shah's initial alliance with agriculture and services was over. The time had come to transform Iran into a modern industrialized nation, the Shah decided. He boasted the immodest and utterly implausible goal of catching up with advanced industrialized nations by 1979.

Policy changed starkly in the wake of the Shah's newly revealed obsession with industrialization. The third and fourth development plans, covering 1962–1967 and 1968–1972, respectively, used tax breaks and preferential credit policies to assist the manufacturing sector. There was little action on the exchange rate front in the 1960s. The rial remained fixed at 76.5 to the dollar throughout the decade. However, the real exchange rate depreciated between 1962 and 1970.[42] The recession of the early 1960s left the Iranian economy with excess productive capacity, which kept inflation unusually low, and below U.S. rates, throughout the decade. The lack of exchange rate changes in this period provides a marked contrast with the Shah's earlier revaluation policies. This nonresponse also differs substantially from Argentina in 1973, when Perón revalued the peso after just a few months

---

42. The real exchange rate, as measured in figure 5.3, depreciated 5.3% over this period. Darvas's (2012) trade-weighted exchange rate index depreciated 12% in this period. These two measures are very strongly correlated ($r = 0.98$) for the period in which the two series overlap (1960–1997).

in which Argentine prices increased more slowly than U.S. prices. Industrialists in Argentina were quite perturbed by the peso's real depreciation in 1973, but this does not appear to have been a concern for Iranian industrialists or their political representatives in the 1960s.

The spike in international oil prices that began in 1973 had a major impact on Iran's oil-rich economy. The increase of oil revenues enabled the Fifth Development Plan, covering the period 1973–1978, to be several times larger than its predecessors. Government spending and the supply of credit rapidly increased between 1973 and 1975. Interest rates were kept at very low rates, which were negative in real terms. The result was an excess demand for credit. The state stepped in to decide who would receive these limited funds, and unsurprisingly, the lion's share went to friends of the Pahlavi family and the regime's newfound allies in the manufacturing sector. Farmers and other less-connected groups were starved of credit. State-allocated credit represented a massive transfer of wealth to the manufacturing sector. Salehi-Isfahani (1989) calculates that credit subsidies accounted for two-thirds of the profits of the manufacturing sector.

The oil price shock led to a massive increase in foreign exchange inflows and put huge upward pressure on the currency. The Iranian government made strong and largely successful efforts to stem the rial's rise. Foreign reserves were rapidly accumulated to prevent appreciation. In 1974 alone, reserves increased 800% (World Bank 2010). In February 1975, Iran abandoned its peg to the dollar and started to manage the currency vis-à-vis the IMF's special drawing rights (SDR) currency basket (Bahmani-Oskooee 2005, 7; Mazarei 1995, 25). The fluctuations against the dollar remained fairly minimal, as the dollar has a heavy weight in the SDR basket, but this new currency regime had the benefit of enhancing flexibility.

Increased inflation combined with a stable rial-dollar exchange rate contributed to an appreciation of the real exchange rate following the oil shock. By the Shah's final year in office (1978), the exchange rate was no longer highly undervalued, but it does not appear overvalued, either (see figure 5.3). By contrast, most other oil exporters in the Middle East had heavily overvalued exchange rates in 1978.[43] Overall, the maintenance of a relatively undervalued exchange rate between 1960 and 1978 reflected the Shah's fixation with the manufacturing sector and his indifference toward the plight of the bazaaris and landlords. Quite atypically, in Iran oil rents "did not undermine industrial development . . . or retard the drive for competitiveness" (Nasr 2000, 113).

The Iranian economy underwent a "tiger-like" miracle between 1960 and 1976. Iran's GDP climbed from $4,300 in 1960 to $11,400 in 1976 (Heston, Summers,

---

43. Overvaluation averaged 19% among the eight Middle East oil exporters in 1978. Other than Iran, the United Arab Emirates was the only other country whose exchange rate was undervalued.

and Aten 2009). Oil income undoubtedly contributed to this growth, but it was not the only cause. Iran's manufacturing sector and its non-oil GDP grew even faster than overall GDP (Pesaran 1982, 504). This period witnessed the emergence of new steel mills, rubber factories, chemical plants, and the birth of the country's first automobile manufacturer (Mazaheri 2008, 589). Simply put, Iran underwent a "minor industrial revolution" (Abrahamian 1982, 430; Nasr 2000, 102).

Unfortunately, the manufacturing sector's success did not spill over to other sectors. The bazaaris were in distress and agriculture experienced difficult times. Both sectors were neglected by the state and unable to access the cheap credit that was available to industrialists. The undervalued exchange rate was also problematic for the bazaar's import merchants because it raised their costs and reduced their profits. Overall, the Shah's financial policies in this period were anathema to the powerful service sector. Groups such as shopkeepers, teachers, and clergymen condemned the Shah and his policies from the early 1960s onward. Ayatollah Khomeini "denounced the regime for . . . neglecting the economic needs of merchants, workers, and peasants" (Abrahamian 1982, 425). The Shah's "uneven treatment [of different sectors] contributed to . . . opposition of a large section of the propertied class to a regime which had engineered the fastest economic boom in Iran's history" (Salehi-Isfahani 1989, 360).

The bazaaris' dislike for the Shah turned into a passionate hatred after 1975. The Iranian economy started to experience problems in 1975, thanks to a weakening oil market. The result was stagflation. Rather than cut government spending to reduce inflation, which topped 27% in 1977, the government chose a different solution: an "Anti-Profiteering Campaign" that was launched in August 1975 and involved sending inspection teams into the bazaars and other businesses to enforce price controls. Offenders were fined and publicly humiliated. Within two weeks, over 7,750 bazaaris were arrested. Over 250,000 businesses faced fines or closures during this campaign, the overwhelming majority of which were retailers and bazaaris. Over the next year and a half, the regime implemented a string of additional policies that antagonized the bazaaris: higher taxes; restrictions on land speculation; and regulation of store hours. The bazaaris reacted by joining the students and others in protest. The bazaaris were also instrumental in getting their allies in the Muslim clergy involved in the anti-regime protests (Abrahamian 1982, 497–498; Keshavarzian 2007, 240–248; Mazaheri 2006; Parsa 1995; Shambayati 1994, 322–324; Smith 2007, 143–146).

The regime altered course somewhat in March 1978 by launching a stabilization plan that helped bring inflation down, but it led to a further contraction in the economy. The construction sector, a major source of employment, was particularly hurt (Clawson and Rubin 2005, 81–82; Looney 1982, 5–6). Construction workers then joined the protest movement in July 1978. Workers in the oil sector joined the protests in September 1978, and more followed after (Moghadam 1996, 82). By the end of 1978, a broad coalition of workers, bazaaris, clergy, and others were organized against the Shah. On January 16, 1979, the Shah left Iran. By the end of the year, a new constitution transformed Iran from a monarchy into an Islamic Republic.

The undervaluation of the Iranian rial between 1960 and 1978 stands at odds with the conditional preference theory, which argues that undervalued exchange rates are unlikely in the absence of a powerful manufacturing sector. The theory gets the preferences correct: the manufacturing sector supported an undervalued exchange rate in Iran, which had state-controlled labor and financial systems. However, the Shah's willingness to adopt exchange rate and other monetary policies that benefited only a weak sector defies my theoretical expectations.

Why did the Shah undervalue the exchange rate? His pro-manufacturing ideology clearly motivated him to adopt financial policies that favored industrial interests. On the other hand, the Shah's ideology was hardly unique. As we saw in chapter 4, Argentine leaders from Juan Perón to Cristina Kirchner adhered to similar ideologies but overvalued their country's exchange rate. Shortly, we will encounter Hashemi Rafsanjani, Iran's president from 1989 to 1997, who shared the monarch's views on the importance of industrial development, but overvalued the rial for most of his tenure. It is also unlikely that the Shah's belief system was radically different in the 1950s when he himself appreciated the real exchange rate. It is difficult to explain Iranian exchange rate policy between 1960 and 1978 without paying attention to ideology, but ideological factors do not distinguish this case from myriad others with overvalued exchange rates.

What distinguishes the Shah from these other political leaders? It is less his ideology than his willingness to ignore domestic political incentives. The Shah gave shockingly little attention to coalition building (Smith 2007, 119). Some view this lack of attention to domestic politics as an "error" (Frank 1984, 297). The Shah himself characterized this as bravery: he wrote that he "wanted a modern country. Moving against the bazaar was typical of the political and social risks I had to take in my drive to modernization" (quoted in Keshavarzian 2007, 134). Mazaheri (2006, 403) hits the nail on the head: "a more prudent leader might have . . . exercised a little restraint" toward the bazaar.

The Shah's fate provides an important lesson about the consequences of ignoring powerful interest groups' preferences. The causes of the Iranian Revolution are incredibly complex and multifaceted, but the Shah's unabashedly antimerchant economic policies, of which an undervalued currency was one component, galvanized opposition to his rule and contributed to the revolution

(Keshavarzian 2007, 240; Looney 1981; Mazaheri 2006; Mazaheri 2008; Parsa 1995). This episode helps illuminate why most rulers are unwilling to adopt exchange rate policies that harm powerful interest groups.

The Islamic Republic: Continuity Amidst Change

The Iranian revolution radically altered the country's political system.[44] The monarchy was replaced with an Islamic Republic whose governance structure combines religious institutions with those of a modern republican state. According to the constitution established in December 1979, the supreme leader is the nation's highest religious official and the state's top political official. The supreme leader has the power to appoint or confirm most other political leaders, including the president, who the constitution specifies as the country's second most powerful official. As the president is generally in charge of economic policy, he is a key player with respect to exchange rate policy. Iran's parliament is responsible for drafting legislation, approving loans, annual budgets, and other policies, though it shares these powers with the Guardian Council, a twelve-member religious body. Postrevolutionary Iran holds regular parliamentary and presidential elections, though they are not free and fair elections; the Guardian Council vets all nominees and regularly rejects candidates.

In spite of the dramatic change in Iran's political regime, the key explanatory variables in this study—the labor system, financial system, and the power of the industrial sector—changed little. Iran's state continued to control finance. If anything, the state expanded its control over the financial system after the revolution. In October 1979, the state nationalized all of the country's thirty-six banks and consolidated them into nine state-owned banks. Valibeigi (1992, 51) shows that nationalization of the banks had the predictable effect of "increased state control over the financial sector."[45] These state-owned banks dominated Iran's financial sector throughout the period under investigation (1979–1997).[46]

The Islamic state also maintained control over labor. Independent labor institutions, known as Worker Councils, existed for a very brief period during and after the revolution. However, within months, the revolutionary government started to attack these Worker Councils and almost all of them were dismantled

---

44. Baktiari (1996), Moslem (2002), and Rakel (2008) provide detailed descriptions of Iran's postrevolutionary political system.

45. Interestingly, Valibeigi (1992) also finds that Islamization of the banking system had little effect on Iran's financial system. Despite Islamic prohibition on the use of interest, Iranian banks skirted this rule by referring to interest charges as "service charges."

46. Systematic data on the prevalence of public banks between 1979 and 1997 is scarce. Gwartney and Lawson's (2009) data suggest that more than 90% of deposits were in state-owned banks.

by mid-1981 (Ladjevardi 1985, 251–254; Moghadam 1996, 86; Rahnema 1992). A new labor law, first proposed in 1982 and enacted in 1990, prohibited the right to strike. This law only permitted workers to organize in Islamic labor councils that were supervised by the Ministry of Labor (Moghadam 1996, 88; Pfeifer 2006, 128). The regime uses these Islamic associations to police factories and create an atmosphere of terror to prevent worker actions (Bayat 1987, 186–190). Iranian labor institutions have changed little since that 1990 law. Iran continues to lack independent labor unions, and it has not ratified international conventions on freedom of association or the right to collective bargaining. Simply put, Iranian labor law "impose[s] severe restrictions on the individual and collective rights of workers" (Moghadam 1996, 88). Iran's collective labor laws are among the most restrictive of all countries.[47]

The revolution also failed to substantially alter the power resources of the manufacturing sector. The economic resources of this sector remained limited. The manufacturing sector still produced a small share of GDP. For example, in 1980, the manufacturing sector's share of GDP was 7.7%, slightly below the 25th percentile of all developing countries between 1975 and 2006. The economic clout of the manufacturing sector pales in comparison to its other industries, particularly the service sector.

Under the Islamic Republic, the organizational resources of the manufacturing sector remained limited. Industrialists did have links to some high-level political officials, particularly Hashemi Rafsanjani and his acolytes. However, Iran's nontradable industries also outdid them in this regard. Two groups within the nontradable sector have close connections to some of the Islamic Republic's top political decision makers.

The first are the import merchants, artisans, and retailers in the bazaars. They are one of the main constituents of the regime's conservative faction, also known as the Traditional Right faction. The leader of this faction, Ali Khamenei, was Iran's president in the 1980s and has been its supreme leader since 1989 (Buchta 2000; Moslem 2002; Rakel 2008).

The revolutionary foundations (*bonyads*) are a second powerful actor with strong interests in the nontradable sector. Iran's 1979 constitution created these religious foundations as independent bodies that are accountable only to the supreme leader. Although their official goal is charity and helping the poor, in reality they operate as giant private monopolies (Farzin 1995, 999; Rakel 2008). The bonyads have economic interests in a variety of sectors, a result of the fact that they control about 35% of Iran's GDP and 40% of the non-oil economy (Buchta

---

47. OECD (2000) data on labor rights places Iran with China in the lowest of four groups. Cingranelli and Richards (2010) make a similar determination on Iran (see table 0.2).

2000, 172; Rakel 2008). Similar to Iran's economy as a whole, the bonyads' main sources of profits are in nontradable industries. For instance, an annual report from 1985–1986 shows that they controlled 68 industrial factories and 17 agricultural firms, 21 construction companies, 75 commercial firms, and over 6,000 properties in Tehran (Buchta 2000, 75). The religious foundations also have impeccable political credentials: many are headed by influential clerics (Buchta 2000, 73) and have powerful patrons in the regime's Radical Left faction (Rakel 2008, 71; Moslem 2002, 44).

The Iranian Revolution had far-reaching effects within and beyond Iran, but it barely changed the power of the manufacturing sector and the state's control of labor and finance. Accordingly, the conditional preference theory expects the manufacturing sector to prefer undervaluation, but to have little ability to convince policymakers to adopt their preferred exchange rate policies. The analysis of postrevolutionary Iran covers two distinct periods: the 1980s, when virtually all of Iran's top political decision makers strongly protected the interests of the service sector; and 1989 to 1997, when Iran's president attempted to implement policies that favored the manufacturing sector.

Manufacturers' Marginalization and Extreme Overvaluation: 1980–1988

During the 1980s, the balance of political power within the Islamic Republic heavily favored nontradable industries. The regime's left-wing faction, which was closely allied with the revolutionary foundations, was dominant throughout the decade. Supreme Leader Ayatollah Khomeini and Prime Minister Mir Hussein Mousavi were the leaders of this left-wing faction, and their followers controlled 120 seats in the first parliament (1980–1984) and an even larger number during the second and third parliaments (1984–1988 and 1988–1989). The conservative faction was the second most powerful group in Iranian politics in the 1980s. The conservatives were strong supporters of the bazaar economy. This faction, led by President Khamenei, controlled about 60 seats in parliament (Baktiari 1996).

The industrial sector had one key ally in government during the 1980s: the speaker of the Iranian Parliament, Hashemi Rafsanjani, and his "pragmatic" faction of parliamentarians. Rafsanjani viewed the East Asian Tigers as the appropriate model for Iran and believed that Iran should adopt Korean-style export-oriented industrialization policies (Buchta 2000; Moslem 2002). Although the manufacturing sector had some allies in the regime, they were far more marginalized than nontradable sectors.

The Islamic Republic's first major shift in exchange rate policy came in May 1980. The authorities devalued the official exchange rate from 82.2 rials/SDR to

92.3 rials/SDR. This official exchange rate, which was used for oil exports, most imports, and public-sector debt, was kept fixed at 92.3 SDR for the remainder of the decade. At the same time, the number of different exchange rates was expanded dramatically. The precise details of the exchange rate regime changed regularly, and there were as many as twelve different exchange rates at certain points in time (Amid and Hadjikhani 2005, 39). At the start of 1991, for example, there were seven different exchange rates: a fixed official exchange rate; two different rates for non-oil exports, both fixed at slightly more depreciated rates; three different exchange rates for different types of "nonessential" imports; and a free market rate that covered all other transactions (Mazarei 1995).

These exchange rates all became massively overvalued during the 1980s (Hakimian and Karshenas 2000, 43; Mazarei 1996, 289; Moslem 2002, 147; Pesaran 1992; Pesaran 2000, 81; Saeidi 2001). Large budget deficits persisted throughout the decade (Mazarei 1996, 298). Subsidies provided to parastatal organizations, such as religious foundations, and a lack of tax receipts from these same organizations, contributed to these fiscal imbalances (Mazarei 1996, 299). The state used its control over the banking system to finance these deficits (Mazarei 1996, 299; Valibeigi 1992, 61). It also used the banking system to channel cheap funds to the construction industry. The construction sector's share of bank credit increased from about 20% before the revolution to over 40% throughout the 1980s; by contrast, industry and mining saw their share of bank loans decline from 50% to 30% over that time (Valibeigi 1992, 64). These expansionary monetary policies contributed to inflation that averaged 20% per year in the 1980s. With the exchange rate fixed against the SDR, the official rial exchange rate appreciated rapidly between 1979 and 1989. Iran's exchange rate in the late 1980s was among the most overvalued exchange rates of modern times. Figure 5.3 shows that the rial was 153% overvalued in 1989.

Some actors opposed the overvalued exchange rate, but they lacked the power to influence policy. Some economists advocated for devaluation, and the Iranian Planning and Budget Organization proposed devaluation in intergovernmental debates in 1982 (Behdad 1988, 1, 18). Hashemi Rafsanjani discussed reducing overvaluation in the fall of 1984, though he ultimately made no policy changes (Lautenschlager 1984). The overvalued exchange rate was anathema to some tradable firms in Iran, such as exporters of carpets, pistachios, dates, and leather. The overvalued exchange rate sharply reduced manufactured exports, and exchange rate policy was consequently one of exporters' main criticisms of the government in the 1980s (Keshavarzian 2007, 201–203). Rug exporters in particular "frequently complain[ed] about the competition from producers in countries such as India and Pakistan" (Lautenschlager 1984, 46). Despite this opposition, no major devaluations occurred.

The government maintained the system of multiple overvalued exchange rates because it generated huge profits for bazaari merchants and religious foundations (Amid and Hadjikhani 2005, 48; Lautenschlager 1986; Mazarei 1996, 297; Saeidi 2001, 231). Overvaluation benefited these groups in two ways. First, the overvalued exchange rate subsidized their large purchases of imported goods (Alizadeh 2002, 276; Farzin 1995, 988; Moslem 2002, 57). Second, since overvaluation produced an excess demand for foreign currency, dollars had to be rationed. Only those with licenses were allowed to purchase foreign currency and imports at the official exchange rate. Licenses were issued primarily to connected groups, and they profited handsomely from the arrangement: they imported goods cheaply at the official overvalued exchange rate and then resold them at much higher prices in the black market (Farzin 1995, 991; Lautenschlager 1986, 41–42; Mazarei 1996, 297; Moslem 2002, 42–46; Pesaran 1992).

Iran's economic policies in the 1980s primarily "benefit[ed] a small group of people in the society that had access to the overvalued exchange rates" (Amid and Hadjikhani 2005, 45). These beneficiaries were concentrated in the nontradable sectors of the economy. The interests of powerful nontradable groups were the main reason Iran's exchange rate was grossly overvalued in the 1980s.

Rafsanjani's Failed Attempt at Undervaluation: 1989–1997

In 1989, the balance of power shifted modestly in the manufacturing sector's direction. The June 1989 death of the Supreme Leader Ayatollah Khomeini deprived the leftist faction of its most powerful advocate. The Assembly of Experts selected President Khamenei to replace Khomeini as supreme leader. Rafsanjani handily won the July 1989 presidential election to replace Khamenei. At the same time, a constitutional referendum abolished the post of prime minister, which eliminated another post controlled by the left-wing faction. Although Rafsanjani was the single most influential policymaker in this period (Moslem 2002, 89), he remained constrained, particularly by the left faction that still dominated the Iranian Parliament. The leftists had 160 seats compared to the Rafsanjani faction's 90 seats, and they controlled all the important parliamentary committees (Baktiari 1996, ch. 5).

President Rafsanjani had a unique vision for the Iranian economy. Whereas the Traditional Right favored laissez-faire economic policies and the Radical Left faction wanted the state to redistribute income to the poor, Rafsanjani envisioned a state that intervened in the economy to promote industrialization. Rafsanjani "desired a modern industrial-based economy integrated into the world economy" (Moslem 2002, 128). The president viewed the state-owned banks as an important instrument for these ends: "In this [Rafsanjani's] scheme, the banks play a vital role in attracting and directing capital into small-scale industrial projects. Critical for the success of this plan is an increase in government taxation through . . . the financial system" (Moslem 2002, 130). In other words, Rafsanjani sought to mimic Park Chung Hee and his export-promotion policies. As in South Korea under Park, manufacturers were able to obtain loans at negative real interest rates in the early 1990s (Pesaran 2000, 80). However, when it came to undervaluing the exchange rate, Rafsanjani was much less successful than Park because he faced much stronger resistance from nontradable industries.

During his first years in office, Rafsanjani modified the multiple exchange rate system in order to improve the manufacturing sector's external competitiveness. Some goods were shifted from the most appreciated official exchange rate to the more depreciated competitive rate; other goods were moved from this latter rate to the even more depreciated free market category (Hakimian and Karshenas 2000, 52; Pesaran 2000, 86). In January 1991, the number of different exchange rates was reduced from seven to three, though the remaining three rates remained worlds apart. The majority of goods continued to be imported at the extremely overvalued official rate of 70 rials/dollar. Other transactions occurred at the much more depreciated rates of either 600 or 1460 rials/dollar (Mazarei 1995; Farzin 1995, 988). Due to these changes, the nominal exchange rate depreciated 110% in weighted average terms between 1989 and 1992.[48]

The depreciation of the real exchange rate was much less drastic. Due to looser-than-planned monetary and fiscal policy, inflation remained high, averaging about 21% per year in this period. These price increases were much more rapid than those targeted by Rafsanjani's first five-year development plan (Hakimian and Karshenas 2000; Pesaran 2000). On balance, the weighted average real exchange rate depreciated only modestly—24% according to data from Hakimian and Karshenas (2000, 47)—barely making a dent in the massively overvalued exchange rate that Rafsanjani inherited. Moreover, the official exchange rate, which remained fixed against the SDR, continued its rapid real appreciation and reached its peak in 1992. Figure 5.3 estimates that Iran's official real exchange rate was a whopping 222% overvalued in 1992.

The economic situation took a turn for the worse in 1992, when oil prices began tumbling. This external shock, combined with the previous trade deficits, produced severe foreign currency shortages. In response, the government tightened import controls and rapidly accumulated short-term foreign debt (Hakimian and Karshenas 2000).

---

48. This calculation is based on data provided by Hakimian and Karshenas (2000, 47).

The increasingly troubling economic situation in 1992 coincided with a more favorable political situation for Rafsanjani. For the first time in the Islamic Republic, the Radical Left faction failed to capture a majority in the 1992 parliamentary elections. While this gave Rafsanjani more room to implement his preferred policies, he did not gain anything close to a free hand in policymaking. The leader of the new parliament, Ali-Akbar Nateq-Nuri, was "strongly protective of the interests of the merchant class [bazaaris]" (Baktiari 1996, 222; Buchta 2000). The Nateq-Nuri faction in Parliament was "opposed to . . . the creation of a modern industrial economy similar to those of the new industrialized countries in Asia" (Moslem 2002, 180).

These modestly looser political constraints convinced Rafsanjani that this was a politically opportune time to try to undervalue the exchange rate (Farzin 1995; Pesaran 2000). Combining the multiple exchange rates into a single unified rate was one of the main unaccomplished goals of Rafsanjani's first five-year plan. The government had been in consultations with the World Bank and IMF, which set a target date of March 1994 for unification. Rafsanjani decided instead to try and unify the exchange rates in March 1993, a full year earlier than targeted.

On March 27, 1993, a single exchange rate was fixed at a rate of 1538 rials/dollar—an effective weighted devaluation of 95.6% (Farzin 1995, 992). Although certainly a large devaluation, many analysts believe that the devaluation was insufficient and the exchange rate was still overvalued (Amid and Hadjikhani 2005, 46; Farzin 1995, 996–997). Moreover, unification was less complete than it appeared because the government earmarked $3.8 trillion to be imported at the old official rate of 70 rials/dollar. Most of these imports were handled by the bonyads—a "concession to the foundations in order to secure their political approval of the exchange reform" (Farzin 1995, 993). This political concession imposed large quasi-fiscal losses on the government, which had to cover the gap (Sundararajan, Lazare, and Williams 2001, 218). To further reduce the bonyads' opposition to these new exchange rate policies, the government directed the state-owned banks to channel extra credit their way (Maloney 2000, 163). Fiscal policy was also used to help cushion the blow from devaluation: the government increased spending more than 50% in 1993 (Hakimian and Karshenas 2000).

At first, the March 1993 exchange rate reforms appeared successful. The government operated a managed float that kept the exchange rate stable, and near its value in the free/black market, from April to September. However, the official fixed rate started to diverge sharply from its free market rate in October. The government ultimately abandoned its unified exchange rate system in December 1993 (Farzin 1995; Sundararajan, Lazare, and Williams 2001; Hakimian and Karshenas 2000). The decision to adopt a unified and depreciated exchange rate in an economically difficult period, and the need to placate powerful opponents of devaluation with inflationary side-payments, made it all but inevitable that this policy would fail. Rafsanjani would have had more success undervaluing the rial if he did not face opposition from so many powerful groups.

A multiple exchange rate system was officially reestablished in May 1994, and it remained in place for the remainder of Rafsanjani's tenure. Monetary policy remained expansionary, with the money supply growing nearly 30% per year from 1994 to 1998 and inflation at 29% per year in this period (Hakimian and Karshenas 2000, 46). According to Pesaran (2000, 79), "the main causes of the excessive monetary expansion and inflation have to be found in the government's unwillingness to oppose the credit demands of politically powerful groups." The composition of credits particularly favored the bonyads because of their "ready access to centers of political power" (Pesaran 2000, 80). High inflation amidst a stable exchange rate resulted, once again, in rapid real exchange rate appreciation after 1993. The rial went from 50% undervalued in 1994 to 22% overvalued in 1997 (see figure 5.3).

The shift of political power in the direction of the manufacturing sector helps explain why Iran's exchange rate was less overvalued in the 1990s than in the 1980s. On the other hand, the continued political and economic dominance of Iran's service sector is the main reason the Iranian exchange rate was overvalued, rather than undervalued, throughout most of Rafsanjani's presidency.

Summary of the Iranian Case

The Iranian case is consistent with most of hypotheses presented in chapter 1, though there are some important and interesting exceptions. Iran has a weak manufacturing sector and state-controlled labor and financial institutions. The conditional preference theory hypothesizes that countries without powerful manufacturing industries tend to have overvalued exchange rates. Iran's exchange rate was, in fact, overvalued for the majority of the period under investigation, and the degree of overvaluation was extraordinary at times. However, this hypothesis cannot explain why Iranian authorities maintained an undervalued exchange rate from 1960 to 1978.

The second hypothesis, that the manufacturing sector is likely to prefer an undervalued exchange rate when the state controls labor and finance, also finds support in the Iranian case. Manufacturing businesses, particularly in the carpet industry, opposed the overvalued exchange rate in the 1980s. In addition, Iranian policymakers who sought to promote the manufacturing sector's interests, such as Mohammad Reza Shah (1960–1978) and Hashemi Rafsanjani (1989–1997), viewed an undervalued exchange rate as being in this group's interest, and made efforts to undervalue the exchange rate. Thus, in Iran, state-controlled institutions coincided with a preference for undervaluation. Although there is limited evidence to explain why this group preferred undervaluation, Iran's labor and financial structures probably contributed to this outcome. Labor-intensive industries, such as carpet producers, had little reason to oppose devaluation because their nonunionized labor force would not be able to agitate for wage increases if the rial depreciated. Rafsanjani's vision of combining undervaluation with cheap credit for manufacturers must have had great appeal to Iran's capital-intensive manufacturing sectors, such as chemicals and metals.

The third hypothesis, that manufacturing sectors with few power resources have limited influence over exchange rate policy, receives strong support in some but not all periods in the case study. Consistent with this argument, Iran's manufacturing sector had little political influence in the 1950s, 1980s, and 1990s. The preferences of Iran's powerful service sector explain why the rial was overvalued in these periods.

Contrary to my expectations, the manufacturing sector received favorable exchange rate and financial policies between 1960 and 1978. This period indicates that resources are not everything. Even non-powerful interest groups receive their preferred exchange rate policies some of the time. At the same time, this case also illustrates the dangers of pursuing exchange rate policies that are not supported by powerful industries. The Shah ignored the preferences of the powerful service sector at his peril. The excessively small support base for his pro-manufacturing policies ultimately hastened his downfall. Had Iran's manufacturing sector been more politically powerful, it is likely that undervalued exchange rates would have persisted far past the 1970s. The political weakness of the Iranian manufacturing sector helps explain why the Iranian rial has often been overvalued and why it was massively overvalued at times.

Conclusions

The case studies of Korea, Mexico, and Iran hold two important lessons for our understanding of exchange rate politics. The first relates to interest group preferences. This chapter provided additional evidence that industries with similar characteristics favor different exchange rate policies in different contexts. Among the contextual factors that shape whether manufacturing firms prefer an undervalued exchange rate, labor and financial market institutions are particularly influential. In Korea and Iran, two countries with state-controlled labor and financial structures, the manufacturing sector tended to favor an undervalued exchange rate. By contrast, manufacturing firms in Mexico, where the state had limited control over labor and finance, usually opposed exchange rate undervaluation.

The second major finding is that powerful industries have greater influence over exchange rate policy than weaker ones. In South Korea and Mexico, where the manufacturing sector controlled many power resources, political decision makers made strong efforts to keep the exchange rate at the level favored by the manufacturing sector. By contrast, exchange rate policymakers in Iran often disregarded the exchange rate preferences of the country's weak manufacturing sector. Policymakers in Iran were just as sensitive to interest group demands, but they were usually more concerned with the preferences of their country's large and well-organized service industries. This chapter shows, once again, that the preferences of powerful interest groups influence whether developing countries maintain an undervalued exchange rate or an overvalued one.

Conclusion

Undervalued exchange rates are appealing for numerous reasons. The economic benefits are often tremendous: undervaluation increases economic growth, reduces unemployment, and lowers the risk of financial crises.[1] An undervalued exchange rate can also bolster a state's geopolitical standing: undervaluation increases a nation's exports and diminishes those of its trading partners, thereby increasing a state's wealth and power in relative terms. It is also widely believed that undervalued exchange rates help politicians curry favor with powerful domestic interest groups. According to conventional wisdom, undervalued exchange rates benefit tradable industries (Frieden 1991a)—industries that tend to be "well represented in the policy process" and "have more sway over [exchange rate] policy than the nontraded sector" (Henning 2006, 123; see also Broz and Frieden 2001, 333; Eichengreen 1996, 152; Frieden 1997, 85; Prasad 2014, 136). These are among the reasons the temptation to adopt undervalued exchange rates often seems irresistible. In reality, however, few developing countries keep their exchange rates undervalued for long periods of time. Far more developing countries intentionally overvalue their exchange rates. This book explains why.

In many ways, the politics of undervaluation is a familiar story of interest group politics. Exchange rate policymakers are more concerned with the interests of particularistic groups than they are with national economic or political interests. Do-

---

1. See the introduction for a more complete discussion and citations to relevant studies.

mestic political theories are also correct that tradable industries often have tremendous influence over exchange rate policy.

However, domestic political theories of exchange rate policy have been led astray by their inaccurate models of interest group preferences. Interest groups are far less supportive of undervalued exchange rates than previous interest group theories have recognized. In particular, tradable industries, such as manufacturing, are not the stalwart supporters of undervaluation that they are usually assumed to be. Undervalued exchange rates have a mixture of positive and negative effects on the manufacturing sector. As a result, many firms in the manufacturing sector are only conditional supporters of an undervalued exchange rate. Sometimes manufacturing firms prefer undervaluation, other times they do not. Undervalued exchange rates are uncommon because interest group support for undervalued exchange rates is limited in most developing countries.

The "conditional preference theory," which I developed and described in this book, argues that the preferences and political influence of interest groups largely determine whether exchange rates are undervalued. The theory is based on two main propositions. First, institutions influence the preferences of the manufacturing sector. Manufacturing firms are more likely to prefer an undervalued exchange rate when rules and decision-making procedures give the state extensive control over labor and financial markets. State-controlled institutions help policymakers shift the costs of undervaluation away from industry and onto banks and workers, which makes an undervalued exchange rate more attractive to the manufacturing sector. Second, powerful manufacturing sectors—sectors that control large amounts of power resources—strongly influence exchange rate policy decisions. By contrast, when the manufacturing sector has fewer power resources than other interest groups, its impact on exchange rate policy tends to be more limited. Based on these two premises, the theory argues that undervalued exchange rates are most likely in countries where state-controlled labor and financial systems coincide with a powerful manufacturing sector.

In this concluding chapter, I review the evidence provided in chapters 2 through 5. The evidence confirms that preferences for undervalued exchange rates are context-dependent, and that powerful interest groups influence decisions about exchange rate policy. Together, these two pieces of evidence indicate that undervalued exchange rates are rare at least in part because they fail to receive solid support from powerful interest groups. After summarizing the evidence, the book ends by considering some broader implications of these findings for social scientists and policymakers.

Summary of the Findings

Different Contexts, Different Preferences

Similar interest groups prefer different exchange rate policies in different circumstances. We saw in chapter 3 that China's manufacturing sector favored devaluation in 1993. However, chapters 4 and 5 showed that the manufacturing sectors of Argentina and Mexico opposed devaluation in 1993. Similarly, in 1974, Korea's manufacturing firms advocated for a devaluation of the currency while their Mexican counterparts were lobbying against devaluation. The variation over time in the exchange rate preferences of the UIA, the main association that represents Argentina's manufacturing sector, is even more striking. In addition to its aforementioned opposition to devaluation in the 1990s, the UIA lobbied against devaluation in 1970, 1980, and 2010. Yet this very same organization was enthusiastic about devaluation in 1967 and between 2001 and 2005. Similar interest groups prefer different exchange rate levels in different circumstances.

What explains the variation in the manufacturing sector's support for undervalued exchange rates across countries and over time? An interest group's preferences depend in part on its internal attributes, or its "production profile" (Lake 2009). In chapter 1, I argued that interest groups tend to be more supportive of undervaluation when their output is internationally tradable and when they are less reliant on imported inputs and debt. Differences in interest groups' production profiles are extremely helpful in explaining why some sectors of the economy are more inclined to support undervaluation than others. However, an exclusive focus on a sector's production profile does not provide a complete explanation for why its preferences vary greatly from one country to another. The main limitation of this argument is that the production profile of the manufacturing sector does not differ much across countries. In each of this book's five case studies, the manufacturing sector produced tradable goods and relied on bank borrowing and imported inputs. Thus, undervaluation should have an ambiguous effect on the profits of the manufacturing sector in all of these countries. And although manufacturers' production profiles are not completely constant, variations in these attributes are not closely related to differences in their preferences. For example, China's manufacturing sector was the strongest supporter of undervaluation even though it is heavily reliant on imported inputs and has below-average levels of export-dependence. Or consider Argentina's manufacturing sector, which was equally supportive of overvaluation in 1973 and in 1993 despite being far more reliant on foreign debt in the latter period. A focus on the production profiles of interest groups is an excellent place to begin the analysis of exchange rate preferences, but it does not suffice for explaining the glaring differences in industrialists' preferences across countries or over time.

A complete explanation of exchange rate preferences requires that one pay attention to the national context facing an interest group. In other words, a sector's preferences depend not only on that sector's production profile but also the broader national economic, political, and institutional context in which that sector finds itself. This book found evidence that three contextual factors account for much of the variation in the manufacturing sector's exchange rate preferences: financial market institutions, labor market institutions, and macroeconomic conditions. These are certainly not the only contextual variables that shape preferences, but they are three of the most important ones. I discuss each of these three variables in turn.

Both quantitative and qualitative evidence demonstrate that the structure of the national financial system has a powerful impact on interest groups' exchange rate preferences. The survey data presented in chapter 2 shows that manufacturing firms tend to prefer undervalued exchange rates to overvalued ones in countries with state-controlled financial systems. By contrast, in private financial systems, most manufacturers hold negative opinions toward undervalued exchange rates.

The case studies of China and South Korea clarify why state control of finance increases industrialists' support for undervalued exchange rates. The authorities in these countries jacked up banks' reserve requirements to exorbitant levels and forced state-owned banks to purchase government bonds at below-market interest rates. These actions imposed sizable losses on state-owned banks and their depositors, but they made it possible for industrial firms to continue to access low-cost funds even while the exchange rate was undervalued. The governments of Korea and China used their control over the financial system to spare the manufacturing sector from some of the potentially large burdens of an undervalued exchange rate.

Argentina and Mexico provide an illuminating contrast. Due to limited state control over the financial system in Argentina and Mexico, those governments were much less successful at insulating their manufacturing sectors from the negative effects of undervalued exchange rates. This helps explain why manufacturing firms in Argentina and Mexico were less supportive of an undervalued exchange rate than their counterparts in China and South Korea.

This book also found some evidence that labor market institutions influence exchange rate preferences. The statistical analyses provided evidence that manufacturing firms hold more favorable opinions of undervalued exchange rates in state-controlled labor systems than in private-controlled ones. However, several of the quantitative models failed to detect any statistically meaningful effect of labor controls on manufacturing firms' preferences.

The case studies provide additional evidence that labor institutions influence exchange rate preferences. Consider the case of Mexico. In the aftermath of several of Mexico's currency devaluations, the country's labor unions lobbied for, and won, large wage increases. This exacerbated the detrimental effect of devaluation on manufacturing firms' operating costs and was part of the reason that Mexican industrialists strongly opposed devaluation in 1976 and 1982. In Argentina, another country with a strong labor movement, similar dynamics followed devaluation in 1975. By contrast, in countries where the state controls labor, workers have been much less successful at convincing policymakers to raise their salaries following devaluations. For example, labor did not win major wage hikes following Korea's devaluations in 1964, 1971, and 1974, or after China's devaluation in 1994. Although labor institutions are probably not as important as financial market institutions, a country's labor system can have a strong effect on firms' exchange rate preferences.

Institutions help explain variation in preferences across countries, but since they change slowly over time they cannot explain why firms' exchange rate preferences often shift from one year to the next. Several of the case studies found that fluctuations in macroeconomic conditions help explain such shifts. Argentina in the early 2000s is a clear example: unprecedented rates of unemployment rendered wages less responsive to devaluation than they usually are in Argentina. Unlike the devaluation of 1975, wages hardly increased at all after Argentina devalued its exchange rate in 2002. This made undervaluation more attractive to Argentine businesses, so industrialists were much keener on an undervalued exchange rate in the early 2000s than they were in other periods. The opposite sort of macroeconomic conditions explain why Chinese manufacturers were less supportive of an undervalued exchange rate in 2006–2007 than they normally are. During this period, an overheating economy and large capital inflows made it nearly impossible for the Chinese government to sustain an undervalued exchange rate while also continuing to channel cheap credit to industrial firms. The manufacturing sector tends to support undervalued exchange rates when economic conditions permit undervaluation to coincide with cheap credit and low wages. Manufacturing firms are less content with undervaluation when keeping the exchange rate undervalued substantially increases their operating expenses.

Economic conditions also influence exchange rate preferences through another, more indirect channel: economic crises enable some states to adopt more interventionist economic policies than is possible in less turbulent conditions. Argentina's severe financial crisis in 2002 opened the door for the government to wipe away industrial firms' foreign debts. Similarly, in Mexico in the 1980s, the severe stress of the debt crisis made it permissible for the government to provide debt relief to manufacturing firms. In both cases, financial repression increased support for undervaluation. Economic crises sometimes increase support for an undervalued exchange rate because they can expand the policy options available to some states.

There are certainly a number of other contextual factors that influence exchange rate preferences. It is beyond the scope of this book to evaluate all such variables. Interestingly, however, a country's development strategy is one contextual factor that appears to have little effect on firms' preferences. Some scholars suggest that protectionist development models, such as import substitution industrialization (ISI), reduce international competition and weaken manufacturers' preference for undervaluation (Crystal 1994; Frieden et al. 2001). However, the link between trade policy and exchange rate preferences is not so clear, either in theory or in reality. As Albert Hirschman (1968, 26–27) points out, even when countries follow ISI, it is "questionable" that overvaluation is desirable for industrialists: "the overvalued exchange rate permitted the acquisition at favorable prices (in domestic currency) of . . . essential industrial materials," but at the same time "the overvalued exchange rate acted as a bar to exports from these industries." Moreover, although trade opening may increase manufacturers' interest in external competitiveness, it may simultaneously increase their reliance on imported inputs, with ambiguous effects overall. The case studies of Argentina and Mexico also suggest that ISI had limited influence on preferences. Those countries' manufacturing firms were equally supportive of overvaluation during the "neoliberal" era as they were during the ISI period.

The essential point is that the manufacturing sector favors an undervalued exchange rate in some situations and opposes this policy in other situations. The rules, decision-making procedures, and economic conditions prevailing in a country's financial and labor markets are among the most important factors that shape the preferences of the manufacturing sector.

The Influence of Interest Group Preferences on Exchange Rate Policy

The preferences of powerful interest groups have a profound influence on whether policymakers keep their exchange rates overvalued or undervalued. Chapter 2 provided statistical evidence that interest groups influence exchange rate policy. Among countries with state-controlled labor and financial institutions, the power of the manufacturing sector is strongly correlated with undervaluation of the exchange rate. The quantitative data suggests that policymakers have a tendency to implement exchange rate policies that are consistent with the preferences of powerful interest groups.

The qualitative evidence also indicates that most exchange rate policymakers are preoccupied with the preferences of powerful interest groups. Iranian leaders overvalued their exchange rate in the 1950s, 1980s, and 1990s, in order to please Iran's large and highly organized commercial and service industries. Policymakers in Argentina and Mexico repeatedly overvalued their exchange rates because powerful manufacturing industries and labor unions opposed devaluation. It is striking that the one brief period (2002 to 2005) in which Argentina undervalued the peso was the only time in forty-seven years that Argentina's industrialists consistently lobbied in favor of an undervalued exchange rate. In South Korea, President Park Chung Hee was only able to sustain the undervalued exchange rate because this policy benefited Korea's large industrial conglomerates.

The case study of China provides particularly compelling evidence that interest groups influence exchange rate policy. China is an authoritarian country where policymakers are insulated from private-sector lobbying to an unusual degree. Although China is among the last places where one would expect interest groups to impact exchange rate policy, chapter 3 showed that such groups strongly influence Chinese exchange rate policy. Whenever China's manufacturing sector lobbied for an undervalued exchange rate, the government responded accordingly. Lobbying by China's manufacturing firms contributed in important ways to several key decisions to undervalue the exchange rate: the 1994 devaluation; exchange rate stabilization in mid-1995; the avoidance of significant appreciation between 2003 and 2006; and the return to a stable exchange rate in mid-2008. The fact that the manufacturing sector's lobbying had an overwhelming impact on exchange rate policy decisions in China, where politicians are relatively autonomous from societal pressures, suggests that few, if any, exchange rate policymakers can ignore the preferences of powerful interest groups.

The evidence presented in chapters 2 through 5 finds that ideas can also influence exchange rate policy in some ways. The common belief that the manufacturing sector is crucial for development is important for exchange rate politics. Pro-industrialization ideology makes it easier for manufacturers to convince policymakers to adopt their preferred exchange rate policies. The widespread belief that undervaluation is superior to overvaluation may also influence exchange rate policy. For example, awareness of the benefits of undervaluation was one of the reasons, though not necessarily the most important, that Park Chung Hee and Mohammad Reza Shah Pahlavi undervalued their exchange rates.

Overall, however, the bulk of the evidence casts doubt on the argument that ideational factors influence decisions about the exchange rate level in developing countries. It is not possible to consider every possible type of ideational explanation. Here, I discuss how the evidence is inconsistent with two of the most popular versions of ideational or constructivist theories of political economy.

The most common constructivist argument suggests that policymakers' ideas and beliefs about exchange rate policy influence their policy choices (Helleiner 2005; McNamara 1998; Morrison 2015; Moschella 2015; Odell 1982). This argument would expect policymakers to keep their exchange rate undervalued if they themselves believe that undervaluation is beneficial for their economies. The evidence presented in this book indicates that policymakers' beliefs about what constitutes ideal exchange rate policy often has little bearing on their decisions about the exchange rate level in developing countries. Many policymakers adopt radically different policies from those that they believe to be optimal. Chinese Premier Wen Jiabao kept the renminbi undervalued despite his belief that appreciation was needed to reduce China's excessive reliance on exports. The opposite occurred in Argentina: nearly all economic ministers since 1966 have believed that Argentina should avoid overvaluation, but almost all of them went on to let the peso become overvalued anyway. Similarly, Hashemi Rafsanjani, Iran's president in the 1990s, wanted to mimic Korea's export-led industrialization strategy but was unsuccessful at sustaining an undervalued currency. More broadly, ideas about exchange rate policy cannot explain variation in exchange rate levels across the developing countries examined here. Since ideas are largely constant—virtually all policymakers recognized the ills of overvaluation—this ideational explanation cannot account for variation across cases. This theory also has difficulty accounting for the prevalence of overvaluation. There is a gaping chasm between most policymakers' actions, which involve overvaluing their exchange rates, and their belief that overvaluation is undesirable.

A second common ideational argument maintains that policymakers' macroeconomic objectives determine their exchange rate policy. Since undervalued exchange rates increase employment but can fuel inflation, some suggest that decisions about the exchange rate level depend on whether policymakers prioritize price stability or employment (e.g., Crystal 1994, 145). Argentina in the 1990s provides one clear example of this logic: Carlos Menem's refusal to devalue the overvalued exchange rate stemmed in part from a widespread fear that it would lead to a resumption of hyperinflation (Schamis 2003; Starr 1997). However, anti-inflationary objectives were not salient in most episodes of overvaluation considered in this book. On the contrary, inflationary macroeconomic policies frequently contribute to overvaluation. During the Echeverría and López Portillo administrations in Mexico, the Onganía, Perón, Videla, and Kirchner administrations in Argentina, and Khamenei's presidency in Iran, loose macroeconomic policies led to rising inflation, which contributed to rapid real exchange rate appreciation. As these examples illustrate, the maintenance of an overvalued exchange rate is not usually a consequence of policymakers holding a strong ideological aversion to inflation.

Although I cannot rule out the possibility that other types of ideas matter, the evidence indicates that policymakers' beliefs about exchange rates and inflation have less impact on exchange rate levels than some authors suggest. When it comes to exchange rate valuation in developing countries, interests are usually more important than ideas.

Why Undervalued Exchange Rates Are Rare: A Demand-Side Explanation

Overvalued exchange rates are more common than undervalued rates because powerful interest groups prefer this outcome in most developing countries. A number of interest groups oppose an undervalued exchange rate. Previous research has highlighted the importance of nontradable industries as key actors that discourage governments from keeping their exchange rates undervalued (Frieden 1991a). Other scholars have emphasized the role of urban consumers that prefer an overvalued exchange rate to enhance their purchasing power (Bates 1981). Opposition to undervaluation from bankers, the service sector, and consumers helps explain why overvalued exchange rates are ubiquitous in developing countries. But this is not the whole story.

To understand why undervalued exchange rates are so rare, it is imperative to consider the preferences of another interest group: the manufacturing sector. The manufacturing sector's lack of support for undervaluation is a key reason that undervalued exchange rates have been relatively uncommon in the developing world. First, the manufacturing sector's preferences often have a strong influence on exchange rate policy. Second, the manufacturing sector frequently dislikes undervalued exchange rates. If the manufacturing sector always favored an undervalued exchange rate, as many scholars assume, far more countries would keep their exchange rates undervalued. For instance, Argentina and Mexico would have been more likely to keep their exchange rates undervalued if their countries' powerful manufacturing sectors did not oppose undervaluation. The manufacturing sector's unwillingness to consistently support undervaluation goes a long way toward explaining why we do not see more undervalued exchange rates.

Implications for Theory: Explaining the Choice of Protectionist Policies

Undervalued exchange rates are a protectionist policy that gives national firms a competitive advantage over their foreign competitors. Thus, undervalued exchange rates and other protectionist policies, such as import tariffs, have similar economic

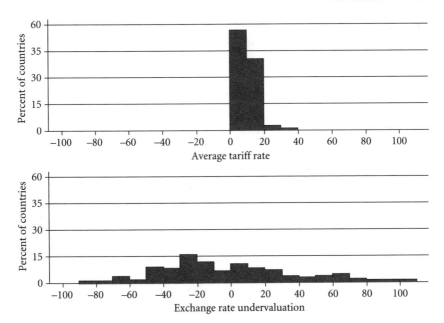

Figure C.1. Trade and exchange rate protectionism in 2006. Average tariff rate is from World Bank (2010). Exchange rate undervaluation is defined as the inverse of real exchange rate overvaluation multiplied by 100. Chapter 2 presents details on the construction of the overvaluation variable.

effects (Broz and Frieden 2001). Given these similar effects, it is puzzling that undervalued exchange rates—also known as "exchange rate protectionism"—are so rare while trade protectionism is nearly omnipresent. I am going to apply this book's theory of exchange rate politics to help us understand why some protectionist instruments are more widely used than others. The answer is that interest groups prefer some protectionist instruments to others. Protectionist instruments that have larger and more unambiguous effects on firms' profits are more popular with interest groups and become more widely used as a result.

Protectionist trade policies remain common. Despite a "rush to free trade" (Rodrik 1994) in the 1980s and 1990s, most developing countries continue to use tariffs to protect local industries. The upper part of figure C.1 displays the distribution of average tariff rates across developing countries in 2006. In that year, over half of developing countries had average tariff rates that were between zero and 10%. Another sizable group of countries maintained tariff rates between 10% and 20%. Very few countries maintained average tariff rates above 20%, and the maximum was 30.2%. Only three countries (Hong Kong, Libya, and Singapore) had average tariff rates of zero in 2006. No country in 2006 had a negative average tariff rate. Today, almost all developing countries maintain mildly protectionist trade policies.

Exchange rate policy follows a distinct pattern from trade policy. The lower panel in figure C.1 presents the distribution of exchange rate levels for an identical sample of developing countries. In this figure, positive values indicate more undervalued exchange rates. The scale is also set to make it more comparable to the tariff data; to give an example, a positive value of 20 implies a 20% undervaluation of the exchange rate, which has similar effects to a 20% tariff. The median and modal country's undervaluation is negative, meaning that the majority of developing countries had "anti-protectionist" (i.e., overvalued) exchange rate policies in 2006.[2] This is roughly equivalent to having a negative average tariff rate, which, to reiterate, did not exist in any country in 2006. This raises the question: Why are tariffs much more widely used as a protectionist instrument than undervalued exchange rates?

One possible answer, suggested by Gowa (1988), is that trade and exchange rate policy feature different dynamics of collective action. This argument suggests that interest groups frequently organize and lobby for tariff protection because tariffs are "excludable," meaning that tariffs can be withheld from industries that do not lobby for them. Interest groups are less likely to lobby for an undervalued exchange rate, according to Gowa (1988, 26), because "devaluation was a distinctly non-excludable good: no individual could be prevented from benefiting from this change, whether or not he contributed to it."

Much of the evidence presented in this book stands at odds with the argument that differences in collective action problems explain why tariffs are more common than undervalued exchange rates.[3] Collective action problems have not prevented interest groups from lobbying for an undervalued exchange rate.[4] For instance, Chinese industrialists often lobbied very effectively for an undervalued exchange rate. The bigger problem with the collective action theory is that interest groups often lobby in opposition to an undervalued exchange rate. Manufacturing firms did this repeatedly in Argentina and Mexico, and they did so occasionally in China and South Korea. The *amount* of lobbying for trade and exchange rate protection differs less than the *direction* of that lobbying. Collec-

---

2. Another noteworthy difference is that highly protectionist exchange rate policies are more common than highly protectionist trade policies in the contemporary global economy.

3. I am not suggesting that collective action issues are unimportant. They likely play an important role in *both* trade and exchange rate policy. My point is that differences *across* the two issues are not primarily driven by differences in collective action problems.

4. One reason is that groups that are already organized should not find it exceedingly costly to lobby for devaluation (Broz and Frieden 2001, 333).

tive action dynamics do not seem to explain why tariffs are more widespread than undervalued exchange rates.[5]

A more important difference between tariffs and undervalued exchange rates is how they affect firms' profits. For import-competing firms, the net benefits of a tariff often exceed the net benefits of an undervalued exchange rate. To understand why, consider a very simple example of how each policy would affect a hypothetical firm that manufactures refrigerators. Both a 25% tariff on refrigerator imports and a 25% devaluation would allow the firm to raise its prices on domestic markets by an equal amount. Hence, both protectionist measures would increase this firm's sales revenue. Although the two policies have identical effects on the firm's revenues, undervalued exchange rates are much more problematic for the cost side of this firm's operations. If the firm uses imported aluminum to build refrigerators, a 25% devaluation would raise its aluminum costs by 25%. And if this firm took out loans that need to be repaid in foreign currency, devaluation also increases the domestic-currency value of those debts by 25%. By contrast, a tariff on refrigerators has no (direct) effect on this firm's input costs or debt burdens.[6] Tariffs and undervalued exchange rates have identical effects on firms' competiveness, but only undervalued exchange rates raise a firm's costs in a substantial way. If asked to choose between these two instruments, this firm would surely prefer a tariff to an undervalued exchange rate. Exchange rate protection is less beneficial to interest groups than trade protection.

The main difference between the two instruments is not interest groups' ability to lobby for these policies, but their desire to do so. Tariff protection can be used in a highly selective manner so that it does not substantially increase firms' costs. Undervalued exchange rates are a far blunter instrument, and as a result, they raise many firms' costs. Some consider tariff protection akin to "doing acupuncture with a fork" because "no matter how carefully you insert one prong, the other is likely to do damage" (Deardorff and Stern 1987, 37). Following this analogy, exchange rate protection would be equivalent to doing acupuncture with a pitchfork: its greater imprecision inflicts a wider array of damages on those it is intended to help. Tariffs are more common than undervalued exchange rates because tariffs receive more interest group support. Protectionist instruments that

---

5. A related argument holds that undervalued exchange rates are relatively rare precisely because countries can achieve the same ends with trade protection (Gowa 1988, 26; see also Copelovitch and Pevehouse 2013). In other words, the possibility of using tariffs negates the need to use protectionist exchange rate policies. However, for the sample of countries used in figure C.1, there is a weak *positive* association between tariff rates and undervalued exchange rates—the opposite of what this substitution argument would expect.

6. This stylized example assumes that one does not simultaneously increase tariffs on intermediate goods. This reflects the reality that tariff rates on final consumer goods are usually much higher than tariffs on intermediate goods (Dornbusch 1992).

can be more narrowly targeted are more popular with interest groups and therefore more widely used.

Implications for Theory: Interests and Institutions in Political Economy

Many theories of international political economy adopt one of two opposing views of preferences. Adherents of the "open economy politics" (OEP) approach assume that an actor's position within the international economy, or its "production profile," dictates its policy preferences (Lake 2009). Jeffry Frieden's (1991a) sectoral theory, which argues that tradable industries prefer undervalued exchange rates and nontradable industries oppose undervaluation, is the most prominent application of this approach to the realm of exchange rate politics. On the other hand, critics of the OEP approach claim that interest groups are highly uncertain about how foreign economic policies affect their profits, and their position in the world economy does not determine their preferences (Abdelal et al. 2010). Opponents of OEP claim that interest group approaches are especially problematic for understanding exchange rate policy because the effects of exchange rates are even more complicated and uncertain than other issues, such as trade policy (Helleiner 2005; McNamara 1998; Morrison 2015; Odell 1982). One implication of this book is that neither the OEP approach nor opponents of that approach provide a satisfactory theory of economic policy preferences.

Consistent with the OEP approach, the evidence I have presented reveals that firms often have clear and comprehensible preferences over exchange rate policy. Industrialists in China and Iran had no trouble identifying their interest in an undervalued exchange rate, for example. Likewise, industrialists in Argentina and Mexico easily recognized that devaluation would increase their debt burdens, input costs, and lower their profits. Policy preferences do correspond with actors' objective material interests—even in an area like exchange rate policy where the distributional effects are less stark and obvious than trade policy. An actor's production profile clearly influences its policy preferences.

On the other hand, preferences cannot be explained solely on the basis of an actor's production profile. Firms with similar characteristics do not always prefer the same value of the exchange rate. There are some circumstances where tradable firms favor an undervalued exchange rate and other times when they want an overvalued exchange rate. The evidence plainly contradicts "the hard core assumption of OEP . . . that interests are determined largely by a unit's production profile or position in the international division of labor" (Lake 2009, 231).

The main alternative to OEP, the "constructivist" approach, which emphasizes nonmaterial sources of preferences, such as ideology, is equally problematic. Constructivists are correct that "many 'similar people' make so many 'dissimilar choices'" (Abdelal et al. 2010, 2). However, contra constructivism, it does not follow that "a purely materialist view of theory is not—and never was—tenable" (Abdelal et al. 2010, 2). By discarding materialism, constructivists are throwing out the baby with the bathwater.

A better solution is to provide more sustenance to OEP's undernourished baby. This book puts forth a third approach to preferences, which retains OEP's focus on material forces but places much more emphasis on contextual factors. When a policy influences an actor's income through multiple opposing channels, contextual factors are likely to determine whether that actor supports or opposes that policy. I have shown that contextual factors, such as macroeconomic conditions and institutions, help explain why industrialists prefer an undervalued exchange rate in some conditions but not others. Incorporating contextual factors that influence preferences should improve scholars' ability to understand interest group preferences in a variety of issue-areas. An accurate explanation of interest group preferences requires attention to an actor's production profile as well as to the features of the political, economic, and institutional environment that the actor inhabits. This advice may seem obvious, but it is not standard scholarly practice.

The conditional preference theory also has important implications regarding the importance of institutions in political economy. Few social scientists dispute the importance of institutions. However, scholars often fail to appreciate some of the important ways in which institutions influence world politics. Conventional wisdom holds that institutions matter because they determine which interest groups' preferences will be given weight by policymakers (Milner 1998; Moravcsik 1997; Lake 2009; Rogowski 1999). This book shows that institutions do much more: they also determine what policies interest groups favor. Labor market and financial market institutions impact exchange rate policy primarily through their effects on interest groups' preferences. This finding echoes previous research in the historical-institutionalist tradition that shows that domestic institutions influence preferences for economic policy.[7] This is obviously not the first study to recognize that institutions matter for their effects on preferences. To give one example, C. Randall Henning's (1994) analysis of exchange rate politics in advanced industrialized nations shows that the structure of the financial system affects whether the financial sector favors or opposes an undervalued exchange

---

7. For further discussion of historical institutionalist theories of preferences, see Farrell and Newman (2010), Fioretos (2011), Thelen (1999), and Thelen and Steinmo (1992).

rate. Still, it is important to reemphasize this point because it remains greatly underappreciated. More sustained attention to the ways in which institutions influence preferences has the potential to greatly enrich our understanding of the political world.

Policy Implications

What, if anything, can be done to improve exchange rate policies in the future? The task is surely a daunting one, but there is enormous room for improvement. Lecturing government officials about the harmful effects of overvalued exchange rates seems pointless. This approach has been tirelessly tried for decades. Policy-makers in the developing world have received a wealth of information about the perils of overvalued exchange rates. They have witnessed, firsthand, how overvalued exchange rates have impaired the competitiveness of local firms, increased unemployment, and generated agonizing financial crises. Developing country policymakers are well aware that overvaluation is not advisable. They do not overvalue their exchange rates because they think it is good for their economies. If the international community wants to help developing countries avoid overvalued exchange rates, a different approach is needed.

Focusing on institutions might prove more effective. This book shows that institutions can have important effects on exchange rate policy. Across the developing world, countries have been more likely to undervalue their exchange rates and less likely to overvalue their exchange rates when rules and decision-making procedures give states extensive control over their labor and financial systems. Thus, the international community might be able to promote more effective exchange rate policies if it encouraged developing countries to reform some of their institutional structures.

If Western governments and the international financial institutions are serious about helping developing countries improve their exchange rate policies, instead of continuing to push developing countries to privatize their state-owned banks and strengthen labor rights, they may need to help developing states expand their control over these arenas. The benefits of state-controlled labor and financial systems can be substantial: they reduce the likelihood that governments overvalue their exchange rates, a policy that tends to be incompatible with sustained economic growth. At the same time, institutional reforms that increase the state's control over labor and finance are no panacea. Nationalizing banks and restricting collective labor rights have a multitude of political, social, and economic effects, many of which are negative. Ultimately, whether state-controlled labor and financial systems cause more harm than good is a decision best made by the citizens of the developing world.

It is equally important to emphasize that institutions that increase the state's control over labor and finance do not always contribute to better exchange rate policies. They only promote undervalued exchange rates and, by extension, export-led development, under certain conditions—namely, in developing countries with powerful manufacturing sectors. State-controlled labor and financial systems contributed to undervaluation and rapid export-oriented growth in China, South Korea, and Taiwan (see also Amsden 1989; Evans 1995; Haggard 1990; Johnson 1987; Wade 1990; Woo 1991). However, similar institutional arrangements have been associated with overvalued exchange rates and economic stagnation in many other countries, including Algeria, Cameroon, Iran, and Tanzania. The institutions that promote good exchange rate policy in one country may not help in another. While the international community might consider being more tolerant of institutional structures that increase state capacity, it would be counterproductive to promote these institutions everywhere and always. Institutional reforms must be sensitive to political context.

Policymakers in the developing world must strive to avoid the mistaken exchange rate policies of the past. With greater help from the international community, they just might succeed. The only way to do so is by paying close attention to the political foundations of economic policymaking.

INTERVIEWS CITED IN CHAPTER 3

CODE	DATE	SECTOR	POSITION	LOCATION
C1	6/12/08	International Organizations	Country Director	U.S. (Telephone)
C2	7/12/08	Government and International Organization	Economist	U.S. (Telephone)
C3	7/21/08	Private (Research/ Consulting)	Managing Director	Beijing
C4	7/21/08	Private (International Business)	Vice President	Beijing
C5	7/21/08	Government	Economist	Beijing
C6	7/22/08	Government	Researcher	Beijing
C7	7/22/08	Journalism	Bureau Chief	Beijing
C8	7/22/08	Government	Associate Researcher	Beijing
C9	7/23/08	Academic	Professor	Beijing
C10	7/23/08	Private (Finance) and International Organization	Economist	Beijing
C11	7/23/08	Government	Director	Beijing
C12	7/28/08	Government	Deputy Chief	Hangzhou
C13	7/28/08	Private (Finance)	Department Head	Shanghai
C14	7/29/08	Private (Finance)	Strategist	Shanghai
C15	7/30/08	Private (International Business)	Chief Representative	Shanghai
C16	7/30/08	Journalism	Bureau Chief	Shanghai
C17	8/6/08	Private (International Business)	Managing Director	Shanghai
C18	8/6/08	Academic	Professor	Shanghai
C19	8/7/08	Private (Industry)	Marketing Director	Shanghai
C20	8/7/08	Journalism	Senior Financial Analyst	Shanghai
C21	8/15/08	Academic	Professor	Shanghai
C22	8/22/08	Government	Researcher	U.S.
C23	3/9/09	Journalism	Managing Editor	Shanghai
C24	3/12/09	Government	Senior Manager	Hong Kong
C25	3/13/09	Government	Department Head	Hong Kong
C26	3/13/09	Private (Consulting)	Senior Counselor	Hong Kong

(continued)

(continued)

CODE	DATE	SECTOR	POSITION	LOCATION
C27	3/16/09	Private (Consulting)	Managing Director	Shanghai
C28	3/17/09	Private (Finance)	Managing Director	Shanghai
C29	3/17/09	Academic	Professor	Shanghai
C30	3/19/09	Journalism	Journalist	Shanghai
C31	3/23/09	Government	Director	Beijing
C32	3/24/09	Government	Economist	Beijing
C33	3/24/09	Government	Deputy Director	Beijing
C34	3/24/09	Government	Researcher	Beijing
C35	3/24/09	Government	Researcher	Beijing
C36	3/25/09	International Organization	Researcher	Beijing
C37	3/25/09	Private (Finance)	Analyst	Beijing
C38	3/27/09	Private (Textiles)	Owner/Manager	Dongguan (Telephone)
C39	3/28/09	Private (Textiles)	CEO	Wenzhou (Telephone)
C40	3/28/09	Government	Director	Beijing
C41	4/2/09	Private (Textiles)	Company President	Hong Kong

Note: Anonymity was granted to interviewees in China in return for discussing potentially sensitive issues.

INTERVIEWS CITED IN CHAPTER 4

CODE	DATE	NAME	POSITION
A1	8/1/07	Ricardo Arriazu	Adviser to Central Bank President (1975–1981)
A2	8/6/07	Catalina Smulovitz	Professor, *Universidad Torcuato di Tella*
A3	8/7/07	Alejandro Bonvecchi	Adviser, Minister of Finance (2000–2001)
A4	8/7/07	Daniel Heymann	Economist, United Nations Economic Commission for Latin America and the Caribbean
A5	8/7/07	Andrés López	Director, *Centro de Investigaciónes Para la Transformación*
A6	8/8/07	Jorge Baldrich	Undersecretary of Economic Policy (1994–1996)
A7	8/9/07	Pablo Guidotti	Director of Central Bank (1994–1996); Deputy Minister of the Economy and Treasury Secretary (1996–1999)
A8	8/10/07	José Maria Fanelli	Senior Researcher, *Centro de Estudios de Estado y Sociedad*
A9	8/13/07	Miguel Kiguel	Deputy General Manager, Central Bank (1994–1996); Undersecretary of Finance and Chief Adviser to Minister of Economy (1996–1999); President, *Banco Hipotecario* (2001–2003)
A10	8/14/07	Sebastián Katz	Undersecretary of Economic Program (2004–2006); Deputy Head of Economic Research, Central Bank
A11	8/15/07	Lucas Llach	Economist, *Universidad Torcuato di Tella*
A12	8/16/07	Pedro Elosegui	Deputy Head of Economic Research, Central Bank
A13	9/16/08	Anonymous	Automobile Exporter Association
A14	9/16/08	Anonymous	Dental products manufacturer
A15	9/18/08	Jorge Avila	Analyst, Treasury Department (1977–1980)
A16	9/18/08	Damian Wilson	Economist, *Asociación de Bancos de la Argentina*
A17	9/19/08	Marta Novick	Undersecretary of Technical Programming and Labor Studies, Ministry of Labor
A18	9/24/08	Anonymous	Senior Analyst, Central Bank
A19	9/24/08	Anonymous	Senior Analyst, Central Bank
A20	9/25/08	Alejandro Bonvecchi	Adviser, Minister of Finance (2000–2001)
A21	9/26/08	Daniel Kostzer	Economist, United Nations Development Programme Argentina
A22	9/26/08	Lucas Llach	Economist, *Universidad Torcuato di Tella*
A23	10/1/08	Sebastián Katz	Undersecretary of Economic Program (2004–2006); Deputy Head of Economic Research, Central Bank
A24	10/8/08	Anonymous	Real Estate Sector
A25	10/10/08	Ezequiel de Freijo	Economist, *Sociedad Rural Argentina*

(continued)

(continued)

CODE	DATE	NAME	POSITION
A26	10/10/08	Alicia Urricariet	Adviser, Institute for Economic Research, *Sociedad Rural Argentina*
A27	10/11/08	Sergio Woyecheszen	Economist, *Union Industrial Argentina*
A28	10/15/08	Roberto Frenkel	Chief Adviser to Minister of Economy (1985–1989); Senior Researcher, *Centro de Estudios de Estado y Sociedad*
A29	10/17/08	Fernando Grasso	Adviser, Industry Secretary (2003–2006); Chief Economist, *Asociación de Industriales Metalúrgicos de la República Argentina*
A30	10/17/08	Mariana Heredia	Researcher, *Instituto de Alto Estudios Sociales*
A31	10/21/08	Anonymous	Researcher, *Cámara de Comercio*
A32	10/23/08	Alberto Rodriguez	Executive Director, *Cámara de la Industria Aceitera de la República Argentina* and *Centro de Exportadores de Cereales*
A33	10/28/08	Antonio Vicenzotti	Director of External Economic Policy, Ministry of Economy
A34	12/22/08 (email)	Juan José Llach	Secretary of Economic Policy (1991–1996); Minister of Education (1999–2000)

Note: All interviews conducted in Buenos Aires. Unless otherwise specified, subject's position refers to position held at the time of the interview.

References

Abdelal, Rawi, Mark Blyth, and Craig Parsons. 2010. *Constructing the International Economy*. Ithaca, NY: Cornell University Press.

Abiad, Abdul, Enrica Detragiache, and Thierry Tressel. 2010. "A New Database of Financial Reforms." *IMF Staff Papers* 57 (2): 281–302.

Abouharb, M. Rodwan, and David Cingranelli. 2007. *Human Rights and Structural Adjustment*. New York: Cambridge University Press.

Abrahamian, Ervand. 1982. *Iran between Two Revolutions*. Princeton, NJ: Princeton University Press.

Acemoglu, Daron, Simon Johnson, James Robinson, and Yunyong Thaicharoen. 2003. "Institutional Causes, Macroeconomic Symptoms." *Journal of Monetary Economics* 50 (1): 49–123.

Adhikari, Ajay, Chek Derashid, and Hao Zhang. 2006. "Public Policy, Political Connections, and Effective Tax Rates." *Journal of Accounting and Public Policy* 25 (5): 574–95.

Aggarwal, Vinod K. 1996. *Debt Games*. New York: Cambridge University Press.

Alderman, Liz. 2011. "Swiss Central Bank Considers Pegging Franc to the Euro." *New York Times*, Aug. 11. http://www.nytimes.com/2011/08/12/business/global/swiss-central-bank-considers-pegging-franc-to-the-euro.html.

Alexander, Robert Jackson. 1962. *Labor Relations in Argentina, Brazil, and Chile*. New York: McGraw-Hill.

Alizadeh, Parvin. 2002. "Iran's Quandary: Economic Reforms and the Structural Trap." *Brown Journal of World Affairs* 9 (2): 267–81.

Ambito Financiero. 1991a. "Tibio Apoyo de UIA al Plan Cavallo." Mar. 31.

——. 1992a. "Riesgosa Jugada de Cavallo." Oct. 28.

——. 1992b. "Cavallo Ahora Profundizara la Convertibilidad con una Virtual Dolarizacion de la Economia." Nov. 17.

——. 1993. "Empresarios de la UIA Darán Apoyo a Reelección de Menem." Mar. 3.

——. 2005a. "El Tipo de Cambio es Crucial para la Coalición con la UIA." Aug. 24.

——. 2005b. "Pudimos Haber Aumentado los Sueldos sin Huelgas." Nov. 25.

——. 2013. "El Blue Subió 21 Centavos a \$10,08." May 7.

Amid, Javad, and Amjad Hadjikhani. 2005. *Trade, Industrialization, and the Firm in Iran*. London: IB Tauris.

Amsden, Alice H. 1989. *Asia's Next Giant*. Oxford: Oxford University Press.

——. 2001. *The Rise of "The Rest."* New York: Oxford University Press.

Amsden, Alice H., and Yoon-Dae Euh. 1993. "South Korea's 1980s Financial Reforms." *World Development* 21 (3): 379–90.

Amuzegar, Jahangir. 1991. *The Dynamics of the Iranian Revolution*. Albany, NY: State University of New York Press.

Anner, Mark, and Teri Caraway. 2010. "International Institutions and Workers' Rights." *Studies in Comparative International Development* 45 (2): 151–69.

Assadi, Morteza. 1990. "Import Substitution and the Structure of the Iranian Economy 1962–1977." *Social Scientist* 18 (5): 30–41.

Aspe, Pedro. 1993. *Economic Transformation the Mexican Way*. Cambridge, MA: MIT Press.

Associated Press. 2010. "G20 Takes Aim at Currency Wars." Oct. 22. http://www.cbc.ca/news/business/g20-takes-aim-at-currency-wars-1.869962.

Auerbach, Nancy Neiman. 2001. *States, Banks, and Markets.* Boulder, CO: Westview Press.

Baer, Werner, Pedro Elosegui, and Andres Gallo. 2002. "The Achievements and Failures of Argentina's Neo-liberal Economic Policies." *Oxford Development Studies* 30 (1): 63–85.

Bahmani-Oskooee, Mohsen. 2005. "History of the Rial and Foreign Exchange Policy in Iran." *Iranian Economic Review* 10 (14): 1–20.

Bai, Chong-En, Jiangyong Lu, and Zhigang Tao. 2006. "Property Rights Protection and Access to Bank Loans." *Economics of Transition* 14 (4): 611–28.

Baktiari, Bahman. 1996. *Parliamentary Politics in Revolutionary Iran.* Gainesville: University Press of Florida.

Balassa, Bela. 1964. "The Purchasing-Power Parity Doctrine: A Reappraisal." *Journal of Political Economy* 72 (6): 584–96.

——. 1983. "Trade Policy in Mexico." *World Development* 11 (9): 795–811.

Baldwin, David A. 1979. "Power Analysis and World Politics." *World Politics* 31 (2): 161–94.

Baliño, Tomas. 1987. "The Argentine Banking Crisis of 1980." *IMF Working Paper* WP/87/77.

Banister, Judith, and George Cook. 2011. "China's Employment and Compensation Costs in Manufacturing through 2008." *Monthly Labor Review* 134 (3): 39–52.

Barrionuevo, Alexei. 2007. "Economic Balancing Act for Argentina's Next Leader." *New York Times,* Nov. 1, A8.

Barth, Jams R., Gerard Caprio, and Ross Levine. 2006. *Rethinking Bank Regulation.* New York: Cambridge University Press.

Bates, Robert. 1981. *Markets and States in Tropical Africa.* Berkeley: University of California Press.

——. 1997. *Open-Economy Politics.* Princeton, NJ: Princeton University Press.

Baumgartner, Frank R., Jeffrey M. Berry, Marie Hojnacki, David C. Kimball, and Beth L. Leech. 2009. *Lobbying and Policy Change: Who Wins, Who Loses, and Why.* Chicago: University of Chicago Press.

Bayat, Assef. 1987. *Workers and Revolution in Iran.* London: Zed Books.

Bazdresch, Carlos, and Santiago Levy. 1991. "Populism and Economic Policy in Mexico, 1970–1982." In *The Macroeconomics of Populism in Latin America,* edited by Rudiger Dornbusch and Sebastian Edwards, 223–62. Chicago: University of Chicago Press.

BCRA. 2007. *Sistema Financiero.* Available at http://www.bcra.gov.ar.

Bearce, David H., and Mark Hallerberg. 2011. "Democracy and De Facto Exchange Rate Regimes." *Economics and Politics* 23 (2): 172–94.

Beck, Nathaniel, and Jonathan N. Katz. 1995. "What to Do (and Not to Do) with Time-Series Cross-Section Data." *American Political Science Review* 89 (3): 634–47.

Beck, Thorsten, Asli Demirgüc-Kunt, and Ross Levine. 2003. "Law, Endowments, and Finance." *Journal of Financial Economics* 70 (2): 137–81.

Behdad, Sohrab. 1988. "Foreign Exchange Gap, Structural Constraints, and the Political Economy of Exchange Rate Determination in Iran." *International Journal of Middle East Studies* 20 (1): 1–21.

Beim, David O., and Charles W. Calomiris. 2001. *Emerging Financial Markets.* New York: McGraw-Hill/Irwin.

Bell, Stephen, and Hui Feng. 2013. *The Rise of the People's Bank of China.* Cambridge, MA: Harvard University Press.

Bellin, Eva. 2002. *Stalled Democracy.* Ithaca, NY: Cornell University Press.

Bennett, Andrew. 2008. "Process Tracing: A Bayesian Perspective." In *The Oxford Hand-book of Political Methodology*, edited by Janet M. Box-Steffensmeier, Henry E. Brady, and David Collier, 702–21. Oxford: Oxford University Press.

Béreau, Sophie, Antonia López Villavicencio, and Valérie Mignon. 2012. "Currency Mis-alignments and Growth." *Applied Economics* 44 (27): 3503–11.

Berg, Andrew, and Yanliang Miao. 2010. "The Real Exchange Rate and Growth Revisited." *IMF Working Paper* WP/10/58.

Berg, Andrew, Jonathan Ostry, and Jeromin Zettelmeyer. 2012. "What Makes Growth Sus-tained?" *Journal of Development Economics* 98 (2): 149–66.

Bergaglio, Pedro. 2005. "Invertir en la Industria Nacional." *Clarín.* Oct. 22.

Bergsten, C. Fred. 2010. "Protectionism by China Is Biggest Since World War II." Oct. 8. http://economix.blogs.nytimes.com/2010/10/08/biggest-protectionism-since-world -war-ii/.

Blomberg, S. Brock, Jeffry Frieden, and Ernesto Stein. 2005. "Sustaining Fixed Rates." *Jour-nal of Applied Economics* 8 (2): 203–25.

Bloomberg. 2003. "Argentina's Prat-Gay Calls Weak Peso Talk 'Nonsense.'" May 28. http://www.bloomberg.com/apps/news?pid=21070001&sid=aCI4xIOPfTYQ.

Blustein, Paul. 2005. *And the Money Kept Rolling In (and Out).* New York: Public Affairs.

Blyth, Mark. 2002. *Great Transformations.* New York: Cambridge University Press.

Bodnar, Gordon M., and William M. Gentry. 1993. "Exchange Rate Exposure and Indus-try Characteristics." *Journal of International Money and Finance* 12 (1): 29–45.

Boehmer, Ekkehart, Robert C. Nash, and Jeffry M. Netter. 2005. "Bank Privatization in De-veloping and Developed Countries." *Journal of Banking & Finance* 29 (8): 1981–2013.

Bolten, Annika. 2009. "Pegs, Politics, and Petrification: Exchange Rate Policy in Argen-tina and Brazil Since the 1980s." PhD diss., London School of Economics and Po-litical Science.

Botero, Juan C., Simeon Djankov, Rafael La Porta, Florecio Lopez-de-Silanes, and Andrei Shliefer. 2004. "The Regulation of Labor." *Quarterly Journal of Economics* 119 (4): 1339–82.

Bottelier, Pieter. 2004. "China's Exchange Rate, U.S.-China Economic Relations and Glo-balization." *China Economic Analysis Working Paper* No. 9.

Bowles, Paul, and Baotai Wang. 2006. "Flowers and Criticism." *Review of International Po-litical Economy* 13 (2): 233–57.

Brahm, Laurence J. 2002. *Zhu Rongji and the Transformation of Modern China.* Singapore: Wiley.

Brennan, James P., and Marcelo Rougier. 2009. *The Politics of National Capitalism: Per-onism and the Argentine Bourgeoisie, 1946–1976.* University Park: Pennsylvania State University Press.

Bresser-Pereira, Luiz Carlos. 2008. "The Dutch Disease and its Neutralization: A Ricard-ian Approach." *Brazilian Journal of Political Economy* 28 (1): 47–71.

Brown, Gilbert T. 1973. *Korean Pricing Policies and Economic Development in the 1960s.* Baltimore: Johns Hopkins University Press.

Broz, J. Lawrence, and Jeffry A. Frieden. 2001. "The Political Economy of International Monetary Relations." *Annual Review of Political Science* 4: 317–43.

Broz, J. Lawrence, Jeffry Frieden, and Stephen Weymouth. 2008. "Exchange-Rate Policy Attitudes: Direct Evidence from Survey Data." *IMF Staff Papers* 55 (3): 417–44.

Buchanan, Paul G. 1995. *State, Labor, Capital.* Pittsburgh: University of Pittsburgh Press.

Buchta, Wilfried. 2000. *Who Rules Iran?* Washington, DC: Washington Institute for Near East Policy.

Bueno de Mesquita, Bruce, Alastair Smith, Randolph M. Siverson, and James D. Morrow. 2003. *The Logic of Political Survival.* Boston: MIT Press.

Buffie, Edward, and Allen Sangines Krause. 1989. "Mexico 1958–86: From Stabilizing Development to the Debt Crisis." In *Developing Country Debt and the World Economy*, edited by Jeffrey D. Sachs, 141–68. Chicago: University of Chicago Press.

Burgueño, Carlos. 2003. "Pidió la UIA Volver a un Dólar de \$3,5." *Ambito Financiero*. Feb. 11.

Burki, Shahid Javed. 1997. "Bad Luck or Bad Policies?" In *Mexico 1994*, edited by Sebastian Edwards and Moisés Naím, 95–124. Washington, DC: Carnegie Endowment for International Peace.

Calomiris, Charles W. 2007. "Devaluation with Contract Redenomination in Argentina." *Annals of Finance* 3 (1): 155–92.

Calvo, Dolores. 2008. "State and Predominant Socioeconomic Actors: The Asymmetric 'Pesification' in Argentina 2001–2002." *Stockholm Papers in Latin American Studies* 4: 1–40.

Calvo, Ernesto, and Maria Victoria Murillo. 2005. "The New Iron Law of Argentine Politics?" In *Argentine Democracy*, edited by Steven Levitsky and Maria Victoria Murillo, 207–26. University Park: Pennsylvania State University Press.

Calvo, Guillermo. 1986. "Fractured Liberalism: Argentina under Martínez de Hoz." *Economic Development and Cultural Change* 34 (3): 511–33.

Calvo, Guillermo A., Leonardo Leiderman, and Carmen M. Reinhart. 1996. "Inflows of Capital to Developing Countries in the 1990s." *Journal of Economic Perspectives* 10 (2): 123–40.

Camp, Roderic Ai. 1989. *Entrepreneurs and Politics in Twentieth-Century Mexico*. New York: Oxford University Press.

Campa, José Manuel, and Linda S. Goldberg. 1997. "The Evolving External Orientation of Manufacturing." *Economic Policy Review* 3 (2): 53–81.

——. 2005. "Exchange Rate Pass-through into Import Prices." *Review of Economics and Statistics* 87 (4): 679–90.

Candelaresi, Cledis. 2003a. "Apostar al Estado Inversor." *Pagina/12*. May 4.

——. 2003b. "Somos Mimados por Kirchner." *Pagina/12*. Nov. 30.

Canitrot, Adolfo. 1994. "Crisis and Transformation of the Argentine State (1978–1992)." In *Democracy, Markets, and Structural Reform in Latin America*, edited by William C. Smith, Carlos H. Acuna, and Eduardo A. Gamarra, 75–104. Miami: North-South Center Press.

Canitrot, Adolfo, and Silvia Junco. 1993. "Macroeconomic Conditions and Trade Liberalization." In *Macroeconomic Conditions and Trade Liberalization*, edited by Adolfo Canitrot and Silvia Junco, 1–30. Washington, DC: Inter-American Development Bank.

Caraway, Teri L. 2009. "Labor Rights in East Asia." *Journal of East Asian Studies* 9 (2): 153–86.

Carrera, Nicolás Iñigo. 2007. "A Century of General Strikes: Strikes in Argentina." In *Strikes Around the World, 1968–2005*, edited by Sjaak van der Velden, Heiner Dribbusch, Dave Lyddon, and Kurt Vandaele, 61–85. Amsterdam: Aksant.

Carrillo Arronte, R. 1987. "The Role of the State and the Entrepreneurial Sector in Mexican Development." In *Government and Private Sector in Contemporary Mexico*, edited by Ricardo Anzaldua and Sylvia Maxfield, 45–63. San Diego, CA: Center for U.S.-Mexican Studies.

Cavallo, Domingo, and Yair Mundlak. 1982. *Agriculture and Economic Growth in an Open Economy*. International Food Policy Research Institute, Research Report No. 36.

Chan, Anita, and Irene Nørlund. 1998. "Vietnamese and Chinese Labour Regimes: On the Road to Divergence." *The China Journal* 40: 173–97.

Chan, Sewell. 2010. "Geithner Calls for Global Cooperation on Currency." *New York Times*, Oct. 6. http://www.nytimes.com/2010/10/07/business/global/07imf.html?hp.

Chandler, Alfred D. 1990. *Scale and Scope: The Dynamics of Industrial Capitalism.* Cambridge, MA: Belknap Press of Harvard University Press.

Chen, Eadie. 2008. "China's MOFCOM Calls for Slower Yuan Rise" *Reuters,* July 14. http://in.reuters.com/article/2008/07/14/china-economy-policy-idINPEK150486200 80714.

Chen, Feng. 2007. "Individual Rights and Collective Rights: Labor's Predicament in China." *Communist and Post-Communist Studies* 40 (1): 59–79.

——. 2009. "Union Power in China Source, Operation, and Constraints." *Modern China* 35 (6): 662–89.

Chen, Ming. 1993. "Analysis of Foreign Exchange Situation in Mainland China in the Near Future." *Liaowang Overseas Edition.* July 5, in *FBIS* July 28, 1993.

Cheung, Peter T. Y. 1998. Introduction to *Provincial Strategies of Economic Reforms in Post-Mao China,* edited by Peter T. Y. Cheung, Jae Ho Chong, Zhimin Lin, and Chae-Ho Chong, 3–46. New York: East Gate.

Chiang, Langi. 2007. "China Bank Lending Curbs Ripple Through Economy." *Reuters,* Nov. 27. http://www.reuters.com/article/2007/11/27/us-china-economy-lending-analysis -idUSPEK23646520071127.

Chin, Gregory, and Eric Helleiner. 2008. "China as a Creditor: A Rising Financial Power?" *Journal of International Affairs* 62 (1): 87–102.

China Daily. 1993a. "Devaluing Drastically Ruled Out." June 6, in *FBIS* June 7, 1993.

——. 1993b. "Foreign Commerce Increases 16.5 Percent." Dec. 8, in *FBIS* Dec. 8, 1993.

——. 1993c. "New Unified Rate Will Help Boost Exports." Dec. 12, in *FBIS* Dec. 13, 1993.

——. 2008. "Govt Unmoved by Slow Exports." July 23, p. 13.

China Labour Bulletin. 2009. *Going It Alone: The Workers' Movement in China (2007–2008).* Hong Kong: CLB Research Report.

Cho, Soon. 1994. *The Dynamics of Korean Economic Development.* Washington, DC: Institute for International Economics.

Choi, Byung-Sun. 1993. "Financial Policy and Big Business in Korea." In *The Politics of Finance in Developing Countries,* edited by Stephan Haggard, Chung H. Lee, and Sylvia Maxfield, 23–54. Ithaca, NY: Cornell University Press.

Choi, Jang Jip. 1989. *Labor and the Authoritarian State.* Seoul: Korea University Press.

Choudhri, Ehsan U., and Dalia S. Hakura. 2006. "Exchange Rate Pass-Through to Domestic Prices: Does the Inflationary Environment Matter?" *Journal of International Money and Finance* 25 (4): 614–39.

Christensen, Darin, and Erik Wibbels. 2014. "Labor Standards, Labor Endowments, and the Evolution of Inequality." *International Studies Quarterly* 58 (2): 362–79.

Chudnovsky, Daniel, and Andrés López. 2007. *The Elusive Quest for Growth in Argentina.* New York: Palgrave MacMillan.

Chung, Wen. 1993. "China Reestablishes Its Exchange Rate Mechanism." *Wen Wei Po.* Feb. 22, in *FBIS* Mar. 4, 1993.

Chwieroth, Jeffrey. 2007. "Neoliberal Economists and Capital Account Liberalization in Emerging Markets." *International Organization* 61 (2): 443–63.

Cingranelli, David L., and David L. Richards. 2010. "The Cingranelli and Richards (CIRI) Human Rights Data Project." *Human Rights Quarterly* 32 (2): 401–24.

Clarín. 1986. "Sourrouille: Los Van a Acompañarnos Planteos Gremiales Por Mucho Tiempo." Feb. 16.

——. 1991a. "Pacto Entre Industriales y Gobierno." Aug. 29.

——. 1991b. "Herrera: 'El Gobierno Debe Cumplir y Bajar los Costos." Oct. 22.

Clawson, Patrick, and Michael Rubin. 2005. *Eternal Iran.* New York: Palgrave Macmillan.

Clifford, Mark. 1994. *Troubled Tiger: Businessmen, Bureaucrats, and Generals in South Korea.* Armonk, NY: ME Sharpe.

Coatz, Diego. 2009. "La Necesidad de Conformar una Estrategia de Largo Plazo." *El Economista*. Jan. 15.

———. 2010. "Primarización e Importactión o Industrialización: Esa es la Cuestión" *Informe Industrial*. Dec. 15.

———. 2011. "El Desafío de la Industrialización." *Revista UIA PyME*. Aug. 25.

Coatz, Diego, and Sergio Woyecheszen. 2013. "Sostener la Demanda." *Pagina/12*. Feb. 4.

Coatz, Diego, Sergio Woyecheszen, and Fernando Garcia Diaz. 2009. "La Necesidad de Repensar una Macro Pro Desarrollo." *El Economista*. July 7.

Coatz, Diego, and Fernando Zack. 2009. "Perspectivas 2010." *El Economista*. Dec. 17.

Cole, David Chamberlin, and Princeton N. Lyman. 1971. *Korean Development*. Cambridge, MA: Harvard University Press.

Cole, David C., and Yung Chul Park. 1983. *Financial Development in Korea, 1945–1978*. Cambridge, MA: Harvard University Press.

Collier, Ruth Berins. 1999. *Paths Toward Democracy*. New York: Cambridge University Press.

Collier, Ruth Berins, and David Collier. 1991. *Shaping the Political Arena*. Princeton, NJ: Princeton University Press.

Collins, Susan M., and Won Am Park. 1989. "External Debt and Macroeconomic Performance in South Korea." In *Developing Country Debt and Economic Performance*, edited by Jeffrey D. Sachs and Susan M. Collins, 121–40. Chicago: University of Chicago Press.

Cook, Maria Lorena. 2007. *The Politics of Labor Reform in Latin America*. University Park: Pennsylvania State University Press.

Cooper, Richard. 1971. *Currency Devaluation in Developing Countries*. Princeton, NJ: Princeton University.

———. 1975. "Prolegomena to the Choice of an International Monetary System." *International Organization* 29 (1): 63–97.

———. 1994. "Korea's Balance of International Payments." In *Macroeconomic Policy and Adjustment in Korea, 1970–1999*, edited by Stephan Haggard, Richard Cooper, Susan Collins, Choongso Kim, and Sung-Tae Ro, 261–94. Cambridge, MA: Harvard University Press.

Copelovitch, Mark, and Jon Pevehouse. 2013. "Ties That Bind? Preferential Trade Agreements and Exchange Rate Policy Choice." *International Studies Quarterly* 57 (2): 385–99.

Cortés Conde, Roberto. 2009. *The Political Economy of Argentina in the Twentieth Century*. New York: Cambridge University Press.

Cottani, Joaquin A., Domingo F. Cavallo, and M. Shahbaz Khan. 1990. "Real Exchange Rate Behavior and Economic Performance in LDCs." *Economic Development and Cultural Change* 39 (1): 61–76.

Cox, Robert W., and Harold Karan Jacobson. 1973. *The Anatomy of Influence: Decision Making in International Organization*. New Haven, CT: Yale University Press.

CNA. 1993. "Economist on Beijing's Single Currency Policy." Feb. 10, in *FBIS* Feb. 11, 1993.

Cruz, Moritz, and Bernard Walters. 2008. "Is the Accumulation of International Reserves Good for Development?" *Cambridge Journal of Economics* 32 (5): 665–81.

Crystal, Jonathan. 1994. "The Politics of Capital Flight: Exit and Exchange Rates in Latin America." *Review of International Studies* 20 (2): 131–47.

Cufré, David. 2003. "La UIA Recreará al G8 para Proteger lo que Ganaron con la Devaluación." *Pagina/12*. Dec. 4.

Cumings, Bruce. 1984. "The Origins and Development of the Northeast Asian Political Economy." *International Organization* 38 (1): 1–40.

Damill, Mario, Roberto Frenkel, and Roxana Maurizio. 2007. "Macroeconomic Policy Changes in Argentina at the Turn of the Century." In *In the Wake of the Crisis*, edited by Marta Novick, Carlos Tomada, Mario Damill, Roberto Frenkel, and Roxana Maurizio, 51–125. Geneva: International Labour Organization.

———. 2011. "Macroeconomic Policy for Full and Productive Employment and Decent Work for All." *Employment Working Paper* No. 109, International Labour Organization.

Darvas, Zsolt. 2012. "Real Effective Exchange Rates for 178 Countries: A New Database." *Bruegel Working Paper* 2012/06.

Deardorff, Alan V., and Robert M. Stern. 1987. "Current Issues in Trade Policy." In *U.S. Trade Policies in a Changing World Economy*, edited by Robert M. Stern, 15–68. Cambridge, MA: MIT Press.

de la Torre, Augusto, Eduardo Levy Yeyati, Sergio Schmuckler. 2003. "Living and Dying with Hard Pegs." *Economía* 3 (2): 43–107.

de Palomino, Mirta L. 1988. *Tradición Y Poder: La Sociedad Rural Argentina (1955–1983)*. Buenos Aires: CISEA.

Deng, Guosheng, and Scott Kennedy. 2010. "Big Business and Industry Association Lobbying in China: The Paradox of Contrasting Styles." *The China Journal* 63: 101–25.

Deyo, Frederic C. 1989. *Beneath the Miracle*. Berkeley: University of California Press.

di Tella, Guido. 1983. *Argentina Under Perón, 1973–76*. New York: St. Martin's Press.

di Tella, Guido, and Carlos Rodríguez Braun. 1990. Introduction to *Argentina, 1946–83: The Economic Ministers Speak*, edited by Guido di Tella and Carlos Rodríguez Braun, 1–30. New York: St. Martin's Press.

Díaz-Bonilla, Eugenio, and Hector E. Schamis. 2001. "From Redistribution to Stability: The Evolution of Exchange Rate Policies in Argentina, 1950–98." In *The Currency Game*, edited by Jeffry Frieden and Ernesto Stein, 65–118. Washington, DC: Inter-American Development Bank.

Dinç, I. Serdar. 2005. "Politicians and Banks: Political Influences on Government-Owned Banks in Emerging Markets." *Journal of Financial Economics* 77 (2): 453–79.

Ding, F. 2010. "Zhejiang Shanghui dasha juxing zhengji yishi [The building of the Zhejiang Merchant Association has an opening ceremony]." *Hangzhou Ribao*, Dec. 2. http://hzdaily.hangzhou.com.cn/hzrb/html/2010-12/02/content_979525.htm.

Dollar, David. 1992. "Outward Oriented Developing Countries Really Do Grow More Rapidly." *Economic Development and Cultural Change* 40 (3): 523–44.

Domínguez, Jorge I. 2011. "The Perfect Dictatorship? Comparing Authoritarian Rule in South Korea and in Argentina, Brazil, Chile, and Mexico." In *The Park Chung Hee Era*, edited by Byung-Kook Kim and Ezra Vogel, 573–602. Cambridge, MA: Harvard University Press.

Dornbusch, Rudiger. 1988. "Mexico: Stabilization, Debt, and Growth." *Economic Policy* 3 (7): 231.

———. 1989. "Argentina after Martínez de Hoz." In *The Political Economy of Argentina*, edited by Guido di Tella and Rudiger Dornbusch, 286–320. Pittsburgh: University of Pittsburgh Press.

———. 1992. "The Case for Trade Liberalization in Developing Countries." *Journal of Economic Perspectives* 6 (1): 69–85.

———. 1997. "The Folly, the Crash, and Beyond: Economic Policies and the Crisis." In *Mexico 1994*, edited by Sebastian Edwards and Moisés Naím, 125–40. Washington, DC: Carnegie Endowment for International Peace.

Drake, Paul W. 1996. *Labor Movements and Dictatorships*. Baltimore: Johns Hopkins University Press.

Dresser, Denise. 1997. "Falling from the Tightrope." In *Mexico 1994*, edited by Sebastian Edwards and Moisés Naím, 55–80. Washington, DC: Carnegie Endowment for International Peace.

Duckenfield, Mark, and Mark Aspinwall. 2010. "Private Interests and Exchange Rate Politics." *European Union Politics* 11 (3): 381–404.

Dye, Howard S. 1955. "Development of the Banco Central in Argentina's Economy." *Southern Economic Journal* 21 (3): 303–18.

Easterly, William. 2001. "The Lost Decades." *Journal of Economic Growth* 6 (2): 135–57.

Economic Information Center of the State Economic and Trade Commission. 1995. "Analysis of China's Current Export Environment." *Jingji Gongzuo Tongxun (Economic Work Newsletter).* May 31, in *FBIS* Aug. 10, 1995.

Economist, The. 2007. "Marital bliss; Argentina." Dec. 15. http://www.economist.com/node/10286016.

——. 2009. "China's Struggling Smaller Firms." Sept. 12. http://www.economist.com/node/14409584.

——. 2011. "Inflated fears; Price rises in China." Jan. 6. http://www.economist.com/node/17851541.

——. 2013. "Don't go Zhou; Monetary policy in China." Mar. 2. http://www.economist.com/news/finance-and-economics/21572805-chinas-central -banker-stays-put-chinese-central-banking-moves-dont-go-zhou.

Eckstein, Harry. 1975. "Case Study and Theory in Political Science." In *Handbook of Political Science*, edited by Fred Greenstein and Nelson W. Polsby, 79–137. Reading, MA: Addison-Wesley.

Edwards, Sebastian. 1989. *Real Exchange Rates, Devaluation, and Adjustment.* Cambridge, MA: MIT Press.

——. 1997. "Bad Luck or Bad Policies? An Economic Analysis of the Crisis." In *Mexico 1994*, edited by Sebastian Edwards and Moisés Naím, 95–124. Washington, DC: Carnegie Endowment for International Peace.

Edwards, Sebastian, and Moisés Naím. 1997. *Mexico 1994: Anatomy of an Emerging-Market Crash.* Washington, DC: Carnegie Endowment for International Peace.

Ehrlich, Sean D. 2007. "Access to Protection." *International Organization* 61 (3): 571–605.

Eichengreen, Barry. 1996. *Globalizing Capital.* Princeton, NJ: Princeton University Press.

——. 2007. "The Real Exchange Rate and Economic Growth." *Social and Economic Studies* 56 (4): 7–20.

Eichengreen, Barry, Ricardo Hausmann, and Ugo Panizza. 2005. "The Pain of Original Sin." In *Other People's Money*, edited by Barry Eichengreen and Ricardo Hausmann, 13–47. Chicago: University of Chicago Press.

El Cronista. 1983. "Politicas Fiscal y Cambiaria, y Deuda Externa." July 28.

——. 1991. "Ofreció la UIA Apoyo a Cavallo Para Afianzar la Estabilidad." May 10.

El Economista. 1991a. "Entrevista Con el Presidente de la UIA, Israel Mahler." May 3.

——. 1991b. "La UIA no Hace Oposición y Apoya la Gestión de Cavallo." May 17.

Enterprise Surveys. Various Years. The World Bank. http://www.enterprisesurveys.org.

Epstein, Rachel A. 2008. "The Social Context in Conditionality: Internationalizing Finance in Postcommunist Europe." *Journal of European Public Policy* 15 (6): 880–98.

Escobar Toledo, Saul. 1987. "Rifts in the Mexican Power Elite, 1976–1986." In *Government and Private Sector in Contemporary Mexico*, edited by Ricardo Anzaldua and Sylvia Maxfield, 65–88. San Diego, CA: Center for U.S.-Mexican Studies.

Etchemendy, Sebastián. 2005. "Old Actors in New Markets." In *Argentine Democracy*, edited by Steven Levitsky and María Victoria Murillo, 62–87. University Park: Pennsylvania State University Press.

Etchemendy, Sebastián, and Ruth Berins Collier. 2007. "Down but Not Out: Union Resurgence and Segmented Neocorporatism in Argentina (2003–2007)." *Politics and Society* 35 (3): 363–401.

Etchemendy, Sebastián, and Candelaria Garay. 2011. "Argentina: Left Populism in Comparative Perspective, 2003–2009." In *The Resurgence of the Latin American Left*, edited by Steven Levitsky and Kenneth M. Roberts, 283–305. Baltimore: Johns Hopkins University Press.

Evans, Peter B. 1995. *Embedded Autonomy*. Princeton, NJ: Princeton University Press.

Faccio, Mara, Ronald W. Masulis, and John McConnell. 2006. "Political Connections and Corporate Bailouts." *Journal of Finance* 61 (6): 2597–2635.

Fairfield, Tasha. 2010. "Business Power and Tax Reform: Taxing Income and Profits in Chile and Argentina." *Latin American Politics and Society* 52 (2): 37–71.

Far Eastern Economic Review. 1974. "Devaluation: Danger of War." Dec. 20, pp. 34–36.

Farrell, Henry, and Abraham L. Newman. 2010. "Making Global Markets: Historical Institutionalism in International Political Economy." *Review of International Political Economy* 17 (4): 609–38.

Farzin, Yeganeh Hossein. 1995. "Foreign Exchange Reform in Iran: Badly Designed, Badly Managed." *World Development* 23 (6): 987–1001.

Fernández, Roque. 1991. "What Have Populists Learned from Hyperinflation?" In *The Macroeconomics of Populism in Latin America*, edited by Rudiger Dornbusch and Sebastián Edwards, 121–49. Chicago: University of Chicago Press.

Filippini, Mariano, and María Angélica Olcese. 1989. "Transitional Economic Policies, 1971–3." In *The Political Economy of Argentina*, edited by Guido di Tella and Rudiger Dornbusch, 189–205. Pittsburgh: University of Pittsburgh Press.

Fioretos, Orfeo. 2011. "Historical Institutionalism in International Relations." *International Organization* 65 (2): 367–99.

Flores Quiroga, Aldo. 2001. "Mexico: Crises and the Domestic Politics of Sustained Liberalization." In *The Political Economy of International Financial Crisis*, edited by Shale Horowitz and Uk Heo, 179–98. Lanham, MD: Rowman and Littlefield.

Foot, Rosemary, and Andrew Walter. 2011. *China, the United States, and Global Order*. New York: Cambridge University Press.

Forbes, Kristin J. 2002. "Cheap Labor Meets Costly Capital: The Impact of Devaluations on Commodity Firms." *Journal of Development Economics* 69 (2): 335–65.

Frank, Charles R., Jr., Kwang Suk Kim, and Larry Westphal. 1975. *Foreign Trade Regimes and Economic Development: South Korea*. New York: Columbia University Press.

Frank, Lawrence P. 1984. "Two Responses to the Oil Boom: Iranian and Nigerian Politics after 1973." *Comparative Politics* 16 (3): 295–314.

Frankel, Jeffrey. 1997. "Sterilization of Money Inflows." *Estudios de Economia* 24 (2): 263–85.

———. 2006. "On the Yuan." *CESifo Economic Studies* 52 (2): 246–75.

Frankel, Jeffrey, and Andrew K. Rose. 1996. "Currency Crashes in Emerging Markets." *Journal of International Economics* 41 (3–4): 351–66.

Frankel, Jeffrey, and George Saravelos. 2012. "Can Leading Indicators Assess Country Vulnerability?" *Journal of International Economics* 87 (2): 216–31.

Frankel, Jeffrey A., and Shang-Jin Wei. 2007. "Assessing China's Exchange Rate Regime." *Economy Policy* 22 (51): 575–627.

Freeman III, Charles W., and Wen Jin Yuan. 2011. "China's Exchange Rate Politics." A Report of the Freeman Chair in China Studies, Center for Strategic and International Studies.

Frenkel, Roberto, and Martin Rapetti. 2006. "Monetary and Exchange Rate Policies in Argentina after the Convertibility Regime Collapse." *Nuevos Documentos CEDES*. Jan. 2006.

Frenkel, Roberto, and Jaime Ros. 2006. "Unemployment and the Real Exchange Rate in Latin America." *World Development* 34 (4): 631–46.

Frenkel, Roberto, and Lance Taylor. 2007. "Real Exchange Rate, Monetary Policy, and Employment." In *Policy Matters*, edited by José Ocampo, Jomo K.S., and Sarbuland Khan, 272–85. New York: Zed Books.

Freund, Caroline, and Martha Denisse Pierola. 2012. "Export Surges." *Journal of Development Economics* 97 (2): 387–95.

Frieden, Jeffry A. 1991a. "Invested Interests: The Politics of National Economic Policies in a World of Global Finance." *International Organization* 45 (4): 425–51.

——. 1991b. *Debt, Development, and Democracy*. Princeton, NJ: Princeton University Press.

——. 1994. "Exchange Rate Politics: Contemporary Lessons from American History." *Review of International Political Economy* 1 (1): 81–103.

——. 1997. "The Politics of Exchange Rates." In *Mexico 1994*, edited by Sebastian Edwards and Moisés Naím, 81–94. New York: Carnegie Endowment for International Peace.

——. 1999. "Actors and Preferences in International Relations." In *Strategic Choice and International Relations*, edited by David Lake and Robert Powell, 39–76. Princeton, NJ: Princeton University Press.

——. 2002. "Real Sources of European Currency Policy." *International Organization* 56 (4): 831–60.

Frieden, Jeffry A., Piero Ghezzi, and Ernesto Stein. 2001. "Politics and Exchange Rates." In *The Currency Game: Exchange Rate Politics in Latin America*, edited by Jeffry Frieden and Ernesto Stein, 21–63. Washington, DC: Inter-American Development Bank.

Frieden, Jeffry, David Leblang, and Neven Valev. 2010. "The Political Economy of Exchange Rate Regimes in Transition Economies." *Review of International Organizations* 5 (1): 1–25.

Galak, Oliver. 2011. "Pide la UIA Bajar Costos y Más Crédito." *La Nación*, Nov. 22.

Galiani, Sebastián, Daniel Heymann, and Mariano Tommasi. 2003. "Great Expectations and Hard Times." *Economía* 3 (2): 109–60.

Gallagher, Kevin P. 2015. "Countervailing Monetary Power: Re-regulating Capital Flows in Brazil and South Korea." *Review of International Political Economy* 22 (1): 77–102.

Gallagher, Mary Elizabeth. 2005. *Contagious Capitalism*. New York: Cambridge University Press.

Gao, Jinshui. 2006. "Dang qian woguo wai hui chu bei you guan wenti tan tao (Analysis of Current Issues about Foreign Reserves)." *Jingji Yanjiu Cankao (Review of Economic Research)* 65: 41–44.

Gereffi, Gary. 2009. "Development Models and Industrial Upgrading in China and Mexico." *European Sociological Review* 25 (1): 37–51.

Gereffi, Gary, John Humphrey, and Timothy Sturgeon. 2005. "The Governance of Global Value Chains." *Review of International Political Economy* 12 (1): 78–104.

Gerschenkron, Alexander. 1962. *Economic Backwardness in Historical Perspective*. Cambridge, MA: Belknap Press of Harvard University Press.

Ghosh, Atish R., Jun Kim, Mahvash S. Qureshi, and Juan Zalduendo. 2012. "Surges." *IMF Working Paper* No. 12/22.

Gibson, Edward. 1996. *Class and Conservative Parties*. Baltimore: Johns Hopkins University Press.

Gil-Díaz, Francisco, and Agustín Carstens. 1997. "Pride and Prejudice." In *Mexico 1994*, edited by Sebastian Edwards and Moisés Naím, 165–200. Washington, DC: Carnegie Endowment for International Peace.

Gilens, Martin, and Benjamin I. Page. 2014. "Testing Theories of American Politics: Elites, Interest Groups, and Average Citizens." *Perspectives on Politics* 12 (3): 564–81.

Gilley, Bruce. 1998. *Tiger on the Brink*. Berkeley: University of California Press.

Gilpin, Robert. 2001. *Global Political Economy*. Princeton, NJ: Princeton University Press.

Giovannini, Alberto, and Martha De Melo. 1993. "Government Revenue from Financial Repression." *American Economic Review* 83 (4): 953–63.

Gluzmann, Pablo, Eduardo Levy-Yeyati, and Federico Sturzenegger. 2012. "Exchange Rate Undervaluation and Economic Growth." *Economics Letters* 117 (3): 666–72.

Goldstein, Avery. 2005. *Rising to the Challenge.* Stanford, CA: Stanford University Press.

Goodfriend, Marvin, and Eswar Prasad. 2006. "A Framework for Independent Monetary Policy in China." *IMF Working Paper* WP/06/112.

Gowa, Joanne. 1988. "Public Goods and Political Institutions." *International Organization* 42 (1): 15–32.

Greenhill, Brian, Layna Mosley, and Aseem Prakash. 2009. "Trade-Based Diffusion of Labor Rights." *American Political Science Review* 103 (4): 669–90.

Grugel, Jean, and Maria Pia Riggirozzi. 2007. "The Return of the State in Argentina." *International Affairs* 83 (1): 87–107.

Guillén, Mauro F. 2001. *The Limits of Convergence.* Princeton, NJ: Princeton University Press.

Gwartney, James, and Robert Lawson. 2009. *Economic Freedom of the World 2009 Annual Report.* Vancouver: The Fraser Institute.

Hacker, Jacob S., and Paul Pierson. 2002. "Business Power and Social Policy." *Politics & Society* 30 (2): 277–325.

Haggard, Stephan. 1990. *Pathways from the Periphery.* Ithaca, NY: Cornell University Press.

———. 1994a. "Macroeconomic Policy through the First Oil Shock, 1970–1975." In *Macroeconomic Policy and Adjustment in Korea, 1970–1999*, edited by Stephan Haggard, Richard Cooper, Susan Collins, Choongso Kim, and Sung-Tae Ro, 23–47. Cambridge, MA: Harvard University Press.

———. 1994b. "From the Heavy Industry Plan to Stabilization." In *Macroeconomic Policy and Adjustment in Korea, 1970–1999*, edited by Stephan Haggard, Richard Cooper, Susan Collins, Choongso Kim, and Sung-Tae Ro, 49–74. Cambridge, MA: Harvard University Press.

Haggard, Stephan, Byung-kook Kim, and Chung-in Moon. 1991. "The Transition to Export-led Growth in South Korea: 1954–1966." *Journal of Asian Studies* 50 (4): 850–73.

Haggard, Stephan, and Sylvia Maxfield. 1996. "The Political Economy of Financial Internationalization in the Developing World." *International Organization* 50 (1): 35–68.

Hakimian, Hassan, and Massoud Karshenas. 2000. "Dilemmas and Prospects for Economic Reform and Reconstruction in Iran." In *Iran's Economy*, edited by Parvin Alizadeh, 29–62. New York: St. Martin's Press.

Hall, Peter A., and David W. Soskice. 2001. *Varieties of Capitalism.* New York: Oxford University Press.

Hamilton, Nora. 1982. *The Limits of State Autonomy: Post-Revolutionary Mexico.* Princeton, NJ: Princeton University Press.

Han, Nae Bok. 1964a. "Austerity." *Far Eastern Economic Review*, Jan. 23, 142–43.

———. 1964b. "Seoul Devalues." *Far Eastern Economic Review*, May 21, 395.

———. 1965. "Floating Rate." *Far Eastern Economic Review*, Apr. 15, 133.

Harvey, Charles, and Stephen R. Lewis. 1990. *Policy Choice and Development Performance in Botswana.* New York: St. Martin's Press.

He, Sui. 1993. "Guangdong Official Sees 'Benefit.'" *Ta Kung Pao*, Dec. 31, in *FBIS* Jan. 3, 1994.

Heath, Jonathan. 1999. *Mexico and the Sexenio Curse.* Washington, DC: Center for Strategic & International Studies.

Helleiner, Eric. 2003. *The Making of National Money.* Ithaca, NY: Cornell University Press.

——. 2005. "A Fixation with Floating." *Canadian Journal of Political Science* 38 (1): 23–44.

Henning, C. Randall. 1994. *Currencies and Politics in the United States, Germany, and Japan.* Washington, DC: Institute for International Economics.

——. 2006. "The Exchange-Rate Weapon and Macroeconomic Conflict." In *International Monetary Power*, edited by David Andrews, 117–38. Ithaca, NY: Cornell University Press.

Henning, C. Randall, and Saori Katada. 2014. "Cooperation without Institutions: The Case of East Asian Currency Arrangements." Unpublished manuscript. American University and University of Southern California.

Herbst, Jeffrey I. 2000. *States and Power in Africa*. Princeton, NJ: Princeton University Press.

Herrerias, Maria J., and Vicente Orts. 2011. "The Driving Forces behind China's Growth." *Economics of Transition* 19 (1): 79–124.

Heston, Alan, Robert Summers, and Bettina Aten. 2009. "Penn World Tables Version 6.3." Center for International Comparisons of Production, Income and Prices, University of Pennsylvania. https://pwt.sas.upenn.edu/php_site/pwt_index.php.

Hirschman, Albert O. 1968. "The Political Economy of Import-Substituting Industrialization in Latin America." *Quarterly Journal of Economics* 82 (1): 1–32.

Hong, Wontack, and Yung Chul Park. 1986. "The Financing of Export-Oriented Growth in South Korea." In *Pacific Growth and Financial Interdependence*, edited by Augustin H. H. Tan and Basant Kapur, 163–82. Sydney: Allen and Unwin.

Howson, Nicholas Calcina. 2009. "China's Restructured Commercial Banks." In *China's Emerging Financial Markets*, edited by Martha Avery, Zhu Min, and Jinqing Cai, 123–63. Singapore: John Wiley & Sons.

Huang, Guobo, and Clement Yuk-Pang Wong. 1996. "Unification of China's Foreign Exchange Rates." *Contemporary Economic Policy* 14 (4): 42–57.

Huang, Yasheng. 2008. *Capitalism with Chinese Characteristics: Entrepreneurship and the State*. New York: Cambridge University Press.

Huizinga, Harry. 1997. "Real Exchange Rate Misalignment and Redistribution." *European Economic Review* 41 (2): 259–77.

Huntington, Samuel P. 1968. *Political Order in Changing Societies*. New Haven, CT: Yale University Press.

Hwang, Don. 1967. "Upside Down Rates." *Far Eastern Economic Review*. Apr. 27, p. 216.

Ikenberry, G. John. 1986. "The Irony of State Strength: Comparative Responses to the Oil Shocks in the 1970s." *International Organization* 40 (1): 105–37.

Ilzetzki, Ethan, Carmen Reinhart, and Kenneth Rogoff. 2008. "Exchange Rate Arrangements Entering the 21st Century." Available at: http://terpconnect.umd.edu/~creinhar/Papers.html.

IMF. 2012. *People's Republic of China 2012 Article IV Consultation*. Washington, DC: International Monetary Fund.

Independent Evaluation Office of the International Monetary Fund. 2004. *The IMF and Argentina, 1991–2001*. Washington, DC: International Monetary Fund.

Jing, Xuecheng. 1995. "Foreign Exchange Reserves Increase; Renminbi Exchange Rate Remains Firm." *Caimao Jingji (Finance and Economics)*. Oct. 11, in *FBIS* Dec. 26, 1995.

Jingji Ribao. 1995. "A Survey of Experts: What Are the Trends in China's Economy in 1995?" Jan. 18, in *FBIS* Apr. 25, 1995.

Johnson, Chalmers. 1987. "Political Institutions and Economic Performance." In *The Political Economy of the New Asian Industrialism*, edited by Frederic C. Deyo, 136–64. Ithaca, NY: Cornell University Press.

Johnson, Simon, Jonathan D. Ostry, and Arvind Subramanian. 2006. "Levers for Growth." *Finance and Development* 43 (1): 28–31.

Jones, Leroy P., and Il Sakong. 1980. *Government, Business, and Entrepreneurship in Economic Development.* Cambridge, MA: Council on East Asian Studies, Harvard University.

Kaifang (Open Magazine). 1995. "Situation in China's Economic Reform for 1995—Zhu Rongji's Closed-Door Speech at End of December 1994." Feb. 2, in *FBIS* May 19, 1995.

Kanenguiser, Martin. 2009. "La UIA Pide Medidas de Reactivación." *La Nación.* Jan. 3.

Kaplan, Stephen B. 2006. "The Political Obstacles to Greater Exchange Rate Flexibility in China." *World Development* 34 (7): 1182–1200.

———. 2013. *Globalization and Austerity Politics in Latin America.* New York: Cambridge University Press.

Karcher, Sebastian, and David A. Steinberg. 2013. "Assessing the Causes of Capital Account Liberalization." *International Studies Quarterly* 57 (1): 128–37.

Karshenas, Massoud. 1990. *Oil, State, and Industrialization in Iran.* New York: Cambridge University Press.

Katouzian, Homa. 1981. *The Political Economy of Modern Iran.* New York: New York University Press.

Katzenstein, Peter J. 1978. Conclusion to *Between Power and Plenty*, edited by Peter J. Katzenstein, 295–336. Madison: University of Wisconsin Press.

Kaufman, Robert R., Carlos Bazdresch, and Blanca Heredia. 1994. "Mexico: Radical Reform in a Dominant Party System." In *Voting for Reform*, edited by Stephan Haggard and Steven B. Webb, 360–410. Washington, DC: World Bank.

Kennedy, Scott. 2005. *The Business of Lobbying in China.* Cambridge, MA: Harvard University Press.

Keshavarzian, Arang. 2007. *Bazaar and State in Iran.* New York: Cambridge University Press.

Kessler, Timothy P. 1998. "Political Capital: Mexican Financial Policy Under Salinas." *World Politics* 51 (1): 36–66.

———. 1999. *Global Capital and National Politics.* Westport, CT: Praeger Publishers.

Khwaja, Asim Ijaz, and Atif Mian. 2005. "Do Lenders Favor Politically Connected Firms?" *Quarterly Journal of Economics* 120 (4): 1371–1411.

Kim, Byung-Kook. 2011. "The Leviathan." In *The Park Chung Hee Era*, edited by Byung-Kook Im and Ezra F. Vogel, 200–232. Cambridge, MA: Harvard University Press.

Kim, Chung-Yum. 2011. *From Despair to Hope: Economic Policymaking in Korea 1945–1979.* Seoul: Korea Development Institute.

Kim, Eun Mee. 1997. *Big Business, Strong State.* Albany: State University of New York Press.

Kim, Eun Mee, and Gil-Sun Park. 2011. "The Chaebol." In *The Park Chung Hee Era*, edited by Byung-Kook Im and Ezra F. Vogel, 265–94. Cambridge, MA: Harvard University Press.

Kim, Kwang Suk. 1991. "The 1964–65 Exchange Rate Reform, Export-Promotion Measures, and Import-Liberalization Program." In *Economic Development in the Republic of Korea*, edited by Lee-Jay Cho and Yoon Hyun Kim, 101–34. Honolulu: University of Hawaii Press.

Kim, Samuel S. 2006. "Chinese Foreign Policy Faces Globalization Challenges." In *New Directions in the Study of China's Foreign Policy*, edited by Alastair Iain Johnston and Robert Ross, 276–306. Stanford, CA: Stanford University Press.

Kim, Wan-Soon. 1991. "The President's Emergency Decree for Economic Stability and Growth (1972)." In *Economic Development in the Republic of Korea*, edited by Lee-Jay Cho and Yoon Hyun Kim, 163–81. Honolulu: University of Hawaii Press.

Kim, Yoon Hyung. 1991. "Policy Response to the Oil Crisis and the Presidential Emergency Decree (1974)." In *Economic Development in the Republic of Korea*, edited by Lee-Jay Cho and Yoon Hyun Kim, 183–206. Honolulu: University of Hawaii Press.

Kinderman, Daniel. 2008. "The Political Economy of Sectoral Exchange Rate Preferences and Lobbying." *Review of International Political Economy* 15 (5): 851–80.

King, Gary, Robert O. Keohane, and Sidney Verba. 1994. *Designing Social Inquiry*. Princeton, NJ: Princeton University Press.

Kirshner, Jonathan. 2003. "Money Is Politics." *Review of International Political Economy* 10 (4): 645–60.

Knight, Sarah Cleeland. 2010. "Divested Interests: Globalization and the New Politics of Exchange Rates." *Business and Politics* 12 (2): 1–28.

Kohli, Atul. 2004. *State-Directed Development*. New York: Cambridge University Press.

Koopman, Robert, Zhi Wang, and Shang-Jin. 2012. "Estimating Domestic Content in Exports When Processing Trade is Pervasive." *Journal of Development Economics* 99 (1): 178–89.

Korpi, Walter. 1985. "Power Resources Approach vs. Action and Conflict." *Sociological Theory* 3 (2): 31–45.

———. 2006. "Power Resources and Employer-centered Approaches in Explanations of Welfare States and Varieties of Capitalism." *World Politics* 58 (2): 167–206.

Krasner, Stephen D. 1978. "United States Commercial and Monetary Policy." In *Between Power and Plenty*, edited by Peter J. Katzenstein, 51–87. Madison: University of Wisconsin Press.

Krieger Vasena, Adalbert. 1990. "Chapter 6." In *Argentina, 1946–83: The Economic Ministers Speak*, edited by Guido di Tella and Carlos Rodríguez Braun, 85–103. New York: St. Martin's Press.

Kritz, Ernesto. 2002. "Poverty and the Labor Market in the Argentine Crisis 1998–2002." *Argentina–Crisis and Poverty 2003: A Poverty Assessment. Background Paper* No. 4.

Krugman, Paul. 2010. "Taking On China." *New York Times*, Mar. 14. http://www.nytimes.com/2010/03/15/opinion/15krugman.html.

Kucera, David. 2002. "Core Labour Standards and Foreign Direct Investment." *International Labour Review* 141 (1–2): 31–69.

Ladjevardi, Habib. 1985. *Labor Unions and Autocracy in Iran*. Syracuse, NY: Syracuse University Press.

Lake, David A. 2009. "Open Economy Politics: A Critical Review." *Review of International Organizations* 4 (3): 219–44.

Lam, Willy Wo-Lap. 1999. *The Era of Jiang Zemin*. New York: Prentice Hall.

Lampton, David M. 1992. "A Plum for a Peach." In *Bureaucracy, Politics, and Decision Making in Post-Mao China*, edited by Kenneth Lieberthal and David M. Lampton, 33–58. Berkeley: University of California Press.

La Nación. 1986. "Sourrouille: Ajustes Cambiarios y en las Tarifas." Apr. 5, p. 14.

———. 1991. "Se Firmó el Acuerdo con la Industria." Sep. 3.

———. 1996. "El futuro de la convertibilidad se instala otra vez en la UIA." Jan. 18. http://www.lanacion.com.ar/171250-el-futuro-de-la-convertibilidad-se-instala-otra-vez-en-la-uia.

———. 1999. "Los Empresarios Defienden el Modelo, Pero dan su Apoyo con Condiciones." May 30. http://www.lanacion.com.ar/140252-los-empresarios-defienden-el-modelo-pero-dan-su-apoyo-con-condiciones.

———. 2002. "Industriales del Interior Pidieron la Pesificación Total." Jan. 26. http://www.lanacion.com.ar/369549-industriales-del-interior-pidieron-la-pesificacion-total.

———. 2007a. "Miceli Dijo que Seguirá el Tipo de Cambio Alto." June 14. http://www.lanacion.com.ar/917286-miceli-dijo-que-seguira-el-tipo-de-cambio-alto.

———. 2007b. "Lousteau Criticó a los Productores por su Falta de Diálogo." Dec. 13. http://www.lanacion.com.ar/970770-lousteau-critico-a-los-productores-por-su-falta-de-dialogo.

——. 2008. "Prometen un Tipo de Cambio Competitivo." Aug. 21. http://www.lanacion.com.ar/1041869-prometen-un-tipo-de-cambio-competitivo.

——. 2010. "Se Suman Reclamos por el Tipo de Cambio." Apr. 14. http://www.lanacion.com.ar/1253999-se-suman-reclamos-por-el-tipo-de-cambio.

——. 2011. "La UIA Dice que no Impulsa 'Ningún Proceso Devaluatorio.'" Nov. 4. http://www.lanacion.com.ar/1420417-la-uia-dice-que-no-impulsa-ningun-proceso-devaluatorio.

La Porta, Rafael, Florencio Lopez-de-Silanes, and Andrei Shleifer. 2002. "Government Ownership of Banks." *Journal of Finance* 57 (1): 265–301.

Lardy, Nicholas R. 1998. *China's Unfinished Economic Revolution*. Washington, DC: Brookings Institution Press.

——. 2012. *Sustaining China's Economic Growth after the Global Financial Crisis*. Washington, DC: Peterson Institute for International Economics.

Lautenschlager, Wolfgang. 1986. "The Effects of an Overvalued Exchange Rate on the Iranian Economy, 1979–1984." *International Journal of Middle East Studies* 18 (1): 31–52.

Lehoucq, Fabrice, Gabriel Negretto, Francisco Aparicio, Benito Nacif, and Allyson Benton. 2008. "Policymaking in Mexico under One-Party Hegemony and Divided Government." In *Policymaking in Latin America*, edited by Ernesto Stein and Mariano Tommasi, 287–328. Washington, DC: Inter-American Development Bank.

Leigh, Lamin, and Richard Podpiera. 2006. "The Rise of Foreign Investment in China's Banks." *IMF Working Paper* WP/06/292.

Levitsky, Steven, and María Victoria Murillo. 2005. "Building Castles in the Sand?" In *Argentine Democracy*, edited by Steven Levitsky and María Victoria Murillo, 21–44. University Park: Pennsylvania State University Press.

Levy-Yeyati, Eduardo, Federico Sturzenegger, and Pablo Alfredo Gluzmann. 2013. "Fear of Appreciation." *Journal of Development Economics* 101: 233–47.

Levy-Yeyati, Eduardo, and Diego Valenzuela. 2007. *La Resurección*. Buenos Aires: Editorial Sudamericana.

Lewis, Paul H. 1990. *The Crisis of Argentine Capitalism*. Chapel Hill: University of North Carolina Press.

Leyba, Carlos Raul Gabriel. 1990. "Chapter 10." In *Argentina, 1946–83: The Economic Ministers Speak*, edited by Guido di Tella and Carlos Rodríguez Braun. New York: St. Martin's Press.

Li, Cheng. 2005. "The New Bipartisanship within the Chinese Communist Party." *Orbis* 49 (3): 387–400.

——. 2009. "China's Team of Rivals." *Foreign Policy* Mar.–Apr. 2009.

Li, Hongbin, Lingsheng Meng, Qian Wang, and Li-An Zhou. 2008. "Political Connections, Financing, and Firm Performance." *Journal of Development Economics* 87 (2): 283–99.

Li, Hongbin, and Li-An Zhou. 2005. "Political Turnover and Economic Performance." *Journal of Public Economics* 89 (9–10): 1743–62.

Li, Pumin. 1995. "Analysis of the 1994 Reform of Foreign Exchange and Trade Management System." *Jingji Yanjiu Cankao (Review of Economic Research)* 4: 29–36.

Lieberman, Evan S. 2005. "Nested Analysis as a Mixed-Method Strategy for Comparative Analysis." *American Political Science Review* 99 (3): 435–52.

Lieberthal, Kenneth. 2004. *Governing China*. 2nd ed. New York: W. W. Norton.

Lieberthal, Kenneth, and Michel Oksenberg. 1988. *Policy Making in China*. Princeton, NJ: Princeton University Press.

Liew, Leong H. 2004. "Policy Elites in the Political Economy of China's Exchange Rate Policymaking." *Journal of Contemporary China* 13 (38): 21–51.

Liew, Leong H., and Harry X. Wu. 2007. *The Making of China's Exchange Rate Policy.* Northampton, MA: Edward Elgar.

Lin, Zhiyuan. 1994. "Conditions and Policies for the Reform of Convertibility of the Renminbi." *Jingji Yanjiu.* Feb. 20, in *FBIS* May 11, 1994.

Lindblom, Charles Edward. 1977. *Politics and Markets.* New York: Basic Books.

Lins, Maria Antonieta del Tedesco. 2012. "State-Owned Banks in Brazil and India." Presented at the annual meeting of the International Studies Association, San Diego, CA.

Liu, Fei. 1996. "Correlation between RMB New Exchange Rate System and Domestic Money Supply." *Caimao Jingji (Finance and Economics).* Dec. 11, in *FBIS* Jan. 31, 1996.

Liu, Li-Gang, and Laurent Pauwels. 2012. "Do External Political Pressures Affect the Renminbi Exchange Rate?" *Journal of International Money and Finance* 31 (6): 1800–1818.

Liu, Xiaoxi. 1995. "On Whether the Inflow of Foreign Capital Produces an Inflationary Effect." *Gaige (Reform).* May 20, in *FBIS* July 28, 1995.

Lizondo, José Saúl. 1989. "Comment." In *The Political Economy of Argentina,* edited by Guido di Tella and Rudiger Dornbusch, 206–12. Pittsburgh: University of Pittsburgh Press.

Ljungwall, Christer, Yi Xiong, and Zou Yutong. 2013. "Central Bank Financial Strength and the Cost of Sterilization in China." *China Economic Review* 25: 105–16.

Looney, Robert E. 1982. *Economic Origins of the Iranian Revolution.* New York: Pergamon Press.

Love, Inessa, and Rida Zaidi. 2010. "Trade Credit, Bank Credit and Financial Crisis." *International Review of Finance* 10 (1): 125–47.

Lu, Jianxin. 2008. "China FX Policy Shift More Rhetoric Than Reality." *Reuters,* May 8. http://www.reuters.com/article/2008/05/08/us-china-yuan-policy-idUSSHA 12085220080508.

Lustig, Nora. 1992. *Mexico: The Remaking of an Economy.* Washington, DC: Brookings Institution.

Machinea, José Luis. 1990. "Stabilization under Alfonsín's Government." *Documento CEDES* No. 42.

Mahoney, James, and Gary Goertz. 2004. "The Possibility Principle: Choosing Negative Cases in Comparative Research." *American Political Science Review* 98 (4): 653–69.

Mai, Shilong. 1993. "Guangdong Economist Views Devaluation of Yuan." *Zhongguo Tongxun She.* June 3, in *FBIS* June 4, 1993.

Maia, José Luis, and Mercedes Kweitel. 2003. "Argentina: Sustainable Output Growth after the Collapse." Manuscript, Dirección Nacional de Politicas Macroeconomicas, Ministerio de Economia-Argentina.

Malesky, Edmund J., and Markus Taussig. 2009. "Where Is Credit Due?" *Journal of Law, Economics, and Organization* 25 (2): 535–78.

Mallon, Richard D., and Juan V. Sourrouille. 1975. *Economic Policymaking in a Conflict Society.* Cambridge, MA: Harvard University Press.

Maloney, Parvin. 2000. "Agents or Obstacles? Parastatal Foundations and Challenges for Iranian Development." In *The Economy of Iran,* edited by Parvin Alizadeh, 145–76. New York: I. B. Tauris.

Marshall, Monty, Keith Jaggers, and Ted Gurr. 2009. "Political Regime Characteristics and Transitions, 1800–2008. Polity IV Project." Vienna, VA: Center for Systemic Peace.

Martín, Mariano. 2005. "La UIA Recibe a Lavagna con Pedidos y Respaldo." *El Cronista.* July 25.

Martínez de Hoz, José Alfredo. 1967. *La Agricultura y la Ganadería Argentina en el Periodo 1930–1960.* Buenos Aires: Editorial Sudamericana.

———. 1990. "Chapter 13." In *Argentina, 1946–83: The Economic Ministers Speak*, edited by Guido di Tella and Carlos Rodríguez Braun, 151–80. New York: St. Martin's Press.

Mason, Edward S., Mahn Je Kim, Dwight H. Perkins, Kwang Suk Kim, and David C. Cole. 1980. *The Economic and Social Modernization of the Republic of Korea*. Cambridge, MA: Harvard University Press.

Maxfield, Sylvia. 1990. *Governing Capital: International Finance and Mexican Politics*. Ithaca, NY: Cornell University Press.

Mazaheri, Nimah. 2006. "State Repression in the Iranian Bazaar, 1975–1977." *Iranian Studies* 39 (3): 401–14.

———. 2008. "An 'Informal' Revolution: State-Business Conflict and Institutional Change in Iran." *Middle Eastern Studies* 44 (4): 585–602.

Mazarei, Adnan. 1995. "The Parallel Market for Foreign Exchange in an Oil Exporting Economy: The Case of Iran, 1978–1990." *IMF Working Paper* No. 95/69.

———. 1996. "The Iranian Economy under the Islamic Republic." *Cambridge Journal of Economics* 20 (3): 289–314.

Mbaye, Samba. 2013. "Currency Undervaluation and Growth: Is There a Productivity Channel?" *International Economics* 133: 8–28.

McGuire, James W. 1997. *Peronism without Perón*. New York: Cambridge University Press.

McKenzie, David J. 2004. "Aggregate Shocks and Urban Labor Market Responses: Evidence from Argentina's Financial Crisis." *Economic Development and Cultural Change* 52 (4): 719–58.

McNamara, Kathleen. 1998. *The Currency of Ideas*. Ithaca, NY: Cornell University Press.

———. 1999. "Consensus and Constraint: Ideas and Capital Mobility in European Monetary Integration." *Journal of Common Market Studies* 37 (3): 455–76.

Meaños, Fernando. 2005. "El Comercio ya Redujo mucho sus Márgenes." *Fortuna*. Aug. 8, pp. 15–18.

Mercado. 1983. "Las Propuestas Económicas de los Partidos." Aug. 18.

Mertha, Andrew. 2009. "'Fragmented Authoritarianism 2.0': Political Pluralization in the Chinese Policy Process." *The China Quarterly* 200: 995–1012.

Micco, Alejandro, Ugo Panizza, and Monica Yañez. 2007. "Bank Ownership and Performance." *Journal of Banking & Finance* 31 (1): 219–241.

Milani, Abbas. 2008. *Eminent Persians*. Syracuse, NY: Syracuse University Press.

Milgrom, Paul, Yingyi Qian, and John Roberts. 1991. "Complementarities, Momentum, and the Evolution of Modern Manufacturing." *American Economic Review* 81 (2): 84–88.

Milner, Helen V. 1998. "Rationalizing Politics." *International Organization* 52 (4): 759–86.

Ming Pao. 1993. "Renminbi Devaluation Downplayed." June 7, in *FBIS* June 7, 1993.

Minushkin, Susan. 2002. "Banqueros and Bolseros." *Journal of Latin American Studies* 34 (4): 915–44.

Mishkin, Frederic C. 2009. "Why We Shouldn't Turn Our Backs on Financial Globalization." *IMF Staff Papers* 56 (1): 139–70.

Moghadam, Valentine M. 1996. "Making History, but Not of Their Own Choosing." In *The Social History of Labor in The Middle East*, edited by Ellis Jay Goldberg, 65–98. Boulder, CO: Westview Press.

Mohanty, Madhusudan S., and Philip Turner. 2005. "Intervention: What Are the Domestic Consequences?" *BIS Papers* 24 (May): 56–81.

Montenegro, Maximilio. 1999. "Lo que la UIA Piensa, Pero no Dice." *Página/12*. Aug. 18.

Moore, Thomas G., and Dixia Yang. 2001. "Empowered and Restrained." In *The Making of Chinese Foreign and Security Policy in the Era of Reform, 1978–2000*, edited by David M. Lampton, 191–229. Stanford, CA: Stanford University Press.

Moravcsik, Andrew. 1997. "Taking Preferences Seriously: A Liberal Theory of International Politics." *International Organization* 51 (4): 513–53.

Morici, Peter, and Evan Schulz. 2001. *Labor Standards in the Global Trading System.* Washington, DC: Economic Strategy Institute.

Morrison, James Ashley. 2012. "Before Hegemony." *International Organization* 66 (3): 395–428.

——. 2015. "Shocking Intellectual Austerity: The Role of Ideas in the Demise of the Gold Standard in Britain." *International Organization* (forthcoming).

Moschella, Manuela. 2015. "Currency Wars in the Advanced World: Resisting Appreciation at a Time of Change in Central Banking Monetary Consensus." *Review of International Political Economy* 22 (1): 134–61.

Moslem, Mehdi. 2002. *Factional Politics in Post-Khomeini Iran.* Syracuse, NY: Syracuse University Press.

Mosley, Layna. 2010. *Labor Rights and Multinational Production.* New York: Cambridge University Press.

Mussa, Michael. 2002. *Argentina and the Fund.* Washington, DC: Peterson Institute.

Naím, Moisés. 1997. "Mexico's Larger Story." In *Mexico 1994: Anatomy of an Emerging Market Crash,* edited by Sebastian Edwards and Moisés Naím, 295–312. Washington, DC: Carnegie Endowment for International Peace.

Naselli, María Irene. 1991. "Una Clase de Ilusión." *Informe Industrial.* Apr., pp. 4–6.

Nasr, Vali. 2000. "Politics within the Late-Pahlavi State." *International Journal of Middle East Studies* 32 (1): 97–122.

Naughton, Barry. 1999. "China: Domestic Restructuring and a New Role in Asia." In *The Politics of the Asian Economic Crisis,* edited by T. J. Pempel, 203–23. Ithaca, NY: Cornell University Press.

——. 2007. *The Chinese Economy.* Cambridge, MA: MIT Press.

Nelson, Stephen, and Peter J. Katzenstein. 2014. "Uncertainty, Risk, and the Financial Crisis of 2008." *International Organization* 48 (2): 361–92.

Neumayer, Eric, and Indra de Soysa. 2006. "Globalization and the Right to Free Association and Collective Bargaining." *World Development* 34 (1): 31–49.

New York Times. 2010. "A Message for China." Oct. 1, A24.

——. 2007. "Sarkozy Pressures China on Yuan's Value." Nov. 25. http://www.nytimes.com/2007/11/25/business/worldbusiness/25iht-yuan.4.8471298.html.

Nichols, Theo, and Wei Zhao. 2010. "Disaffection with Trade Unions in China." *Industrial Relations Journal* 41 (1): 19–33.

Nogués, Julio J. 1986. *The Nature of Argentina's Policy Reforms during 1976–81.* Washington, DC: World Bank.

Nye, Joseph S. 2004. *Soft Power.* New York: Public Affairs.

Oatley, Thomas. 2010. "Real Exchange Rates and Trade Protectionism." *Business and Politics* 12 (2): 1–17.

Oberst, Tomás. "La Economía Argentina Según Carlos Moyano Llerena." *Revista Ensayos de Política Económica* 3: 1–16.

Obstfeld, Maurice, and Kenneth Rogoff. 2009. *Global Imbalances and the Financial Crisis.* Proceedings, Federal Reserve Bank of San Francisco.

Odell, John S. 1982. *U.S. International Monetary Policy.* Princeton, NJ: Princeton University Press.

O'Donnell, Guillermo. 1978. "State and Alliances in Argentina, 1956–76." *Journal of Development Studies* 15 (1): 3–33.

——. 1988. *Bureaucratic Authoritarianism.* Berkeley: University of California Press.

OECD. 2000. *International Trade and Core Labour Standards.* Paris: Organization for Economic Cooperation and Development.

Ogle, George E. 1990. *South Korea: Dissent within the Economic Miracle.* London: Zed Books.

Olivera, Franciso. 2008. "Los Industriales Piden una Nueva Devaluación del Peso." *La Nación.* Nov. 25.

Olson, Mancur. 1965. *The Logic of Collective Action.* Cambridge, MA: Harvard University Press.

———. 1993. "Dictatorship, Democracy, and Development." *American Political Science Review* 87 (3): 567–76.

Ortiz, Guillermo, and Leopoldo Solís. 1979. "Financial Structure and Exchange Rate Experience." *Journal of Development Economics* 6 (4): 515–48.

Página/12. 1995. "La UIA y Cavallo Discuten Sobre Los Salarios." July 22.

Panorama. 1993. "Una Devaluacíon no Duraría ni Tres Días." Oct., pp. 8–12.

Park, Yung Chul. 1991. "The Development of Financial Institutions and the Role of Government in Credit Allocation." In *Economic Development in the Republic of Korea,* edited by Lee-Jay Cho and Yoon Hyun Kim, 45–72. Honolulu: University of Hawaii Press.

Parsa, Misagh. 1995. "Entrepreneurs and Democratization: Iran and the Philippines." *Comparative Studies in Society and History* 37 (4): 803–30.

Pascó-Font, Alberto, and Piero Ghezzi. 2001. "Exchange Rates and Interest Groups in Peru, 1950–1996." In *The Currency Game,* edited by Jeffry Frieden and Ernesto Stein, 249–77. Washington, DC: Inter-American Development Bank.

Pastore, José María Dagnino. 1990. "Chapter 7." In *Argentina, 1946–83: The Economic Ministers Speak,* edited by Guido di Tella and Carlos Rodríguez Braun, 104–10. New York: St. Martin's Press.

PBC. 2003. *China Monetary Policy Report.* Available at: http://www.pbc.gov.cn.

———. 2007. *China Monetary Policy Report, Quarter 3, 2007.* Available at: http://www.pbc.gov.cn.

———. 2010. *China Monetary Policy Report, Quarter 1, 2010.* Available at: http://www.pbc.gov.cn.

People's Daily. 1994. "What Does the Reunification of the Renminbi Foreign Exchange Rates Mean?" Jan. 12, in *FBIS* Jan. 19, 1994.

———. 2007. "The Central Economic Work Conference Convenes in Beijing." Dec. 6.

Pepinsky, Thomas B. 2009. *Economic Crises and the Breakdown of Authoritarian Regimes.* New York: Cambridge University Press.

Peralta Ramos, Monica. 1992. "Economic Policy and Distributional Conflict among Business Groups in Argentina." In *The New Argentine Democracy,* edited by Edward Epstein, 97–123. Westport, CT: Praeger.

Pesaran, M. Hashem. 1982. "The System of Dependent Capitalism in Pre- and Post-Revolutionary Iran." *International Journal of Middle East Studies* 14 (4): 501–22.

———. 1992. "The Iranian Foreign Exchange Policy and the Black Market for Dollars." *International Journal of Middle East Studies* 24 (1): 101–25.

———. 2000. "Economic Trends and Macroeconomic Policies in Post-Revolutionary Iran." In *Iran's Economy,* edited by Parvin Alizadeh, 63–99. New York: St. Martin's Press.

Petrei, A. Humberto, and James Tybout. 1985. "Microeconomic Adjustments in Argentina During 1976–1981: The Importance of Changing Levels of Financial Subsidies." *World Development* 13 (8): 949–67.

Pettis, Michael. 2007. "China's Last Option: Let the Yuan Soar." *Far Eastern Economic Review* 170 (5): 10–15.

Pfeifer, Karen. 2006. "Islam and Labor Law." In *Islam and the Everyday World,* edited by Sohrab Behdad and Farhad Nomani, 113–40. London: Routledge.

Pick, Daniel H., and Thomas L. Vollrath. 1994. "Real Exchange Rate Misalignment and Agricultural Export Performance in Developing Countries." *Economic Development and Cultural Change* 42 (3): 555–71.

Podpiera, Richard. 2006. "Progress in China's Banking Sector Reform" *IMF Working Paper* WP/06/71.

Polak, Jacques J. 1991. "The Changing Nature of IMF Conditionality." *OECD Development Centre Working Paper* No. 41.

Prasad, Eswar S. 2014. *The Dollar Trap*. Princeton, NJ: Princeton University Press.

Radetzki, Marian. 2008. *A Handbook of Primary Commodities in the Global Economy*. New York: Cambridge University Press.

Rahnema, Saeed. 1992. "Work Councils in Iran." *Economic and Industrial Democracy* 13 (1): 69–94.

Rakel, Eva Patricia. 2008. *Power, Islam, and Political Elite in Iran*. Boston: Brill.

Ramírez, Carlos D. 2013. "The Political Economy of 'Currency Manipulation' Bashing." *China Economic Review* 27: 227–37.

Ramírez de la O, Rogelio. 1996. "The Mexican Peso Crisis and Recession of 1994–1995." In *The Mexican Peso Crisis*, edited by Riordan Roett, 11–32. Boulder, CO: Lynne Rienner Publishers.

Ranis, Peter. 1992. *Argentine Workers*. Pittsburgh: University of Pittsburgh Press.

Razin, Ofair, and Susan M Collins. 1999. "Real-Exchange-Rate Misalignments and Growth." In *The Economics of Globalization*, edited by Assaf Razin and Efraim Sadka, 85–122. New York: Cambridge University Press.

Rebossio, Alejandro. 2005. "El Gobierno Frena el Alza del Gasto para Atacar la Inflación." *La Nación*. Oct. 29. http://www.lanacion.com.ar/751754-el-gobierno-frena-el-alza-del-gasto-para-atacar-la-inflacion.

——. 2007. "Un Hombre de la Industria y, Sobre Todo, un Hombre del Presidente." *La Nación*. July 17. http://www.lanacion.com.ar/926415-un-hombre-de-la-industria-y-sobre-todo-un-hombre-del-presidente.

——. 2008. "Señal Contundente, pero Coyuntural." *La Nación*. May 29. http://www.lanacion.com.ar/1016556-senal-contundente-pero-coyuntural.

Reinhardt, Dennis, Luca Antonio Ricci, and Thierry Tressel. 2013. "International Capital Flows and Development." *Journal of International Economics* 91 (2): 235–51.

Reinhart, Carmen M., and Vincent R. Reinhart. 1998. "Some Lessons for Policy Makers Who Deal with the Mixed Blessing of Capital Inflows." In *Capital Flows and Financial Crises*, edited by Miles Kahler, 93–127. Manchester: Council of Foreign Relations.

——. 2008. "Capital Inflows and Reserve Accumulation." *National Bureau of Economic Research Working Paper* No. 13842.

Reinhart, Carmen M., and Kenneth Rogoff. 2009. *This Time Is Different*. Princeton, NJ: Princeton University Press.

Reynolds, Clark W. 1978. "Why Mexico's 'Stabilizing Development' Was Actually Destabilizing (with Some Implications for the Future)." *World Development* 6 (7): 1005–18.

Richardson, Neal P. 2009. "Export-Oriented Populism: Commodities and Coalitions in Argentina." *Studies in Comparative International Development* 44 (3): 228–55.

Riedel, James, Jing Jin, and Jian Gao. 2007. *How China Grows*. Princeton, NJ: Princeton University Press.

Riggi, Horacio. 2004. "Los Empresarios Quieren que la Baja de Retenciones Abarque a Toda la Industria." *El Cronista*. Dec. 27.

Rodríguez, José María. 2007. "El Producto Potencial de la Argentina." Unpublished manuscript, Universidad Nacional de Córdoba.

Rodrik, Dani. 1994. "The Rush to Free Trade in the Developing World." In *Voting for Reform*, edited by Stephan Haggard and Steven Webb, 61–88. New York: Oxford University Press.

——. 1996. "Labor Standards in International Trade." In *Emerging Agenda for Global Trade*, edited by Robert Z. Lawrence, Dani Rodrik, and John Whalley, 35–80. Washington, DC: Overseas Development Council.

——. 2008. "The Real Exchange Rate and Economic Growth." *Brookings Papers on Economic Activity* 2: 365–412.

——. 2010. "Making Room for China in the World Economy." *American Economic Review* 100 (2): 89–93.

Rogoff, Kenneth. 1996. "The Purchasing Power Parity Puzzle." *Journal of Economic Literature* 34 (2): 647–68.

Rogowski, Ronald. 1999. "Institutions as Constraints on Strategic Choice." In *Strategic Choice and International Relations*, edited by David A. Lake and Robert Powell, 115–36. Princeton, NJ: Princeton University Press.

Roubini, Nouriel, and Stephen Mihm. 2010. *Crisis Economics*. New York: Penguin Press.

Roubini, Nouriel, and Xavier Sala-i-Martin. 1992. "Financial Repression and Economic Growth." *Journal of Development Economics* 39 (1): 5–30.

Rozenwurcel, Guillermo, and Leonardo Bleger. 1998. "Argentina's Banking Sector in the Nineties." *The World Economy* 21 (3): 369–96.

Saeidi, Ali A. 2001. "Charismatic Political Authority and Populist Economics in Post-Revolutionary Iran." *Third World Quarterly* 22 (2): 219–36.

Salehi-Isfahani, Djavad. 1989. "The Political Economy of Credit Subsidy in Iran, 1973–1978." *International Journal of Middle East Studies* 21 (3): 359–79.

Samuelson, Paul A. 1964. "Theoretical Notes on Trade Problems." *Review of Economics and Statistics* 46 (2): 145–54.

Sanguinetti, Pablo, and Christian Volpe Martincus. 2004. "Does Trade Liberalization Favor Industrial De-concentration?" Manuscript, Universidad Torcuato di Tella and University of Bonn.

Sapienza, Paola. 2004. "The Effects of Government Ownership on Bank Lending." *Journal of Financial Economics* 72 (2): 357–84.

Schamis, Hector. 1999. "Distributional Coalitions and the Politics of Economic Reform in Latin America." *World Politics* 51 (2): 236–68.

——. 2003. "The Political Economy of Currency Boards." In *Monetary Orders*, edited by Jonathan Kirshner, 125–50. Ithaca, NY: Cornell University Press.

Schattschneider, E. E. 1935. *Politics, Pressures, and the Tariff*. New York: Prentice Hall.

Schlagheck, James L. 1977. *The Political, Economic, and Labor Climate in Mexico*. Philadelphia: University of Pennsylvania.

Schneider, Ben Ross. 2004. *Business Politics and the State in Twentieth-Century Latin America*. New York: Cambridge University Press.

——. 2010. "Business Politics in Latin America." In *Oxford Handbook of Business and Government*, edited by David Coen, Graham Wilson, and Wyn Grant, 307–29. New York: Oxford University Press.

——. 2013. *Hierarchical Capitalism in Latin America*. New York: Cambridge University Press.

Schumer, Charles E., and Lindsey O. Graham. 2005. "Will It Take a Tariff to Free the Yuan?" *New York Times*, June 8. http://www.nytimes.com/2005/06/08/opinion/08schumer.html.

Schvarzer, Jorge. 1986. *La Política Económica de Martínez de Hoz*. Buenos Aires: CISEA.

——. 1991. *Empresarios del Pasado: La Unión Industrial Argentina*. Buenos Aires: CISEA.

Seawright, Jason, and John Gerring. 2008. "Case Selection Techniques in Case Study Research." *Political Research Quarterly* 61 (2): 294.

Sehinkman, Diego. 2013. "José de Mendiguren: 'Soy Optimista, pero hay Cosas por Corregir." *La Nación*, Mar. 30.

Shambayati, Hootan. 1994. "The Rentier State, Interest Groups, and the Paradox of Autonomy." *Comparative Politics* 26 (3): 307–31.

Shao, Yun. 1993. "A Unified Exchange Rate to Be Implemented in China Next Year Will Be an Important Step for Free Conversion of Renminbi." *Zhongguo Tongxun She.* Dec. 1, in *FBIS* Dec. 7, 1993.

Sharma, Shalendra. 2003. *The Asian Financial Crisis.* Manchester: Manchester University Press.

Shih, Victor. 2007. "Partial Reform Equilibrium, Chinese Style." *Comparative Political Studies* 40 (10): 1238–62.

——. 2008. *Factions and Finance in China.* New York: Cambridge University Press.

——. 2011. "'Goldilocks' Liberalization: The Uneven Path toward Interest Rate Reform in China." *Journal of East Asian Studies* 11 (3): 437–65.

Shirk, Susan L. 1993. *The Political Logic of Economic Reform in China.* Berkeley: University of California Press.

——. 1994. *How China Opened Its Door.* Washington, DC: Brookings Institution Press.

Sikkink, Kathryn. 1991. *Ideas and Institutions: Developmentalism in Brazil and Argentina.* Ithaca, NY: Cornell University Press.

Silva, Eduardo. 1993. "Capitalist Coalitions, the State, and Neoliberal Economic Restructuring: Chile, 1973–88." *World Politics* 45 (4): 526–59.

Singer, David A. 2010. "Migrant Remittances and Exchange Rate Regimes in the Developing World." *American Political Science Review* 104 (2): 307–23.

Skocpol, Theda. 1985. "Bringing the State Back In." In *Bringing the State Back In,* edited by Peter B. Evans, Dietrich Rueschemeyer, and Theda Skocpol, 3–37. New York: Cambridge University Press.

Smith, Benjamin B. 2007. *Hard Times in the Lands of Plenty.* Ithaca, NY: Cornell University Press.

Smith, Peter H. 1997. "Political Dimensions of the Peso Crisis." In *Mexico 1994,* edited by Sebastian Edwards and Moisés Naím, 31–54. Washington, DC: Carnegie Endowment for International Peace.

Smith, William C. 1989. *Authoritarianism and the Crisis of Argentine Political Economy.* Stanford, CA: Stanford University Press.

——. 1990. "Democracy, Distributional Conflicts, and Macroeconomic Policymaking in Argentina, 1983–89." *Journal of Interamerican Studies and World Affairs* 32 (2): 1–42.

Snow, Peter G., and Luigi Manzetti. 1993. *Political Forces in Argentina.* Westport, CT: Praeger.

Solís, Leopoldo. 1981. *Economic Policy Reform in Mexico.* New York: Pergamon.

Somos. 1986. "Porque Ahora: Plan Austral, Fase II." Feb. 12.

Spiller, Pablo T., and Mariano Tommasi. 2007. *The Institutional Foundations of Public Policy in Argentina.* New York: Cambridge University Press.

Standard Chartered. 2004. "CNY Revaluation: Economically Yes; Politically, Now Debating." *On the Ground-China.* Standard Chartered Bank, Shanghai. Nov. 18.

——. 2007a. "Calling All PBoC FX Sterilisation Geeks." *On the Ground China.* Standard Chartered Bank, Shanghai. June 18.

——. 2007b. "Mild Revisions to Our CNY Forecasts." *FX Alert Chinese Yuan.* Standard Chartered Bank, Shanghai. July 20.

——. 2007c. "More Inflation, More Hikes, More Sleepless Nights." *On the Ground China.* Standard Chartered Bank, Shanghai. Dec. 20.

——. 2008a. "CNY May Be Being Managed on a NEER Basis." *FX Alert Chinese Yuan.* Standard Chartered Bank, Shanghai. May 14.

——. 2008b. "We Strike Gold in the Q1 PBoC Report." *On the Ground China.* Standard Chartered Bank, Shanghai. May 16.

———. 2008c. "State of the Art: PBOC Sterilisation Update." *On the Ground China*. Standard Chartered Bank, Shanghai. June 18.

Starr, Pamela K. 1997. "Government Coalitions and the Viability of Currency Boards." *Journal of Interamerican Studies and World Affairs* 39 (2): 83–133.

———. 1999. "Capital Flows, Fixed Exchange rates, and Political Survival." In *Markets and Democracy in Latin America*, edited by Philip Oxhorn and Pamela K. Starr, 203–38. Boulder, CO: Lynne Rienner.

Steinberg, David A., and Krishan Malhotra. 2014. "The Effect of Authoritarian Regime Type on Exchange Rate Policy." *World Politics* 66 (3): 491–529.

Steinfeld, Edward S. 1998. "The Asian Financial Crisis." *Washington Quarterly* 21: 37–52.

Steinmo, Sven. 1989. "Political Institutions and Tax Policy in the United States, Sweden, and Britain." *World Politics* 41 (4): 500–535.

Story, Dale. 1986. *Industry, the State, and Public Policy in Mexico*. Austin: University of Texas Press.

Stubbs, Richard. 1999. "War and Economic Development: Export-Oriented Industrialization in East and Southeast Asia." *Comparative Politics* 31 (3): 337–55.

Sturgeon, Timothy, Johannes Van Biesebroeck, and Gary Gereffi. 2008. "Value Chains, Networks, and Clusters." *Journal of Economic Geography* 8 (3): 297–321.

Sturzenegger, Federico A. 1991. "Description of a Populist Experience: Argentina, 1973–1976." In *The Macroeconomics of Populism in Latin America*, edited by Rudiger Dornbusch and Sebastián Edwards, 77–120. Chicago: University of Chicago Press.

Su, Yunqin, and Lin Sen. 1995. "A Synthesis of Views on Inflation." *Caimao Jingji (Finance and Economics)*. June 11, in FBIS Sep. 19, 1995.

Subramanian, Arvind. 2010. *New PPP-based Estimates of Renminbi Undervaluation and Policy Implications*. Washington, DC: Peterson Institute for International Economics Policy Brief.

Sun, Lujun. 1995. "Some Thoughts on Central Bank's Regulation of Foreign Exchange." *Jingji Yanjiu Cankao (Review of Economic Research)* 193: 2–8.

Sun, Mingchun. 1995. "Adjustment in Management of Renminbi Exchange Rates and Related Policies" *Guanli Shijie (Management World)*. Mar. 24, in FBIS June 9, 1995.

Sundararajan, Vasudevan, Michel Lazare, and Sherwyn Williams. 2001. "Exchange Rate Unification, the Equilibrium Real Exchange Rate, and the Choice of Exchange Rate Regime." In *Macroeconomic Issues and Policies in the Middle East and North Africa*, edited by Zubair Iqbal, 213–52. Washington, DC: International Monetary Fund.

Ta Kung Po. 1993. "Zhu Rongji Says Exchange Rate Alignment to Begin." Nov. 24, in FBIS Nov. 29, 1993.

Taylor, Alan M., and Mark P. Taylor. 2004. "The Purchasing Power Parity Debate." *Journal of Economic Perspectives* 18 (4): 135–58.

Taylor, Bill, and Qi Li. 2007. "Is the ACFTU a Union and Does It Matter?" *Journal of Industrial Relations* 49 (5): 701–15.

Teitelbaum, Emmanuel. 2010. "Measuring Trade Union Rights through Violations Recorded in Textual Sources." *Political Research Quarterly* 63 (2): 461–74.

Ten Kate, Adriaan. 1992. "Trade Liberalization and Economic Stabilization in Mexico." *World Development* 20 (5): 659–72.

Thelen, Kathleen. 1999. "Historical Institutionalism in Comparative Politics." *Annual Review of Political Science* 2: 369–404.

Thelen, Kathleen, and Sven Steinmo. 1992. "Historical Institutionalism in Comparative Politics." In *Structuring Politics*, edited by Sven Steinmo, Kathleen Thelen, and Frank Longstreth, 1–32. New York: Cambridge University Press.

Thompson, John K. 1979. *Inflation, Financial Markets, and Economic Development*. Greenwich, CT: Jai Press.

Tiempo. 1986. "Lavagna Anunció las Medidas Económicas que Impulsarán la Reactivación con Estabilidad." Feb. 11.

Todaro, Michael P., and Stephen C. Smith. 2003. *Economic Development*. Boston: Addison-Wesley.

Tomada, Carlos, and Marta Novick. 2007. "Argentina 2003–2006." In *In the Wake of the Crisis*, edited by Marta Novick, Carlos Tomada, Mario Damill, Roberto Frenkel, and Roxana Maurizio, 1–49. Geneva: International Labour Organization.

Tomz, Michael, Jason Wittenberg, and Gary King. 2003. "CLARIFY: Software for Interpreting and Presenting Statistical Results." *Journal of Statistical Software* 8 (1): 1–30.

Tsai, Kellee S. 2007. *Capitalism without Democracy*. Ithaca, NY: Cornell University Press.

Tybout, James R. 2000. "Manufacturing Firms in Developing Countries: How Well Do They Do, and Why?" *Journal of Economic Literature* 38 (1): 11–44.

Upward, Richard, Zheng Wang, and Jinghai Zheng. 2013. "Weighting China's Export Basket." *Journal of Comparative Economics* 41(2): 527–43.

Valibeigi, Mehrdad. 1992. "Banking and Credit Rationing under the Islamic Republic of Iran." *Iranian Studies* 25 (3–4): 51–65.

Vu, Tuong. 2010. *Paths to Development in Asia*. New York: Cambridge University Press.

Wade, Robert. 1990. *Governing the Market*. Princeton, NJ: Princeton University Press.

Waldner, David. 1999. *State Building and Late Development*. Ithaca, NY: Cornell University Press.

Walter, Carl, and Fraser Howie. 2011. *Red Capitalism*. Hoboken, NJ: John Wiley & Sons.

Walter, Stefanie. 2008. "A New Approach for Determining Exchange-Rate Level Preferences." *International Organization* 62 (3): 405–38.

Wang, Hongying. 2003. "China's Exchange Rate Policy in the Aftermath of the Asian Financial Crisis." In *Monetary Orders*, edited by Jonathan Kirshner, 153–71. Ithaca, NY: Cornell University Press.

Wang, Songqi. 2006. "Ren Min Bi Da Fu Sheng Zhi Li Da Yu Bi (The Benefit of RMB Dramatic Appreciation Outweighs Disadvantage)." *Gai Ge Nei Can* (*Internal Reference for Economic Reform*) 33: 19–22.

Wang, Zixian. 1993. "An Analysis of Fluctuation Trend of Renminbi Exchange Rate" *Jingji Cankao Bao*. July 5, in *FBIS* Aug. 4, 1993.

Wen, Jiabao. 2007. "Government Work Report." http://english.people.com.cn/200703/07/eng20070307_355189.html.

Wen, Mei. 2004. "Relocation and Agglomeration of Chinese Industry." *Journal of Development Economics* 73 (1): 329–47.

Wen Pei Wo. 1993. "Unification of Renminbi Exchange Rates Well Received in Various Localities." Dec. 31, in *FBIS* Jan. 3, 1994.

Weymouth, Stephen. 2012. "Firm Lobbying and Influence in Developing Countries." *Business and Politics* 14 (4): 1–26.

Williamson, John. 1990. "What Washington Means by Policy Reform." In *Latin American Adjustment*, edited by John Williamson, 7–20. Washington, DC: Institute for International Economics.

Woo, Jung-En. 1991. *Race to the Swift*. New York: Columbia University Press.

Woo-Cumings, Meredith. 1999. "Introduction." In *The Developmental State*, edited by Meredith Woo-Cumings, 1–31. Ithaca, NY: Cornell University Press.

Woodruff, David M. 2005. "Boom, Gloom, Doom." *Politics and Society* 33 (1): 3–45.

Wong, Edward, and Mark Landler. 2010. "China Rejects U.S. Complaints on Its Currency." *New York Times*, Feb. 5. http://www.nytimes.com/2010/02/05/world/asia/05diplo.html.

World Bank. 2004. *Global Development Finance*. Washington, DC: World Bank.

——. 2010. *World Development Indicators.* Online database.

Wright, Logan. 2008. "The Yuan, Three Years Later." Stone & McCarthy Research Associates. July 23.

——. 2009. *The Elusive Price for Stability: Ideas and Interests in the Reform of China's Exchange Rate Regime.* PhD diss., Department of Political Science, George Washington University.

Wuhan PBC. 1995. "A View of the Effects of the New Exchange Rate Policy in 1994." *Review of Economic Research* 28: 38–46.

Wynia, Gary W. 1978. *Argentina in the Postwar Era.* Albuquerque: University of New Mexico Press.

Xin, Zhiming. 2008. "Yuan Set Lower 5 Days in a Row." *China Daily.* Aug. 6.

Xinhua. 1993a. "State Takes Steps to Stabilize Exchange Rate." Mar. 11, in *FBIS* Mar. 11, 1993.

——. 1993b. "Zhu Rongji Discusses Foreign Exchange Control." Aug. 3, in *FBIS* Aug. 4, 1993.

——. 1993c. "Experts: Time 'Ripe' for Unified Yuan Exchange Rate." Oct. 21, in *FBIS* Oct. 21, 1993.

——. 1994. "New Foreign Exchange System Taking Shape." Apr. 1, in *FBIS* Apr. 4, 1994.

——. 1995. "Zhu Rongji Comments on Renminbi Convertibility." Dec. 9, in *FBIS* Dec. 11, 1995.

——. 1998. "Official Denies U.S. Charge on Export Tax Refunds." Nov. 20 (Retrieved from Access World News Database).

——. 2008. "Premier Wen Jiabao Inspects Jiangsu." July 7.

Xiong, Sihao. 1993. "Keeping China's Development on Track." *Beijing Review.* Nov. 15–21, in *FBIS* Nov. 22, 1993.

Xu, Lin. 2008. "Push Forward Scientific Development in the Midst of Liberalizing Thinking: A True Account of Xi Jinping's Inspection of Guangdong." *Guangzhou Ribao (Guangzhou Daily).* July 7.

Yang, Dennis Tao, Vivian Weijia Chen, and Ryan Monarch. 2010. "Rising Wages: Has China Lost Its Global Labor Advantage?" *Pacific Economic Review* 15 (4): 482–504.

Yang, Fan. 1995. "China's Export Tariff Rebates and Foreign Exchange Rate Stabilization Problems." *Caimao Jingji (Finance and Economics).* Dec. 11, in *FBIS* Jan. 31, 1996.

——. 1996. "Several Issues Concerning Renminbi Exchange Rate." *Guanli Shijie (Management World).* Mar. 24, in *FBIS* July 17, 1996.

——. 2005. "Shei Zai Xia Zhu Ren Min Bi (Who Is Betting on RMB Appreciation)." *Gai Ge Nei Can (Internal Reference for Economic Reform)* 16: 18–21.

Yang, Liu. 1994. "As the Unified Exchange Rate Increases the Cost of Foreign Debts, the Central Government Adopts Measures to Help Localities Make Repayments." *Ming Pao.* Jan. 5, in *FBIS* Jan. 6, 1994.

Yu, Jun. 1994. "Experts Suggest Carrying through the Plan for Free Exchange of Renminbi at an Early Date." *Zhongguo Xinwen She.* Feb. 22, in *FBIS* Mar. 7, 1994.

Yu, Yongding. 2003. "Eradicate the Fear of RMB Revaluation." *Guoji jingji pinglun (International Economic Review)* 9–10: 1–10.

——. 2008. "Downturn's Upside." *Caijing Annual Edition*, pp. 11–12.

Zamora, Stephen. 1984. "Peso-Dollar Economics and the Imposition of Foreign Exchange Controls in Mexico." *American Journal of Comparative Law* 32 (1): 99–154.

Zhang, Liqun. 1994. "Analysis of Key Problems in Current Economy." *Jingji Cankao Bao.* Nov. 29, in *FBIS* Jan. 12, 1995.

Zhang, Ming. 2012. "Chinese Stylized Sterilization: The Cost-sharing Mechanism and Financial Repression." *China & World Economy* 20 (2): 41–58.

Zhang, Xiaohua. 2008. "Li Keqiang: Strengthen the Vitality of Firms and Renew Developmental Models; Preserve the Stable and Relatively Fast Development of the Economy." *People's Daily*, Jul. 9. http://cpc.people.com.cn/GB/64093/64094/7486459.html.

Zhang, Shuguang. 2005. "Ren Min Bi Sheng Zhi Chong Ji Le Shei (Who was affected by RMB appreciation)." *Gai Ge Nei Can (Internal Reference for Economic Reform)* 17: 10–14.

Zhong, Wei. 2004. "Jv E Wai Hui Chu Bei Bi Yuan Da Yu Li (The disadvantages of holding big amount of foreign reserve far outweigh the advantages)." *Gai Ge Nei Can (Internal Reference for Economic Reform)* 6: 17–19.

Zhou, L. 2010. "Beijing Zhejiang Shanghui fuhuizhang Chen Jin jiaoshou kan 'xinzheng' (The vice head of the Beijing Zhejiang Merchants' Association Professor Chen Jin examines 'new policies')." *Sina.com*.

Zhu, Min. 2009. "Overview." In *China's Emerging Financial Markets*, edited by Martha Avery, Zhu Min, and Jinqing Cai, xxiii–liii. Singapore: John Wiley & Sons.

Index

Locators in *italic* refer to figures/tables